AMONGST the LIBERAL Elite

THE ROAD TRIP EXPLORING SOCIETAL INEQUITIES SOLIDIFIED BY TRUMP (RESIST)

Written by Elly Lonon · Art design by Joan Reilly
with
Pencils by Miguel Yurrita · Inks by Theresa Chiechi

pH **powerHouse Books**

Brooklyn, NY

To our Villages.

Thanks for supporting and inspiring us.

It really did take each and every one of you.

Chapter 1

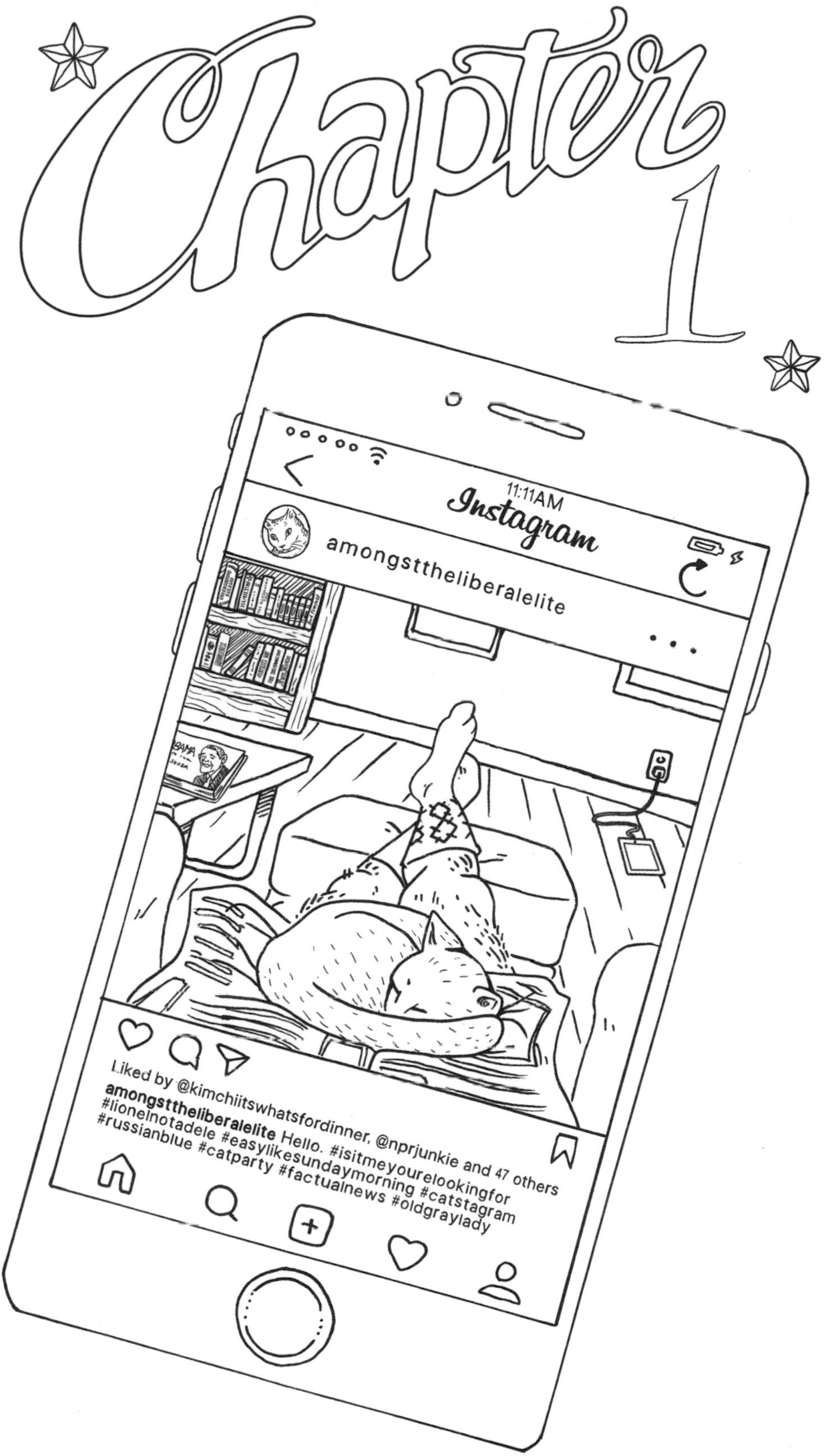

11:11AM
Instagram
amongsttheliberalelite
Liked by @kimchiitswhatsfordinner, @nprjunkie and 47 others
amongsttheliberalelite Hello. #isitmeyourelookingfor #lionelnotadele #easylikesundaymorning #catstagram #russianblue #catparty #factualnews #oldgraylady

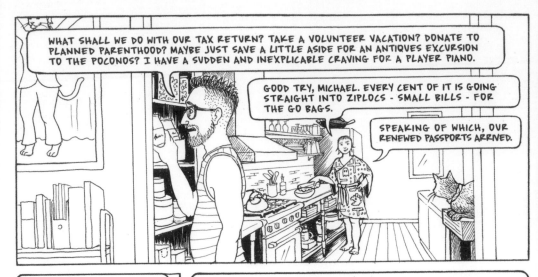

WHAT SHALL WE DO WITH OUR TAX RETURN? TAKE A VOLUNTEER VACATION? DONATE TO PLANNED PARENTHOOD? MAYBE JUST SAVE A LITTLE ASIDE FOR AN ANTIQUES EXCURSION TO THE POCONOS? I HAVE A SUDDEN AND INEXPLICABLE CRAVING FOR A PLAYER PIANO.

GOOD TRY, MICHAEL. EVERY CENT OF IT IS GOING STRAIGHT INTO ZIPLOCS - SMALL BILLS - FOR THE GO BAGS.

SPEAKING OF WHICH, OUR RENEWED PASSPORTS ARRIVED.

OH, COME ON, ALEX. WE'VE BEEN WORKING SO HARD. WE DESERVE A LITTLE SAVASANA.

THOUGH I SUPPOSE WE SHOULD KEEP IT DOMESTIC. IF ANY GOVERNMENT OFFICIALS LOOK THROUGH MY SOCIAL MEDIA, THEY'LL NEVER LET ME BACK IN THE COUNTRY.

I KNOW - LET'S RENT ONE OF THOSE VW CAMPERS AND TAKE A "RECONNECT WITH AMERICA" ROAD TRIP! WE'LL HAVE OUR OWN TINY HOUSE ON WHEELS!

NO.

SERIOUSLY. I'VE NEVER SEEN THE GRAND CANYON, HAVE YOU?

THERE WAS THAT MINDFULNESS RETREAT AND DETOX AT LAKE MEAD THAT COINCIDED WITH THE VERNAL EQUINOX, BUT AFTER ALL THAT PEYOTE, I CAN'T REMEMBER IF WE EVER MADE IT OUT OF THE LODGE, MUCH LESS THE GROUNDS.

THAT'S A NO. WHAT ABOUT MT. RUSHMORE?

Fweeee

A GIANT GRANITE EDIFICE CELEBRATING THE PATRIARCHY? THANKS BUT NO THANKS.

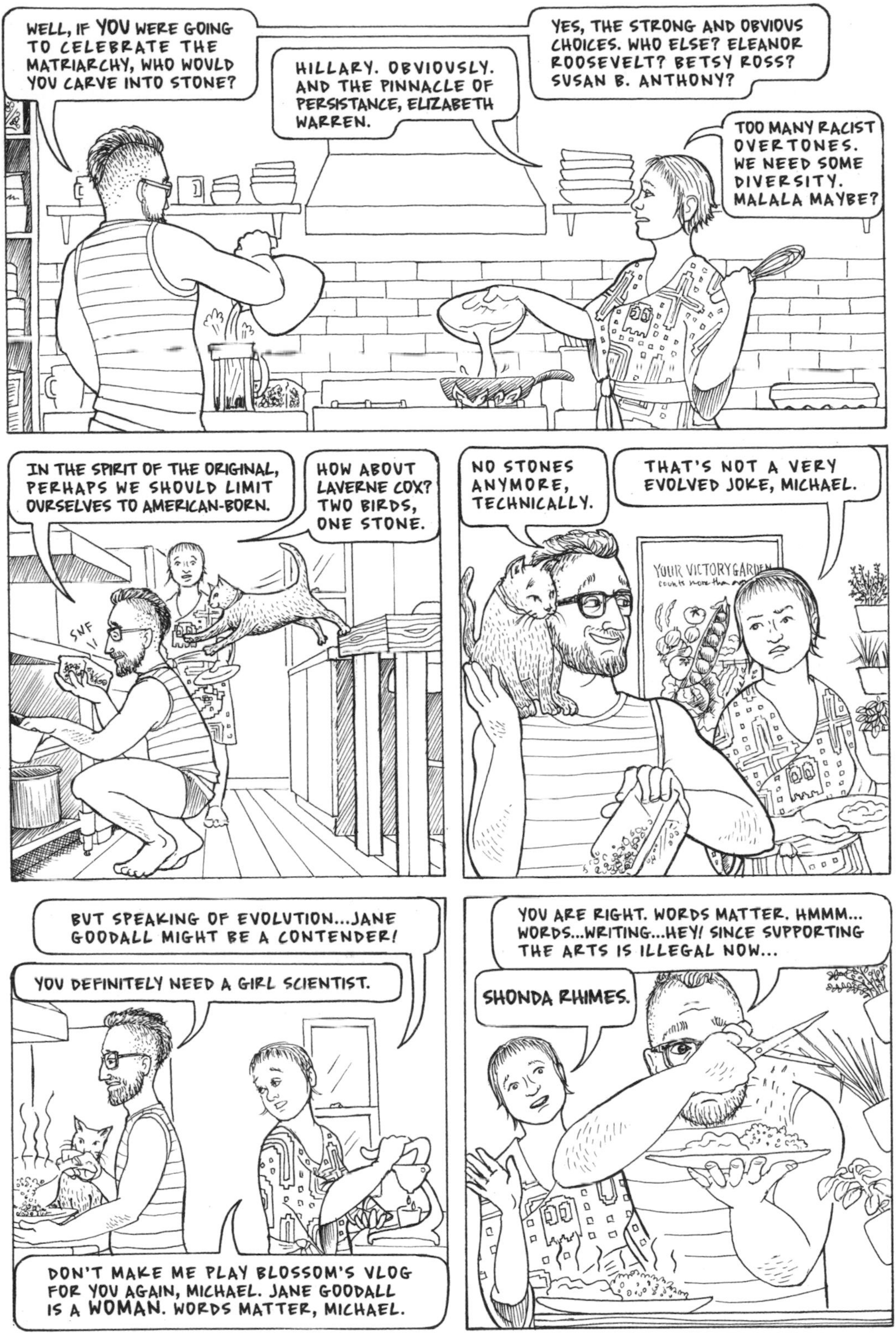
WELL, IF YOU WERE GOING TO CELEBRATE THE MATRIARCHY, WHO WOULD YOU CARVE INTO STONE?
HILLARY. OBVIOUSLY. AND THE PINNACLE OF PERSISTANCE, ELIZABETH WARREN.
YES, THE STRONG AND OBVIOUS CHOICES. WHO ELSE? ELEANOR ROOSEVELT? BETSY ROSS? SUSAN B. ANTHONY?
TOO MANY RACIST OVERTONES. WE NEED SOME DIVERSITY. MALALA MAYBE?
IN THE SPIRIT OF THE ORIGINAL, PERHAPS WE SHOULD LIMIT OURSELVES TO AMERICAN-BORN.
HOW ABOUT LAVERNE COX? TWO BIRDS, ONE STONE.
SNF
NO STONES ANYMORE, TECHNICALLY.
THAT'S NOT A VERY EVOLVED JOKE, MICHAEL.
YOUR VICTORY GARDEN
BUT SPEAKING OF EVOLUTION...JANE GOODALL MIGHT BE A CONTENDER!
YOU DEFINITELY NEED A GIRL SCIENTIST.
DON'T MAKE ME PLAY BLOSSOM'S VLOG FOR YOU AGAIN, MICHAEL. JANE GOODALL IS A WOMAN. WORDS MATTER, MICHAEL.
YOU ARE RIGHT. WORDS MATTER. HMMM... WORDS...WRITING...HEY! SINCE SUPPORTING THE ARTS IS ILLEGAL NOW...
SHONDA RHIMES.

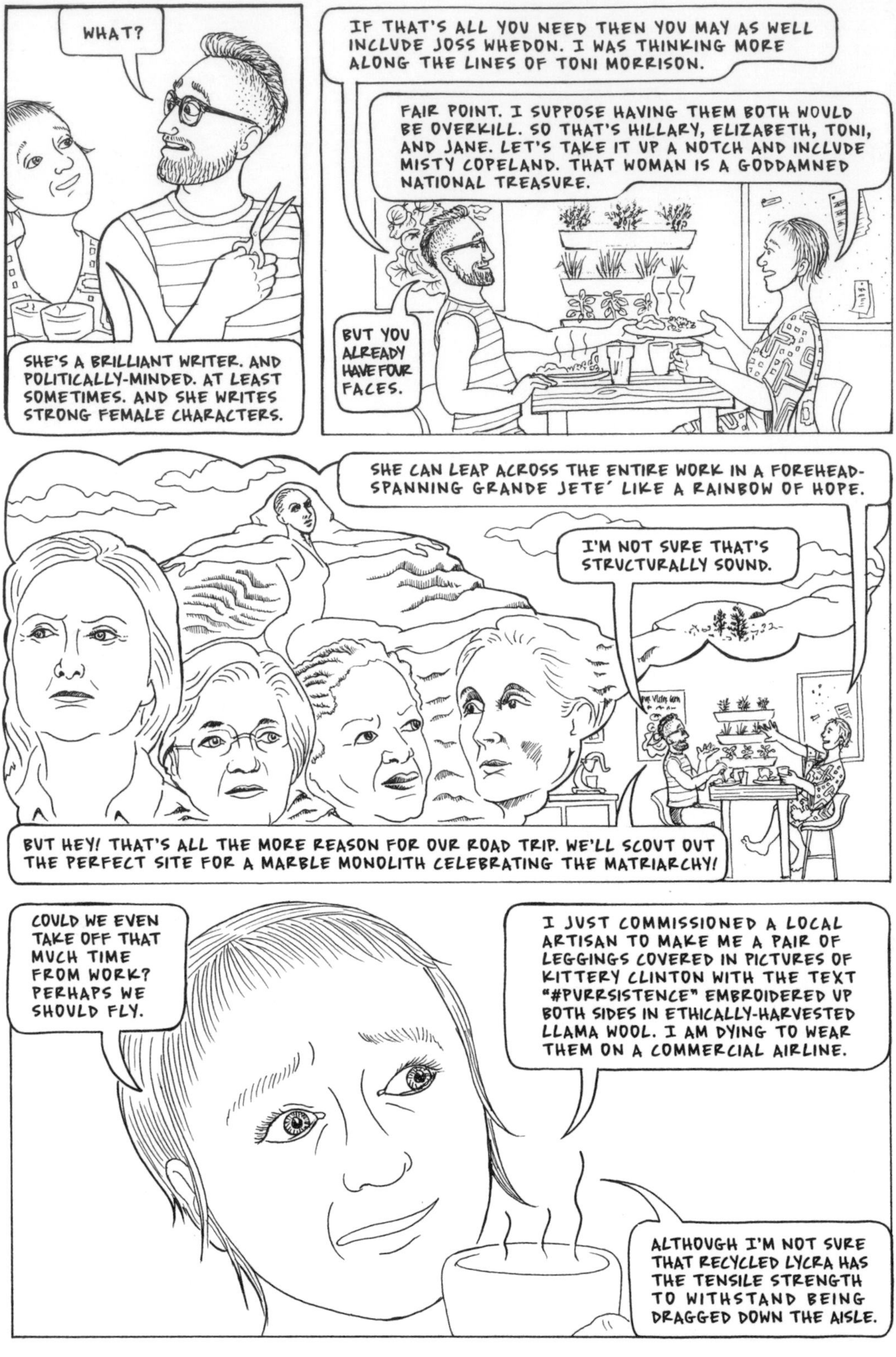
WHAT?
SHE'S A BRILLIANT WRITER. AND POLITICALLY-MINDED. AT LEAST SOMETIMES. AND SHE WRITES STRONG FEMALE CHARACTERS.
IF THAT'S ALL YOU NEED THEN YOU MAY AS WELL INCLUDE JOSS WHEDON. I WAS THINKING MORE ALONG THE LINES OF TONI MORRISON.
FAIR POINT. I SUPPOSE HAVING THEM BOTH WOULD BE OVERKILL. SO THAT'S HILLARY, ELIZABETH, TONI, AND JANE. LET'S TAKE IT UP A NOTCH AND INCLUDE MISTY COPELAND. THAT WOMAN IS A GODDAMNED NATIONAL TREASURE.
BUT YOU ALREADY HAVE FOUR FACES.
SHE CAN LEAP ACROSS THE ENTIRE WORK IN A FOREHEAD-SPANNING GRANDE JETE' LIKE A RAINBOW OF HOPE.
I'M NOT SURE THAT'S STRUCTURALLY SOUND.
BUT HEY! THAT'S ALL THE MORE REASON FOR OUR ROAD TRIP. WE'LL SCOUT OUT THE PERFECT SITE FOR A MARBLE MONOLITH CELEBRATING THE MATRIARCHY!
COULD WE EVEN TAKE OFF THAT MUCH TIME FROM WORK? PERHAPS WE SHOULD FLY.
I JUST COMMISSIONED A LOCAL ARTISAN TO MAKE ME A PAIR OF LEGGINGS COVERED IN PICTURES OF KITTERY CLINTON WITH THE TEXT "#PURRSISTENCE" EMBROIDERED UP BOTH SIDES IN ETHICALLY-HARVESTED LLAMA WOOL. I AM DYING TO WEAR THEM ON A COMMERCIAL AIRLINE.
ALTHOUGH I'M NOT SURE THAT RECYCLED LYCRA HAS THE TENSILE STRENGTH TO WITHSTAND BEING DRAGGED DOWN THE AISLE.

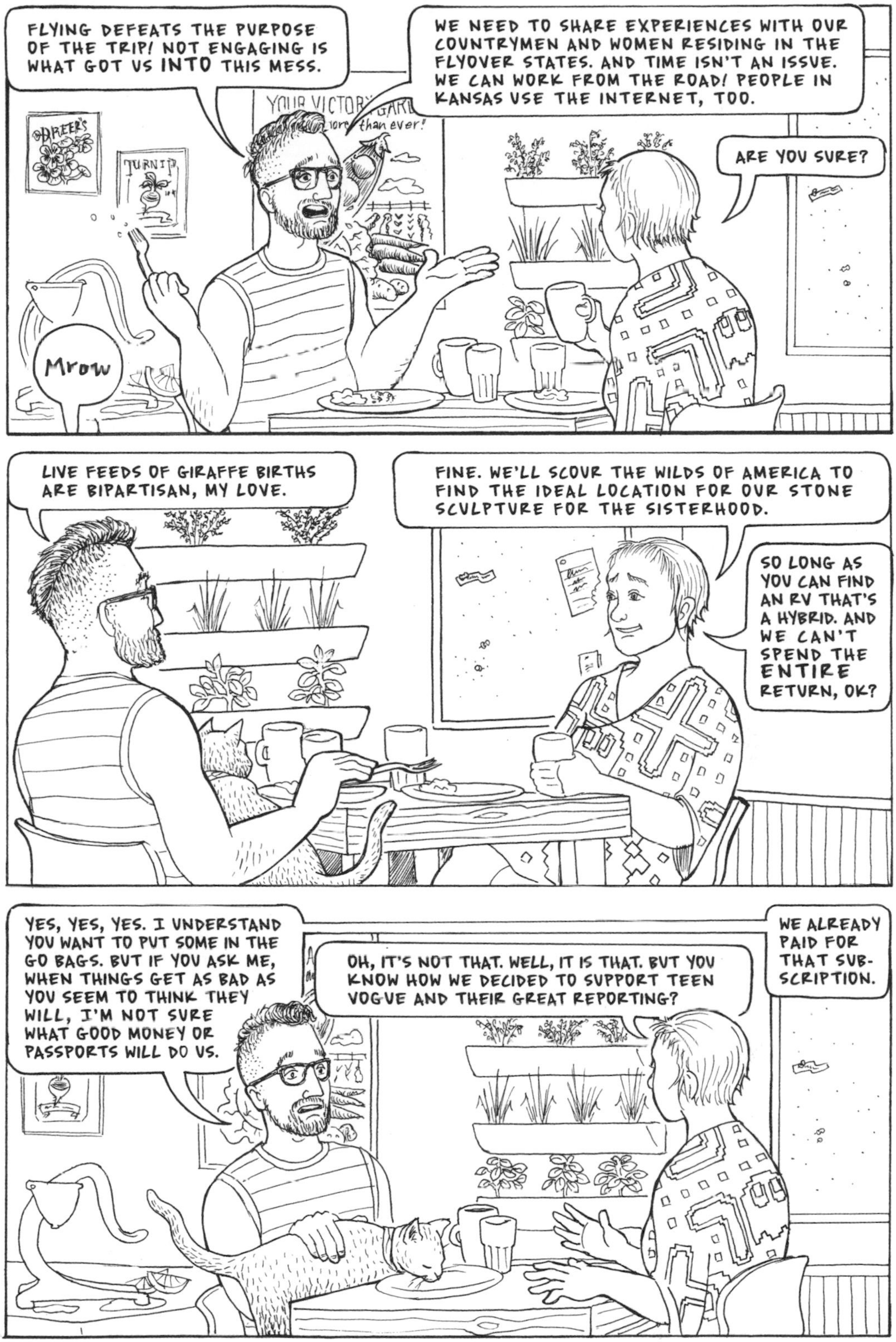
FLYING DEFEATS THE PURPOSE OF THE TRIP! NOT ENGAGING IS WHAT GOT US INTO THIS MESS.
WE NEED TO SHARE EXPERIENCES WITH OUR COUNTRYMEN AND WOMEN RESIDING IN THE FLYOVER STATES. AND TIME ISN'T AN ISSUE. WE CAN WORK FROM THE ROAD! PEOPLE IN KANSAS USE THE INTERNET, TOO.
YOUR VICTORY GARD
than ever!
DREER'S
TURNIP
ARE YOU SURE?
Mrow
LIVE FEEDS OF GIRAFFE BIRTHS ARE BIPARTISAN, MY LOVE.
FINE. WE'LL SCOUR THE WILDS OF AMERICA TO FIND THE IDEAL LOCATION FOR OUR STONE SCULPTURE FOR THE SISTERHOOD.
SO LONG AS YOU CAN FIND AN RV THAT'S A HYBRID. AND WE CAN'T SPEND THE ENTIRE RETURN, OK?
YES, YES, YES. I UNDERSTAND YOU WANT TO PUT SOME IN THE GO BAGS. BUT IF YOU ASK ME, WHEN THINGS GET AS BAD AS YOU SEEM TO THINK THEY WILL, I'M NOT SURE WHAT GOOD MONEY OR PASSPORTS WILL DO US.
OH, IT'S NOT THAT. WELL, IT IS THAT. BUT YOU KNOW HOW WE DECIDED TO SUPPORT TEEN VOGUE AND THEIR GREAT REPORTING?
WE ALREADY PAID FOR THAT SUBSCRIPTION.

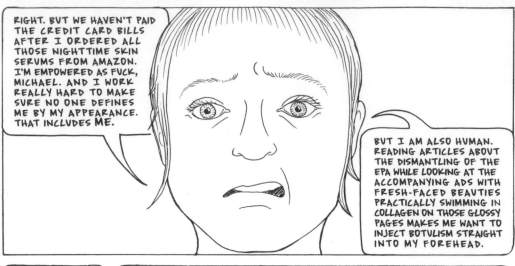

RIGHT. BUT WE HAVEN'T PAID THE CREDIT CARD BILLS AFTER I ORDERED ALL THOSE NIGHTTIME SKIN SERUMS FROM AMAZON. I'M EMPOWERED AS FUCK, MICHAEL. AND I WORK REALLY HARD TO MAKE SURE NO ONE DEFINES ME BY MY APPEARANCE. THAT INCLUDES ME.

BUT I AM ALSO HUMAN. READING ARTICLES ABOUT THE DISMANTLING OF THE EPA WHILE LOOKING AT THE ACCOMPANYING ADS WITH FRESH-FACED BEAUTIES PRACTICALLY SWIMMING IN COLLAGEN ON THOSE GLOSSY PAGES MAKES ME WANT TO INJECT BOTULISM STRAIGHT INTO MY FOREHEAD.

YOU SHOULD BE ASHAMED OF YOURSELF.

I KNOW! BUT THESE FUCKING AGE SPOTS ARE THE RESULT OF THE FUCKING DEPLETED OZONE LAYER WHICH IS THE FUCKING GOVERNMENT'S FAULT AND NOW THE COMMANDER-IN-CHIEF'S PLATFORM IS THAT A WOMAN ISN'T WORTH ACKNOWLEDGING UNLESS SHE'S AT LEAST A SEVEN AND IF YOU CATCH ME IN ONE OF MY WEAK, SHALLOW MOMENTS I MIGHT ADMIT THAT SOMETIMES I MISS BEING CATCALLED.

Y GARDEN than ever!

I AM GOING THROUGH SOME THINGS RIGHT NOW, MICHAEL. BEING A WOMAN IS VERY CONFUSING.

NO. I MEANT YOU SHOULD BE ASHAMED ABOUT USING AMAZON. WE PROMISED WE WOULD QUIT.

I KNOW, BUT I USED AMAZON SMILE! SO I AUTOMATICALLY MADE A DONATION TO PBS!

DOES THIS MEAN YOU'LL STOP RUNNING THAT MENSTRUAL CUP THROUGH THE DISHWASHER NOW?

IF YOU STOP EMPTYING YOUR NETI POT INTO THE KITCHEN SINK.

TO CELEBRATE, I BOUGHT THOSE PERIOD PANTIES, TOO. THEY SEEMED BETTER FOR THE GO BAGS.

THAT'S MY GIRL.

GODDAMMIT, MICHAEL. WOMAN.

8

Chapter 2

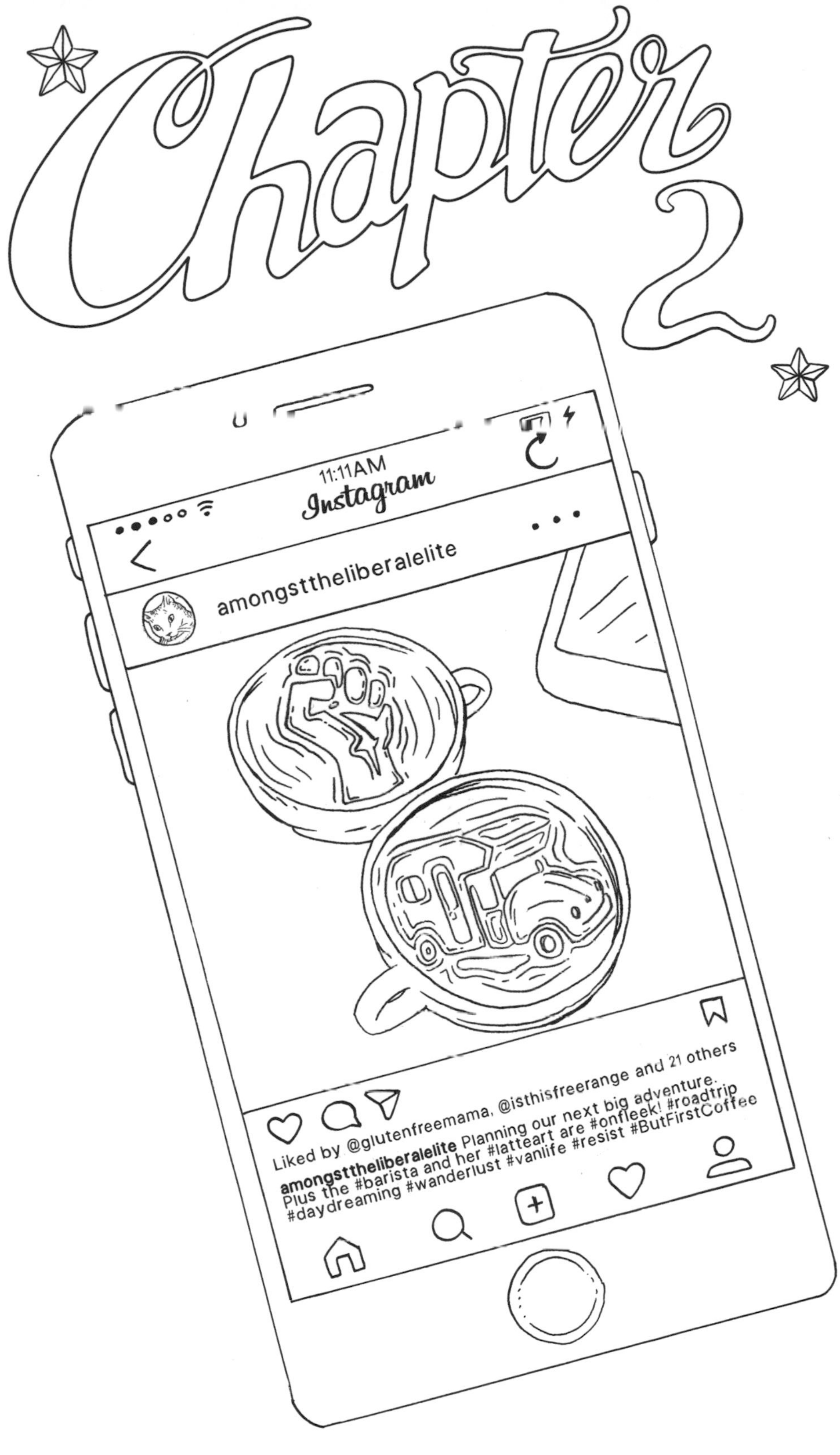

11:11AM
Instagram
amongsttheliberalelite
Liked by @glutenfreemama, @isthisfreerange and 21 others
amongsttheliberalelite Planning our next big adventure.
Plus the #barista and her #latteart are #onfleek! #roadtrip
#daydreaming #wanderlust #vanlife #resist #ButFirstCoffee

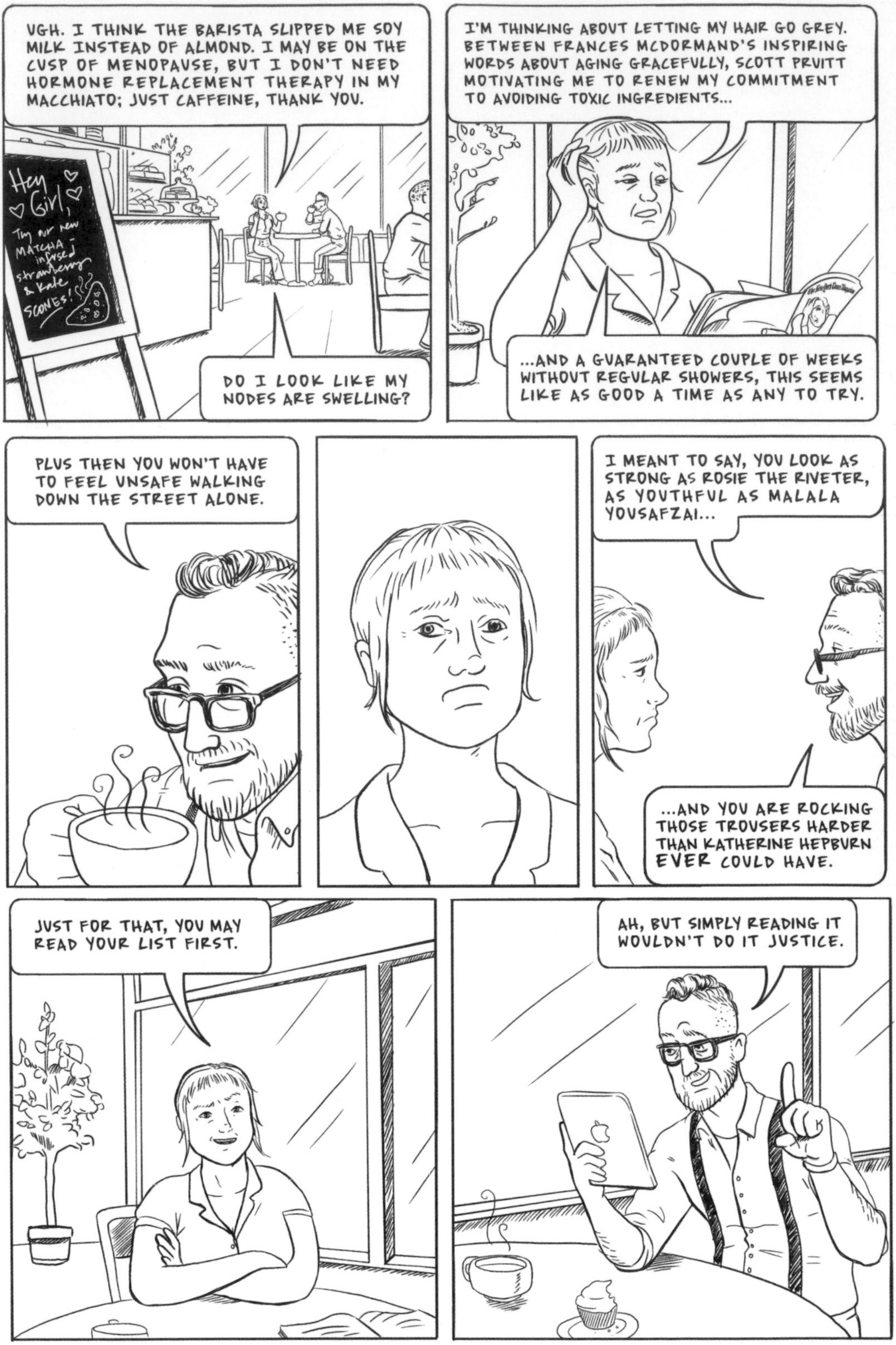

UGH. I THINK THE BARISTA SLIPPED ME SOY MILK INSTEAD OF ALMOND. I MAY BE ON THE CUSP OF MENOPAUSE, BUT I DON'T NEED HORMONE REPLACEMENT THERAPY IN MY MACCHIATO; JUST CAFFEINE, THANK YOU.
Hey Girl, Try our new MATCHA-infused strawberry & kale SCONES!
DO I LOOK LIKE MY NODES ARE SWELLING?
I'M THINKING ABOUT LETTING MY HAIR GO GREY. BETWEEN FRANCES MCDORMAND'S INSPIRING WORDS ABOUT AGING GRACEFULLY, SCOTT PRUITT MOTIVATING ME TO RENEW MY COMMITMENT TO AVOIDING TOXIC INGREDIENTS...
...AND A GUARANTEED COUPLE OF WEEKS WITHOUT REGULAR SHOWERS, THIS SEEMS LIKE AS GOOD A TIME AS ANY TO TRY.
PLUS THEN YOU WON'T HAVE TO FEEL UNSAFE WALKING DOWN THE STREET ALONE.
I MEANT TO SAY, YOU LOOK AS STRONG AS ROSIE THE RIVETER, AS YOUTHFUL AS MALALA YOUSAFZAI...
...AND YOU ARE ROCKING THOSE TROUSERS HARDER THAN KATHERINE HEPBURN EVER COULD HAVE.
JUST FOR THAT, YOU MAY READ YOUR LIST FIRST.
AH, BUT SIMPLY READING IT WOULDN'T DO IT JUSTICE.

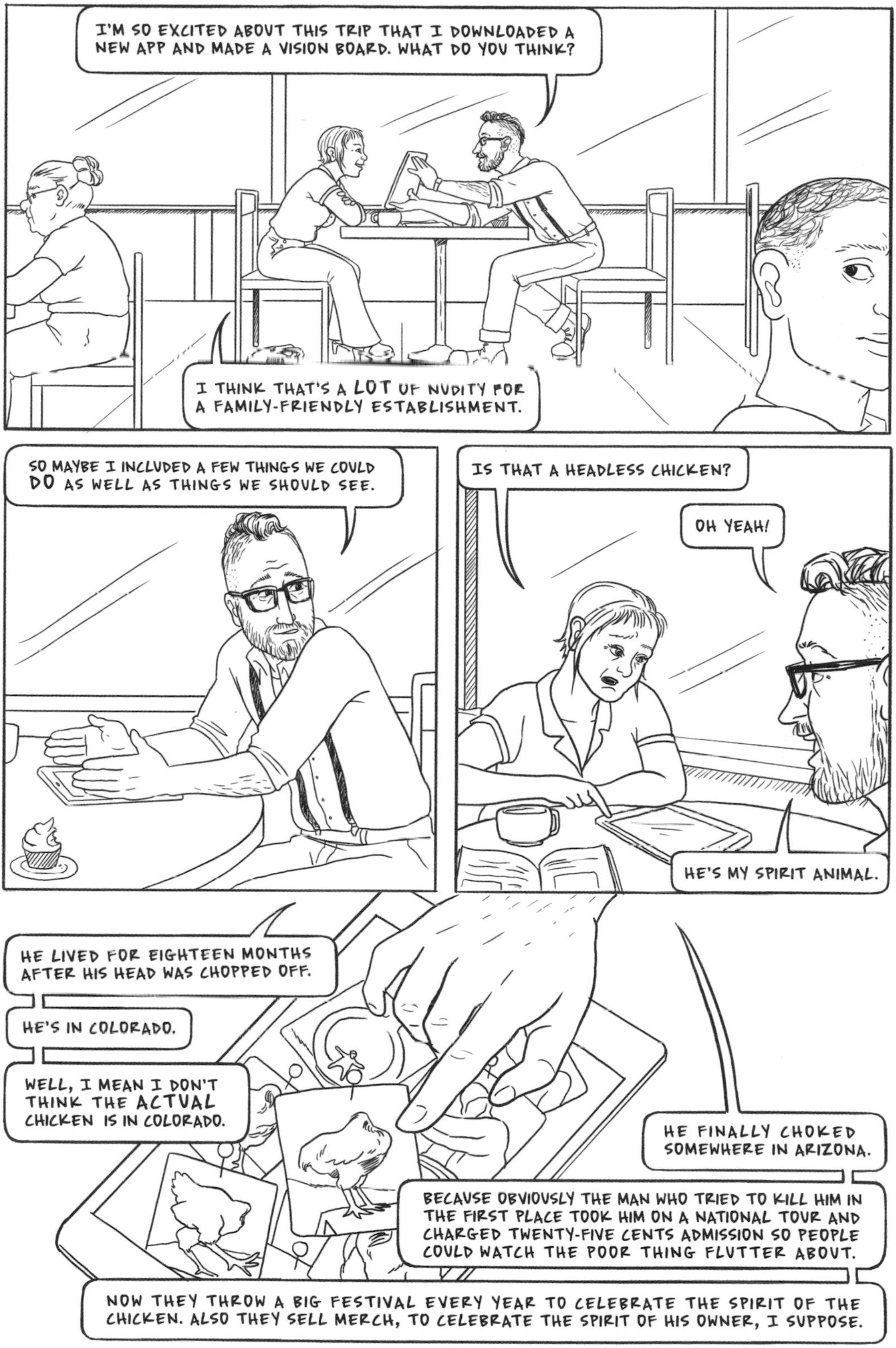
I'M SO EXCITED ABOUT THIS TRIP THAT I DOWNLOADED A NEW APP AND MADE A VISION BOARD. WHAT DO YOU THINK?
I THINK THAT'S A LOT OF NUDITY FOR A FAMILY-FRIENDLY ESTABLISHMENT.
SO MAYBE I INCLUDED A FEW THINGS WE COULD DO AS WELL AS THINGS WE SHOULD SEE.
IS THAT A HEADLESS CHICKEN?
OH YEAH!
HE'S MY SPIRIT ANIMAL.
HE LIVED FOR EIGHTEEN MONTHS AFTER HIS HEAD WAS CHOPPED OFF.
HE'S IN COLORADO.
WELL, I MEAN I DON'T THINK THE ACTUAL CHICKEN IS IN COLORADO.
HE FINALLY CHOKED SOMEWHERE IN ARIZONA.
BECAUSE OBVIOUSLY THE MAN WHO TRIED TO KILL HIM IN THE FIRST PLACE TOOK HIM ON A NATIONAL TOUR AND CHARGED TWENTY-FIVE CENTS ADMISSION SO PEOPLE COULD WATCH THE POOR THING FLUTTER ABOUT.
NOW THEY THROW A BIG FESTIVAL EVERY YEAR TO CELEBRATE THE SPIRIT OF THE CHICKEN. ALSO THEY SELL MERCH, TO CELEBRATE THE SPIRIT OF HIS OWNER, I SUPPOSE.

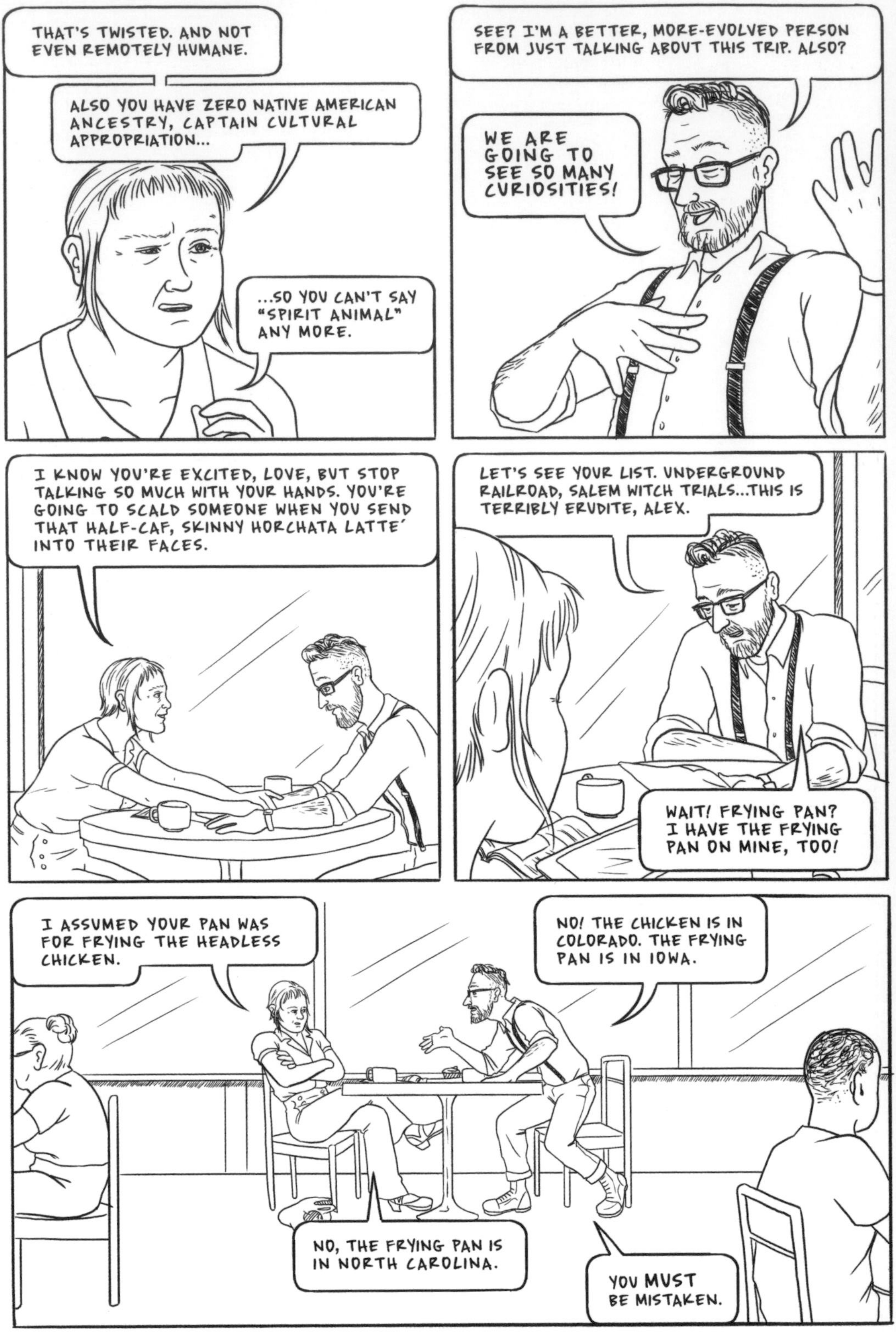
THAT'S TWISTED. AND NOT EVEN REMOTELY HUMANE.
ALSO YOU HAVE ZERO NATIVE AMERICAN ANCESTRY, CAPTAIN CULTURAL APPROPRIATION...
...SO YOU CAN'T SAY "SPIRIT ANIMAL" ANY MORE.
SEE? I'M A BETTER, MORE-EVOLVED PERSON FROM JUST TALKING ABOUT THIS TRIP. ALSO?
WE ARE GOING TO SEE SO MANY CURIOSITIES!
I KNOW YOU'RE EXCITED, LOVE, BUT STOP TALKING SO MUCH WITH YOUR HANDS. YOU'RE GOING TO SCALD SOMEONE WHEN YOU SEND THAT HALF-CAF, SKINNY HORCHATA LATTE´ INTO THEIR FACES.
LET'S SEE YOUR LIST. UNDERGROUND RAILROAD, SALEM WITCH TRIALS...THIS IS TERRIBLY ERUDITE, ALEX.
WAIT! FRYING PAN? I HAVE THE FRYING PAN ON MINE, TOO!
I ASSUMED YOUR PAN WAS FOR FRYING THE HEADLESS CHICKEN.
NO! THE CHICKEN IS IN COLORADO. THE FRYING PAN IS IN IOWA.
NO, THE FRYING PAN IS IN NORTH CAROLINA.
YOU MUST BE MISTAKEN.

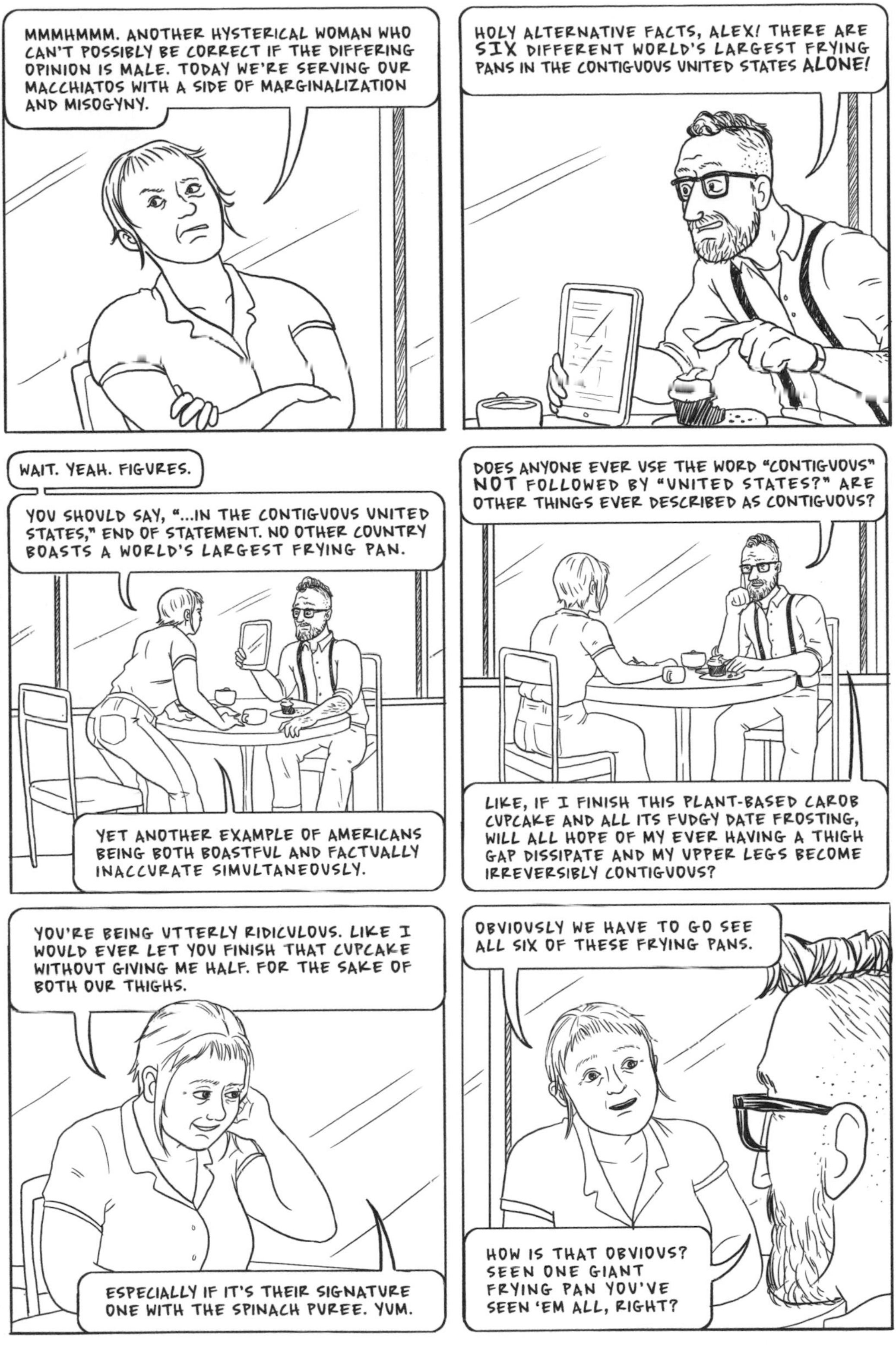
MMMHMMM. ANOTHER HYSTERICAL WOMAN WHO CAN'T POSSIBLY BE CORRECT IF THE DIFFERING OPINION IS MALE. TODAY WE'RE SERVING OUR MACCHIATOS WITH A SIDE OF MARGINALIZATION AND MISOGYNY.
HOLY ALTERNATIVE FACTS, ALEX! THERE ARE SIX DIFFERENT WORLD'S LARGEST FRYING PANS IN THE CONTIGUOUS UNITED STATES ALONE!
WAIT. YEAH. FIGURES.
YOU SHOULD SAY, "...IN THE CONTIGUOUS UNITED STATES," END OF STATEMENT. NO OTHER COUNTRY BOASTS A WORLD'S LARGEST FRYING PAN.
YET ANOTHER EXAMPLE OF AMERICANS BEING BOTH BOASTFUL AND FACTUALLY INACCURATE SIMULTANEOUSLY.
DOES ANYONE EVER USE THE WORD "CONTIGUOUS" NOT FOLLOWED BY "UNITED STATES?" ARE OTHER THINGS EVER DESCRIBED AS CONTIGUOUS?
LIKE, IF I FINISH THIS PLANT-BASED CAROB CUPCAKE AND ALL ITS FUDGY DATE FROSTING, WILL ALL HOPE OF MY EVER HAVING A THIGH GAP DISSIPATE AND MY UPPER LEGS BECOME IRREVERSIBLY CONTIGUOUS?
YOU'RE BEING UTTERLY RIDICULOUS. LIKE I WOULD EVER LET YOU FINISH THAT CUPCAKE WITHOUT GIVING ME HALF. FOR THE SAKE OF BOTH OUR THIGHS.
ESPECIALLY IF IT'S THEIR SIGNATURE ONE WITH THE SPINACH PUREE. YUM.
OBVIOUSLY WE HAVE TO GO SEE ALL SIX OF THESE FRYING PANS.
HOW IS THAT OBVIOUS? SEEN ONE GIANT FRYING PAN YOU'VE SEEN 'EM ALL, RIGHT?

WELL IF THAT ISN'T A METAPHOR FOR OUR FELLOW COUNTRYPERSONS' ABHORRENCE OF DIVERSITY, I DON'T KNOW WHAT IS. I BET EACH ONE OF THOSE FRYING PANS IS A UNIQUE CELEBRATION OF THE COMMUNITY THAT MADE IT, THAT EACH IS SEASONED WITH THE CULTURE THAT INSPIRED IT, THAT EACH IS...

...STICKY WITH RANCID OIL.

YEAH, PROBABLY. BUT EACH ONE WITH A DIFFERENT OIL.

ANYWAY FUCK KELLYANNE'S ALTERNATIVE FACTS AND 45'S FAKE NEWS. WE OWE IT TO THE AMERICAN PEOPLE....

TO ONCE AND FOR ALL INDEPENDENTLY VERIFY THESE CLAIMS OF WORLD'S-LARGEST-NESS AND DETERMINE THE SINGLE, UNIMPEACHABLE WINNER.

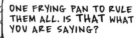

ONE FRYING PAN TO RULE THEM ALL. IS THAT WHAT YOU ARE SAYING?

WOULD BEING RULED BY A GIANT FRYING PAN BE MUCH WORSE THAN OUR CURRENT SITUATION?

GUESS NOT.

GREAT! IT'S DECIDED.

AND IF WE MUST FOREGO SEEING HISTORICAL SITES AND GEOGRAPHICAL WONDERS TO DO SO, THEN SO BE IT.

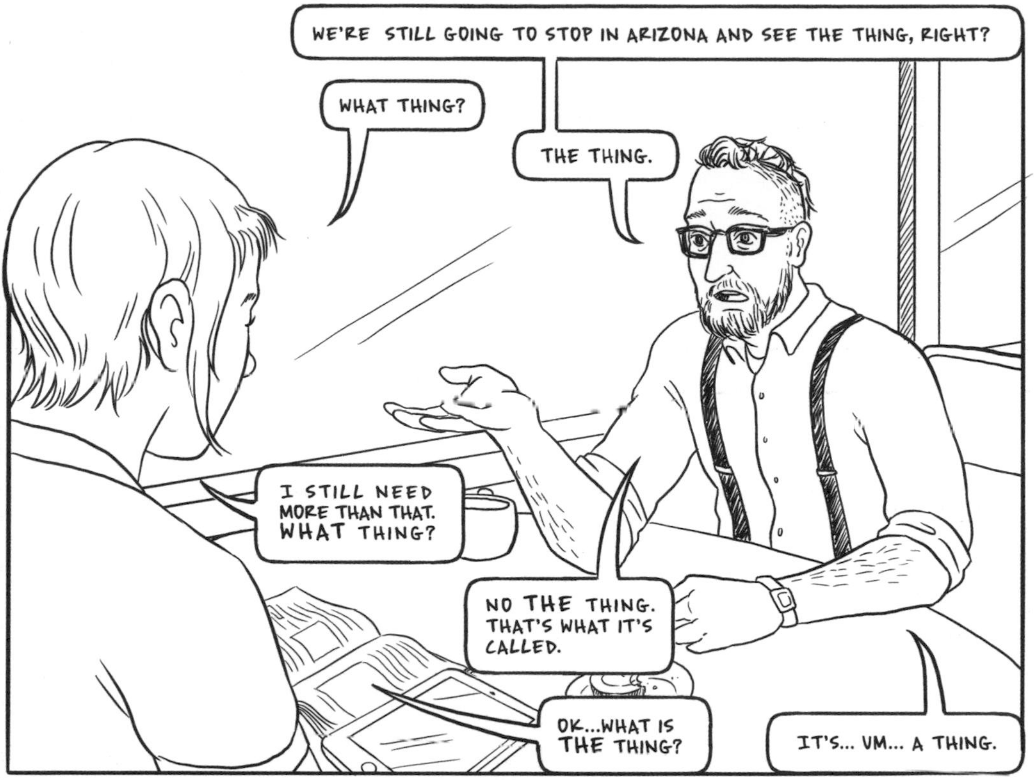

WE'RE STILL GOING TO STOP IN ARIZONA AND SEE THE THING, RIGHT?
WHAT THING?
THE THING.
I STILL NEED MORE THAN THAT. WHAT THING?
NO THE THING. THAT'S WHAT IT'S CALLED.
OK...WHAT IS THE THING?
IT'S... UM... A THING.

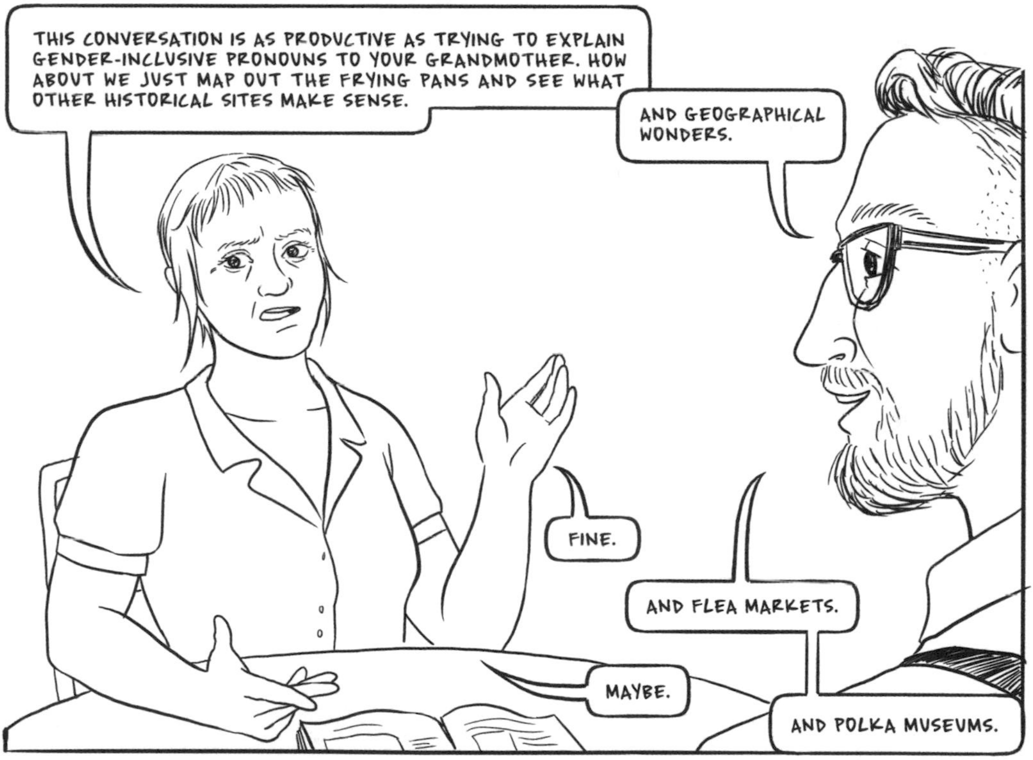

THIS CONVERSATION IS AS PRODUCTIVE AS TRYING TO EXPLAIN GENDER-INCLUSIVE PRONOUNS TO YOUR GRANDMOTHER. HOW ABOUT WE JUST MAP OUT THE FRYING PANS AND SEE WHAT OTHER HISTORICAL SITES MAKE SENSE.
AND GEOGRAPHICAL WONDERS.
FINE.
AND FLEA MARKETS.
MAYBE.
AND POLKA MUSEUMS.

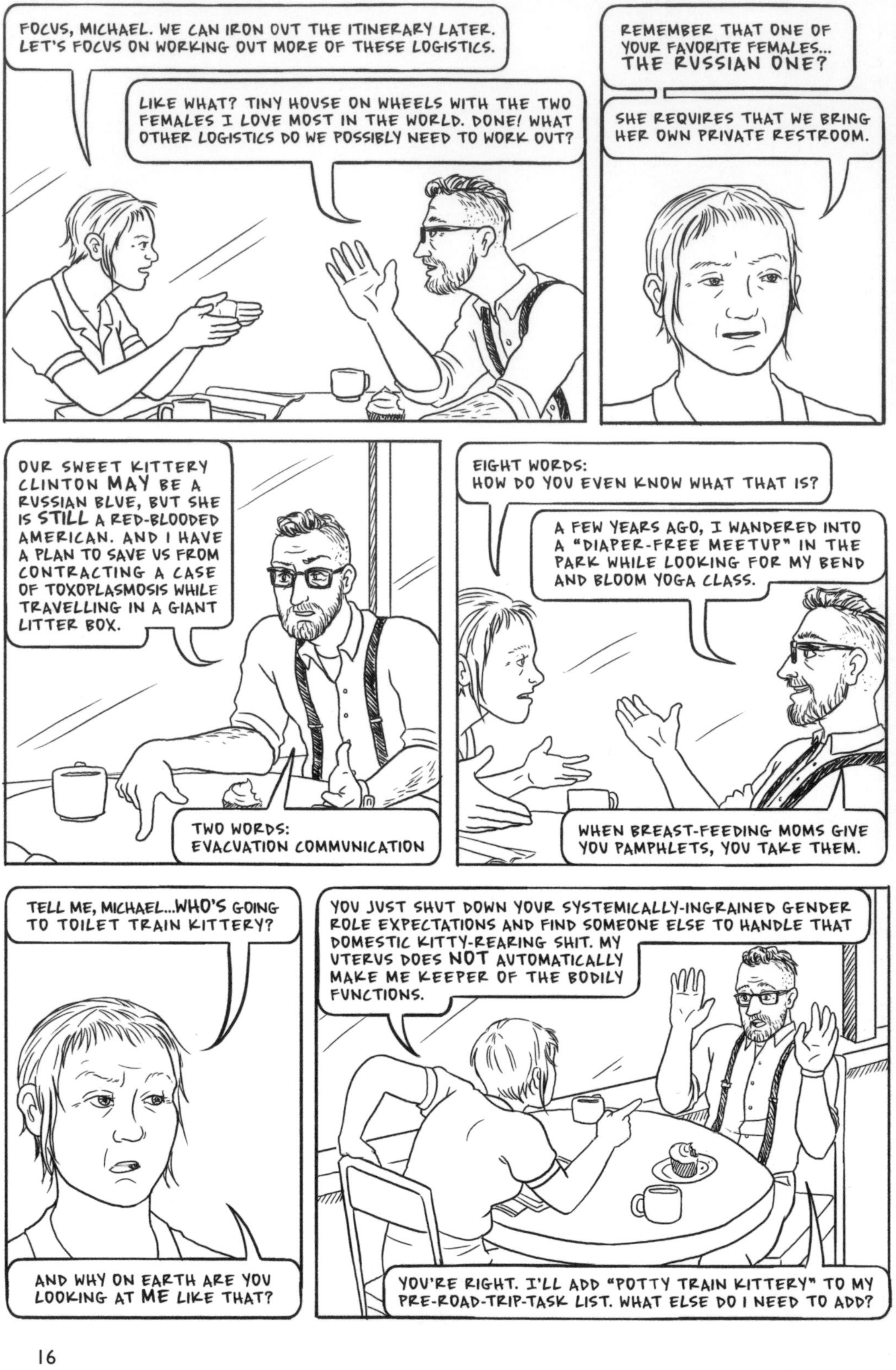
FOCUS, MICHAEL. WE CAN IRON OUT THE ITINERARY LATER. LET'S FOCUS ON WORKING OUT MORE OF THESE LOGISTICS.
LIKE WHAT? TINY HOUSE ON WHEELS WITH THE TWO FEMALES I LOVE MOST IN THE WORLD. DONE! WHAT OTHER LOGISTICS DO WE POSSIBLY NEED TO WORK OUT?
REMEMBER THAT ONE OF YOUR FAVORITE FEMALES... THE RUSSIAN ONE?
SHE REQUIRES THAT WE BRING HER OWN PRIVATE RESTROOM.
OUR SWEET KITTERY CLINTON MAY BE A RUSSIAN BLUE, BUT SHE IS STILL A RED-BLOODED AMERICAN. AND I HAVE A PLAN TO SAVE US FROM CONTRACTING A CASE OF TOXOPLASMOSIS WHILE TRAVELLING IN A GIANT LITTER BOX.
TWO WORDS: EVACUATION COMMUNICATION
EIGHT WORDS: HOW DO YOU EVEN KNOW WHAT THAT IS?
A FEW YEARS AGO, I WANDERED INTO A "DIAPER-FREE MEETUP" IN THE PARK WHILE LOOKING FOR MY BEND AND BLOOM YOGA CLASS.
WHEN BREAST-FEEDING MOMS GIVE YOU PAMPHLETS, YOU TAKE THEM.
TELL ME, MICHAEL...WHO'S GOING TO TOILET TRAIN KITTERY?
AND WHY ON EARTH ARE YOU LOOKING AT ME LIKE THAT?
YOU JUST SHUT DOWN YOUR SYSTEMICALLY-INGRAINED GENDER ROLE EXPECTATIONS AND FIND SOMEONE ELSE TO HANDLE THAT DOMESTIC KITTY-REARING SHIT. MY UTERUS DOES NOT AUTOMATICALLY MAKE ME KEEPER OF THE BODILY FUNCTIONS.
YOU'RE RIGHT. I'LL ADD "POTTY TRAIN KITTERY" TO MY PRE-ROAD-TRIP-TASK LIST. WHAT ELSE DO I NEED TO ADD?

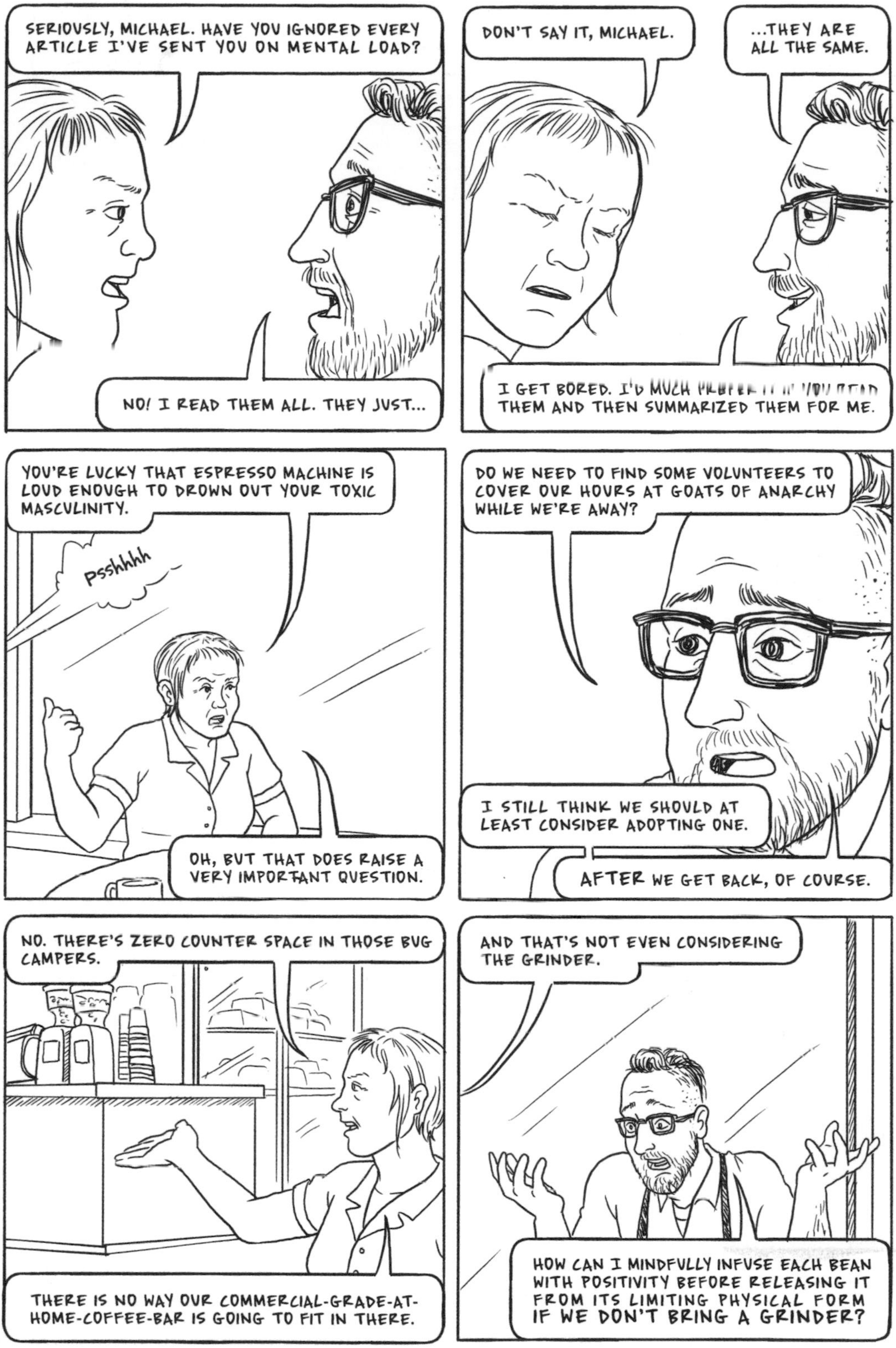

SERIOUSLY, MICHAEL. HAVE YOU IGNORED EVERY ARTICLE I'VE SENT YOU ON MENTAL LOAD?
NO! I READ THEM ALL. THEY JUST...
DON'T SAY IT, MICHAEL.
...THEY ARE ALL THE SAME.
I GET BORED. I'D MUCH
THEM AND THEN SUMMARIZED THEM FOR ME.
YOU'RE LUCKY THAT ESPRESSO MACHINE IS LOUD ENOUGH TO DROWN OUT YOUR TOXIC MASCULINITY.
psshhhh
OH, BUT THAT DOES RAISE A VERY IMPORTANT QUESTION.
DO WE NEED TO FIND SOME VOLUNTEERS TO COVER OUR HOURS AT GOATS OF ANARCHY WHILE WE'RE AWAY?
I STILL THINK WE SHOULD AT LEAST CONSIDER ADOPTING ONE.
AFTER WE GET BACK, OF COURSE.
NO. THERE'S ZERO COUNTER SPACE IN THOSE BUG CAMPERS.
THERE IS NO WAY OUR COMMERCIAL-GRADE-AT-HOME-COFFEE-BAR IS GOING TO FIT IN THERE.
AND THAT'S NOT EVEN CONSIDERING THE GRINDER.
HOW CAN I MINDFULLY INFUSE EACH BEAN WITH POSITIVITY BEFORE RELEASING IT FROM ITS LIMITING PHYSICAL FORM IF WE DON'T BRING A GRINDER?

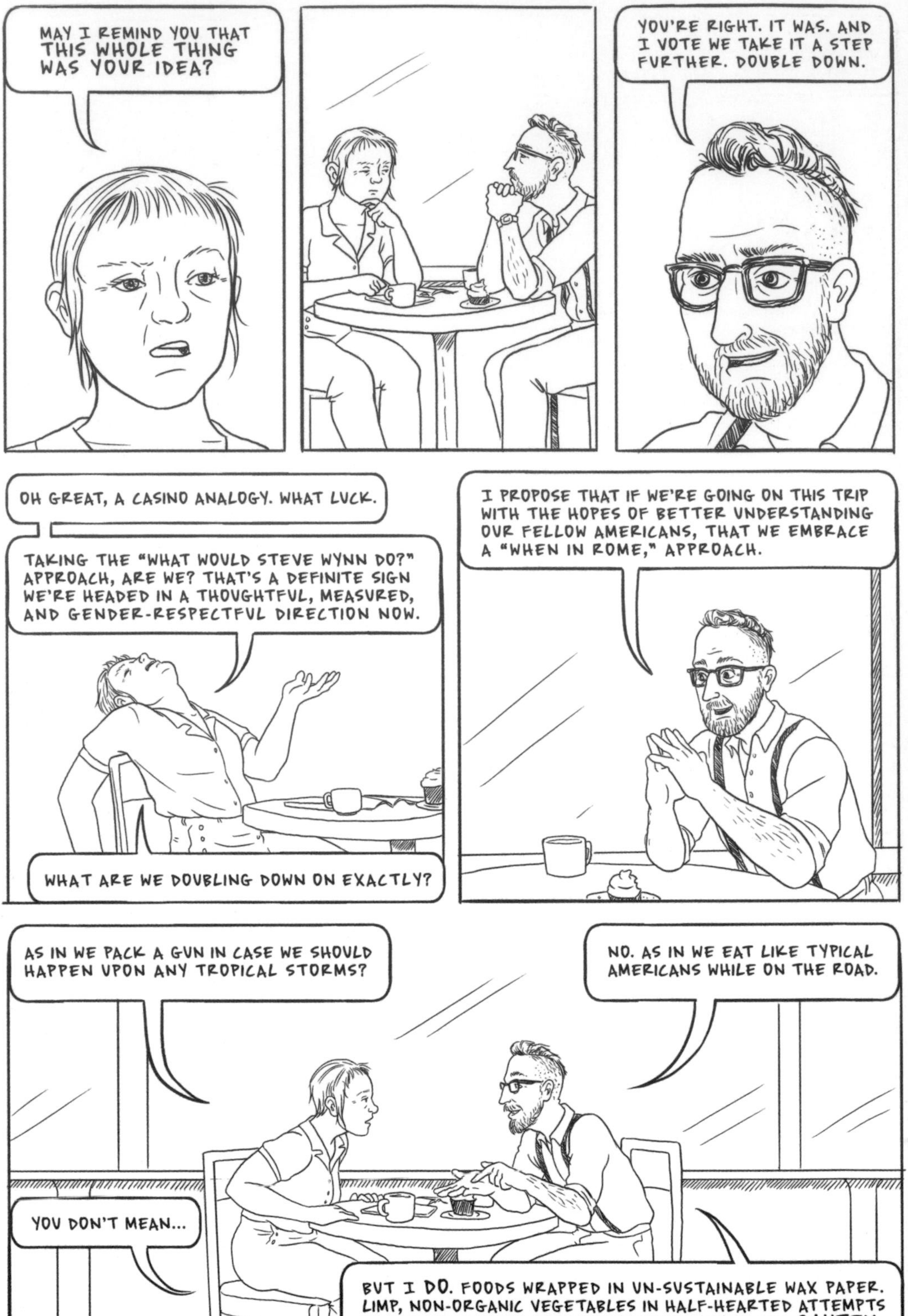
MAY I REMIND YOU THAT THIS WHOLE THING WAS YOUR IDEA?
YOU'RE RIGHT. IT WAS. AND I VOTE WE TAKE IT A STEP FURTHER. DOUBLE DOWN.
OH GREAT, A CASINO ANALOGY. WHAT LUCK.
TAKING THE "WHAT WOULD STEVE WYNN DO?" APPROACH, ARE WE? THAT'S A DEFINITE SIGN WE'RE HEADED IN A THOUGHTFUL, MEASURED, AND GENDER-RESPECTFUL DIRECTION NOW.
WHAT ARE WE DOUBLING DOWN ON EXACTLY?
I PROPOSE THAT IF WE'RE GOING ON THIS TRIP WITH THE HOPES OF BETTER UNDERSTANDING OUR FELLOW AMERICANS, THAT WE EMBRACE A "WHEN IN ROME," APPROACH.
AS IN WE PACK A GUN IN CASE WE SHOULD HAPPEN UPON ANY TROPICAL STORMS?
NO. AS IN WE EAT LIKE TYPICAL AMERICANS WHILE ON THE ROAD.
YOU DON'T MEAN...
BUT I DO. FOODS WRAPPED IN UN-SUSTAINABLE WAX PAPER. LIMP, NON-ORGANIC VEGETABLES IN HALF-HEARTED ATTEMPTS AT SALADS. COMTEMPORARY GRAINS. HAPPY MEALS. GLUTEN.

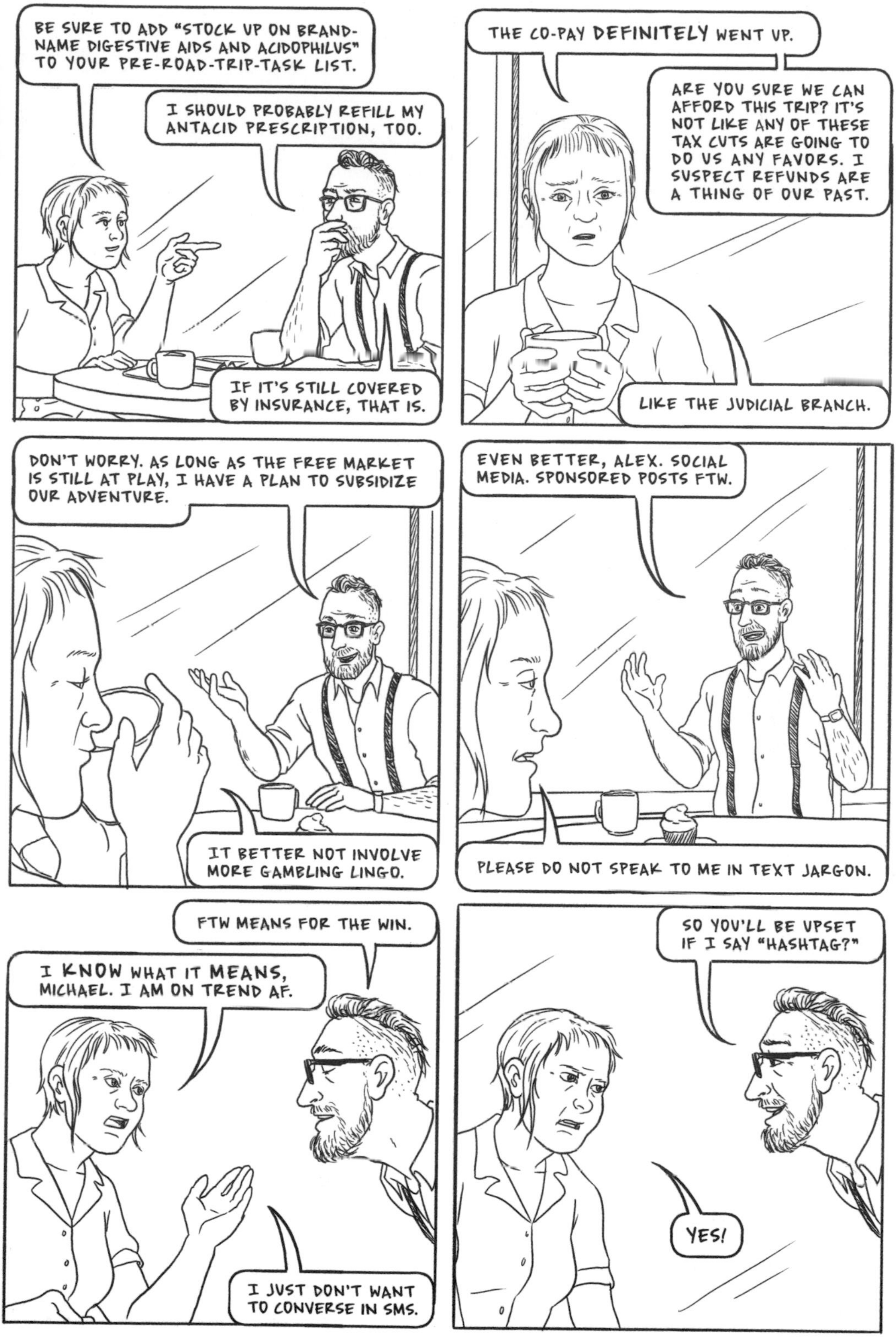
BE SURE TO ADD "STOCK UP ON BRAND-NAME DIGESTIVE AIDS AND ACIDOPHILUS" TO YOUR PRE-ROAD-TRIP-TASK LIST.
I SHOULD PROBABLY REFILL MY ANTACID PRESCRIPTION, TOO.
IF IT'S STILL COVERED BY INSURANCE, THAT IS.
THE CO-PAY DEFINITELY WENT UP.
ARE YOU SURE WE CAN AFFORD THIS TRIP? IT'S NOT LIKE ANY OF THESE TAX CUTS ARE GOING TO DO US ANY FAVORS. I SUSPECT REFUNDS ARE A THING OF OUR PAST.
LIKE THE JUDICIAL BRANCH.
DON'T WORRY. AS LONG AS THE FREE MARKET IS STILL AT PLAY, I HAVE A PLAN TO SUBSIDIZE OUR ADVENTURE.
IT BETTER NOT INVOLVE MORE GAMBLING LINGO.
EVEN BETTER, ALEX. SOCIAL MEDIA. SPONSORED POSTS FTW.
PLEASE DO NOT SPEAK TO ME IN TEXT JARGON.
FTW MEANS FOR THE WIN.
I KNOW WHAT IT MEANS, MICHAEL. I AM ON TREND AF.
I JUST DON'T WANT TO CONVERSE IN SMS.
SO YOU'LL BE UPSET IF I SAY "HASHTAG?"
YES!

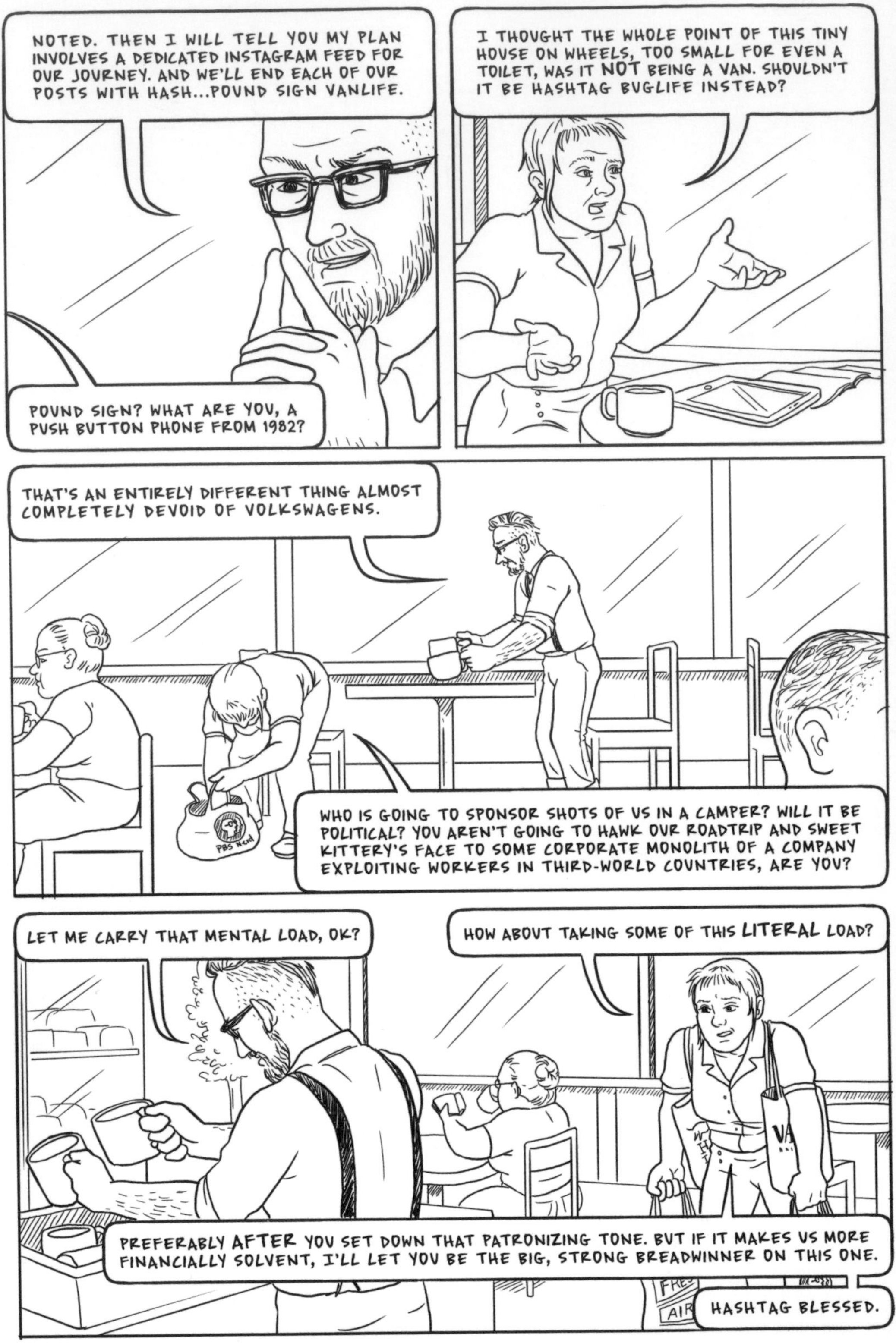
NOTED. THEN I WILL TELL YOU MY PLAN INVOLVES A DEDICATED INSTAGRAM FEED FOR OUR JOURNEY. AND WE'LL END EACH OF OUR POSTS WITH HASH...POUND SIGN VANLIFE.
POUND SIGN? WHAT ARE YOU, A PUSH BUTTON PHONE FROM 1982?
I THOUGHT THE WHOLE POINT OF THIS TINY HOUSE ON WHEELS, TOO SMALL FOR EVEN A TOILET, WAS IT NOT BEING A VAN. SHOULDN'T IT BE HASHTAG BUGLIFE INSTEAD?
THAT'S AN ENTIRELY DIFFERENT THING ALMOST COMPLETELY DEVOID OF VOLKSWAGENS.
PBS Nerd
WHO IS GOING TO SPONSOR SHOTS OF US IN A CAMPER? WILL IT BE POLITICAL? YOU AREN'T GOING TO HAWK OUR ROADTRIP AND SWEET KITTERY'S FACE TO SOME CORPORATE MONOLITH OF A COMPANY EXPLOITING WORKERS IN THIRD-WORLD COUNTRIES, ARE YOU?
LET ME CARRY THAT MENTAL LOAD, OK?
HOW ABOUT TAKING SOME OF THIS LITERAL LOAD?
PREFERABLY AFTER YOU SET DOWN THAT PATRONIZING TONE. BUT IF IT MAKES US MORE FINANCIALLY SOLVENT, I'LL LET YOU BE THE BIG, STRONG BREADWINNER ON THIS ONE.
HASHTAG BLESSED.

Chapter 3

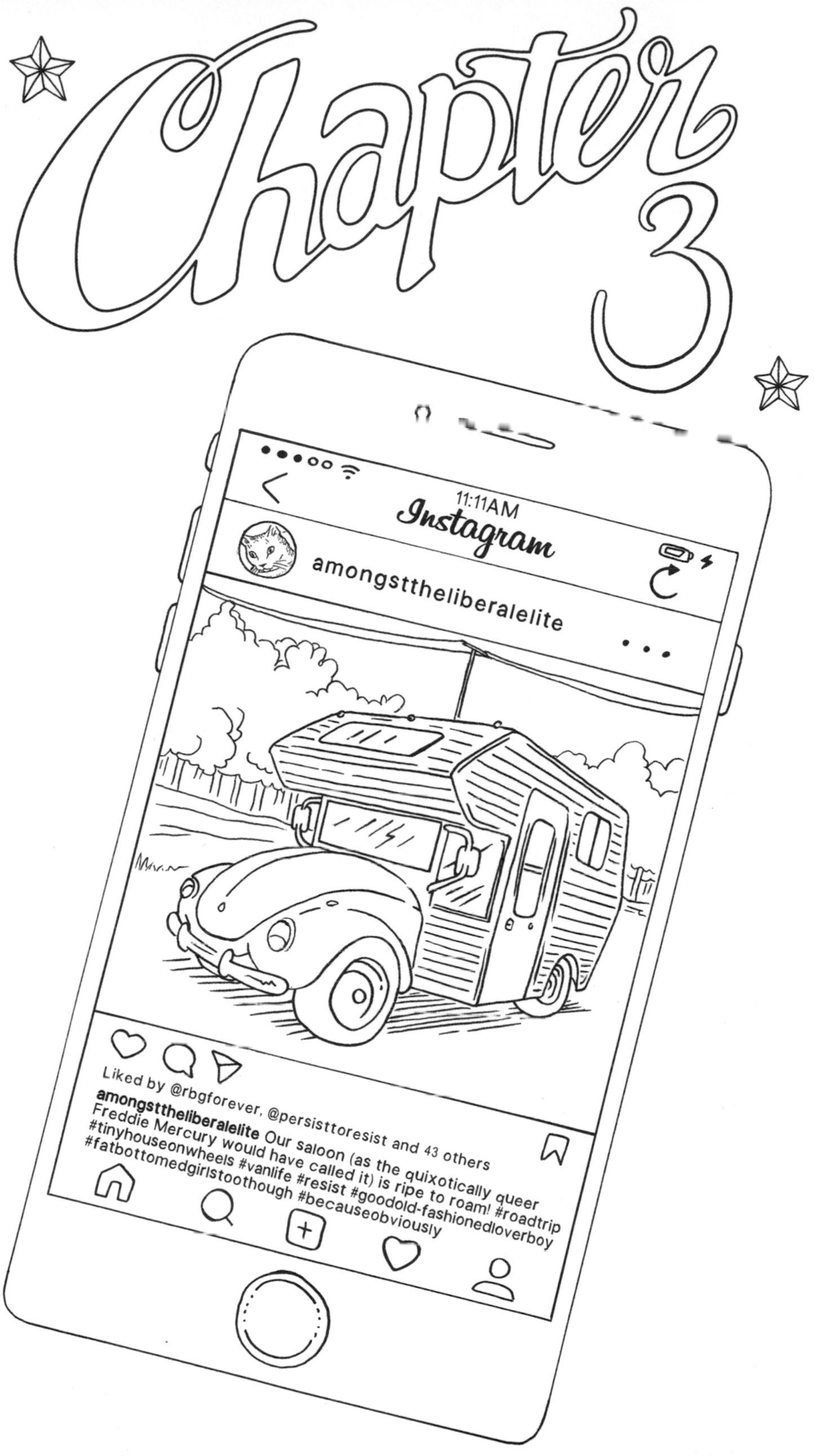
11:11AM
Instagram
amongsttheliberalelite
Liked by @rbgforever, @persisttoresist and 43 others
amongsttheliberalelite Our saloon (as the quixotically queer Freddie Mercury would have called it) is ripe to roam! #roadtrip #tinyhouseonwheels #vanlife #resist #goodold-fashionedloverboy #fatbottomedgirlstoothough #becauseobviously

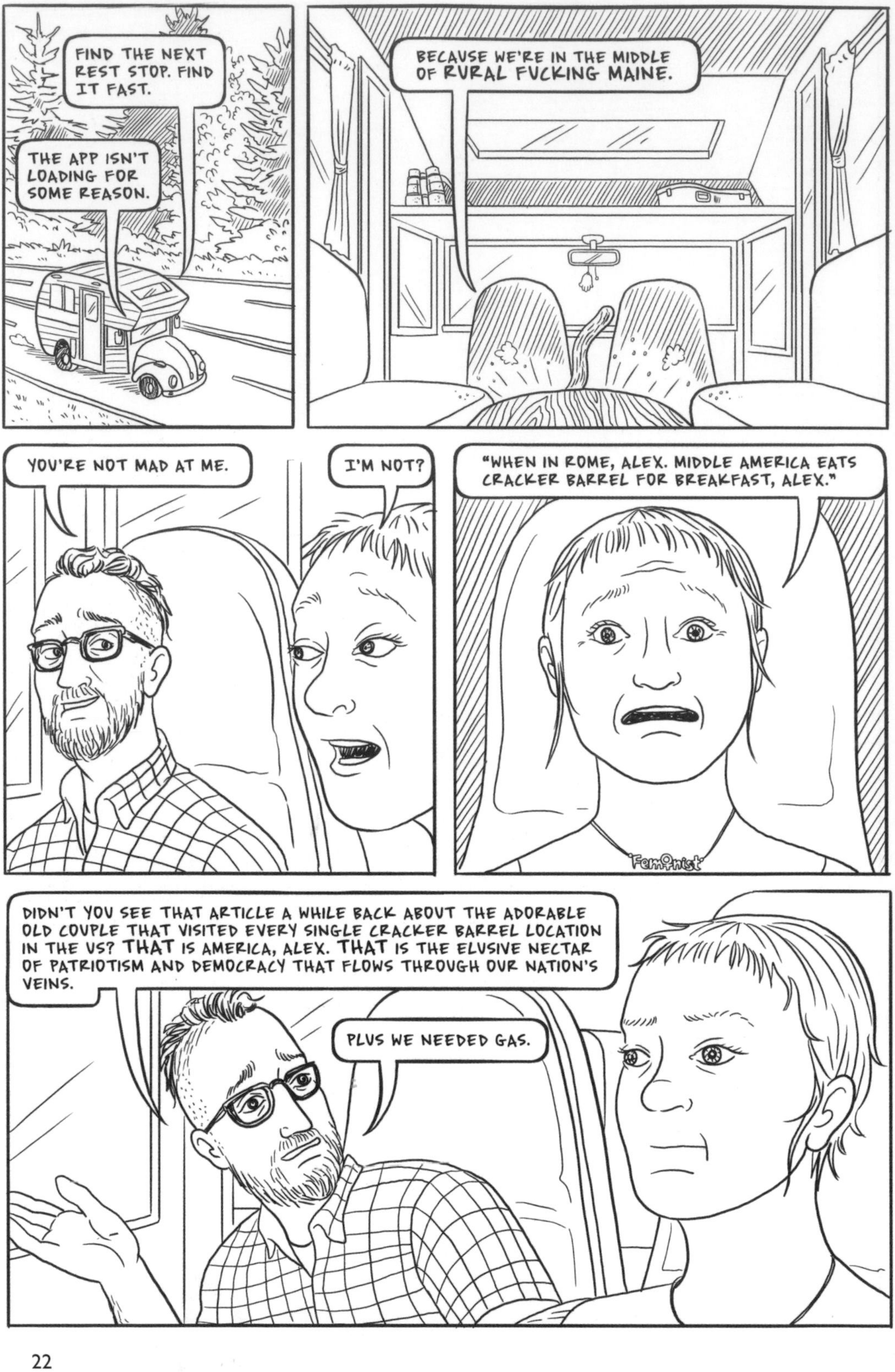
FIND THE NEXT REST STOP. FIND IT FAST.
THE APP ISN'T LOADING FOR SOME REASON.
BECAUSE WE'RE IN THE MIDDLE OF RURAL FUCKING MAINE.
YOU'RE NOT MAD AT ME.
I'M NOT?
"WHEN IN ROME, ALEX. MIDDLE AMERICA EATS CRACKER BARREL FOR BREAKFAST, ALEX."
Feminist
DIDN'T YOU SEE THAT ARTICLE A WHILE BACK ABOUT THE ADORABLE OLD COUPLE THAT VISITED EVERY SINGLE CRACKER BARREL LOCATION IN THE US? THAT IS AMERICA, ALEX. THAT IS THE ELUSIVE NECTAR OF PATRIOTISM AND DEMOCRACY THAT FLOWS THROUGH OUR NATION'S VEINS.
PLUS WE NEEDED GAS.

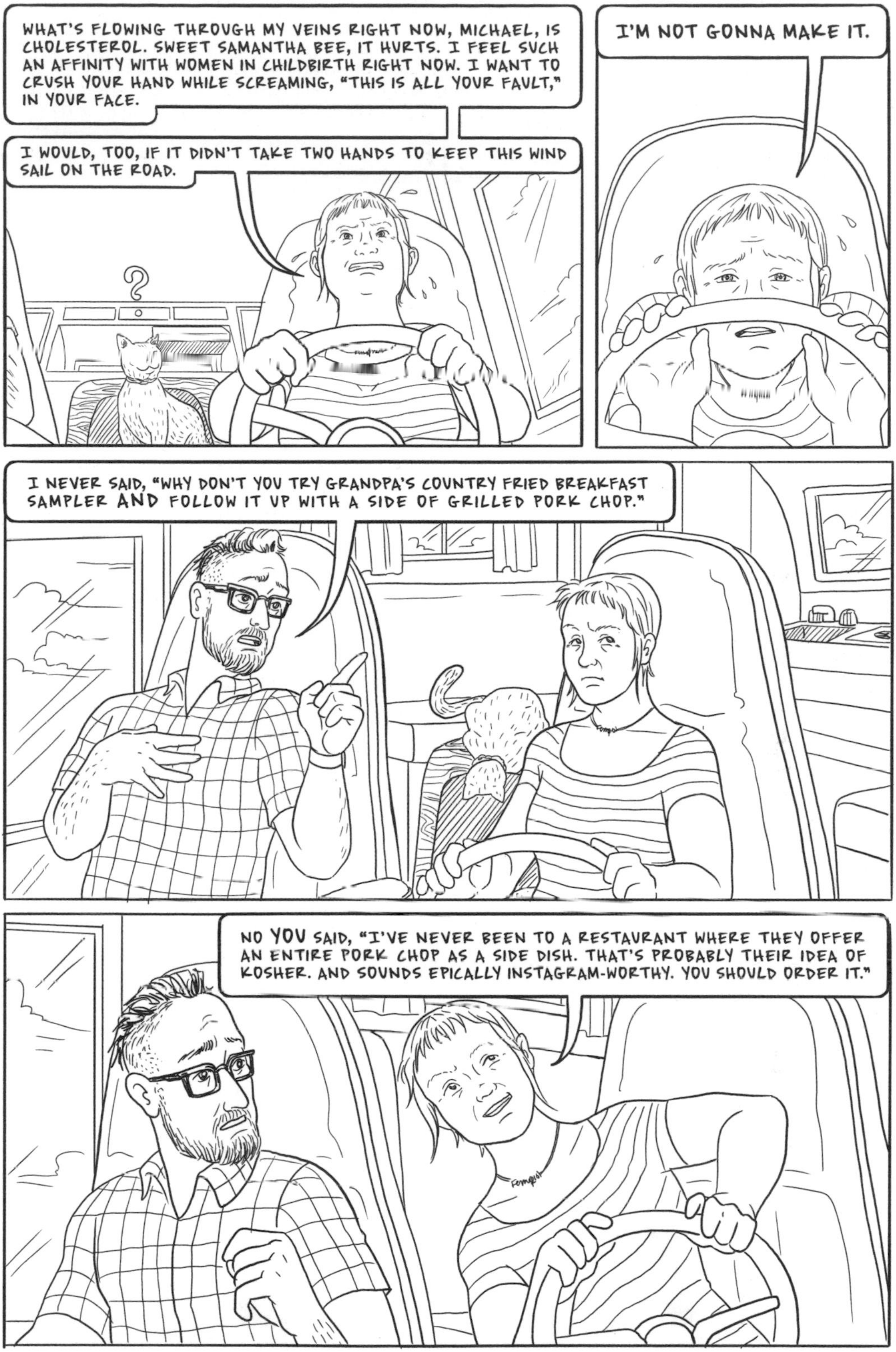
WHAT'S FLOWING THROUGH MY VEINS RIGHT NOW, MICHAEL, IS CHOLESTEROL. SWEET SAMANTHA BEE, IT HURTS. I FEEL SUCH AN AFFINITY WITH WOMEN IN CHILDBIRTH RIGHT NOW. I WANT TO CRUSH YOUR HAND WHILE SCREAMING, "THIS IS ALL YOUR FAULT," IN YOUR FACE.
I WOULD, TOO, IF IT DIDN'T TAKE TWO HANDS TO KEEP THIS WIND SAIL ON THE ROAD.
?
I'M NOT GONNA MAKE IT.
I NEVER SAID, "WHY DON'T YOU TRY GRANDPA'S COUNTRY FRIED BREAKFAST SAMPLER AND FOLLOW IT UP WITH A SIDE OF GRILLED PORK CHOP."
NO YOU SAID, "I'VE NEVER BEEN TO A RESTAURANT WHERE THEY OFFER AN ENTIRE PORK CHOP AS A SIDE DISH. THAT'S PROBABLY THEIR IDEA OF KOSHER. AND SOUNDS EPICALLY INSTAGRAM-WORTHY. YOU SHOULD ORDER IT."

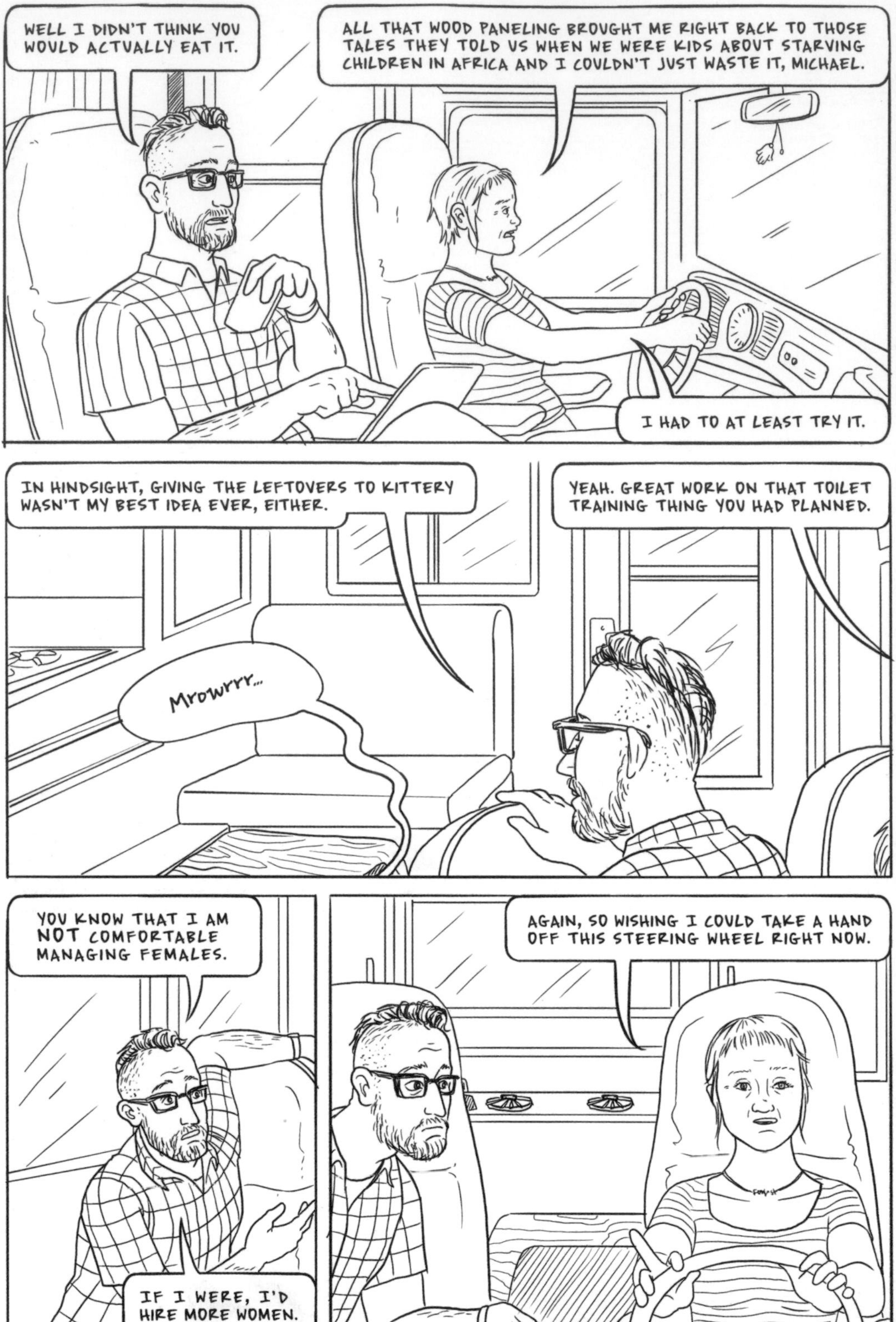
WELL I DIDN'T THINK YOU WOULD ACTUALLY EAT IT.
ALL THAT WOOD PANELING BROUGHT ME RIGHT BACK TO THOSE TALES THEY TOLD US WHEN WE WERE KIDS ABOUT STARVING CHILDREN IN AFRICA AND I COULDN'T JUST WASTE IT, MICHAEL.
I HAD TO AT LEAST TRY IT.
IN HINDSIGHT, GIVING THE LEFTOVERS TO KITTERY WASN'T MY BEST IDEA EVER, EITHER.
Mrowrrr...
YEAH. GREAT WORK ON THAT TOILET TRAINING THING YOU HAD PLANNED.
YOU KNOW THAT I AM NOT COMFORTABLE MANAGING FEMALES.
IF I WERE, I'D HIRE MORE WOMEN.
AGAIN, SO WISHING I COULD TAKE A HAND OFF THIS STEERING WHEEL RIGHT NOW.

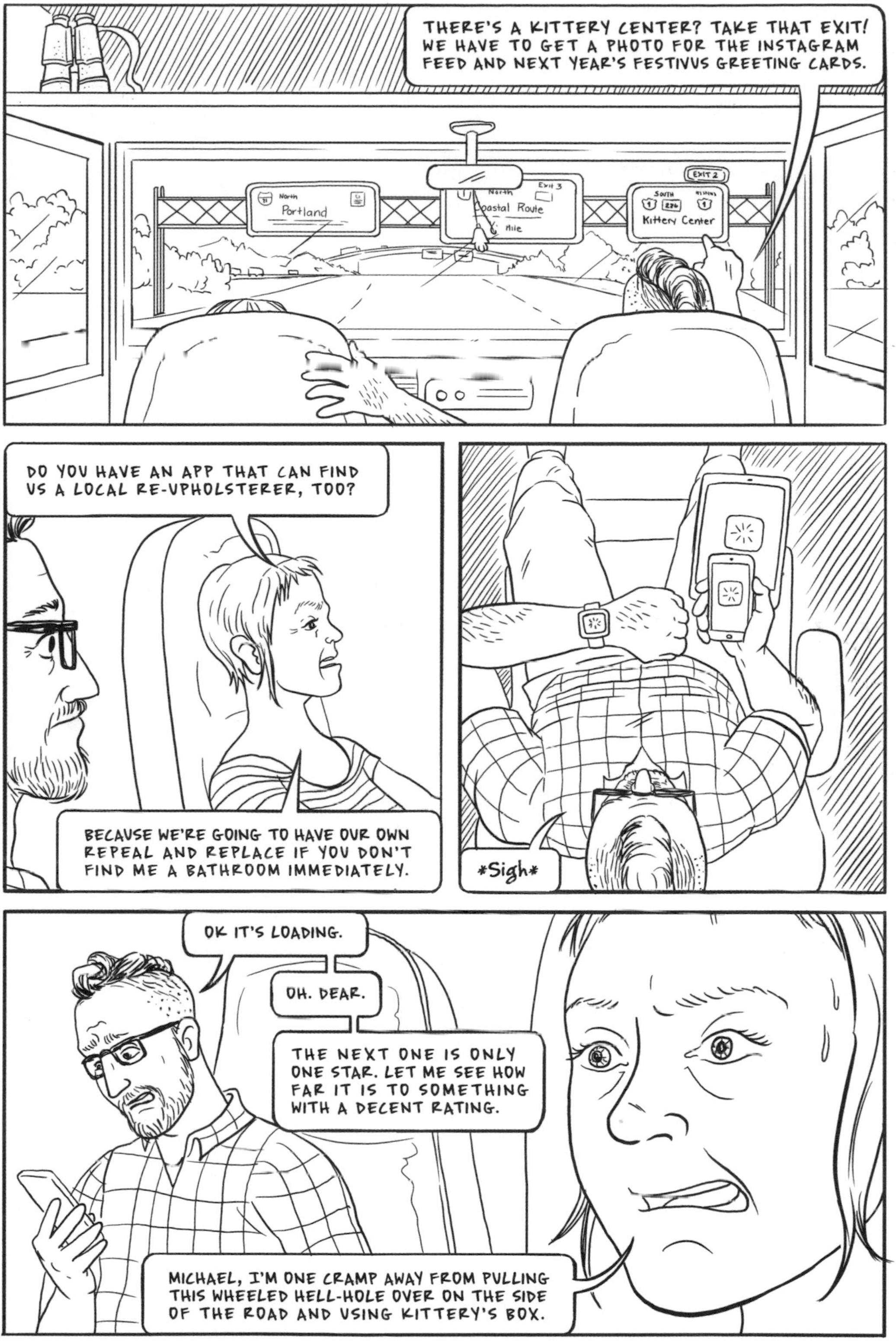
THERE'S A KITTERY CENTER? TAKE THAT EXIT! WE HAVE TO GET A PHOTO FOR THE INSTAGRAM FEED AND NEXT YEAR'S FESTIVUS GREETING CARDS.
North
Portland
North
Exit 3
Coastal Route
EXIT 2
SOUTH
Kittery Center
DO YOU HAVE AN APP THAT CAN FIND US A LOCAL RE-UPHOLSTERER, TOO?
BECAUSE WE'RE GOING TO HAVE OUR OWN REPEAL AND REPLACE IF YOU DON'T FIND ME A BATHROOM IMMEDIATELY.
Sigh
OK IT'S LOADING.
OH. DEAR.
THE NEXT ONE IS ONLY ONE STAR. LET ME SEE HOW FAR IT IS TO SOMETHING WITH A DECENT RATING.
MICHAEL, I'M ONE CRAMP AWAY FROM PULLING THIS WHEELED HELL-HOLE OVER ON THE SIDE OF THE ROAD AND USING KITTERY'S BOX.

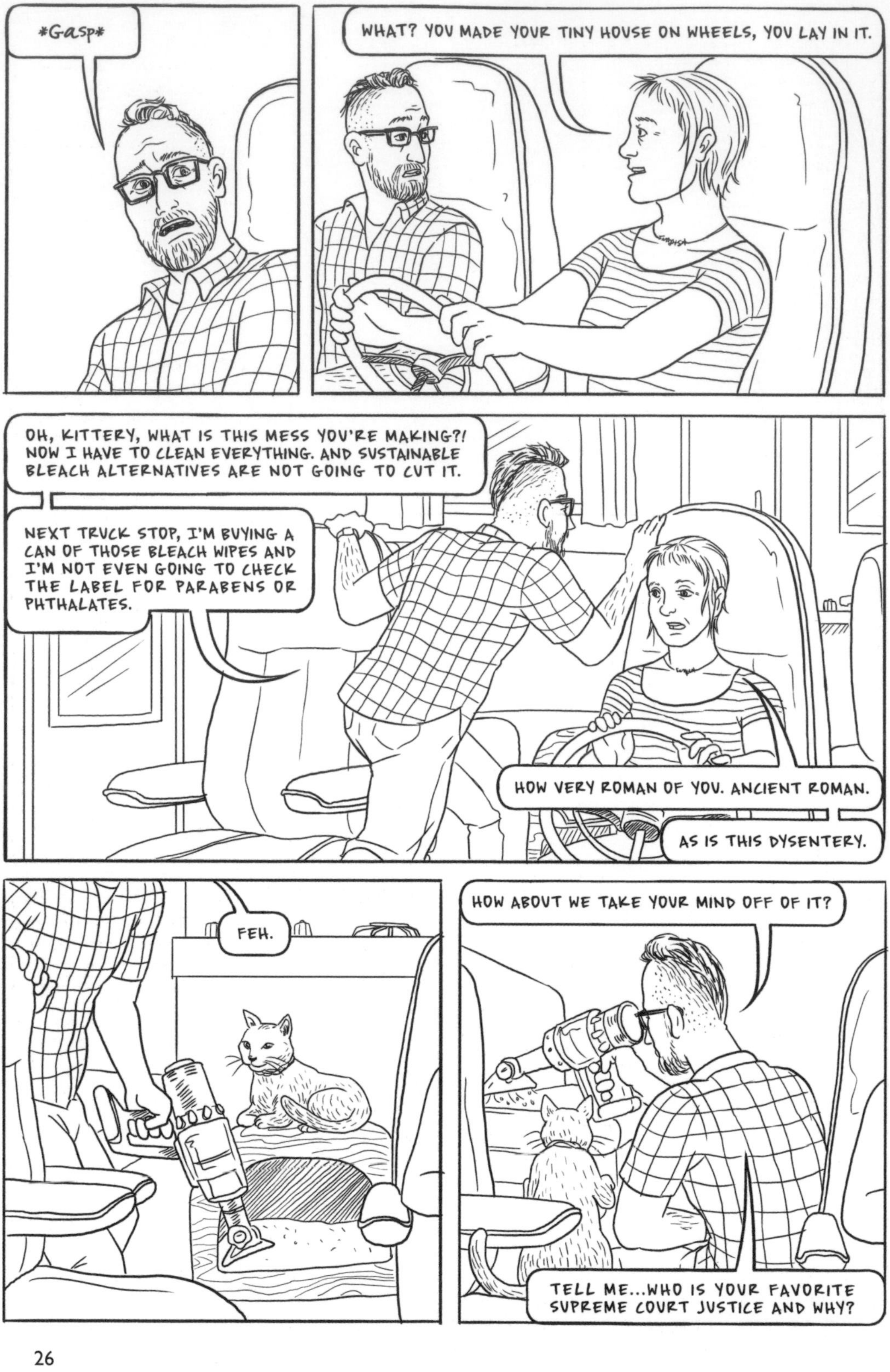
Gasp
WHAT? YOU MADE YOUR TINY HOUSE ON WHEELS, YOU LAY IN IT.
OH, KITTERY, WHAT IS THIS MESS YOU'RE MAKING?! NOW I HAVE TO CLEAN EVERYTHING. AND SUSTAINABLE BLEACH ALTERNATIVES ARE NOT GOING TO CUT IT.
NEXT TRUCK STOP, I'M BUYING A CAN OF THOSE BLEACH WIPES AND I'M NOT EVEN GOING TO CHECK THE LABEL FOR PARABENS OR PHTHALATES.
HOW VERY ROMAN OF YOU. ANCIENT ROMAN.
AS IS THIS DYSENTERY.
FEH.
HOW ABOUT WE TAKE YOUR MIND OFF OF IT?
TELL ME...WHO IS YOUR FAVORITE SUPREME COURT JUSTICE AND WHY?

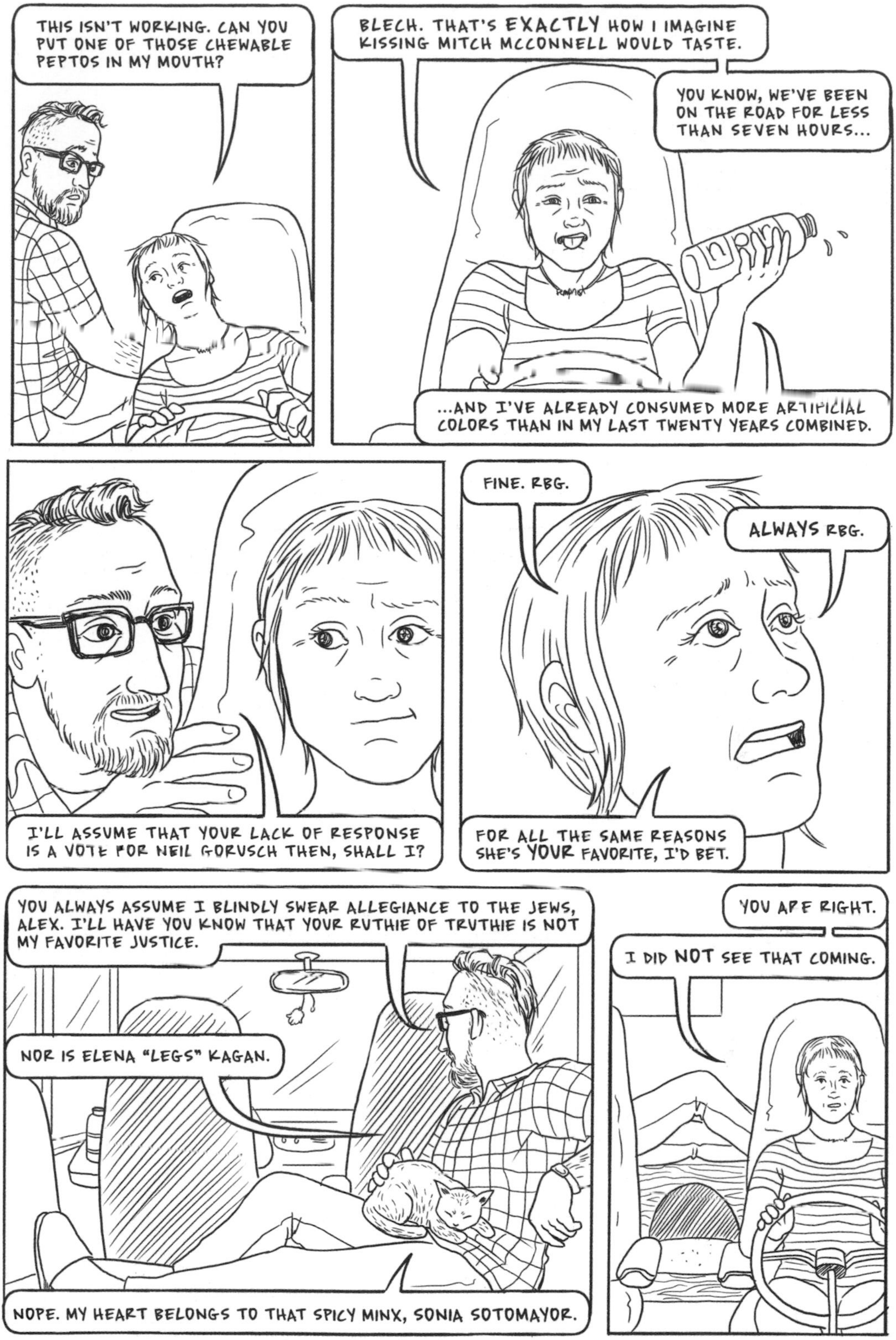
THIS ISN'T WORKING. CAN YOU PUT ONE OF THOSE CHEWABLE PEPTOS IN MY MOUTH?
BLECH. THAT'S EXACTLY HOW I IMAGINE KISSING MITCH MCCONNELL WOULD TASTE.
YOU KNOW, WE'VE BEEN ON THE ROAD FOR LESS THAN SEVEN HOURS...
...AND I'VE ALREADY CONSUMED MORE ARTIFICIAL COLORS THAN IN MY LAST TWENTY YEARS COMBINED.
I'LL ASSUME THAT YOUR LACK OF RESPONSE IS A VOTE FOR NEIL GORUSCH THEN, SHALL I?
FINE. RBG.
ALWAYS RBG.
FOR ALL THE SAME REASONS SHE'S YOUR FAVORITE, I'D BET.
YOU ALWAYS ASSUME I BLINDLY SWEAR ALLEGIANCE TO THE JEWS, ALEX. I'LL HAVE YOU KNOW THAT YOUR RUTHIE OF TRUTHIE IS NOT MY FAVORITE JUSTICE.
NOR IS ELENA "LEGS" KAGAN.
NOPE. MY HEART BELONGS TO THAT SPICY MINX, SONIA SOTOMAYOR.
YOU ARE RIGHT.
I DID NOT SEE THAT COMING.

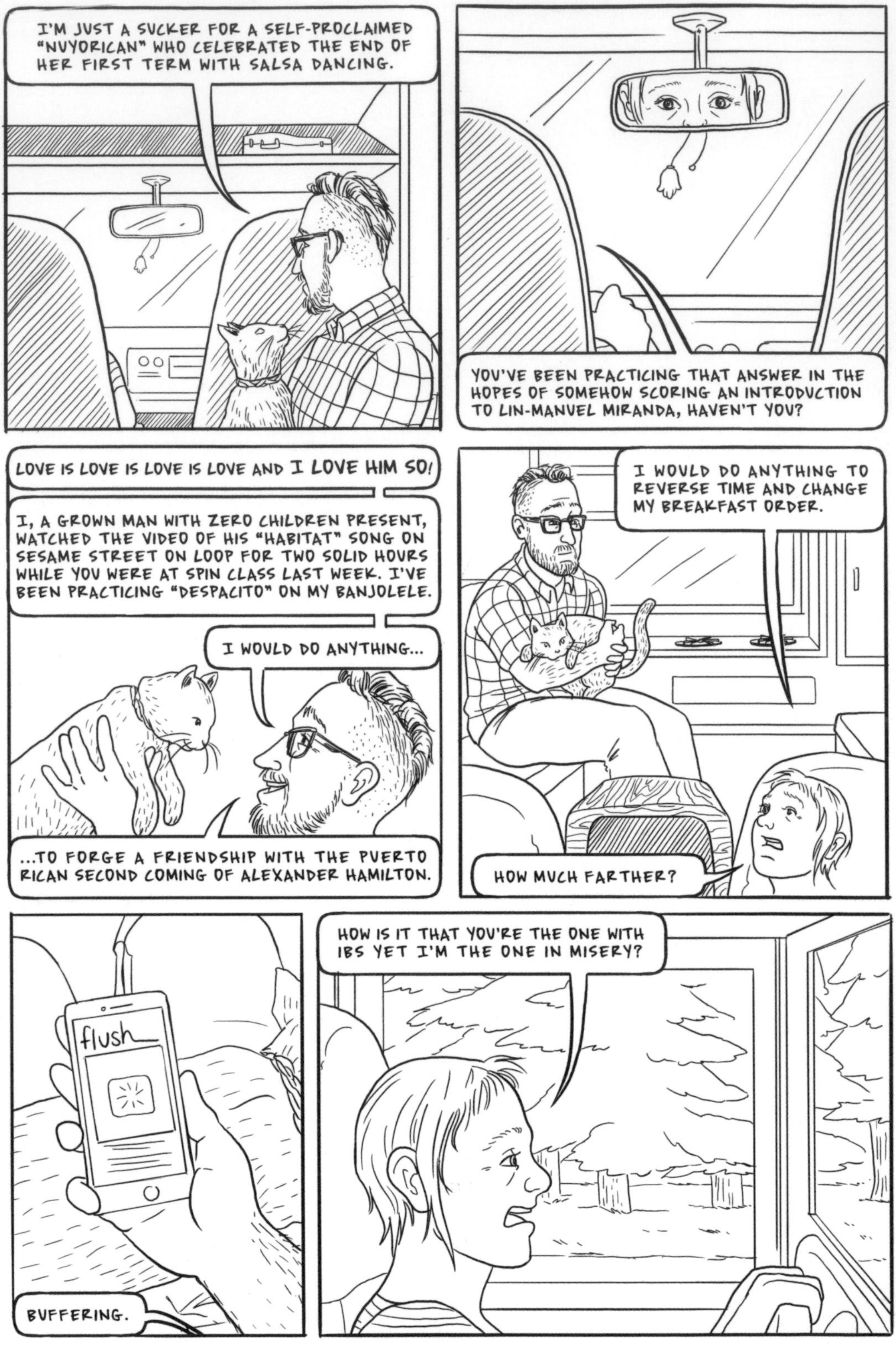
I'M JUST A SUCKER FOR A SELF-PROCLAIMED "NUYORICAN" WHO CELEBRATED THE END OF HER FIRST TERM WITH SALSA DANCING.
YOU'VE BEEN PRACTICING THAT ANSWER IN THE HOPES OF SOMEHOW SCORING AN INTRODUCTION TO LIN-MANUEL MIRANDA, HAVEN'T YOU?
LOVE IS LOVE IS LOVE IS LOVE AND I LOVE HIM SO!
I, A GROWN MAN WITH ZERO CHILDREN PRESENT, WATCHED THE VIDEO OF HIS "HABITAT" SONG ON SESAME STREET ON LOOP FOR TWO SOLID HOURS WHILE YOU WERE AT SPIN CLASS LAST WEEK. I'VE BEEN PRACTICING "DESPACITO" ON MY BANJOLELE.
I WOULD DO ANYTHING...
...TO FORGE A FRIENDSHIP WITH THE PUERTO RICAN SECOND COMING OF ALEXANDER HAMILTON.
I WOULD DO ANYTHING TO REVERSE TIME AND CHANGE MY BREAKFAST ORDER.
HOW MUCH FARTHER?
flush
BUFFERING.
HOW IS IT THAT YOU'RE THE ONE WITH IBS YET I'M THE ONE IN MISERY?

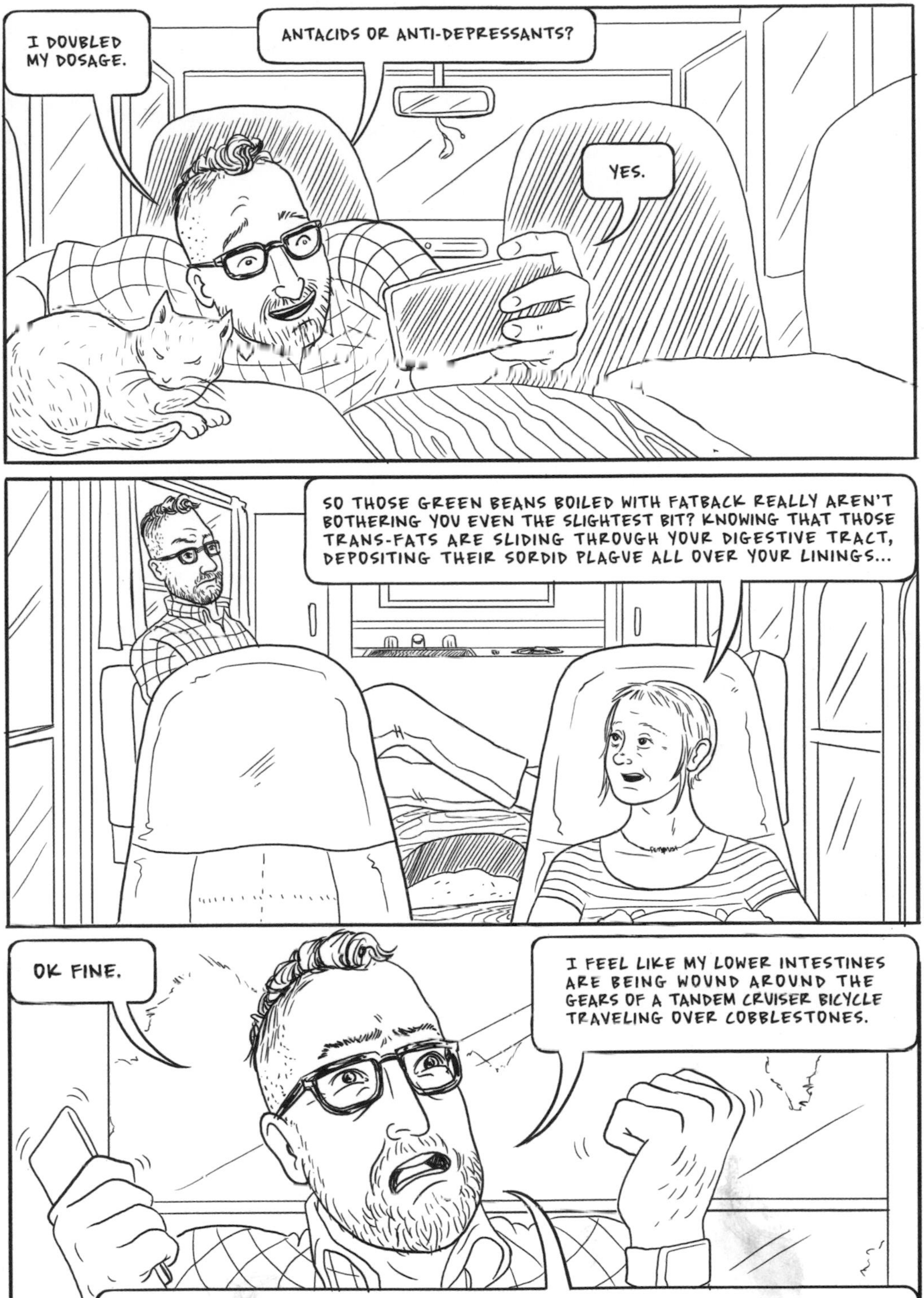
I DOUBLED MY DOSAGE.
ANTACIDS OR ANTI-DEPRESSANTS?
YES.
SO THOSE GREEN BEANS BOILED WITH FATBACK REALLY AREN'T BOTHERING YOU EVEN THE SLIGHTEST BIT? KNOWING THAT THOSE TRANS-FATS ARE SLIDING THROUGH YOUR DIGESTIVE TRACT, DEPOSITING THEIR SORDID PLAGUE ALL OVER YOUR LININGS...
OK FINE.
I FEEL LIKE MY LOWER INTESTINES ARE BEING WOUND AROUND THE GEARS OF A TANDEM CRUISER BICYCLE TRAVELING OVER COBBLESTONES.
I'M BASICALLY DOING DUDE KEGELS RIGHT NOW TO KEEP MYSELF FROM FLOODING MY HEMP-WOVEN, MUSTACHE-TWIRLING TOUCAN-PATTERNED BIKINI BRIEFS WITH FECES. BUT I WILL BE DAMNED IF I'M GOING TO SIT IN A ONE-STAR REST STOP.

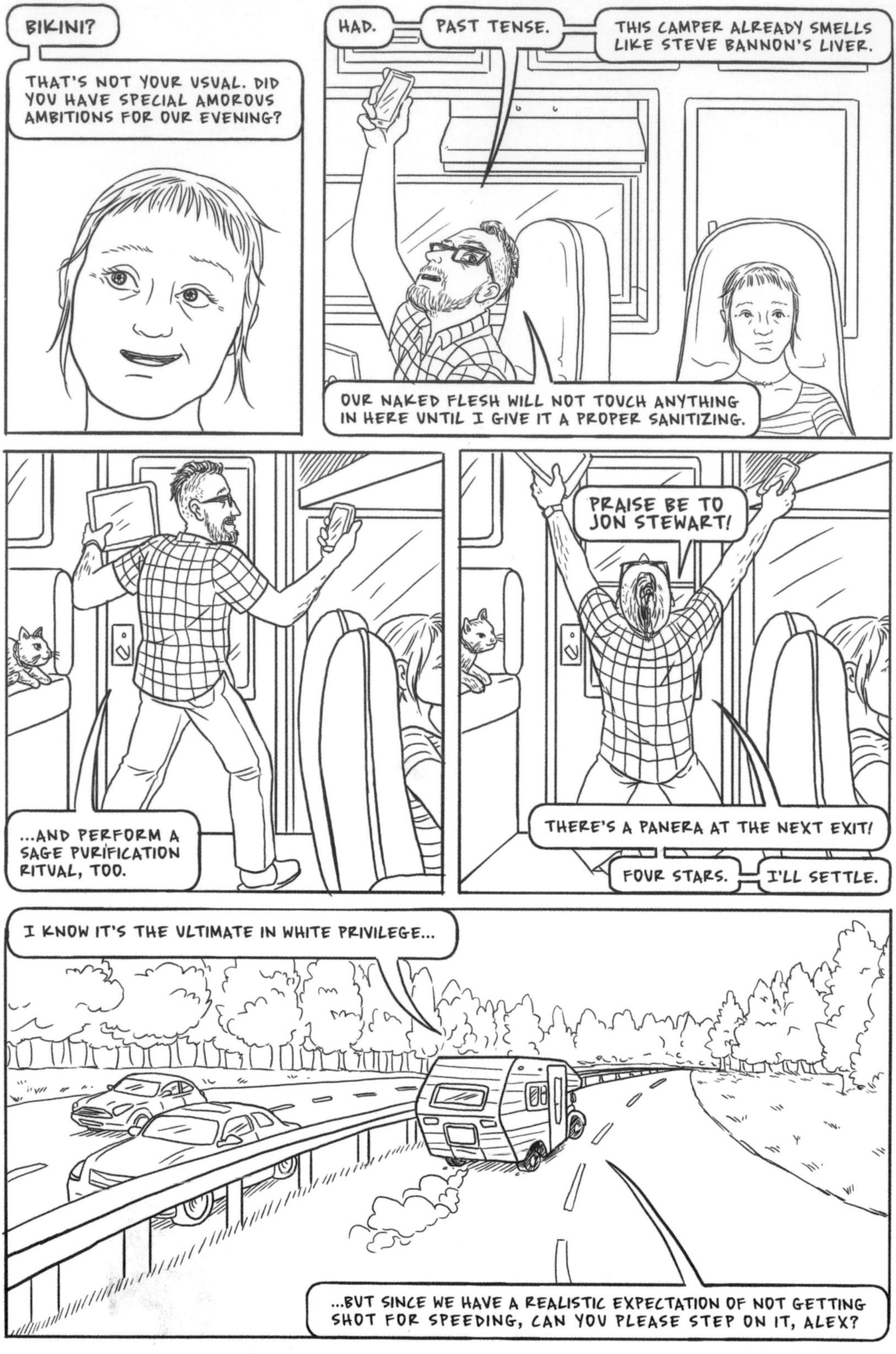
BIKINI?
THAT'S NOT YOUR USUAL. DID YOU HAVE SPECIAL AMOROUS AMBITIONS FOR OUR EVENING?
HAD.
PAST TENSE.
THIS CAMPER ALREADY SMELLS LIKE STEVE BANNON'S LIVER.
OUR NAKED FLESH WILL NOT TOUCH ANYTHING IN HERE UNTIL I GIVE IT A PROPER SANITIZING.
...AND PERFORM A SAGE PURIFICATION RITUAL, TOO.
PRAISE BE TO JON STEWART!
THERE'S A PANERA AT THE NEXT EXIT!
FOUR STARS.
I'LL SETTLE.
I KNOW IT'S THE ULTIMATE IN WHITE PRIVILEGE...
...BUT SINCE WE HAVE A REALISTIC EXPECTATION OF NOT GETTING SHOT FOR SPEEDING, CAN YOU PLEASE STEP ON IT, ALEX?

Chapter 4

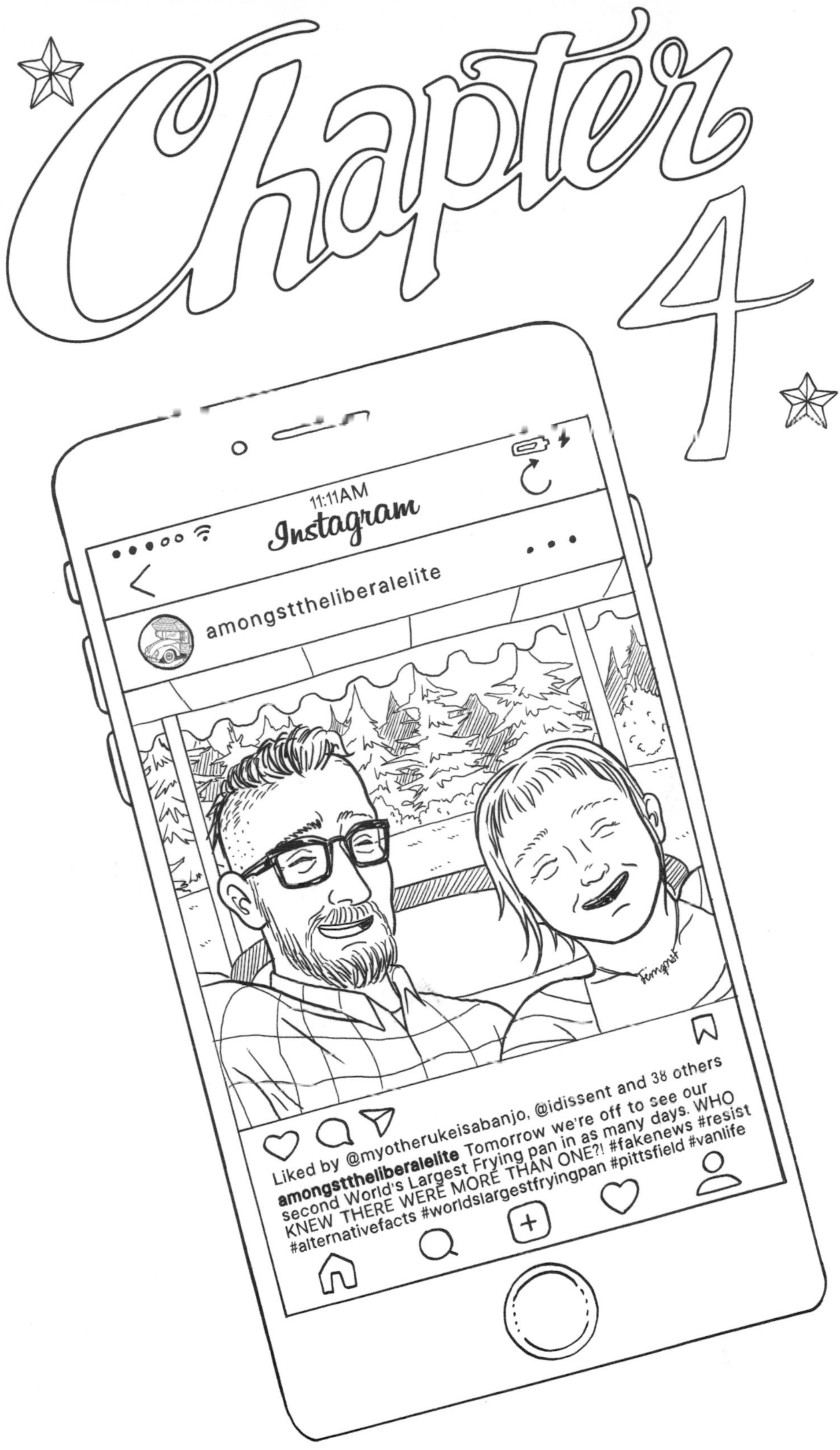
11:11AM
Instagram
amongsttheliberalelite
amongsttheliberalelite
Liked by @myotherukeisabanjo, @idissent and 38 others
amongsttheliberalelite Tomorrow we're off to see our second World's Largest Frying pan in as many days. WHO KNEW THERE WERE MORE THAN ONE?! #fakenews #resist #alternativefacts #worldslargestfryingpan #pittsfield #vanlife

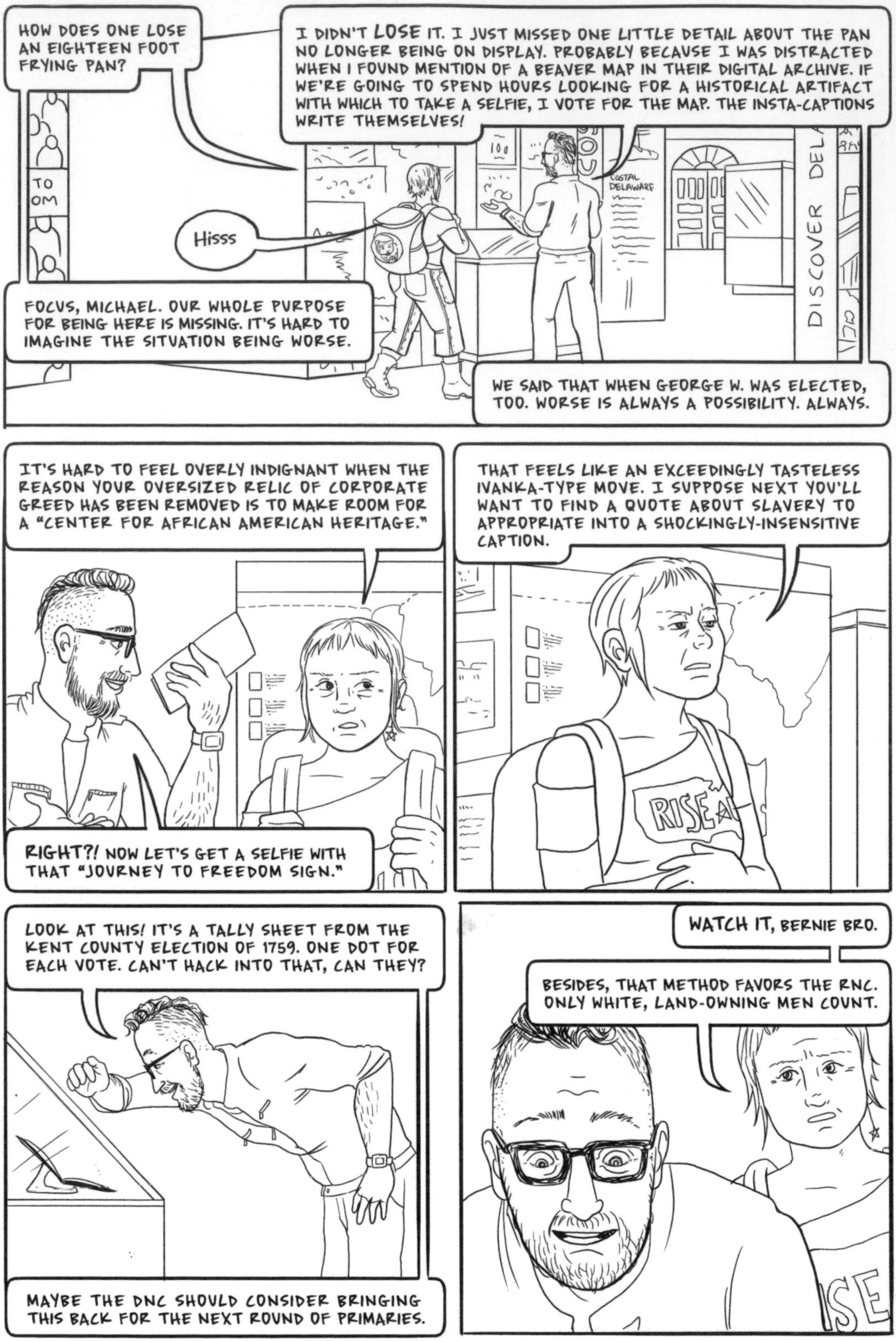
HOW DOES ONE LOSE AN EIGHTEEN FOOT FRYING PAN?
I DIDN'T LOSE IT. I JUST MISSED ONE LITTLE DETAIL ABOUT THE PAN NO LONGER BEING ON DISPLAY. PROBABLY BECAUSE I WAS DISTRACTED WHEN I FOUND MENTION OF A BEAVER MAP IN THEIR DIGITAL ARCHIVE. IF WE'RE GOING TO SPEND HOURS LOOKING FOR A HISTORICAL ARTIFACT WITH WHICH TO TAKE A SELFIE, I VOTE FOR THE MAP. THE INSTA-CAPTIONS WRITE THEMSELVES!
Hisss
COSTAL DELAWARE
DISCOVER DELA
FOCUS, MICHAEL. OUR WHOLE PURPOSE FOR BEING HERE IS MISSING. IT'S HARD TO IMAGINE THE SITUATION BEING WORSE.
WE SAID THAT WHEN GEORGE W. WAS ELECTED, TOO. WORSE IS ALWAYS A POSSIBILITY. ALWAYS.
IT'S HARD TO FEEL OVERLY INDIGNANT WHEN THE REASON YOUR OVERSIZED RELIC OF CORPORATE GREED HAS BEEN REMOVED IS TO MAKE ROOM FOR A "CENTER FOR AFRICAN AMERICAN HERITAGE."
RIGHT?! NOW LET'S GET A SELFIE WITH THAT "JOURNEY TO FREEDOM SIGN."
THAT FEELS LIKE AN EXCEEDINGLY TASTELESS IVANKA-TYPE MOVE. I SUPPOSE NEXT YOU'LL WANT TO FIND A QUOTE ABOUT SLAVERY TO APPROPRIATE INTO A SHOCKINGLY-INSENSITIVE CAPTION.
RISE
LOOK AT THIS! IT'S A TALLY SHEET FROM THE KENT COUNTY ELECTION OF 1759. ONE DOT FOR EACH VOTE. CAN'T HACK INTO THAT, CAN THEY?
MAYBE THE DNC SHOULD CONSIDER BRINGING THIS BACK FOR THE NEXT ROUND OF PRIMARIES.
WATCH IT, BERNIE BRO.
BESIDES, THAT METHOD FAVORS THE RNC. ONLY WHITE, LAND-OWNING MEN COUNT.

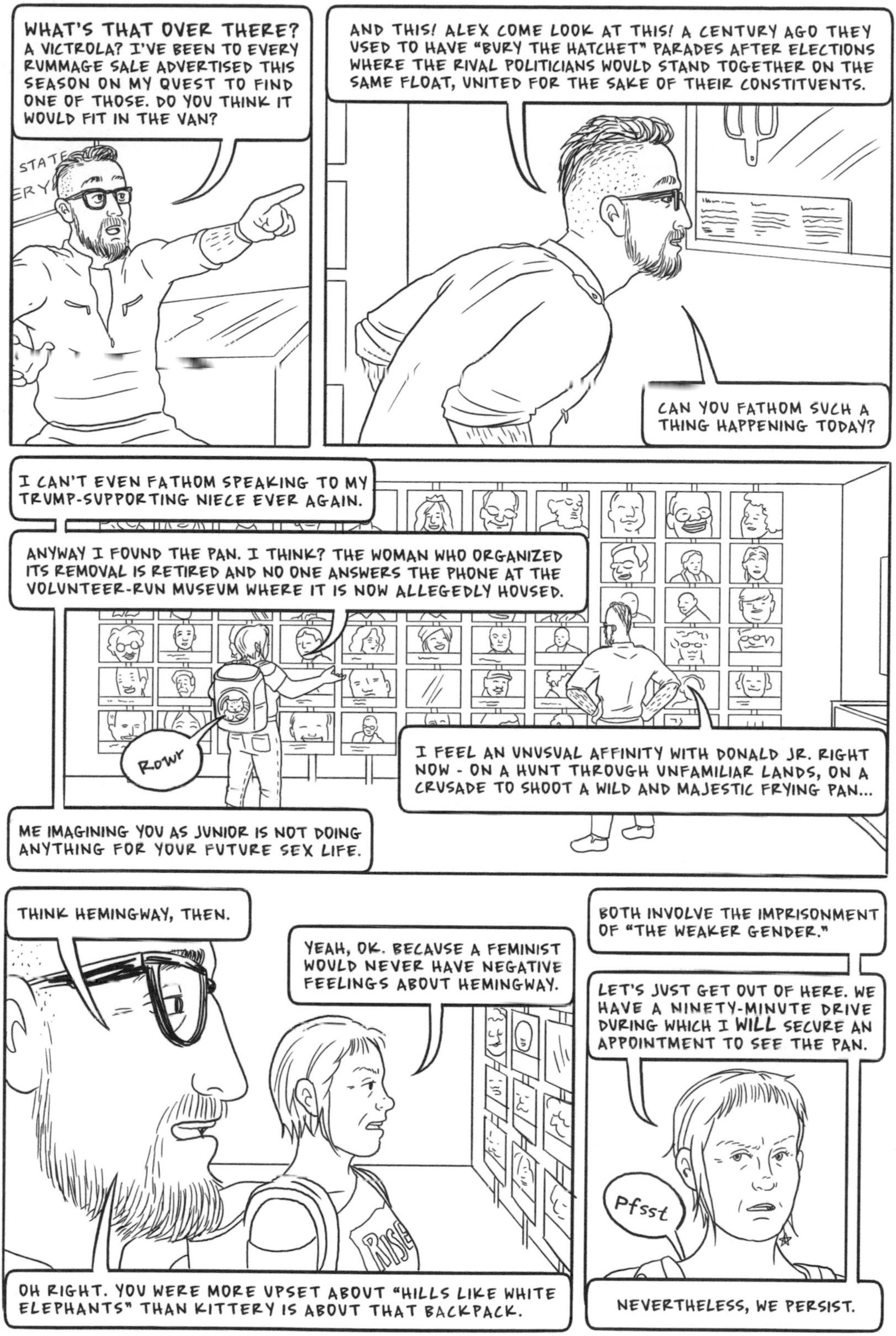
WHAT'S THAT OVER THERE? A VICTROLA? I'VE BEEN TO EVERY RUMMAGE SALE ADVERTISED THIS SEASON ON MY QUEST TO FIND ONE OF THOSE. DO YOU THINK IT WOULD FIT IN THE VAN?
AND THIS! ALEX COME LOOK AT THIS! A CENTURY AGO THEY USED TO HAVE "BURY THE HATCHET" PARADES AFTER ELECTIONS WHERE THE RIVAL POLITICIANS WOULD STAND TOGETHER ON THE SAME FLOAT, UNITED FOR THE SAKE OF THEIR CONSTITUENTS.
CAN YOU FATHOM SUCH A THING HAPPENING TODAY?
I CAN'T EVEN FATHOM SPEAKING TO MY TRUMP-SUPPORTING NIECE EVER AGAIN.
ANYWAY I FOUND THE PAN. I THINK? THE WOMAN WHO ORGANIZED ITS REMOVAL IS RETIRED AND NO ONE ANSWERS THE PHONE AT THE VOLUNTEER-RUN MUSEUM WHERE IT IS NOW ALLEGEDLY HOUSED.
Rowr
I FEEL AN UNUSUAL AFFINITY WITH DONALD JR. RIGHT NOW - ON A HUNT THROUGH UNFAMILIAR LANDS, ON A CRUSADE TO SHOOT A WILD AND MAJESTIC FRYING PAN...
ME IMAGINING YOU AS JUNIOR IS NOT DOING ANYTHING FOR YOUR FUTURE SEX LIFE.
THINK HEMINGWAY, THEN.
YEAH, OK. BECAUSE A FEMINIST WOULD NEVER HAVE NEGATIVE FEELINGS ABOUT HEMINGWAY.
RISE
OH RIGHT. YOU WERE MORE UPSET ABOUT "HILLS LIKE WHITE ELEPHANTS" THAN KITTERY IS ABOUT THAT BACKPACK.
BOTH INVOLVE THE IMPRISONMENT OF "THE WEAKER GENDER."
LET'S JUST GET OUT OF HERE. WE HAVE A NINETY-MINUTE DRIVE DURING WHICH I WILL SECURE AN APPOINTMENT TO SEE THE PAN.
Pfsst
NEVERTHELESS, WE PERSIST.

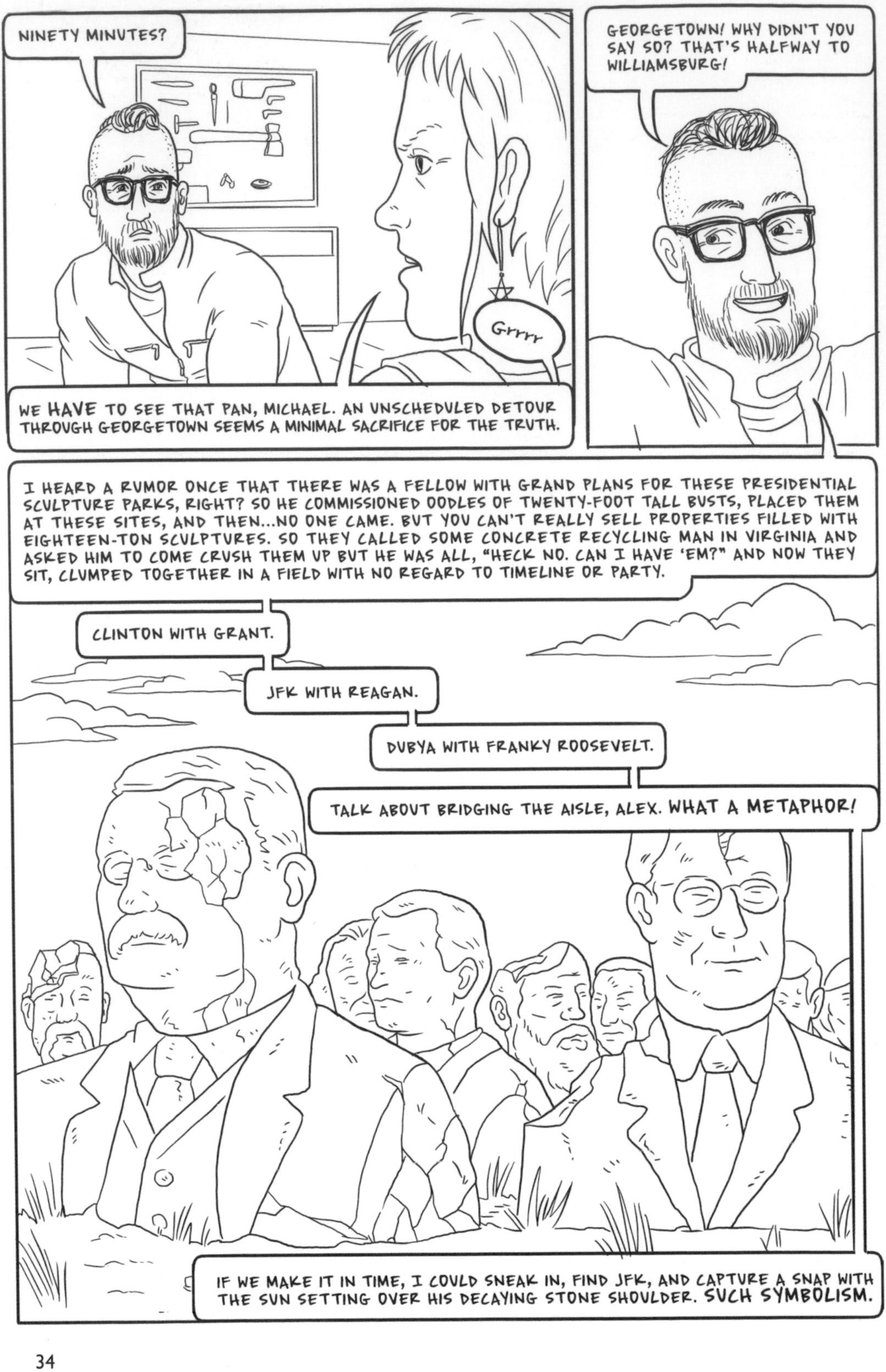
NINETY MINUTES?
Grrrr
WE HAVE TO SEE THAT PAN, MICHAEL. AN UNSCHEDULED DETOUR THROUGH GEORGETOWN SEEMS A MINIMAL SACRIFICE FOR THE TRUTH.
GEORGETOWN! WHY DIDN'T YOU SAY SO? THAT'S HALFWAY TO WILLIAMSBURG!
I HEARD A RUMOR ONCE THAT THERE WAS A FELLOW WITH GRAND PLANS FOR THESE PRESIDENTIAL SCULPTURE PARKS, RIGHT? SO HE COMMISSIONED OODLES OF TWENTY-FOOT TALL BUSTS, PLACED THEM AT THESE SITES, AND THEN...NO ONE CAME. BUT YOU CAN'T REALLY SELL PROPERTIES FILLED WITH EIGHTEEN-TON SCULPTURES. SO THEY CALLED SOME CONCRETE RECYCLING MAN IN VIRGINIA AND ASKED HIM TO COME CRUSH THEM UP BUT HE WAS ALL, "HECK NO. CAN I HAVE 'EM?" AND NOW THEY SIT, CLUMPED TOGETHER IN A FIELD WITH NO REGARD TO TIMELINE OR PARTY.
CLINTON WITH GRANT.
JFK WITH REAGAN.
DUBYA WITH FRANKY ROOSEVELT.
TALK ABOUT BRIDGING THE AISLE, ALEX. WHAT A METAPHOR!
IF WE MAKE IT IN TIME, I COULD SNEAK IN, FIND JFK, AND CAPTURE A SNAP WITH THE SUN SETTING OVER HIS DECAYING STONE SHOULDER. SUCH SYMBOLISM.

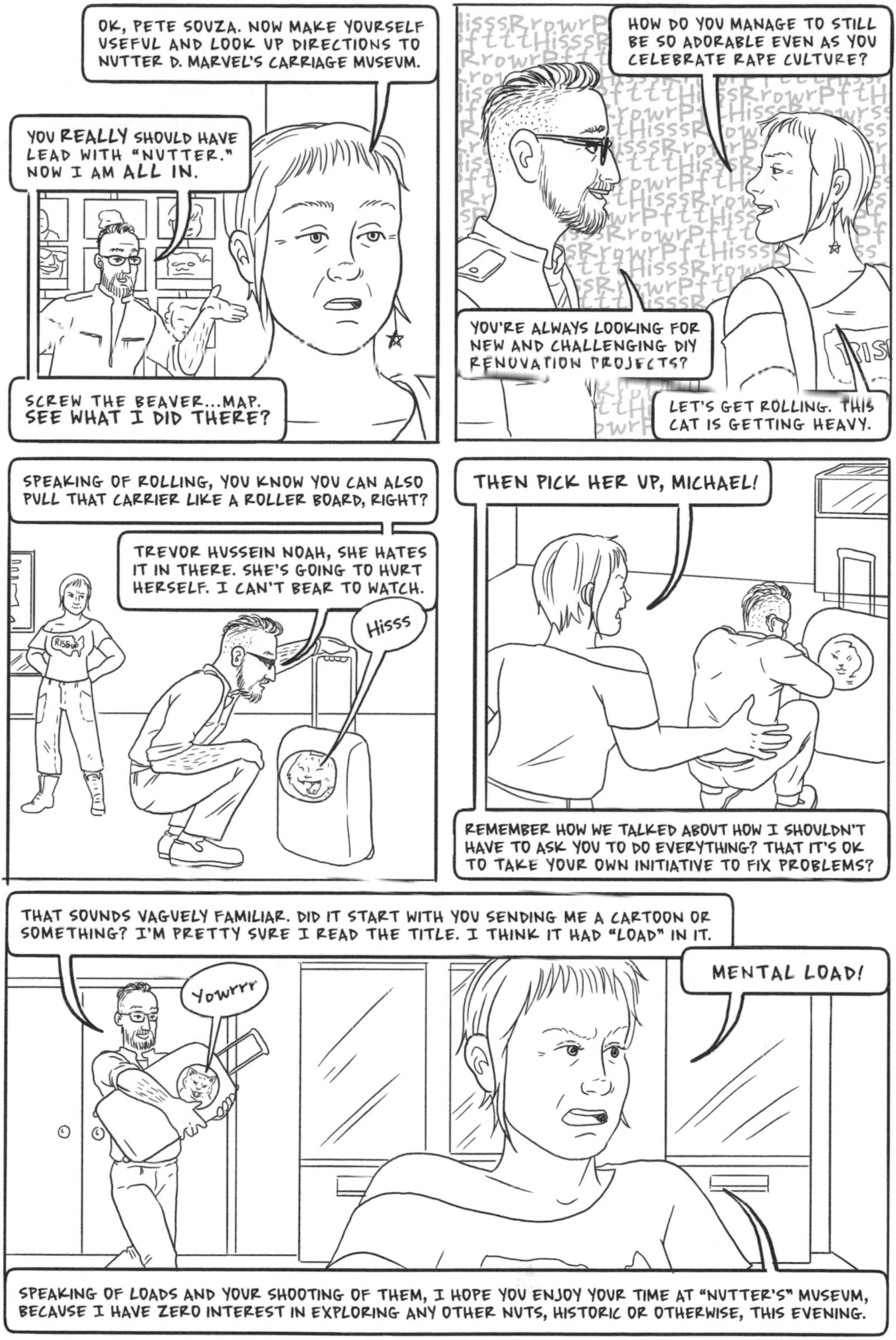
OK, PETE SOUZA. NOW MAKE YOURSELF USEFUL AND LOOK UP DIRECTIONS TO NUTTER D. MARVEL'S CARRIAGE MUSEUM.
YOU REALLY SHOULD HAVE LEAD WITH "NUTTER." NOW I AM ALL IN.
SCREW THE BEAVER...MAP. SEE WHAT I DID THERE?
HOW DO YOU MANAGE TO STILL BE SO ADORABLE EVEN AS YOU CELEBRATE RAPE CULTURE?
YOU'RE ALWAYS LOOKING FOR NEW AND CHALLENGING DIY RENOVATION PROJECTS?
LET'S GET ROLLING. THIS CAT IS GETTING HEAVY.
SPEAKING OF ROLLING, YOU KNOW YOU CAN ALSO PULL THAT CARRIER LIKE A ROLLER BOARD, RIGHT?
TREVOR HUSSEIN NOAH, SHE HATES IT IN THERE. SHE'S GOING TO HURT HERSELF. I CAN'T BEAR TO WATCH.
Hisss
THEN PICK HER UP, MICHAEL!
REMEMBER HOW WE TALKED ABOUT HOW I SHOULDN'T HAVE TO ASK YOU TO DO EVERYTHING? THAT IT'S OK TO TAKE YOUR OWN INITIATIVE TO FIX PROBLEMS?
THAT SOUNDS VAGUELY FAMILIAR. DID IT START WITH YOU SENDING ME A CARTOON OR SOMETHING? I'M PRETTY SURE I READ THE TITLE. I THINK IT HAD "LOAD" IN IT.
Yowrrr
MENTAL LOAD!
SPEAKING OF LOADS AND YOUR SHOOTING OF THEM, I HOPE YOU ENJOY YOUR TIME AT "NUTTER'S" MUSEUM, BECAUSE I HAVE ZERO INTEREST IN EXPLORING ANY OTHER NUTS, HISTORIC OR OTHERWISE, THIS EVENING.

Chapter 5

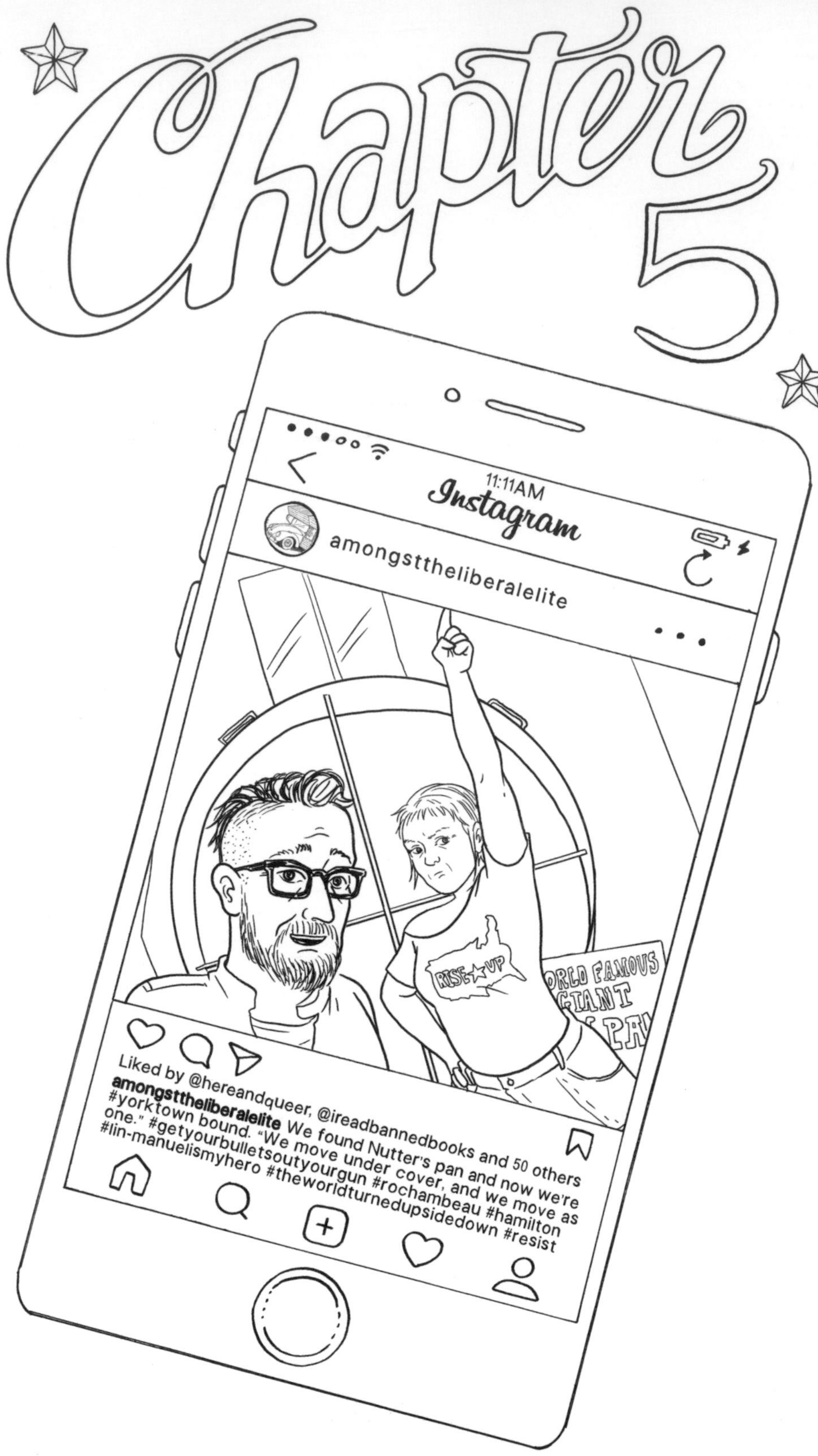

11:11AM
Instagram
amongsttheliberalelite
RISE UP
WORLD FAMOUS
GIANT
Liked by @hereandqueer, @ireadbannedbooks and 50 others
amongsttheliberalelite We found Nutter's pan and now we're #yorktown bound. "We move under cover, and we move as one." #getyourbulletsoutyourgun #rochambeau #hamilton #lin-manuelismyhero #theworldturnedupsidedown #resist

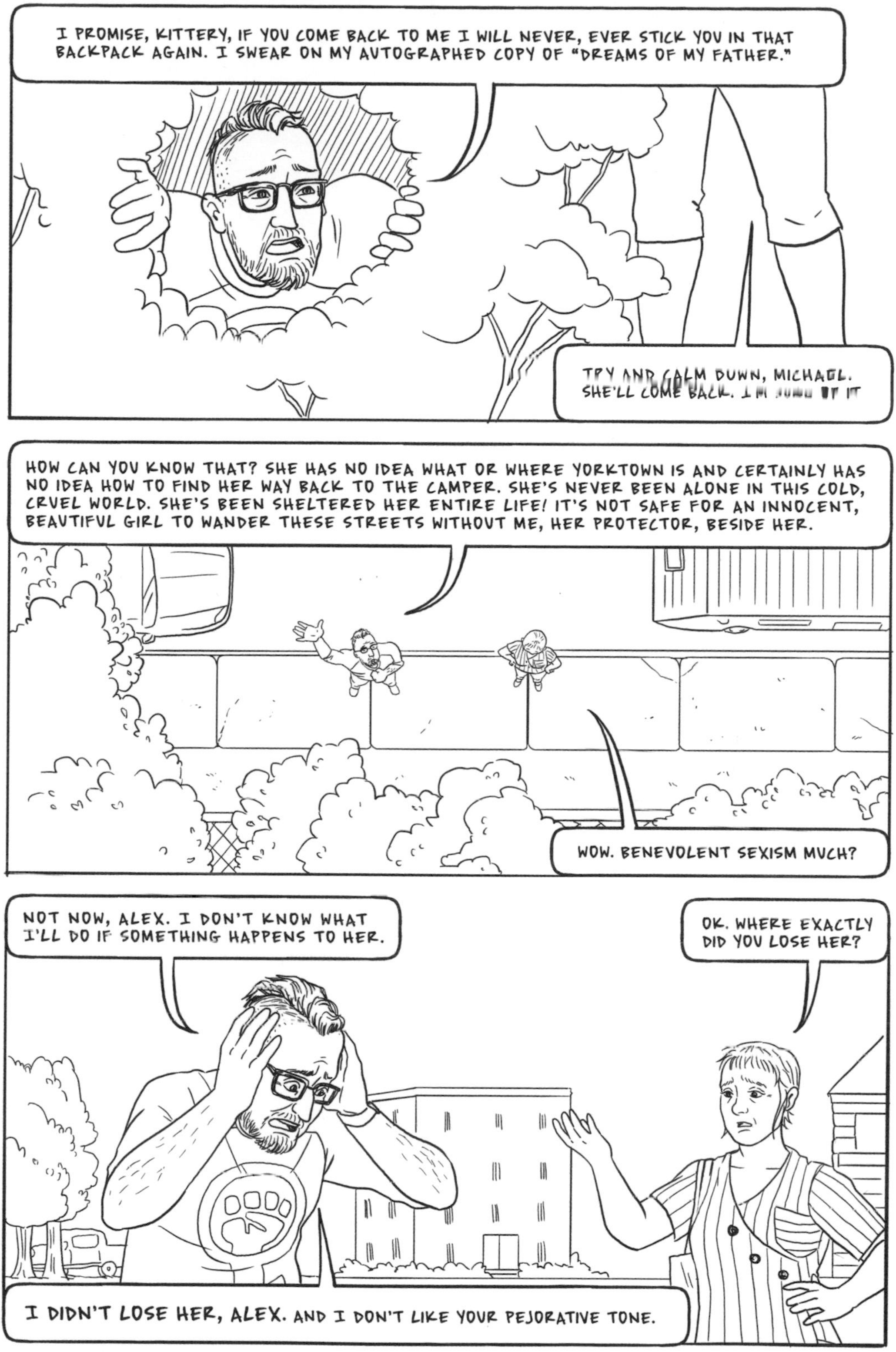
I PROMISE, KITTERY, IF YOU COME BACK TO ME I WILL NEVER, EVER STICK YOU IN THAT BACKPACK AGAIN. I SWEAR ON MY AUTOGRAPHED COPY OF "DREAMS OF MY FATHER."
TRY AND CALM DOWN, MICHAEL. SHE'LL COME BACK.
HOW CAN YOU KNOW THAT? SHE HAS NO IDEA WHAT OR WHERE YORKTOWN IS AND CERTAINLY HAS NO IDEA HOW TO FIND HER WAY BACK TO THE CAMPER. SHE'S NEVER BEEN ALONE IN THIS COLD, CRUEL WORLD. SHE'S BEEN SHELTERED HER ENTIRE LIFE! IT'S NOT SAFE FOR AN INNOCENT, BEAUTIFUL GIRL TO WANDER THESE STREETS WITHOUT ME, HER PROTECTOR, BESIDE HER.
WOW. BENEVOLENT SEXISM MUCH?
NOT NOW, ALEX. I DON'T KNOW WHAT I'LL DO IF SOMETHING HAPPENS TO HER.
OK. WHERE EXACTLY DID YOU LOSE HER?
I DIDN'T LOSE HER, ALEX. AND I DON'T LIKE YOUR PEJORATIVE TONE.

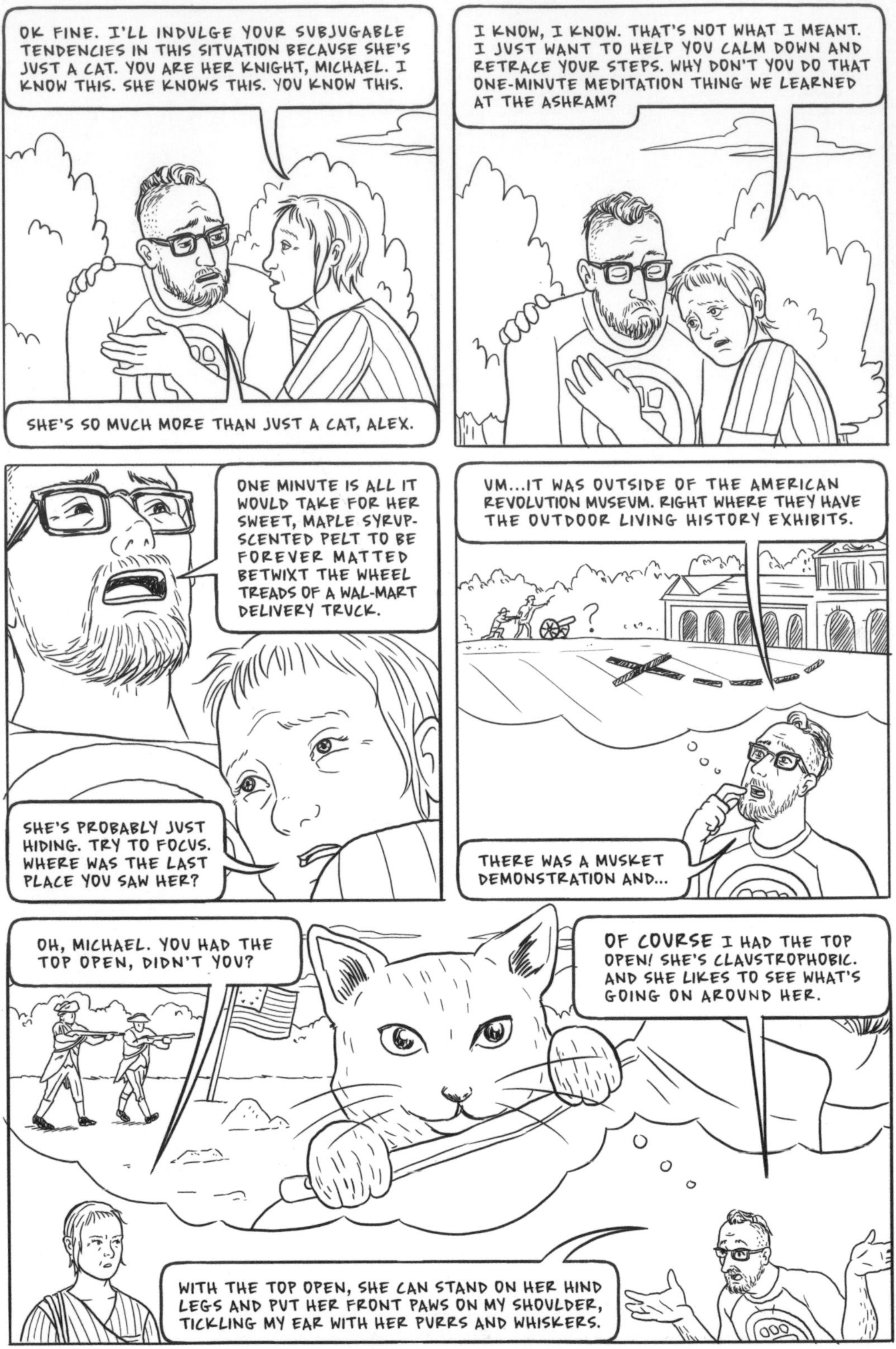
OK FINE. I'LL INDULGE YOUR SUBJUGABLE TENDENCIES IN THIS SITUATION BECAUSE SHE'S JUST A CAT. YOU ARE HER KNIGHT, MICHAEL. I KNOW THIS. SHE KNOWS THIS. YOU KNOW THIS.
SHE'S SO MUCH MORE THAN JUST A CAT, ALEX.
I KNOW, I KNOW. THAT'S NOT WHAT I MEANT. I JUST WANT TO HELP YOU CALM DOWN AND RETRACE YOUR STEPS. WHY DON'T YOU DO THAT ONE-MINUTE MEDITATION THING WE LEARNED AT THE ASHRAM?
ONE MINUTE IS ALL IT WOULD TAKE FOR HER SWEET, MAPLE SYRUP-SCENTED PELT TO BE FOREVER MATTED BETWIXT THE WHEEL TREADS OF A WAL-MART DELIVERY TRUCK.
SHE'S PROBABLY JUST HIDING. TRY TO FOCUS. WHERE WAS THE LAST PLACE YOU SAW HER?
UM...IT WAS OUTSIDE OF THE AMERICAN REVOLUTION MUSEUM. RIGHT WHERE THEY HAVE THE OUTDOOR LIVING HISTORY EXHIBITS.
?
THERE WAS A MUSKET DEMONSTRATION AND...
OH, MICHAEL. YOU HAD THE TOP OPEN, DIDN'T YOU?
OF COURSE I HAD THE TOP OPEN! SHE'S CLAUSTROPHOBIC. AND SHE LIKES TO SEE WHAT'S GOING ON AROUND HER.
WITH THE TOP OPEN, SHE CAN STAND ON HER HIND LEGS AND PUT HER FRONT PAWS ON MY SHOULDER, TICKLING MY EAR WITH HER PURRS AND WHISKERS.

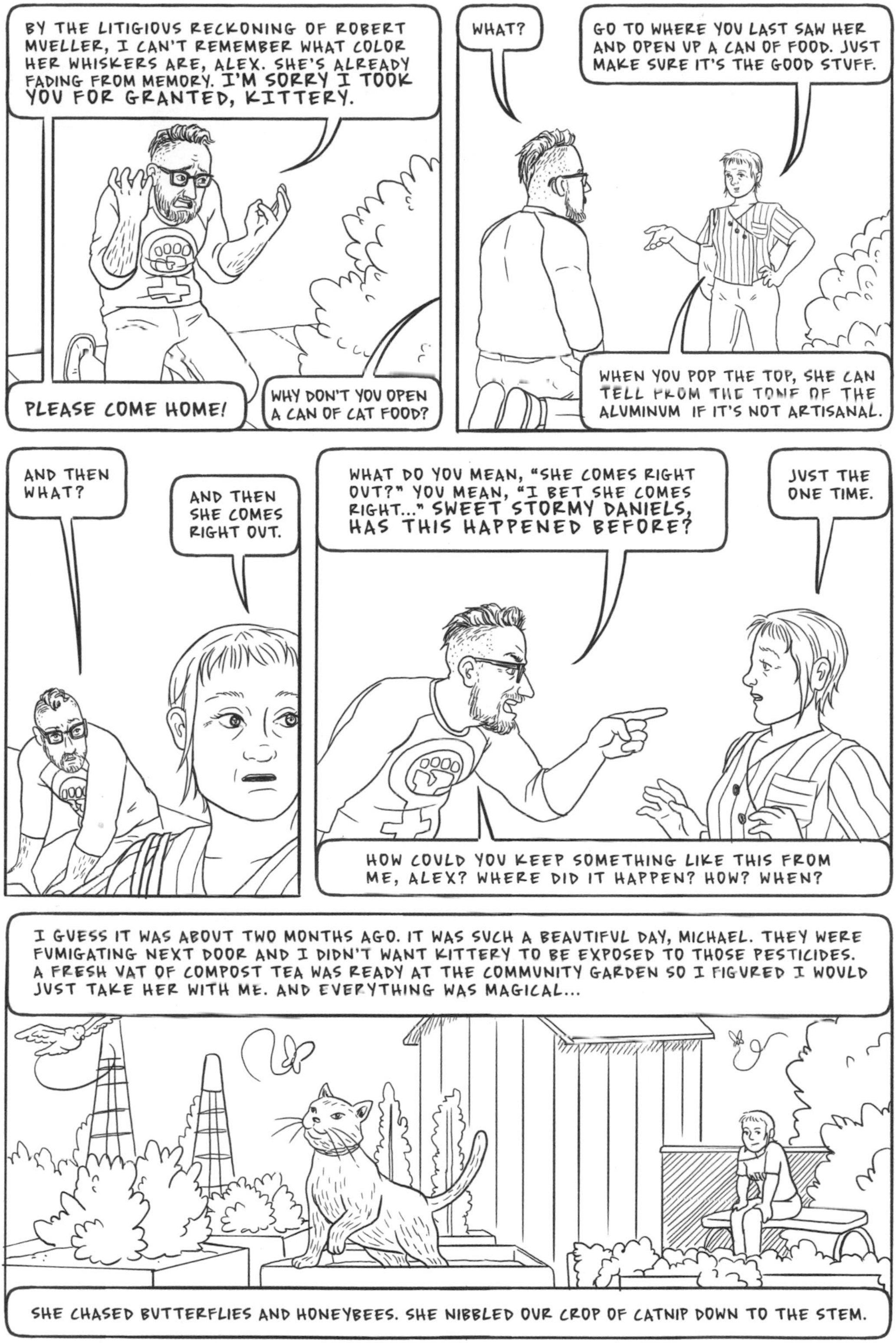
BY THE LITIGIOUS RECKONING OF ROBERT MUELLER, I CAN'T REMEMBER WHAT COLOR HER WHISKERS ARE, ALEX. SHE'S ALREADY FADING FROM MEMORY. I'M SORRY I TOOK YOU FOR GRANTED, KITTERY.
PLEASE COME HOME!
WHY DON'T YOU OPEN A CAN OF CAT FOOD?
WHAT?
GO TO WHERE YOU LAST SAW HER AND OPEN UP A CAN OF FOOD. JUST MAKE SURE IT'S THE GOOD STUFF.
WHEN YOU POP THE TOP, SHE CAN TELL FROM THE TONE OF THE ALUMINUM IF IT'S NOT ARTISANAL.
AND THEN WHAT?
AND THEN SHE COMES RIGHT OUT.
WHAT DO YOU MEAN, "SHE COMES RIGHT OUT?" YOU MEAN, "I BET SHE COMES RIGHT..." SWEET STORMY DANIELS, HAS THIS HAPPENED BEFORE?
JUST THE ONE TIME.
HOW COULD YOU KEEP SOMETHING LIKE THIS FROM ME, ALEX? WHERE DID IT HAPPEN? HOW? WHEN?
I GUESS IT WAS ABOUT TWO MONTHS AGO. IT WAS SUCH A BEAUTIFUL DAY, MICHAEL. THEY WERE FUMIGATING NEXT DOOR AND I DIDN'T WANT KITTERY TO BE EXPOSED TO THOSE PESTICIDES. A FRESH VAT OF COMPOST TEA WAS READY AT THE COMMUNITY GARDEN SO I FIGURED I WOULD JUST TAKE HER WITH ME. AND EVERYTHING WAS MAGICAL...
SHE CHASED BUTTERFLIES AND HONEYBEES. SHE NIBBLED OUR CROP OF CATNIP DOWN TO THE STEM.

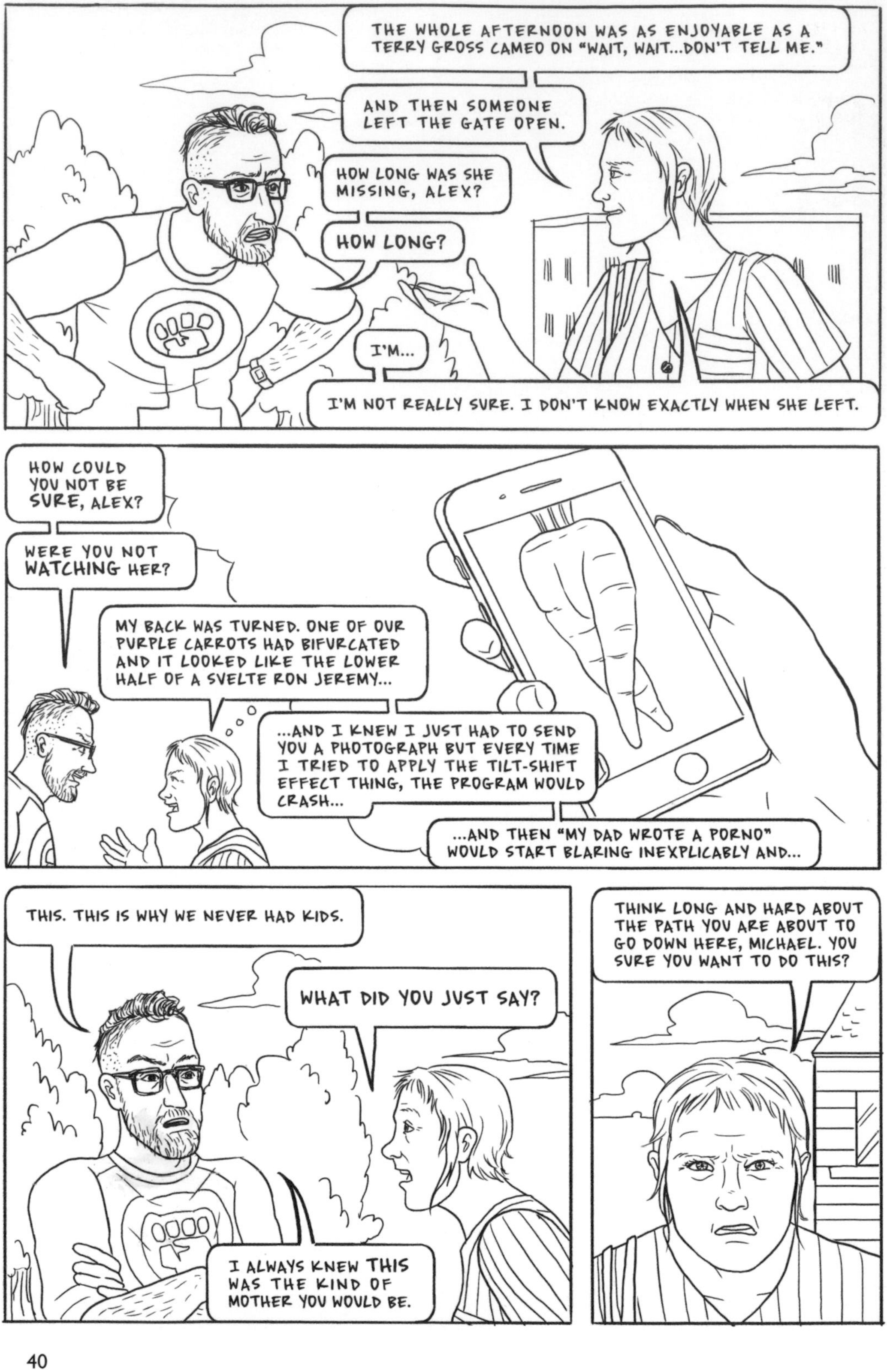
THE WHOLE AFTERNOON WAS AS ENJOYABLE AS A TERRY GROSS CAMEO ON "WAIT, WAIT...DON'T TELL ME."
AND THEN SOMEONE LEFT THE GATE OPEN.
HOW LONG WAS SHE MISSING, ALEX?
HOW LONG?
I'M...
I'M NOT REALLY SURE. I DON'T KNOW EXACTLY WHEN SHE LEFT.
HOW COULD YOU NOT BE SURE, ALEX?
WERE YOU NOT WATCHING HER?
MY BACK WAS TURNED. ONE OF OUR PURPLE CARROTS HAD BIFURCATED AND IT LOOKED LIKE THE LOWER HALF OF A SVELTE RON JEREMY...
...AND I KNEW I JUST HAD TO SEND YOU A PHOTOGRAPH BUT EVERY TIME I TRIED TO APPLY THE TILT-SHIFT EFFECT THING, THE PROGRAM WOULD CRASH...
...AND THEN "MY DAD WROTE A PORNO" WOULD START BLARING INEXPLICABLY AND...
THIS. THIS IS WHY WE NEVER HAD KIDS.
WHAT DID YOU JUST SAY?
I ALWAYS KNEW THIS WAS THE KIND OF MOTHER YOU WOULD BE.
THINK LONG AND HARD ABOUT THE PATH YOU ARE ABOUT TO GO DOWN HERE, MICHAEL. YOU SURE YOU WANT TO DO THIS?

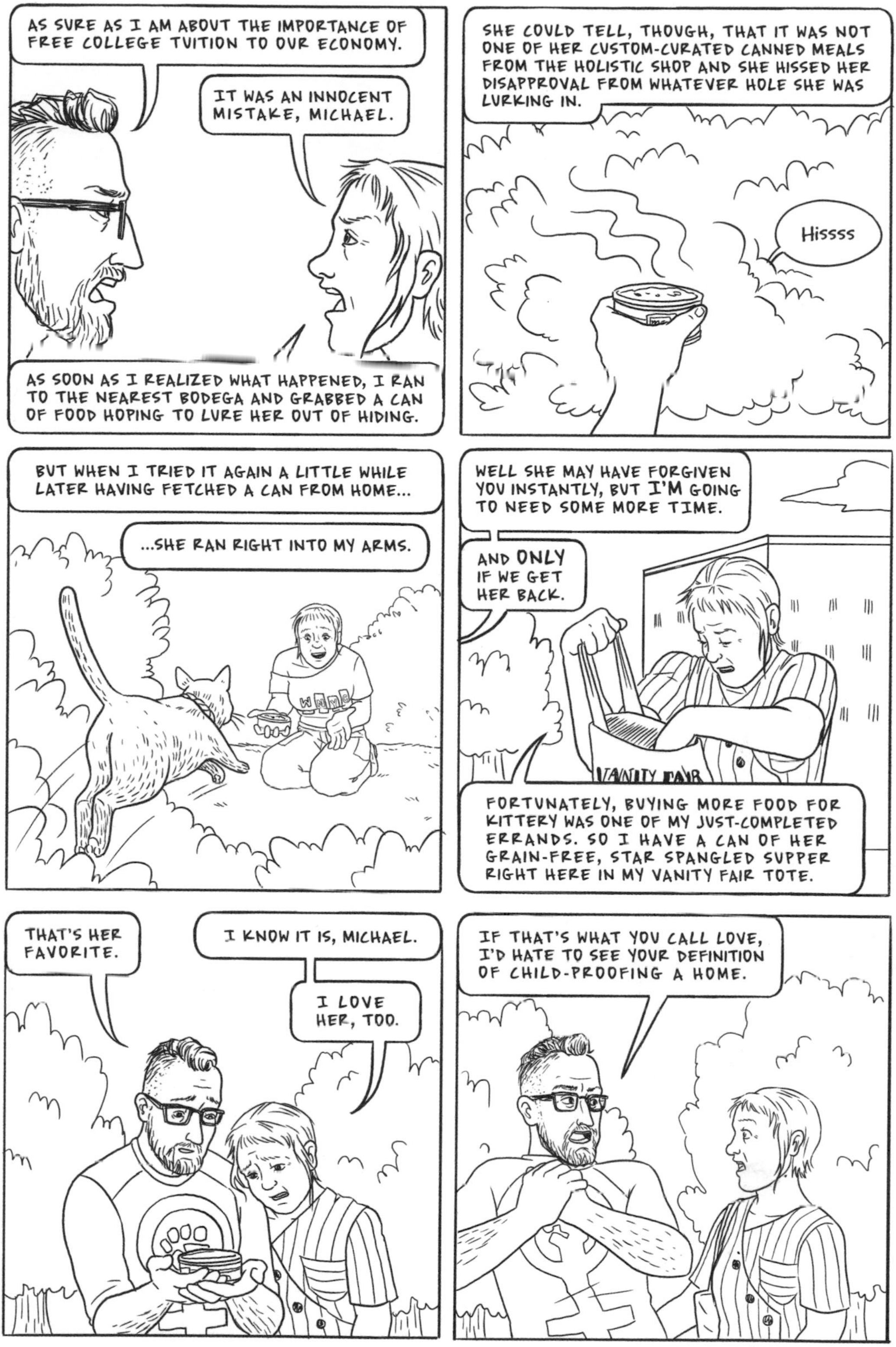
AS SURE AS I AM ABOUT THE IMPORTANCE OF FREE COLLEGE TUITION TO OUR ECONOMY.
IT WAS AN INNOCENT MISTAKE, MICHAEL.
AS SOON AS I REALIZED WHAT HAPPENED, I RAN TO THE NEAREST BODEGA AND GRABBED A CAN OF FOOD HOPING TO LURE HER OUT OF HIDING.
SHE COULD TELL, THOUGH, THAT IT WAS NOT ONE OF HER CUSTOM-CURATED CANNED MEALS FROM THE HOLISTIC SHOP AND SHE HISSED HER DISAPPROVAL FROM WHATEVER HOLE SHE WAS LURKING IN.
Hissss
BUT WHEN I TRIED IT AGAIN A LITTLE WHILE LATER HAVING FETCHED A CAN FROM HOME...
...SHE RAN RIGHT INTO MY ARMS.
WELL SHE MAY HAVE FORGIVEN YOU INSTANTLY, BUT I'M GOING TO NEED SOME MORE TIME.
AND ONLY IF WE GET HER BACK.
VANITY FAIR
FORTUNATELY, BUYING MORE FOOD FOR KITTERY WAS ONE OF MY JUST-COMPLETED ERRANDS. SO I HAVE A CAN OF HER GRAIN-FREE, STAR SPANGLED SUPPER RIGHT HERE IN MY VANITY FAIR TOTE.
THAT'S HER FAVORITE.
I KNOW IT IS, MICHAEL.
I LOVE HER, TOO.
IF THAT'S WHAT YOU CALL LOVE, I'D HATE TO SEE YOUR DEFINITION OF CHILD-PROOFING A HOME.

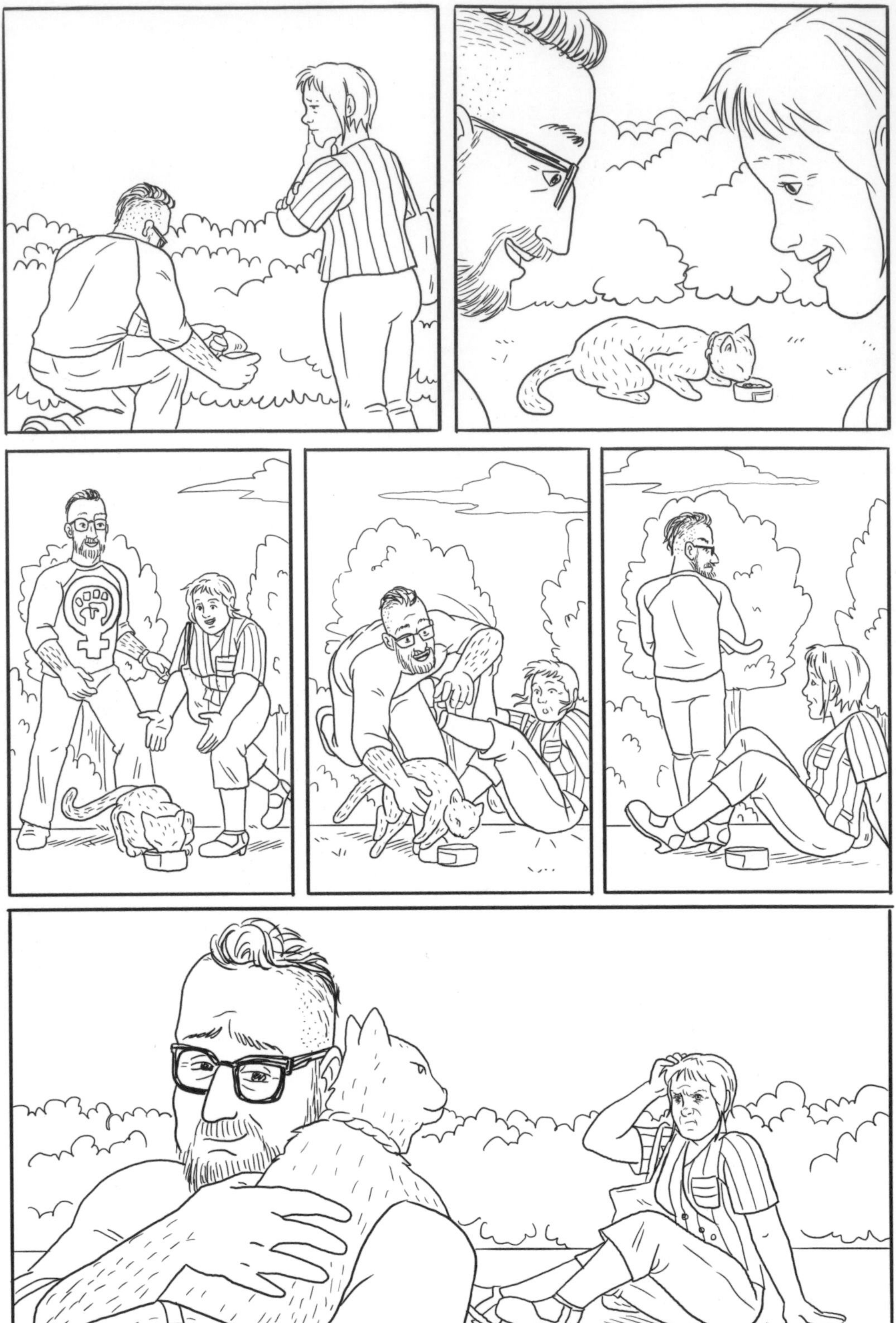

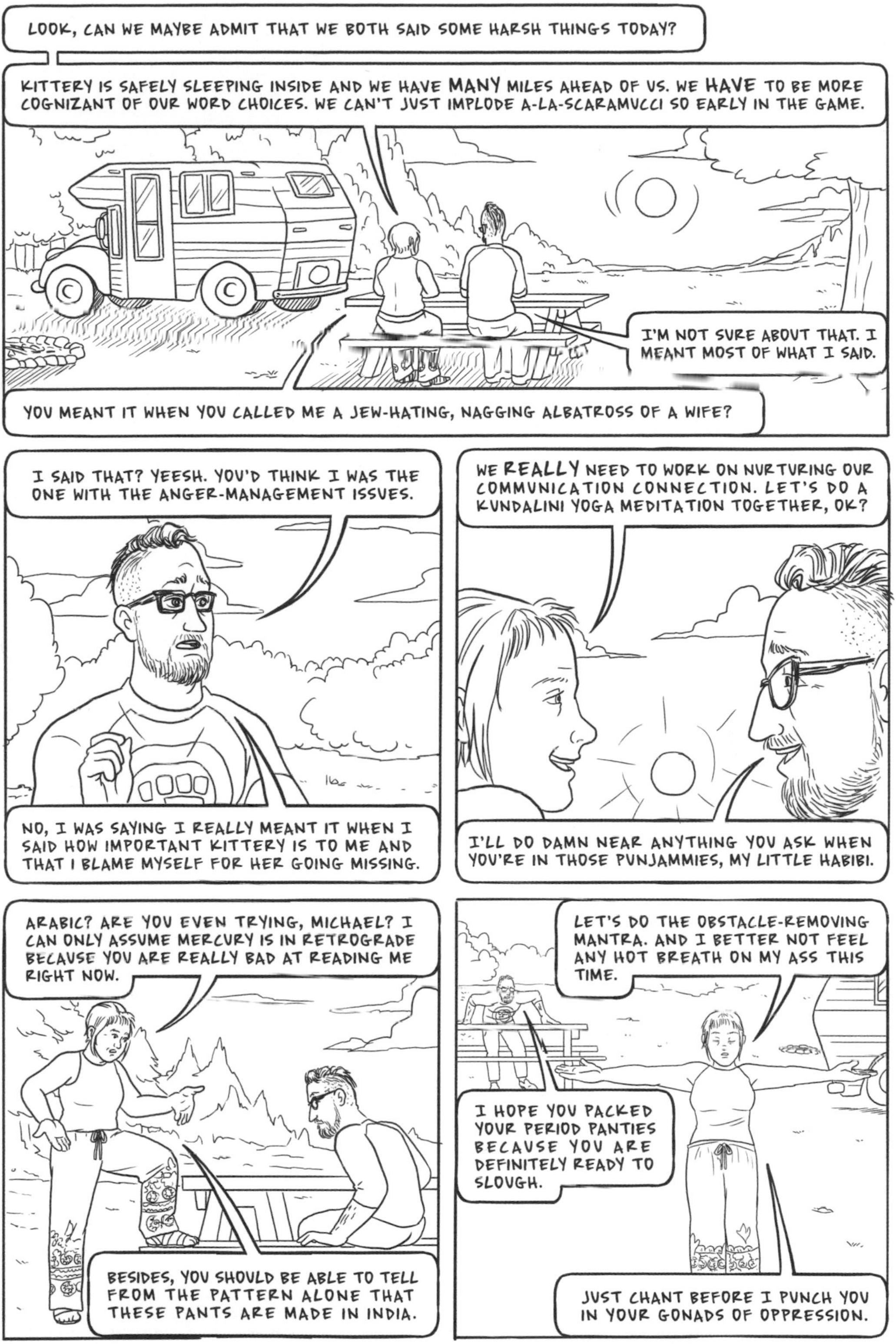
LOOK, CAN WE MAYBE ADMIT THAT WE BOTH SAID SOME HARSH THINGS TODAY?
KITTERY IS SAFELY SLEEPING INSIDE AND WE HAVE MANY MILES AHEAD OF US. WE HAVE TO BE MORE COGNIZANT OF OUR WORD CHOICES. WE CAN'T JUST IMPLODE A-LA-SCARAMUCCI SO EARLY IN THE GAME.
I'M NOT SURE ABOUT THAT. I MEANT MOST OF WHAT I SAID.
YOU MEANT IT WHEN YOU CALLED ME A JEW-HATING, NAGGING ALBATROSS OF A WIFE?
I SAID THAT? YEESH. YOU'D THINK I WAS THE ONE WITH THE ANGER-MANAGEMENT ISSUES.
NO, I WAS SAYING I REALLY MEANT IT WHEN I SAID HOW IMPORTANT KITTERY IS TO ME AND THAT I BLAME MYSELF FOR HER GOING MISSING.
WE REALLY NEED TO WORK ON NURTURING OUR COMMUNICATION CONNECTION. LET'S DO A KUNDALINI YOGA MEDITATION TOGETHER, OK?
I'LL DO DAMN NEAR ANYTHING YOU ASK WHEN YOU'RE IN THOSE PUNJAMMIES, MY LITTLE HABIBI.
ARABIC? ARE YOU EVEN TRYING, MICHAEL? I CAN ONLY ASSUME MERCURY IS IN RETROGRADE BECAUSE YOU ARE REALLY BAD AT READING ME RIGHT NOW.
BESIDES, YOU SHOULD BE ABLE TO TELL FROM THE PATTERN ALONE THAT THESE PANTS ARE MADE IN INDIA.
LET'S DO THE OBSTACLE-REMOVING MANTRA. AND I BETTER NOT FEEL ANY HOT BREATH ON MY ASS THIS TIME.
I HOPE YOU PACKED YOUR PERIOD PANTIES BECAUSE YOU ARE DEFINITELY READY TO SLOUGH.
JUST CHANT BEFORE I PUNCH YOU IN YOUR GONADS OF OPPRESSION.

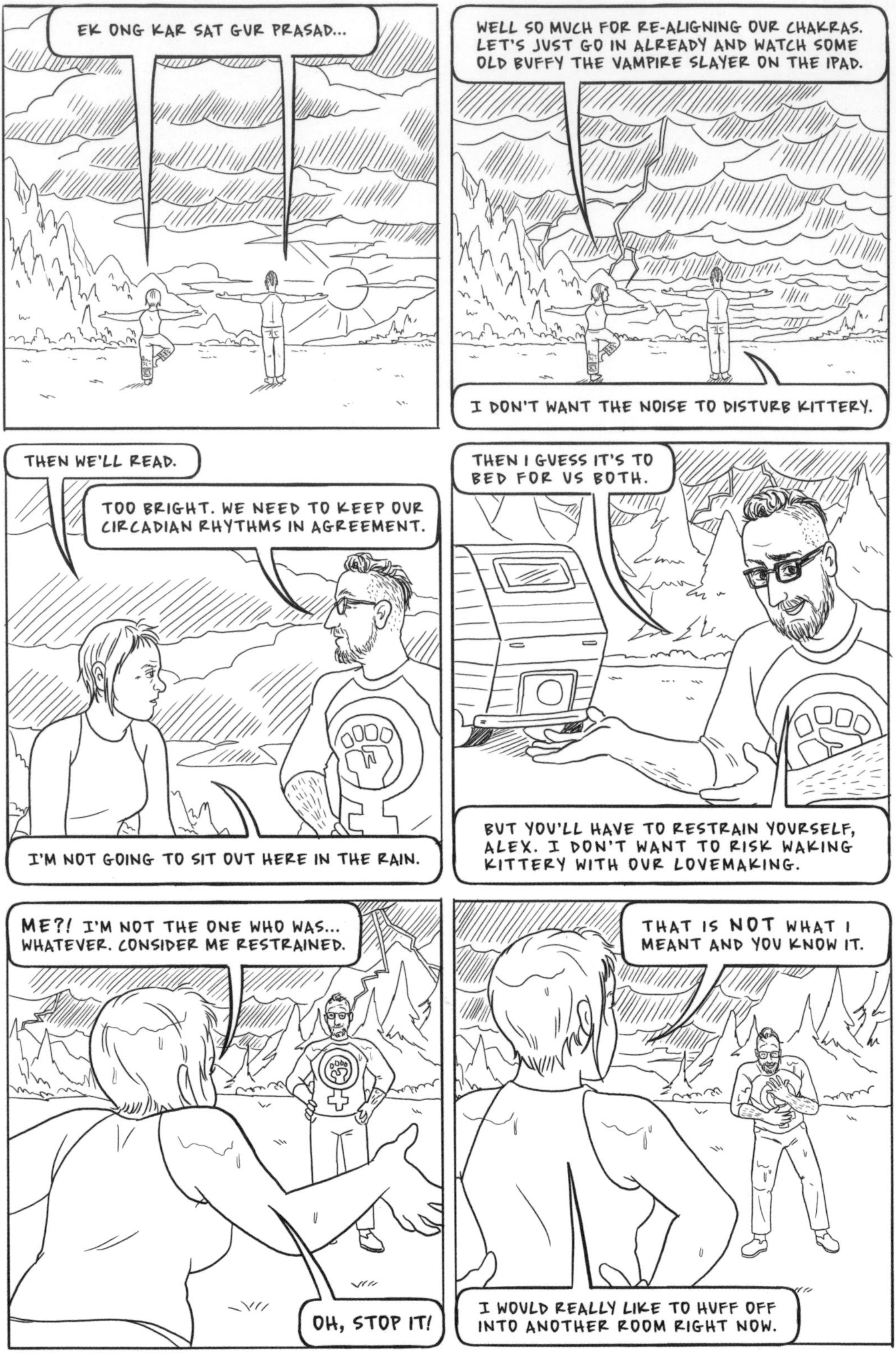
EK ONG KAR SAT GUR PRASAD...
WELL SO MUCH FOR RE-ALIGNING OUR CHAKRAS. LET'S JUST GO IN ALREADY AND WATCH SOME OLD BUFFY THE VAMPIRE SLAYER ON THE IPAD.
I DON'T WANT THE NOISE TO DISTURB KITTERY.
THEN WE'LL READ.
TOO BRIGHT. WE NEED TO KEEP OUR CIRCADIAN RHYTHMS IN AGREEMENT.
I'M NOT GOING TO SIT OUT HERE IN THE RAIN.
THEN I GUESS IT'S TO BED FOR US BOTH.
BUT YOU'LL HAVE TO RESTRAIN YOURSELF, ALEX. I DON'T WANT TO RISK WAKING KITTERY WITH OUR LOVEMAKING.
ME?! I'M NOT THE ONE WHO WAS... WHATEVER. CONSIDER ME RESTRAINED.
OH, STOP IT!
THAT IS NOT WHAT I MEANT AND YOU KNOW IT.
I WOULD REALLY LIKE TO HUFF OFF INTO ANOTHER ROOM RIGHT NOW.

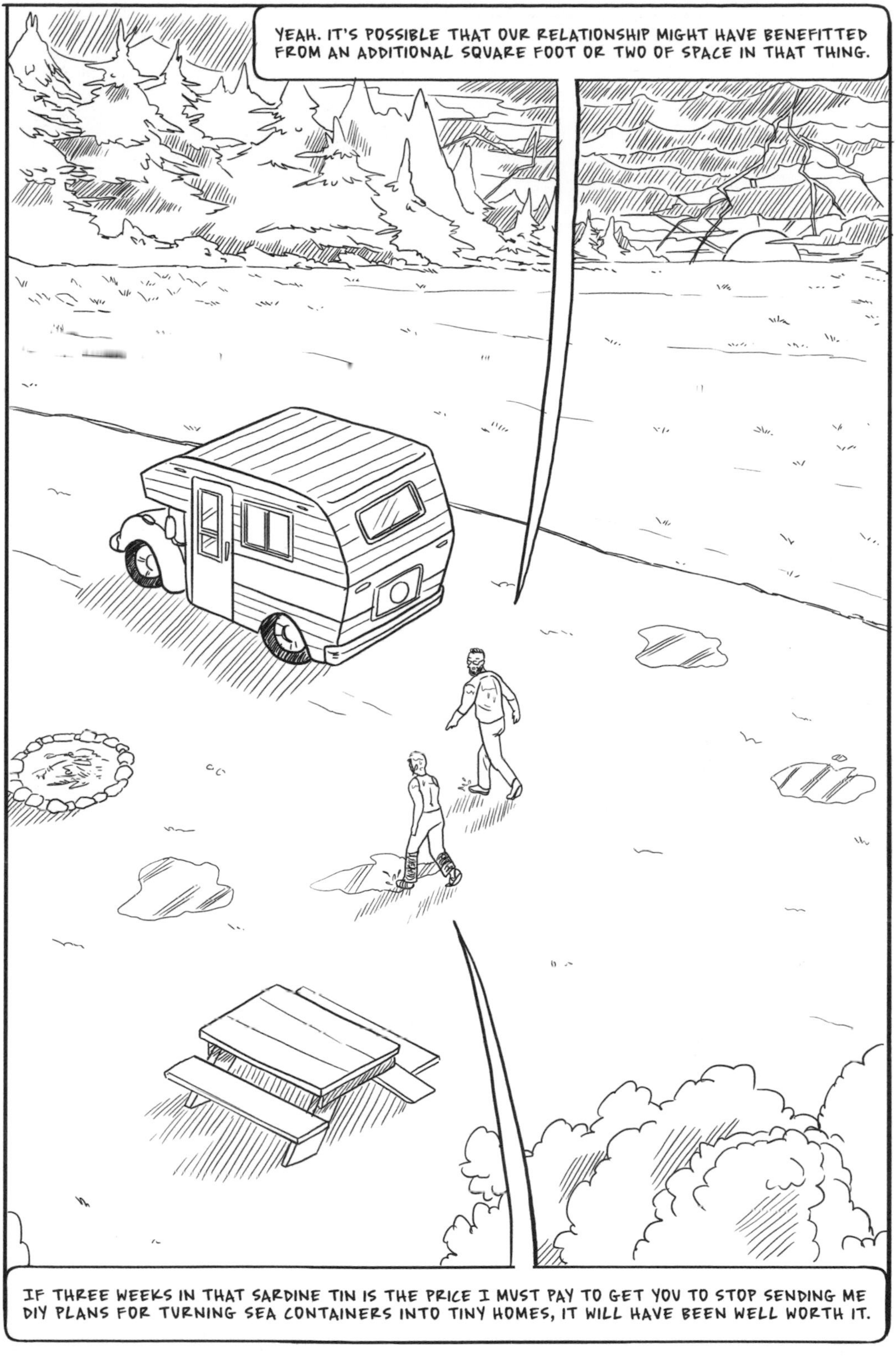
YEAH. IT'S POSSIBLE THAT OUR RELATIONSHIP MIGHT HAVE BENEFITTED FROM AN ADDITIONAL SQUARE FOOT OR TWO OF SPACE IN THAT THING.
IF THREE WEEKS IN THAT SARDINE TIN IS THE PRICE I MUST PAY TO GET YOU TO STOP SENDING ME DIY PLANS FOR TURNING SEA CONTAINERS INTO TINY HOMES, IT WILL HAVE BEEN WELL WORTH IT.

Chapter 6

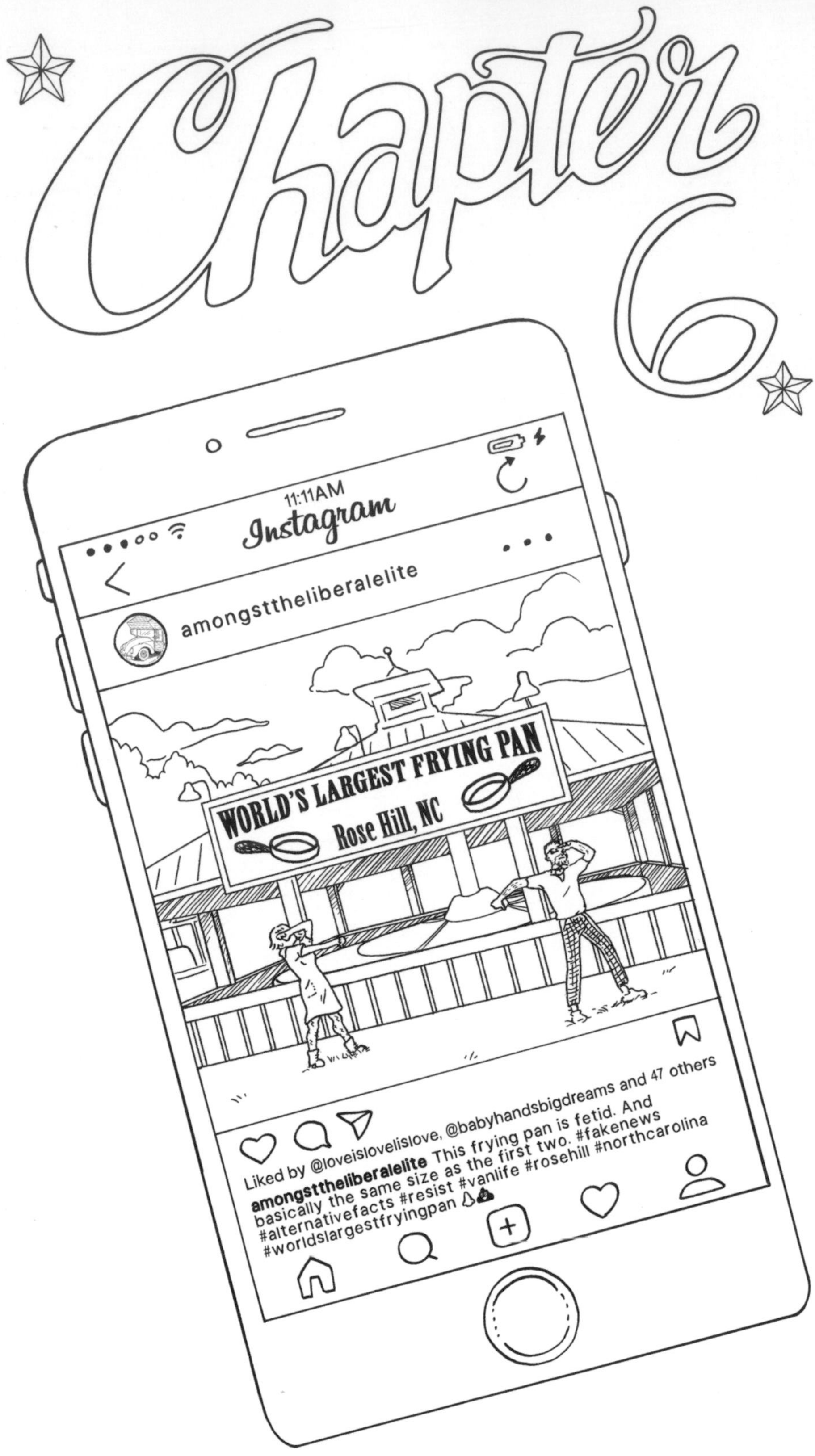

11:11AM
Instagram
amongsttheliberalelite
amongsttheliberalelite
WORLD'S LARGEST FRYING PAN
Rose Hill, NC
Liked by @loveislovelislove, @babyhandsbigdreams and 47 others
amongsttheliberalelite This frying pan is fetid. And basically the same size as the first two. #fakenews #alternativefacts #resist #vanlife #rosehill #northcarolina #worldslargestfryingpan

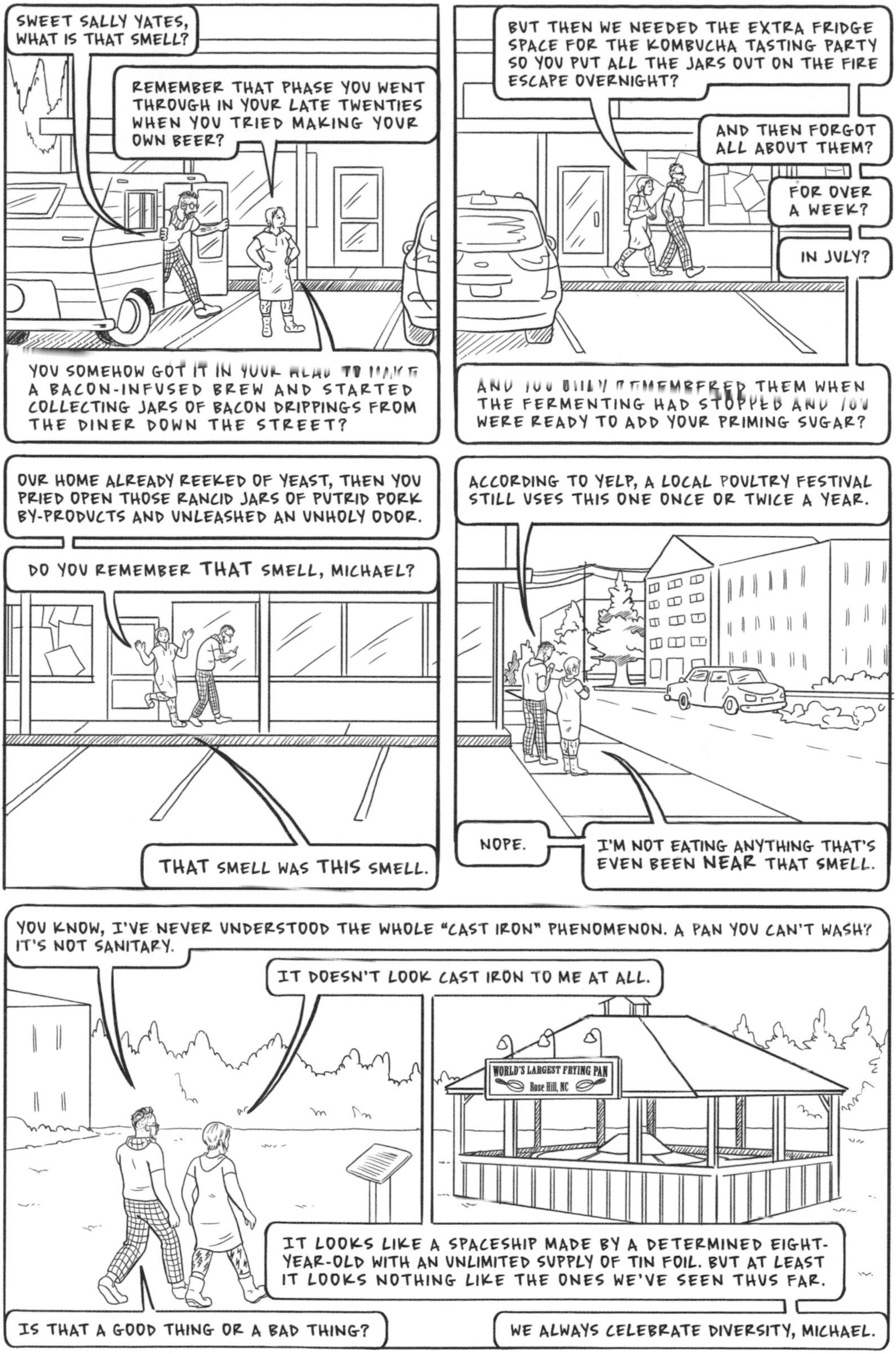

SWEET SALLY YATES, WHAT IS THAT SMELL?
REMEMBER THAT PHASE YOU WENT THROUGH IN YOUR LATE TWENTIES WHEN YOU TRIED MAKING YOUR OWN BEER?
YOU SOMEHOW GOT IT IN YOUR HEAD TO MAKE A BACON-INFUSED BREW AND STARTED COLLECTING JARS OF BACON DRIPPINGS FROM THE DINER DOWN THE STREET?
BUT THEN WE NEEDED THE EXTRA FRIDGE SPACE FOR THE KOMBUCHA TASTING PARTY SO YOU PUT ALL THE JARS OUT ON THE FIRE ESCAPE OVERNIGHT?
AND THEN FORGOT ALL ABOUT THEM?
FOR OVER A WEEK?
IN JULY?
AND YOU ONLY REMEMBERED THEM WHEN THE FERMENTING HAD STOPPED AND YOU WERE READY TO ADD YOUR PRIMING SUGAR?
OUR HOME ALREADY REEKED OF YEAST, THEN YOU PRIED OPEN THOSE RANCID JARS OF PUTRID PORK BY-PRODUCTS AND UNLEASHED AN UNHOLY ODOR.
DO YOU REMEMBER THAT SMELL, MICHAEL?
THAT SMELL WAS THIS SMELL.
ACCORDING TO YELP, A LOCAL POULTRY FESTIVAL STILL USES THIS ONE ONCE OR TWICE A YEAR.
NOPE.
I'M NOT EATING ANYTHING THAT'S EVEN BEEN NEAR THAT SMELL.
YOU KNOW, I'VE NEVER UNDERSTOOD THE WHOLE "CAST IRON" PHENOMENON. A PAN YOU CAN'T WASH? IT'S NOT SANITARY.
IT DOESN'T LOOK CAST IRON TO ME AT ALL.
WORLD'S LARGEST FRYING PAN
Rose Hill, NC
IT LOOKS LIKE A SPACESHIP MADE BY A DETERMINED EIGHT-YEAR-OLD WITH AN UNLIMITED SUPPLY OF TIN FOIL. BUT AT LEAST IT LOOKS NOTHING LIKE THE ONES WE'VE SEEN THUS FAR.
IS THAT A GOOD THING OR A BAD THING?
WE ALWAYS CELEBRATE DIVERSITY, MICHAEL.

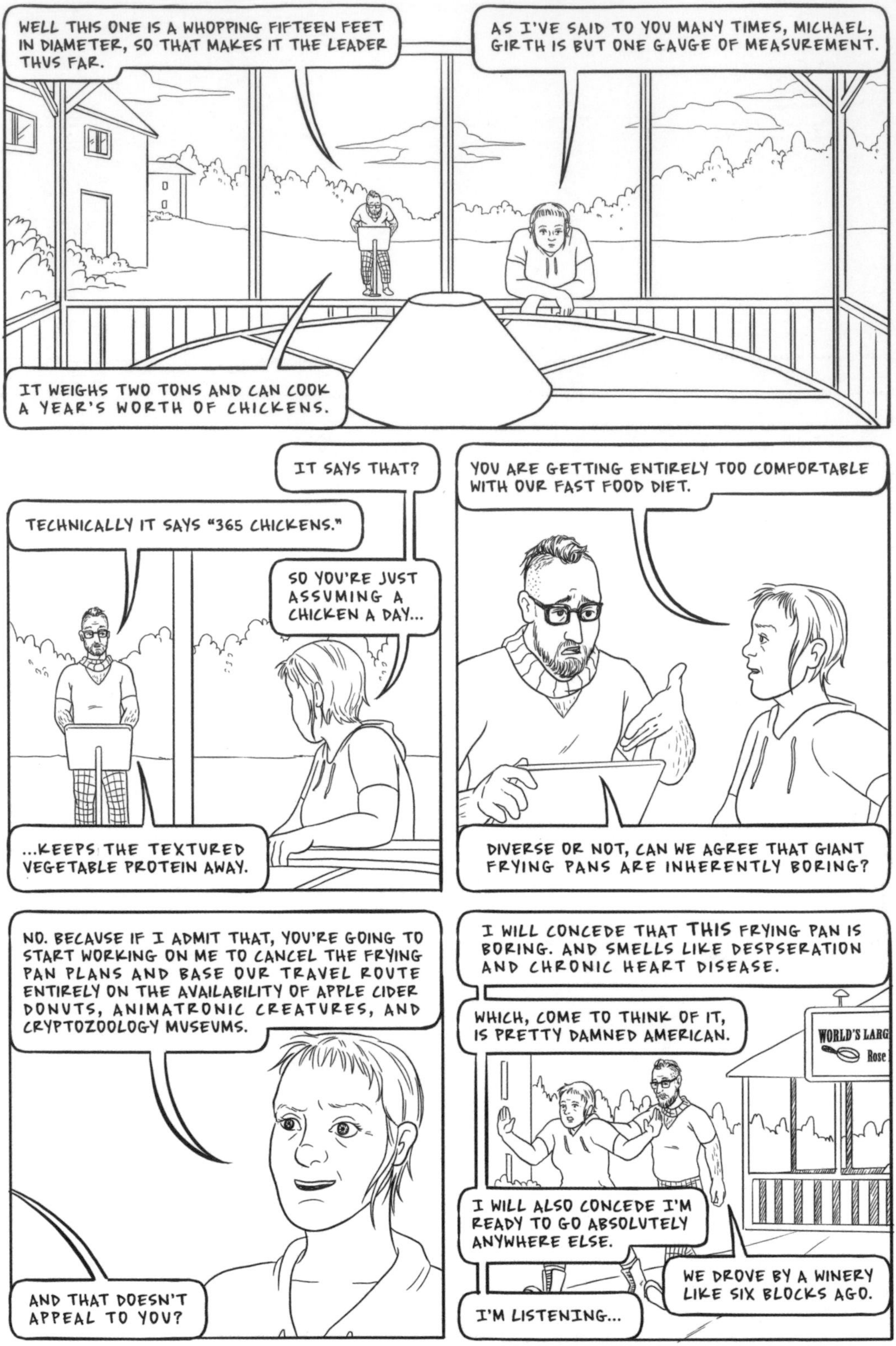
WELL THIS ONE IS A WHOPPING FIFTEEN FEET IN DIAMETER, SO THAT MAKES IT THE LEADER THUS FAR.
AS I'VE SAID TO YOU MANY TIMES, MICHAEL, GIRTH IS BUT ONE GAUGE OF MEASUREMENT.
IT WEIGHS TWO TONS AND CAN COOK A YEAR'S WORTH OF CHICKENS.
IT SAYS THAT?
TECHNICALLY IT SAYS "365 CHICKENS."
SO YOU'RE JUST ASSUMING A CHICKEN A DAY...
...KEEPS THE TEXTURED VEGETABLE PROTEIN AWAY.
YOU ARE GETTING ENTIRELY TOO COMFORTABLE WITH OUR FAST FOOD DIET.
DIVERSE OR NOT, CAN WE AGREE THAT GIANT FRYING PANS ARE INHERENTLY BORING?
NO. BECAUSE IF I ADMIT THAT, YOU'RE GOING TO START WORKING ON ME TO CANCEL THE FRYING PAN PLANS AND BASE OUR TRAVEL ROUTE ENTIRELY ON THE AVAILABILITY OF APPLE CIDER DONUTS, ANIMATRONIC CREATURES, AND CRYPTOZOOLOGY MUSEUMS.
AND THAT DOESN'T APPEAL TO YOU?
I WILL CONCEDE THAT THIS FRYING PAN IS BORING. AND SMELLS LIKE DESPSERATION AND CHRONIC HEART DISEASE.
WHICH, COME TO THINK OF IT, IS PRETTY DAMNED AMERICAN.
I WILL ALSO CONCEDE I'M READY TO GO ABSOLUTELY ANYWHERE ELSE.
WE DROVE BY A WINERY LIKE SIX BLOCKS AGO.
I'M LISTENING...

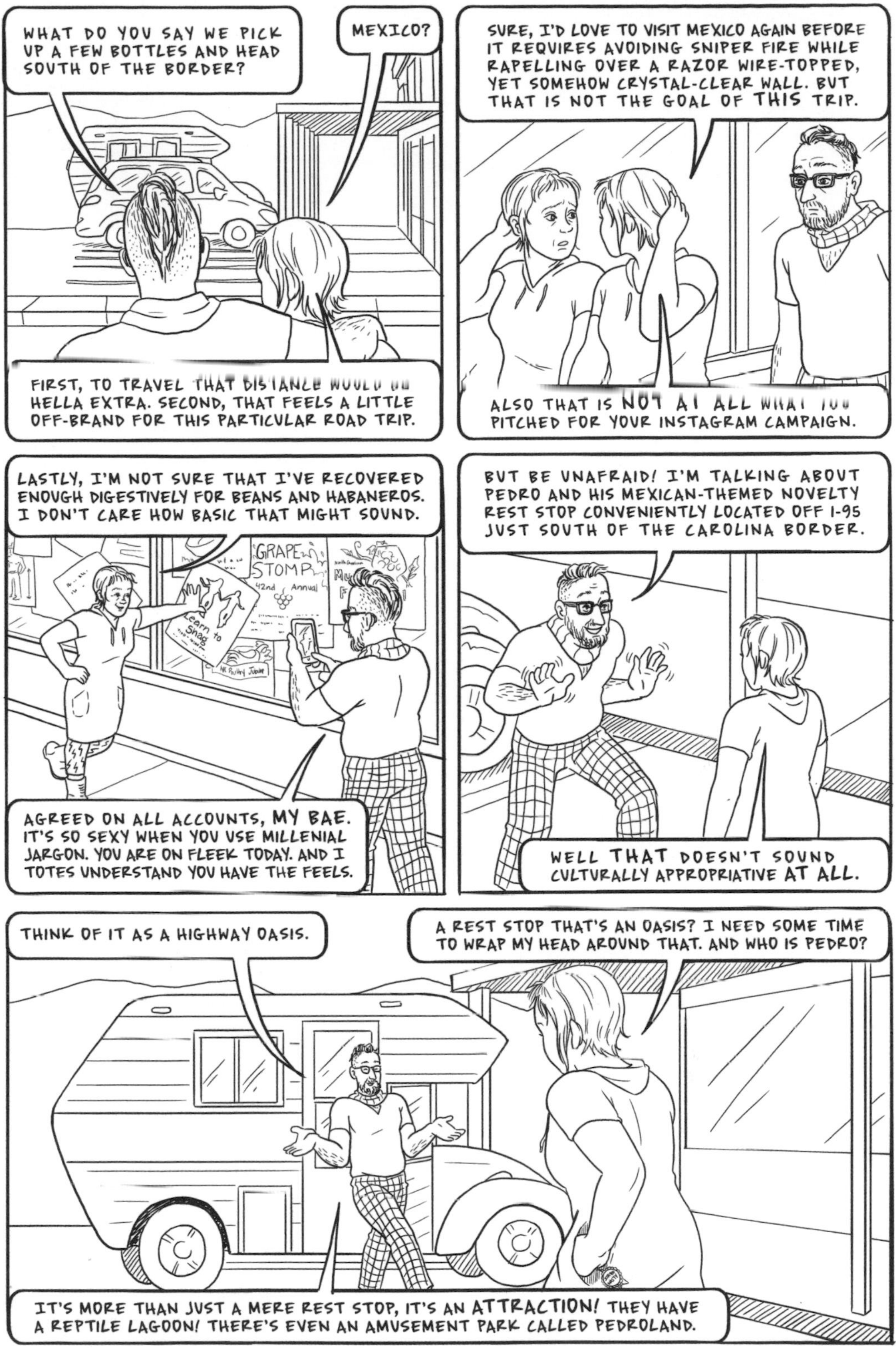
WHAT DO YOU SAY WE PICK UP A FEW BOTTLES AND HEAD SOUTH OF THE BORDER?
MEXICO?
FIRST, TO TRAVEL THAT DISTANCE WOULD BE HELLA EXTRA. SECOND, THAT FEELS A LITTLE OFF-BRAND FOR THIS PARTICULAR ROAD TRIP.
SURE, I'D LOVE TO VISIT MEXICO AGAIN BEFORE IT REQUIRES AVOIDING SNIPER FIRE WHILE RAPELLING OVER A RAZOR WIRE-TOPPED, YET SOMEHOW CRYSTAL-CLEAR WALL. BUT THAT IS NOT THE GOAL OF THIS TRIP.
ALSO THAT IS NOT AT ALL WHAT YOU PITCHED FOR YOUR INSTAGRAM CAMPAIGN.
LASTLY, I'M NOT SURE THAT I'VE RECOVERED ENOUGH DIGESTIVELY FOR BEANS AND HABANEROS. I DON'T CARE HOW BASIC THAT MIGHT SOUND.
GRAPE STOMP
42nd Annual
Learn to Snag
AGREED ON ALL ACCOUNTS, MY BAE. IT'S SO SEXY WHEN YOU USE MILLENIAL JARGON. YOU ARE ON FLEEK TODAY. AND I TOTES UNDERSTAND YOU HAVE THE FEELS.
BUT BE UNAFRAID! I'M TALKING ABOUT PEDRO AND HIS MEXICAN-THEMED NOVELTY REST STOP CONVENIENTLY LOCATED OFF I-95 JUST SOUTH OF THE CAROLINA BORDER.
WELL THAT DOESN'T SOUND CULTURALLY APPROPRIATIVE AT ALL.
THINK OF IT AS A HIGHWAY OASIS.
A REST STOP THAT'S AN OASIS? I NEED SOME TIME TO WRAP MY HEAD AROUND THAT. AND WHO IS PEDRO?
IT'S MORE THAN JUST A MERE REST STOP, IT'S AN ATTRACTION! THEY HAVE A REPTILE LAGOON! THERE'S EVEN AN AMUSEMENT PARK CALLED PEDROLAND.

AND WAIT UNTIL YOU HEAR ABOUT THE SOMBRERO OBSERVATION TOWER. THE LOCALS CALL IT THE EIFFEL TOWER OF THE SOUTH.

I FEEL PRETTY CONFIDENT I KNOW WHO THEY VOTED FOR IN 2016.

I BET YOU'RE RIGHT. FROM AN ANTHROPOLOGICAL STANDPOINT, WE BASICALLY HAVE TO GO. NOW THAT IS AN ON-BRAND STOP, AMIRIGHT?

AND PEDRO?

HE'S THE NINETY-SEVEN-FOOT MASCOT. WE CAN DRIVE THROUGH HIS LEGS. PHOTO OPPORTUNITY, ALEX.

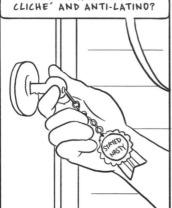

PEDRO. REALLY? COULD THEY NOT COME UP WITH SOMETHING A LITTLE MORE CLICHE' AND ANTI-LATINO?

STAYED NASTY

THERE WAS AN ACTUAL PEDRO THAT THE ORIGINAL OWNER BROUGHT BACK WITH HIM FROM A SHOPPING TRIP TO MEXICO.

OR MAYBE THAT WAS PANCHO? IT'S BEEN A WHILE SINCE I READ THE WIKIPEDIA ENTRY.

I NEVER THOUGHT YOU'D GO FOR IT SO I DIDN'T BOTHER WITH CONDUCTING MY USUAL EXHAUSTIVE WIKI-BASED RESEARCH. NOT THAT WIKIPEDIA IS A REPUTABLE SOURCE OF INFORMATION ANYWAY. I DON'T TRUST ANYTHING WIKI ANYMORE.

DID I MENTION THERE'S A CAMPGROUND ON SITE? I KNOW IT LACKS THE GRAVITAS OF THE ART INSTALLATION YOU WANTED TO SEE IN LOUISIANA WITH THE GARDEN PLOTS THE SIZE OF SOLITARY CONFINEMENT JAIL CELLS, BUT IT IS JUST A FEW HOURS AWAY AND...

wqfs

IS THERE A HOTEL?

THERE IS. TECHNICALLY IT'S A MOTOR LODGE. WITH AN ACCOMMODATING PET POLICY. AND SOMETHING CALLED "THE PLEASURE DOME."

IF YOU CAN GET ME A LOW-SULFITE WINE AND AN HOUR ALONE IN A BATHTUB, I'M IN.

REALLY?!

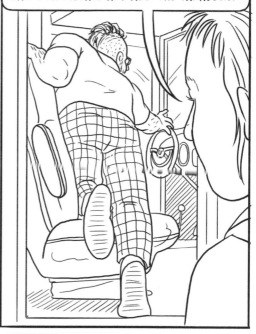

AND YOU HAVE TO PROMISE TO BATHE YOURSELF AND KITTERY. AND DO A LOAD OF LAUNDRY. EVEN IF THE ONLY SOAP AVAILABLE HAS SODIUM LAURETH SULFATE AND ALL THE PARABENS.

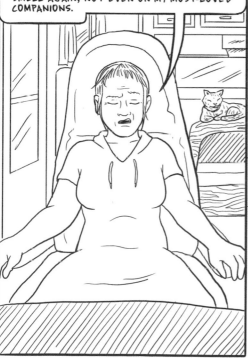

BECAUSE I DON'T EVER WANT TO SMELL THIS SMELL AGAIN, NOT EVEN ON MY MOST-LOVED COMPANIONS.

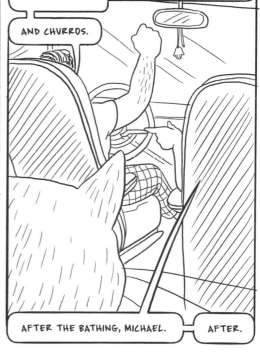

DONE AND DONE. OH ALEX, I AM GOING TO SHOWER YOU WITH THE SWEET SMELL OF MY LOVE TONIGHT.

AND CHURROS.

AFTER THE BATHING, MICHAEL.

AFTER.

Chapter 7

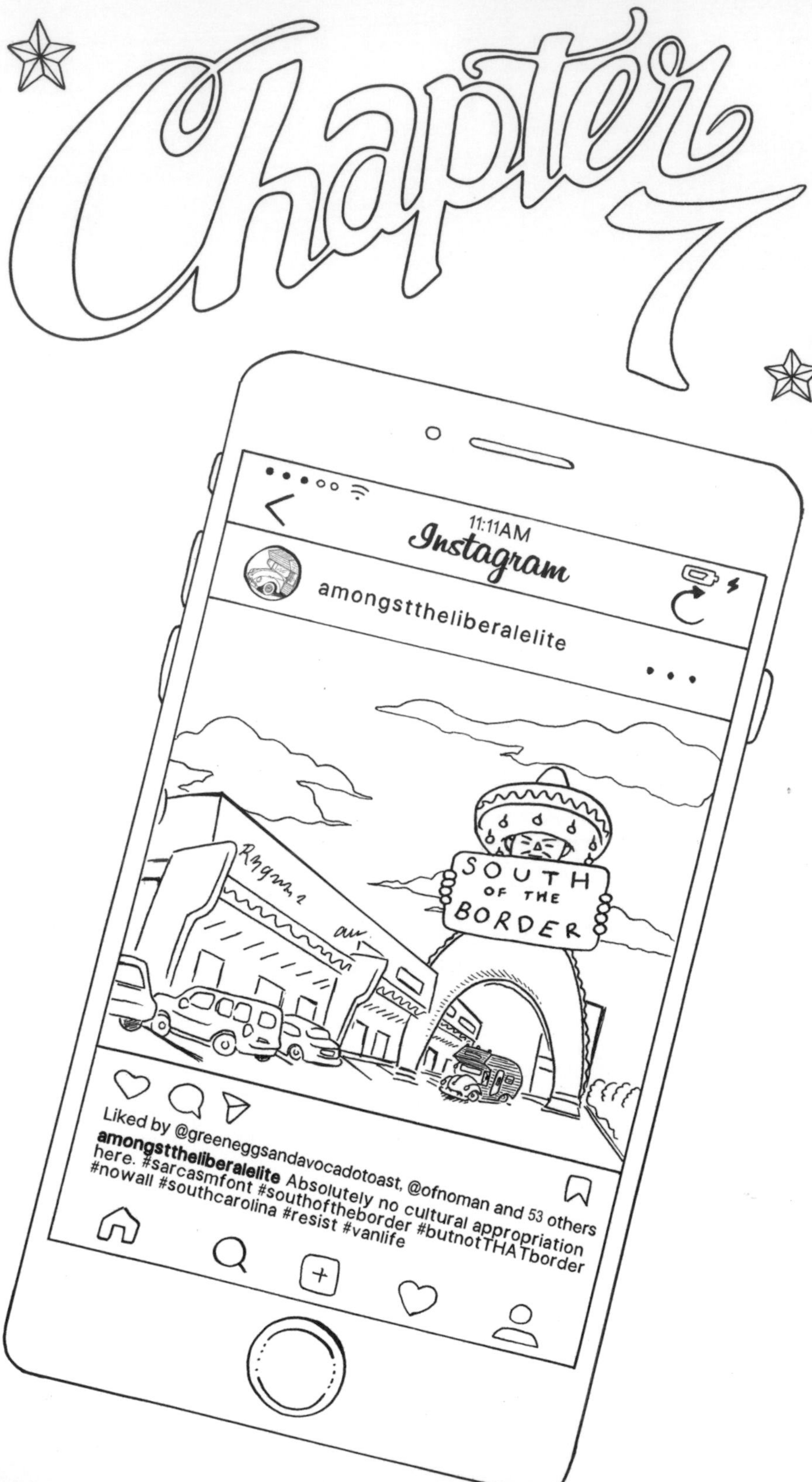
11:11AM
Instagram
amongsttheliberalelite
SOUTH OF THE BORDER
Liked by @greeneggsandavocadotoast, @ofnoman and 53 others
amongsttheliberalelite Absolutely no cultural appropriation here. #sarcasmfont #southoftheborder #butnotTHATborder #nowall #southcarolina #resist #vanlife

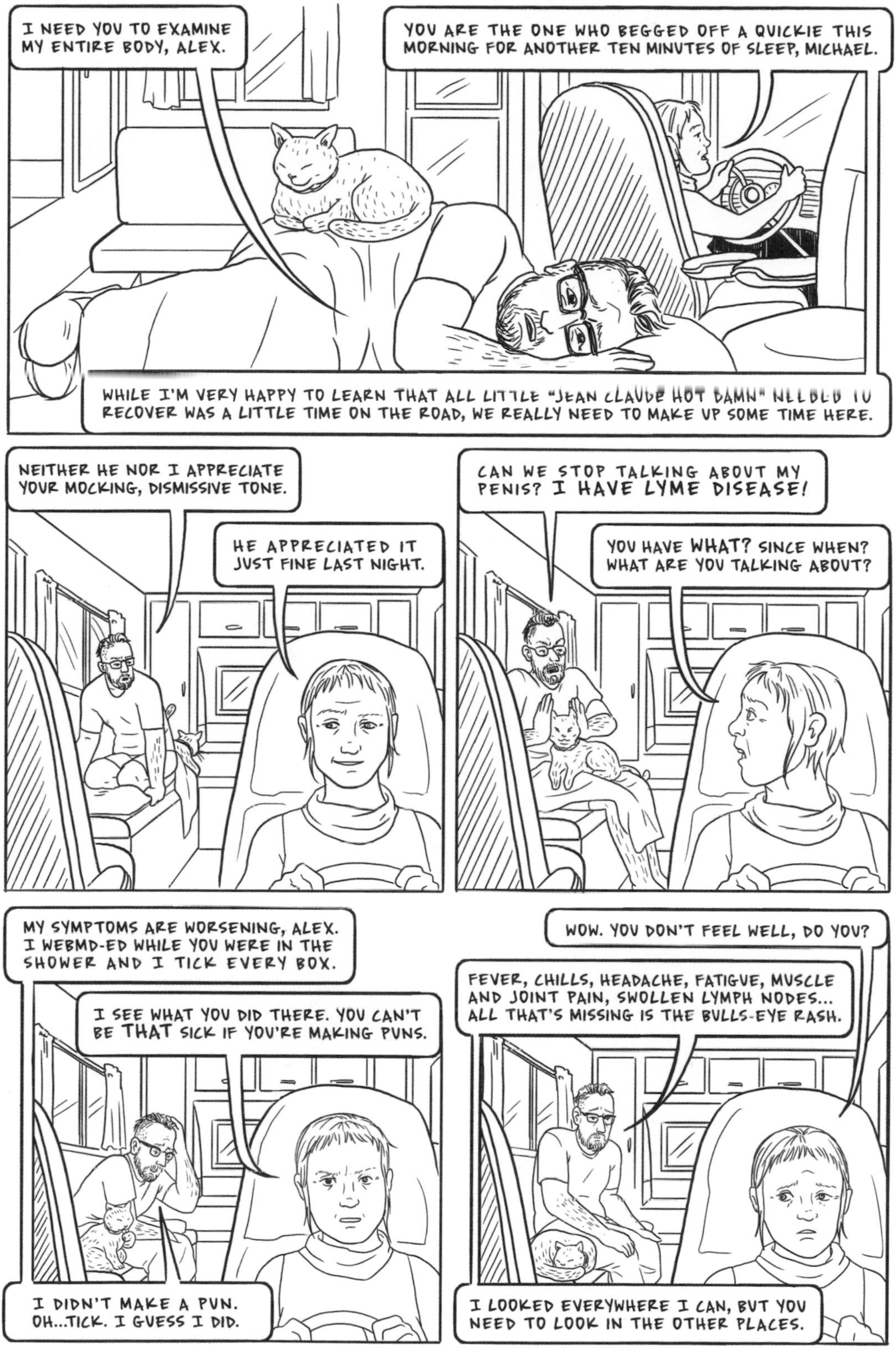
I NEED YOU TO EXAMINE MY ENTIRE BODY, ALEX.
YOU ARE THE ONE WHO BEGGED OFF A QUICKIE THIS MORNING FOR ANOTHER TEN MINUTES OF SLEEP, MICHAEL.
WHILE I'M VERY HAPPY TO LEARN THAT ALL LITTLE "JEAN CLAUDE HOT DAMN" NEEDED TO RECOVER WAS A LITTLE TIME ON THE ROAD, WE REALLY NEED TO MAKE UP SOME TIME HERE.
NEITHER HE NOR I APPRECIATE YOUR MOCKING, DISMISSIVE TONE.
HE APPRECIATED IT JUST FINE LAST NIGHT.
CAN WE STOP TALKING ABOUT MY PENIS? I HAVE LYME DISEASE!
YOU HAVE WHAT? SINCE WHEN? WHAT ARE YOU TALKING ABOUT?
MY SYMPTOMS ARE WORSENING, ALEX. I WEBMD-ED WHILE YOU WERE IN THE SHOWER AND I TICK EVERY BOX.
I SEE WHAT YOU DID THERE. YOU CAN'T BE THAT SICK IF YOU'RE MAKING PUNS.
I DIDN'T MAKE A PUN. OH...TICK. I GUESS I DID.
WOW. YOU DON'T FEEL WELL, DO YOU?
FEVER, CHILLS, HEADACHE, FATIGUE, MUSCLE AND JOINT PAIN, SWOLLEN LYMPH NODES... ALL THAT'S MISSING IS THE BULLS-EYE RASH.
I LOOKED EVERYWHERE I CAN, BUT YOU NEED TO LOOK IN THE OTHER PLACES.

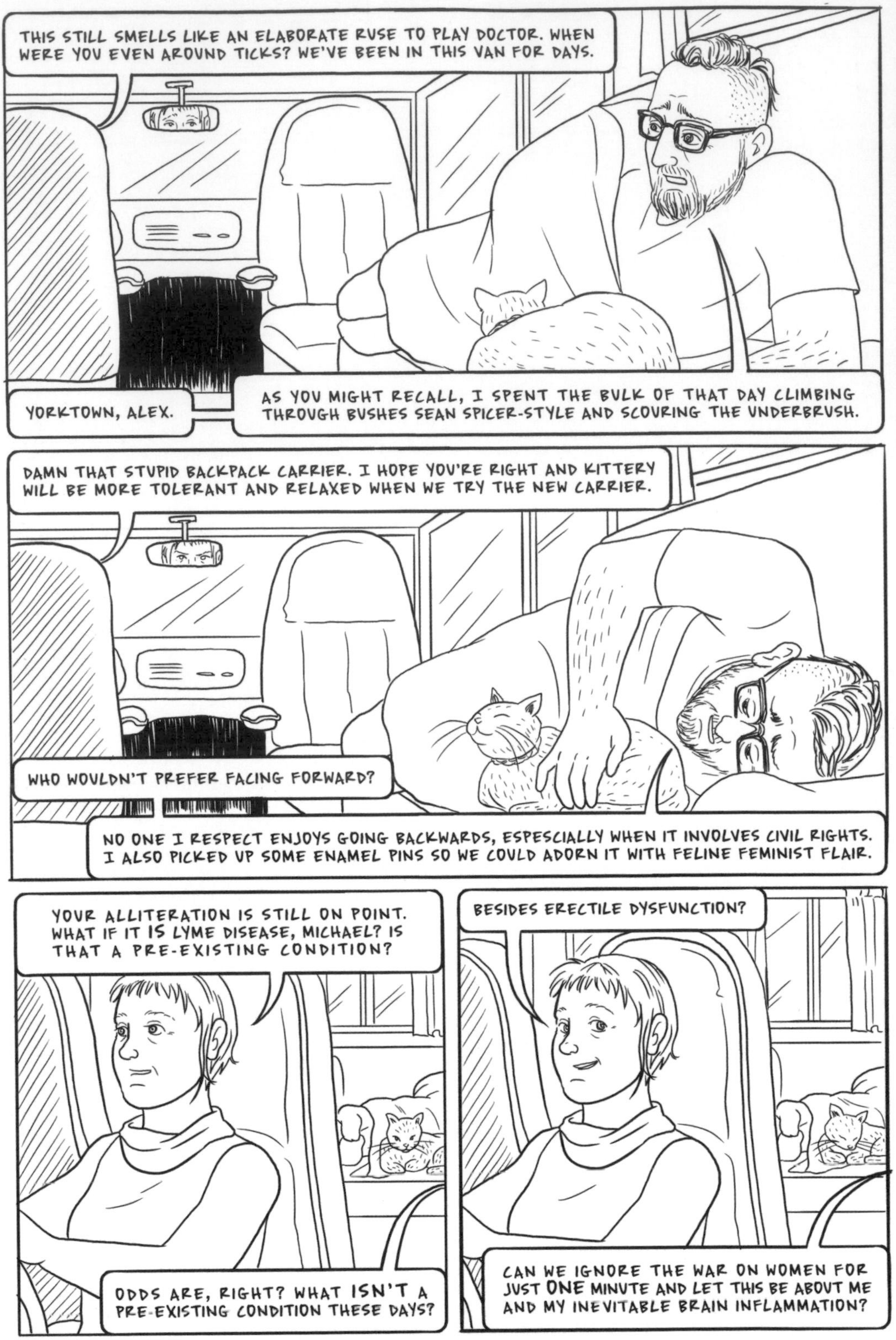

THIS STILL SMELLS LIKE AN ELABORATE RUSE TO PLAY DOCTOR. WHEN WERE YOU EVEN AROUND TICKS? WE'VE BEEN IN THIS VAN FOR DAYS.
YORKTOWN, ALEX.
AS YOU MIGHT RECALL, I SPENT THE BULK OF THAT DAY CLIMBING THROUGH BUSHES SEAN SPICER-STYLE AND SCOURING THE UNDERBRUSH.
DAMN THAT STUPID BACKPACK CARRIER. I HOPE YOU'RE RIGHT AND KITTERY WILL BE MORE TOLERANT AND RELAXED WHEN WE TRY THE NEW CARRIER.
WHO WOULDN'T PREFER FACING FORWARD?
NO ONE I RESPECT ENJOYS GOING BACKWARDS, ESPESCIALLY WHEN IT INVOLVES CIVIL RIGHTS. I ALSO PICKED UP SOME ENAMEL PINS SO WE COULD ADORN IT WITH FELINE FEMINIST FLAIR.
YOUR ALLITERATION IS STILL ON POINT. WHAT IF IT IS LYME DISEASE, MICHAEL? IS THAT A PRE-EXISTING CONDITION?
ODDS ARE, RIGHT? WHAT ISN'T A PRE-EXISTING CONDITION THESE DAYS?
BESIDES ERECTILE DYSFUNCTION?
CAN WE IGNORE THE WAR ON WOMEN FOR JUST ONE MINUTE AND LET THIS BE ABOUT ME AND MY INEVITABLE BRAIN INFLAMMATION?

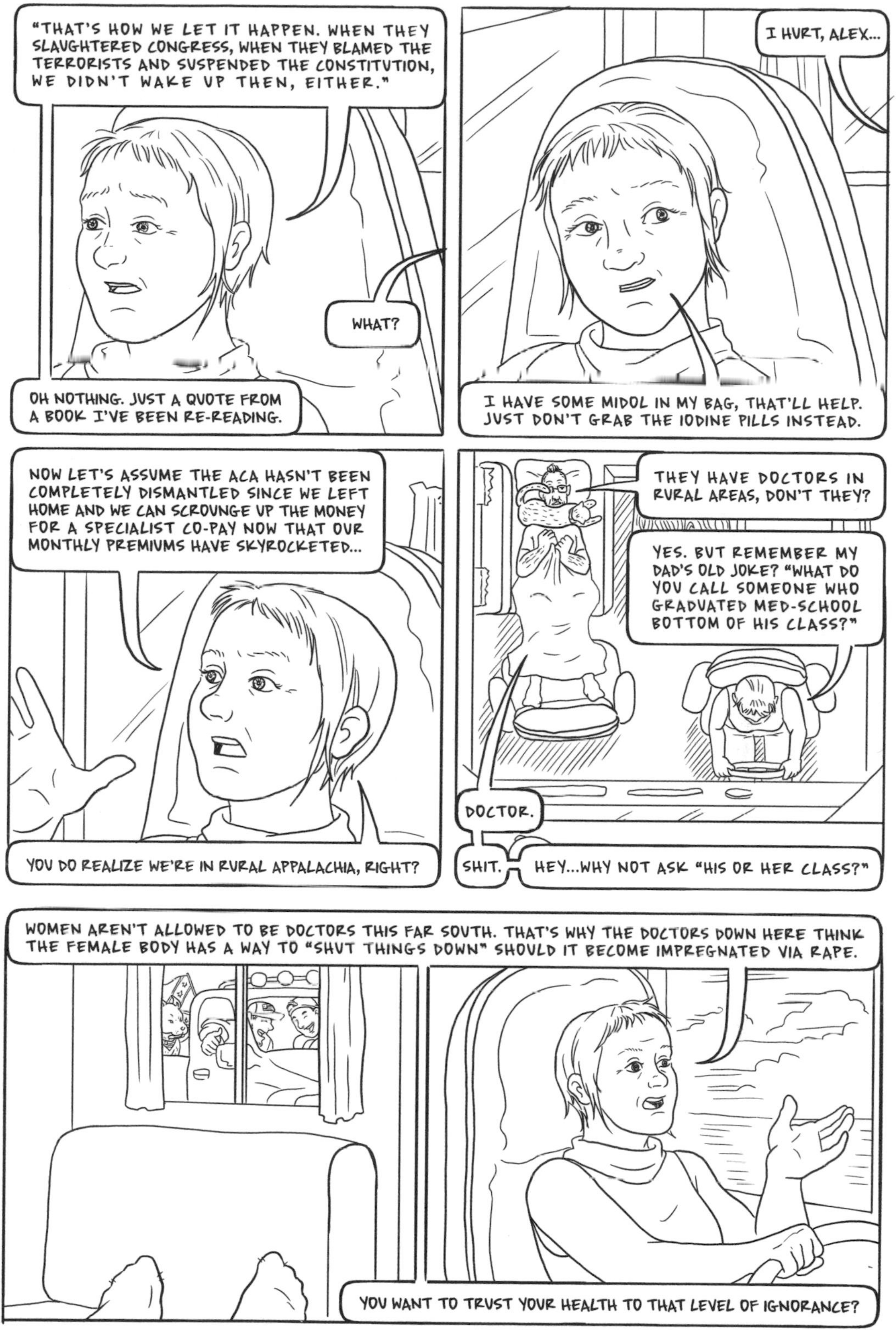

"THAT'S HOW WE LET IT HAPPEN. WHEN THEY SLAUGHTERED CONGRESS, WHEN THEY BLAMED THE TERRORISTS AND SUSPENDED THE CONSTITUTION, WE DIDN'T WAKE UP THEN, EITHER."
WHAT?
OH NOTHING. JUST A QUOTE FROM A BOOK I'VE BEEN RE-READING.
I HURT, ALEX...
I HAVE SOME MIDOL IN MY BAG, THAT'LL HELP. JUST DON'T GRAB THE IODINE PILLS INSTEAD.
NOW LET'S ASSUME THE ACA HASN'T BEEN COMPLETELY DISMANTLED SINCE WE LEFT HOME AND WE CAN SCROUNGE UP THE MONEY FOR A SPECIALIST CO-PAY NOW THAT OUR MONTHLY PREMIUMS HAVE SKYROCKETED...
YOU DO REALIZE WE'RE IN RURAL APPALACHIA, RIGHT?
THEY HAVE DOCTORS IN RURAL AREAS, DON'T THEY?
YES. BUT REMEMBER MY DAD'S OLD JOKE? "WHAT DO YOU CALL SOMEONE WHO GRADUATED MED-SCHOOL BOTTOM OF HIS CLASS?"
DOCTOR.
SHIT.
HEY...WHY NOT ASK "HIS OR HER CLASS?"
WOMEN AREN'T ALLOWED TO BE DOCTORS THIS FAR SOUTH. THAT'S WHY THE DOCTORS DOWN HERE THINK THE FEMALE BODY HAS A WAY TO "SHUT THINGS DOWN" SHOULD IT BECOME IMPREGNATED VIA RAPE.
YOU WANT TO TRUST YOUR HEALTH TO THAT LEVEL OF IGNORANCE?

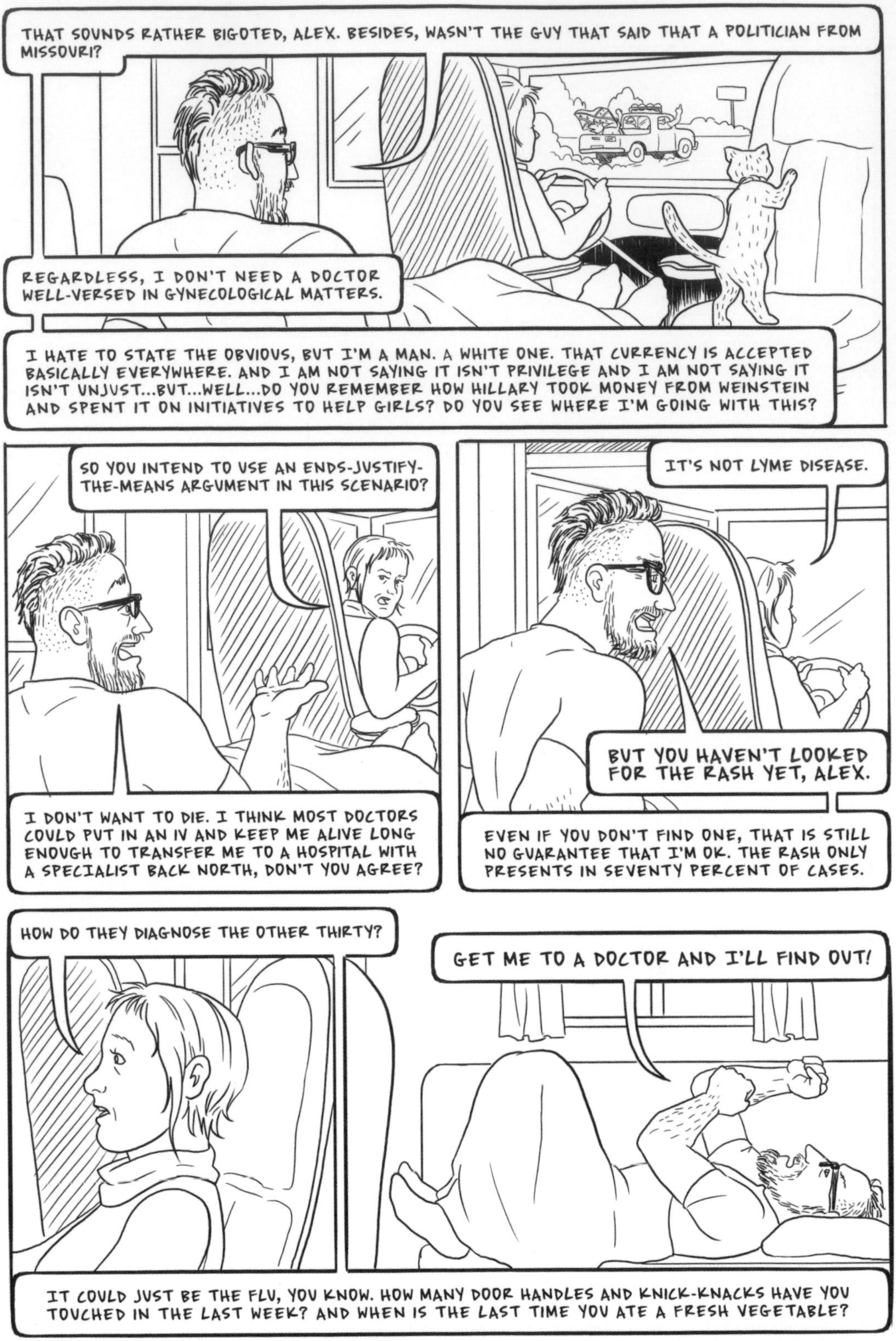
THAT SOUNDS RATHER BIGOTED, ALEX. BESIDES, WASN'T THE GUY THAT SAID THAT A POLITICIAN FROM MISSOURI?
REGARDLESS, I DON'T NEED A DOCTOR WELL-VERSED IN GYNECOLOGICAL MATTERS.
I HATE TO STATE THE OBVIOUS, BUT I'M A MAN. A WHITE ONE. THAT CURRENCY IS ACCEPTED BASICALLY EVERYWHERE. AND I AM NOT SAYING IT ISN'T PRIVILEGE AND I AM NOT SAYING IT ISN'T UNJUST...BUT...WELL...DO YOU REMEMBER HOW HILLARY TOOK MONEY FROM WEINSTEIN AND SPENT IT ON INITIATIVES TO HELP GIRLS? DO YOU SEE WHERE I'M GOING WITH THIS?
SO YOU INTEND TO USE AN ENDS-JUSTIFY-THE-MEANS ARGUMENT IN THIS SCENARIO?
I DON'T WANT TO DIE. I THINK MOST DOCTORS COULD PUT IN AN IV AND KEEP ME ALIVE LONG ENOUGH TO TRANSFER ME TO A HOSPITAL WITH A SPECIALIST BACK NORTH, DON'T YOU AGREE?
IT'S NOT LYME DISEASE.
BUT YOU HAVEN'T LOOKED FOR THE RASH YET, ALEX.
EVEN IF YOU DON'T FIND ONE, THAT IS STILL NO GUARANTEE THAT I'M OK. THE RASH ONLY PRESENTS IN SEVENTY PERCENT OF CASES.
HOW DO THEY DIAGNOSE THE OTHER THIRTY?
GET ME TO A DOCTOR AND I'LL FIND OUT!
IT COULD JUST BE THE FLU, YOU KNOW. HOW MANY DOOR HANDLES AND KNICK-KNACKS HAVE YOU TOUCHED IN THE LAST WEEK? AND WHEN IS THE LAST TIME YOU ATE A FRESH VEGETABLE?

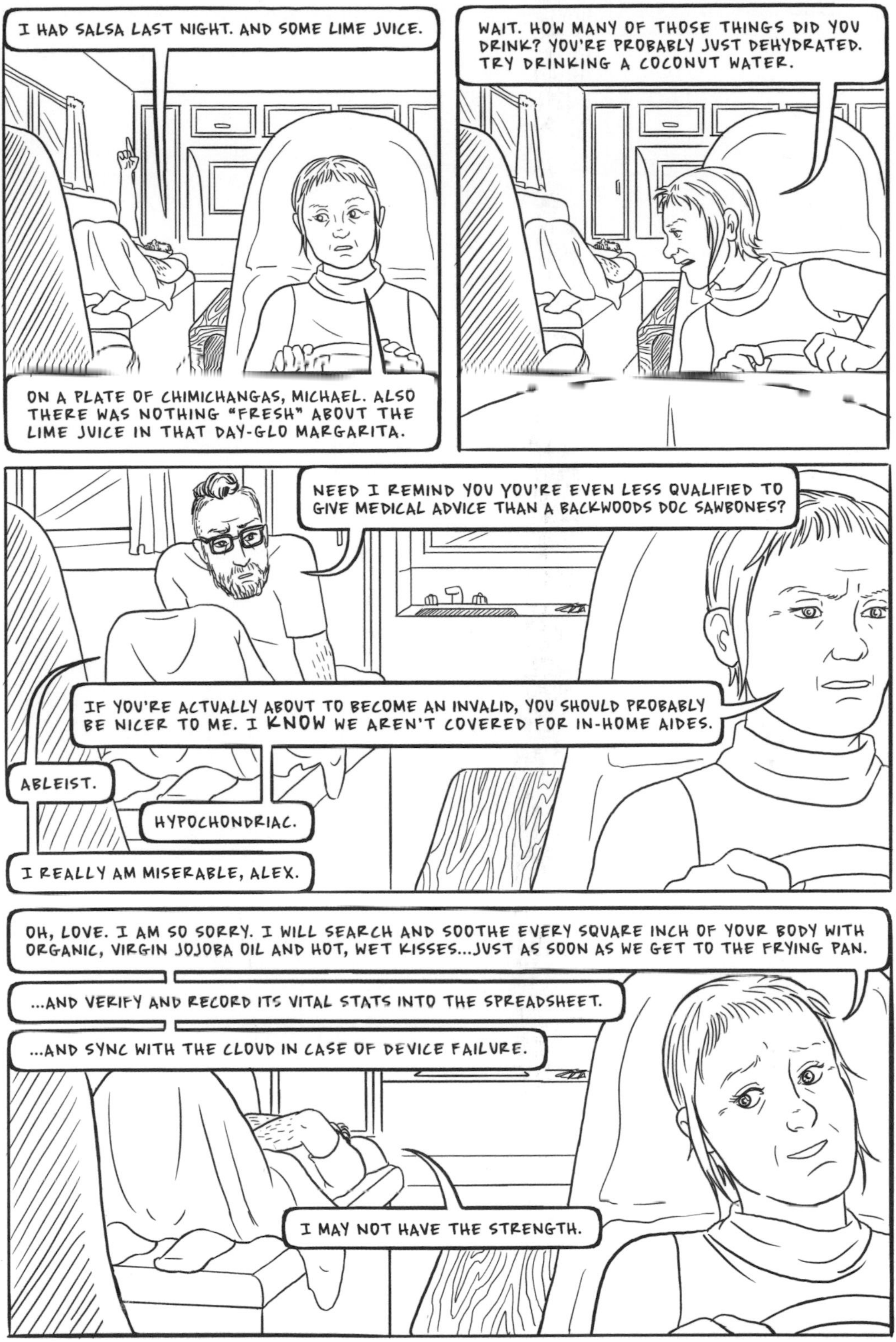

I HAD SALSA LAST NIGHT. AND SOME LIME JUICE.
ON A PLATE OF CHIMICHANGAS, MICHAEL. ALSO THERE WAS NOTHING "FRESH" ABOUT THE LIME JUICE IN THAT DAY-GLO MARGARITA.
WAIT. HOW MANY OF THOSE THINGS DID YOU DRINK? YOU'RE PROBABLY JUST DEHYDRATED. TRY DRINKING A COCONUT WATER.
NEED I REMIND YOU YOU'RE EVEN LESS QUALIFIED TO GIVE MEDICAL ADVICE THAN A BACKWOODS DOC SAWBONES?
IF YOU'RE ACTUALLY ABOUT TO BECOME AN INVALID, YOU SHOULD PROBABLY BE NICER TO ME. I KNOW WE AREN'T COVERED FOR IN-HOME AIDES.
ABLEIST.
HYPOCHONDRIAC.
I REALLY AM MISERABLE, ALEX.
OH, LOVE. I AM SO SORRY. I WILL SEARCH AND SOOTHE EVERY SQUARE INCH OF YOUR BODY WITH ORGANIC, VIRGIN JOJOBA OIL AND HOT, WET KISSES...JUST AS SOON AS WE GET TO THE FRYING PAN.
...AND VERIFY AND RECORD ITS VITAL STATS INTO THE SPREADSHEET.
...AND SYNC WITH THE CLOUD IN CASE OF DEVICE FAILURE.
I MAY NOT HAVE THE STRENGTH.

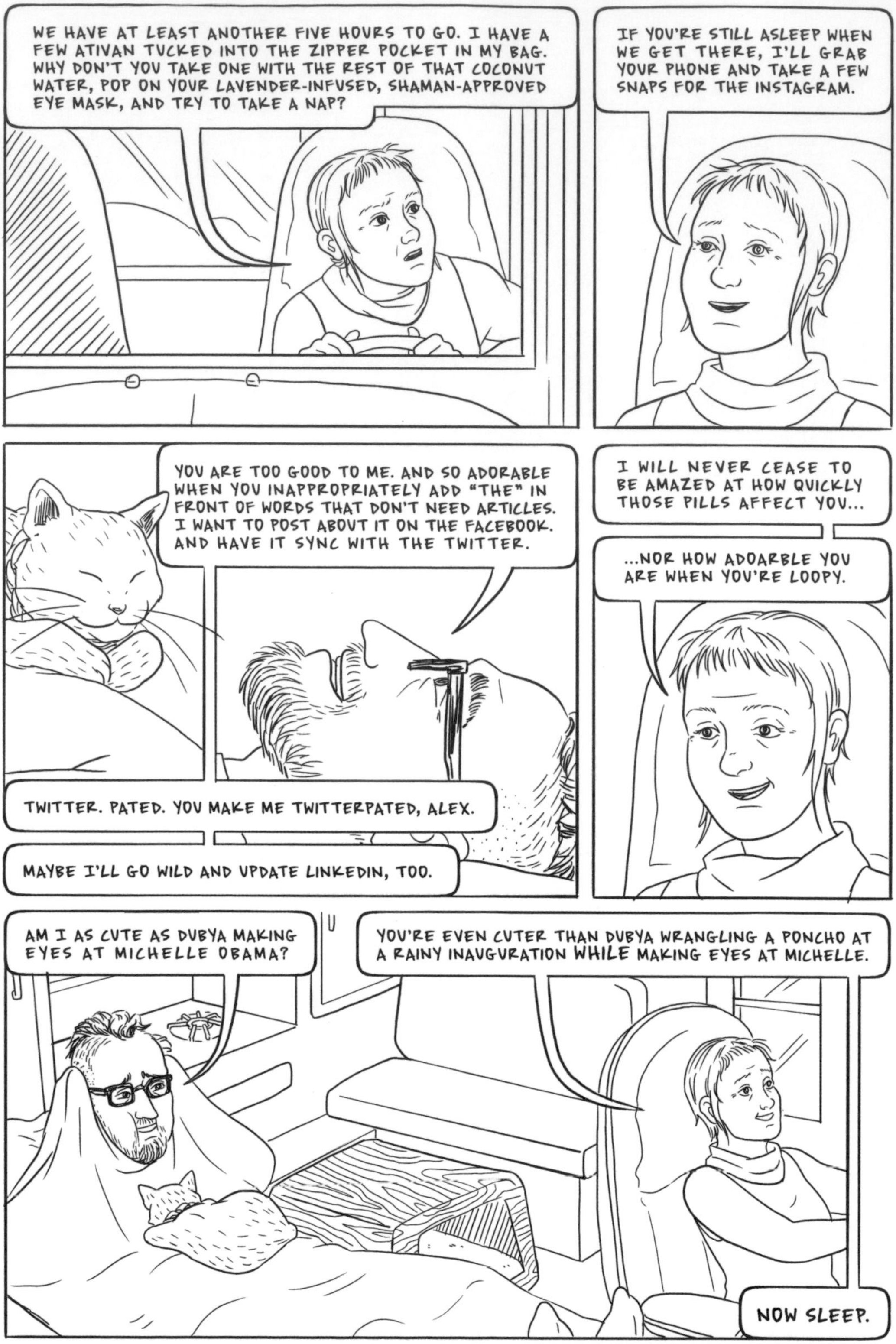
WE HAVE AT LEAST ANOTHER FIVE HOURS TO GO. I HAVE A FEW ATIVAN TUCKED INTO THE ZIPPER POCKET IN MY BAG. WHY DON'T YOU TAKE ONE WITH THE REST OF THAT COCONUT WATER, POP ON YOUR LAVENDER-INFUSED, SHAMAN-APPROVED EYE MASK, AND TRY TO TAKE A NAP?
IF YOU'RE STILL ASLEEP WHEN WE GET THERE, I'LL GRAB YOUR PHONE AND TAKE A FEW SNAPS FOR THE INSTAGRAM.
YOU ARE TOO GOOD TO ME. AND SO ADORABLE WHEN YOU INAPPROPRIATELY ADD "THE" IN FRONT OF WORDS THAT DON'T NEED ARTICLES. I WANT TO POST ABOUT IT ON THE FACEBOOK. AND HAVE IT SYNC WITH THE TWITTER.
TWITTER. PATED. YOU MAKE ME TWITTERPATED, ALEX.
MAYBE I'LL GO WILD AND UPDATE LINKEDIN, TOO.
I WILL NEVER CEASE TO BE AMAZED AT HOW QUICKLY THOSE PILLS AFFECT YOU...
...NOR HOW ADOARBLE YOU ARE WHEN YOU'RE LOOPY.
AM I AS CUTE AS DUBYA MAKING EYES AT MICHELLE OBAMA?
YOU'RE EVEN CUTER THAN DUBYA WRANGLING A PONCHO AT A RAINY INAUGURATION WHILE MAKING EYES AT MICHELLE.
NOW SLEEP.

Chapter 8

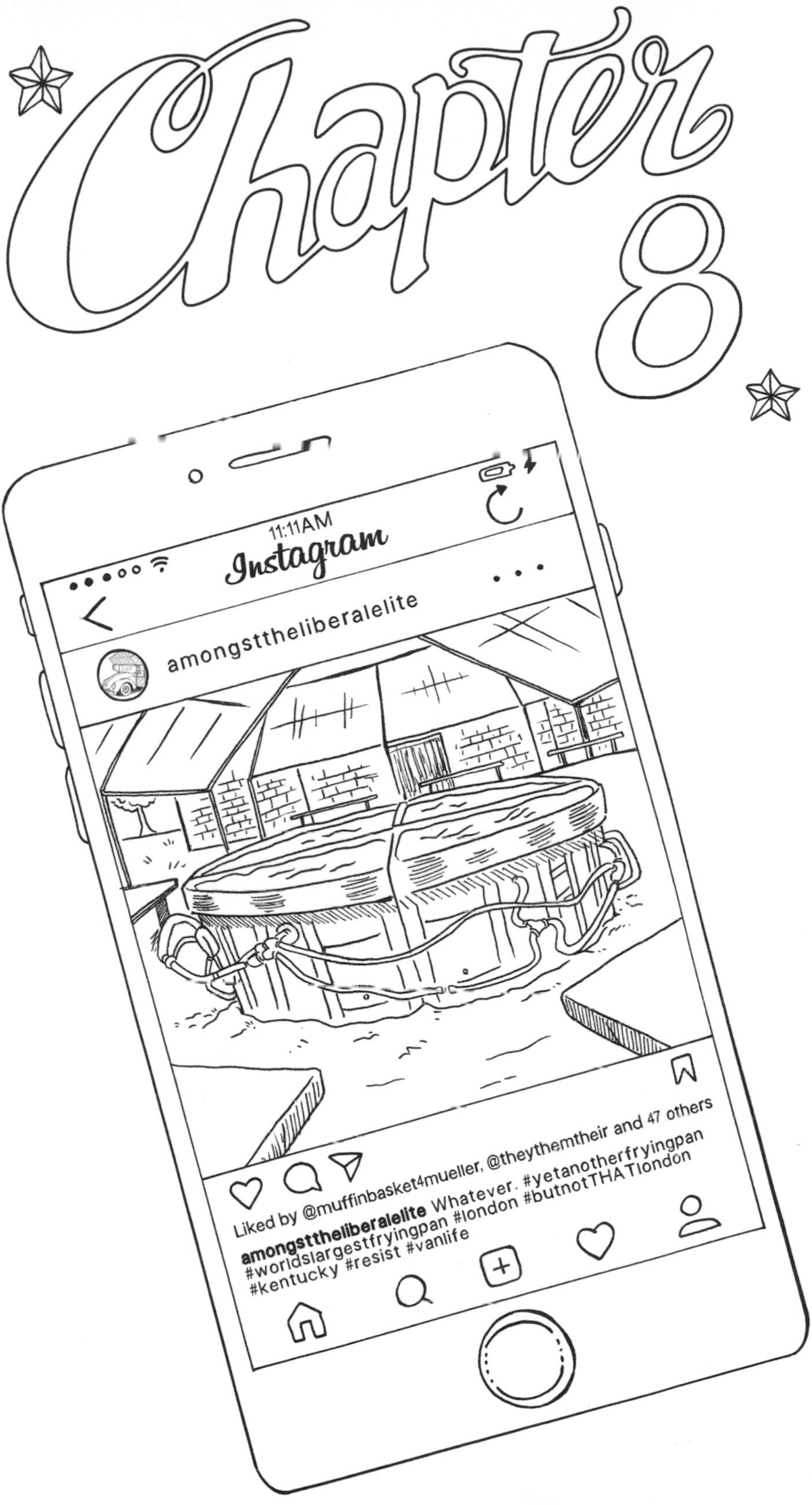
11:11AM
Instagram
amongsttheliberalelite
Liked by @muffinbasket4mueller, @theythemtheir and 47 others
amongsttheliberalelite Whatever. #yetanotherfryingpan #worldslargestfryingpan #london #butnotTHATlondon #kentucky #resist #vanlife

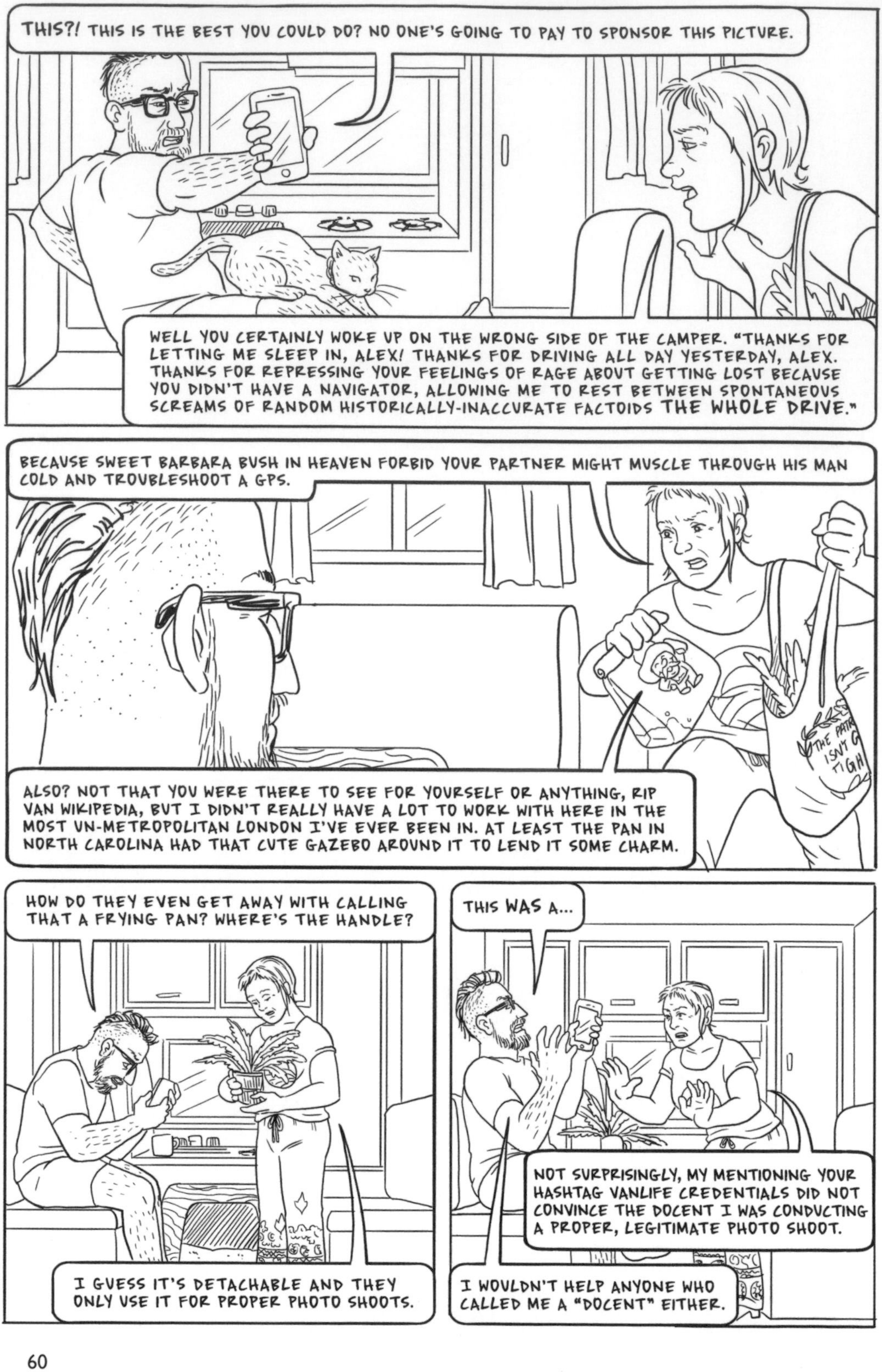
THIS?! THIS IS THE BEST YOU COULD DO? NO ONE'S GOING TO PAY TO SPONSOR THIS PICTURE.
WELL YOU CERTAINLY WOKE UP ON THE WRONG SIDE OF THE CAMPER. "THANKS FOR LETTING ME SLEEP IN, ALEX! THANKS FOR DRIVING ALL DAY YESTERDAY, ALEX. THANKS FOR REPRESSING YOUR FEELINGS OF RAGE ABOUT GETTING LOST BECAUSE YOU DIDN'T HAVE A NAVIGATOR, ALLOWING ME TO REST BETWEEN SPONTANEOUS SCREAMS OF RANDOM HISTORICALLY-INACCURATE FACTOIDS THE WHOLE DRIVE."
BECAUSE SWEET BARBARA BUSH IN HEAVEN FORBID YOUR PARTNER MIGHT MUSCLE THROUGH HIS MAN COLD AND TROUBLESHOOT A GPS.
ALSO? NOT THAT YOU WERE THERE TO SEE FOR YOURSELF OR ANYTHING, RIP VAN WIKIPEDIA, BUT I DIDN'T REALLY HAVE A LOT TO WORK WITH HERE IN THE MOST UN-METROPOLITAN LONDON I'VE EVER BEEN IN. AT LEAST THE PAN IN NORTH CAROLINA HAD THAT CUTE GAZEBO AROUND IT TO LEND IT SOME CHARM.
HOW DO THEY EVEN GET AWAY WITH CALLING THAT A FRYING PAN? WHERE'S THE HANDLE?
I GUESS IT'S DETACHABLE AND THEY ONLY USE IT FOR PROPER PHOTO SHOOTS.
THIS WAS A...
NOT SURPRISINGLY, MY MENTIONING YOUR HASHTAG VANLIFE CREDENTIALS DID NOT CONVINCE THE DOCENT I WAS CONDUCTING A PROPER, LEGITIMATE PHOTO SHOOT.
I WOULDN'T HELP ANYONE WHO CALLED ME A "DOCENT" EITHER.

INSTAGRAM SNAPS ARE **NOT** THE POINT OF THIS EXERCISE, MICHAEL. WE ARE NOT GOING TO BESTOW THE CROWN OF "WORLD'S LARGEST FRYING PAN" BASED ON AESTHETIC AND PHOTOGENIC QUALITIES.

SINCE YOU FORGOT TO ASK, I'LL VOLUNTEER ITS SPECIFICS: TEN FEET SIX INCHES IN DIAMETER, WEIGHS SEVEN HUNDRED POUNDS, CAN COOK 885 QUARTERS OF CHICKEN AT ONE TIME, AND REQUIRES THREE HUNDRED GALLONS OF PEANUT OIL TO DO SO.

SEVEN HUNDRED POUNDS OF UNIDENTIFIABLE HIDEOUSNESS. SAFE BET WE WON'T BE USING THE NOFILTER HASHTAG WITH THIS POST.

I BET IF I'D BEEN THERE, THEY WOULD HAVE PUT THE HANDLE ON.

PROBABLY SO, YOU CONDESCENDING FUCK. THE GUY I TALKED TO KEPT CALLING ME "SUGAR TITS" AND ASKING IF I COULD EVER IMAGINE HAVING A FAMILY BIG ENOUGH TO NEED A DEEP FRYER OF THAT SIZE.

THEN HE ASSURED ME THAT HE POSSESSED THE VIRILITY TO PROVIDE ME WITH SUCH A FAMILY AND EVEN OFFERED TO GIVE ME A "TEST DRIVE."

OF COURSE, ALL THAT WAS AFTER HE ASSUMED I COULDN'T POSSIBLY KNOW HOW TO WORK THE CAMERA ON YOUR PHONE...

...AND INSISTED ON DOING IT **FOR** ME. SO BE SURE TO TAG WHATEVER PHOTO YOU POST WITH THE HASHTAGS METOO AND MANSPLAINED.

OH! SO THESE FIRST PHOTOS ARE **HIS**, THEN?

HA! THAT EXPLAINS THE CLEAVAGE SHOT. THESE LATER ONES ARE MUCH BETTER AND I CAN TOTALLY SEE EVIDENCE OF YOUR EYE FOR COMPOSITION. I CAN MAKE YOURS WORK. THE SITUATION IS NOT AS DIRE AS I THOUGHT.

THAT'S YOUR TAKEAWAY FROM WHAT I JUST SHARED WITH YOU?

NOT TO BE CALLOUSED, BABE, BUT WERE YOU HOPING FOR SHOCK OR SURPRISE? JEALOUSY? I'M NOT WALKING INTO A FIGHT ABOUT MY AUDACITY TO CLAIM YOU AS MY OWN AND TERRITORIAL PISSING AND ALL THOSE OTHER TOPICS YOU ARE CLEARLY WAITING TO WHIP OUT THIS MORNING. BESIDES...

OH, IT'S JUST THIS NEW BRA I...

...YOUR TITS WERE PRETTY MAGNIFICENT YESTERDAY.

NO. I AM **MORE** THAN MY TITS, MICHAEL.

I MEAN BREASTS.

...BUT ALSO REMIND ME TO ORDER MORE OF THOSE BRAS.

SHIT. WE CAN'T AMAZON PRIME ON THE ROAD, CAN WE?

LET'S JUST GO HOME.

WHAT?

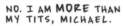

I'M TIRED OF FRYING PANS. OF BEING SO FAR AWAY FROM THE COMFORTS OF HOME. AND MY PRIMARY CARE PHYSICIAN.

BUT I THOUGHT YOU WERE FEELING BETTER.

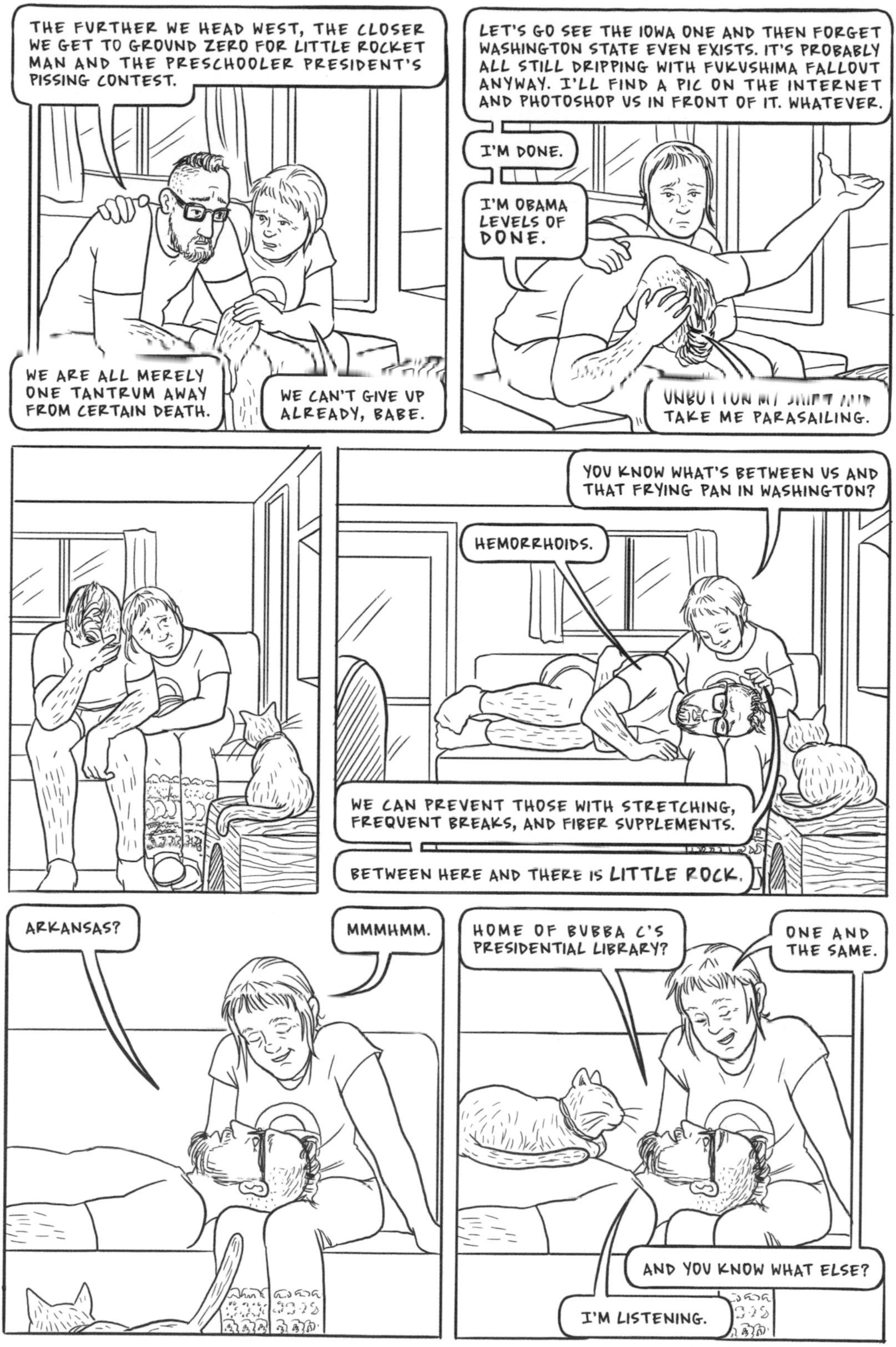

THE FURTHER WE HEAD WEST, THE CLOSER WE GET TO GROUND ZERO FOR LITTLE ROCKET MAN AND THE PRESCHOOLER PRESIDENT'S PISSING CONTEST.
WE ARE ALL MERELY ONE TANTRUM AWAY FROM CERTAIN DEATH.
WE CAN'T GIVE UP ALREADY, BABE.
LET'S GO SEE THE IOWA ONE AND THEN FORGET WASHINGTON STATE EVEN EXISTS. IT'S PROBABLY ALL STILL DRIPPING WITH FUKUSHIMA FALLOUT ANYWAY. I'LL FIND A PIC ON THE INTERNET AND PHOTOSHOP US IN FRONT OF IT. WHATEVER.
I'M DONE.
I'M OBAMA LEVELS OF DONE.
TAKE ME PARASAILING.
YOU KNOW WHAT'S BETWEEN US AND THAT FRYING PAN IN WASHINGTON?
HEMORRHOIDS.
WE CAN PREVENT THOSE WITH STRETCHING, FREQUENT BREAKS, AND FIBER SUPPLEMENTS.
BETWEEN HERE AND THERE IS LITTLE ROCK.
ARKANSAS?
MMMHMM.
HOME OF BUBBA C'S PRESIDENTIAL LIBRARY?
ONE AND THE SAME.
AND YOU KNOW WHAT ELSE?
I'M LISTENING.

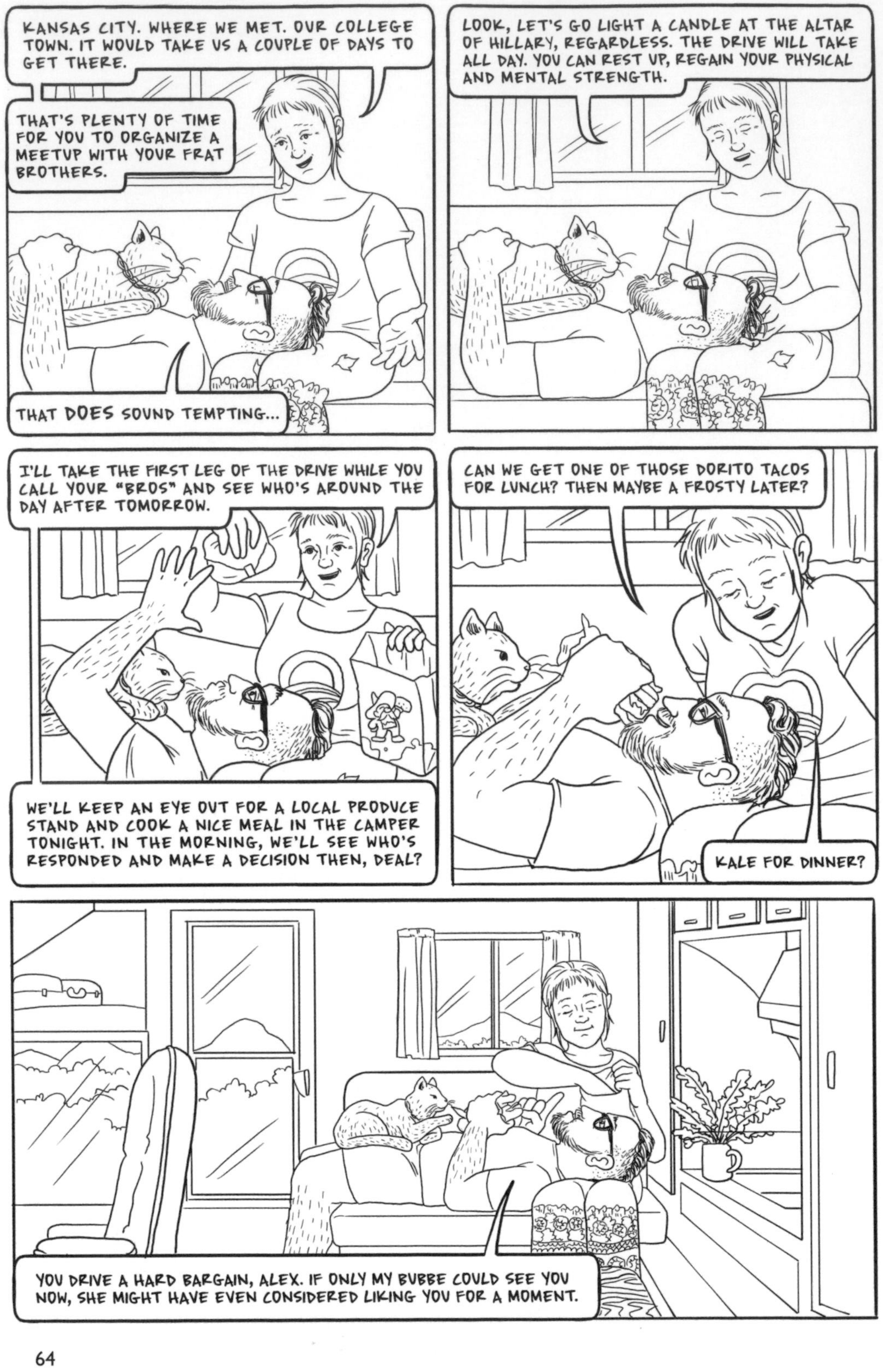

KANSAS CITY. WHERE WE MET. OUR COLLEGE TOWN. IT WOULD TAKE US A COUPLE OF DAYS TO GET THERE.
THAT'S PLENTY OF TIME FOR YOU TO ORGANIZE A MEETUP WITH YOUR FRAT BROTHERS.
THAT DOES SOUND TEMPTING...
LOOK, LET'S GO LIGHT A CANDLE AT THE ALTAR OF HILLARY, REGARDLESS. THE DRIVE WILL TAKE ALL DAY. YOU CAN REST UP, REGAIN YOUR PHYSICAL AND MENTAL STRENGTH.
I'LL TAKE THE FIRST LEG OF THE DRIVE WHILE YOU CALL YOUR "BROS" AND SEE WHO'S AROUND THE DAY AFTER TOMORROW.
WE'LL KEEP AN EYE OUT FOR A LOCAL PRODUCE STAND AND COOK A NICE MEAL IN THE CAMPER TONIGHT. IN THE MORNING, WE'LL SEE WHO'S RESPONDED AND MAKE A DECISION THEN, DEAL?
CAN WE GET ONE OF THOSE DORITO TACOS FOR LUNCH? THEN MAYBE A FROSTY LATER?
KALE FOR DINNER?
YOU DRIVE A HARD BARGAIN, ALEX. IF ONLY MY BUBBE COULD SEE YOU NOW, SHE MIGHT HAVE EVEN CONSIDERED LIKING YOU FOR A MOMENT.

Chapter 9

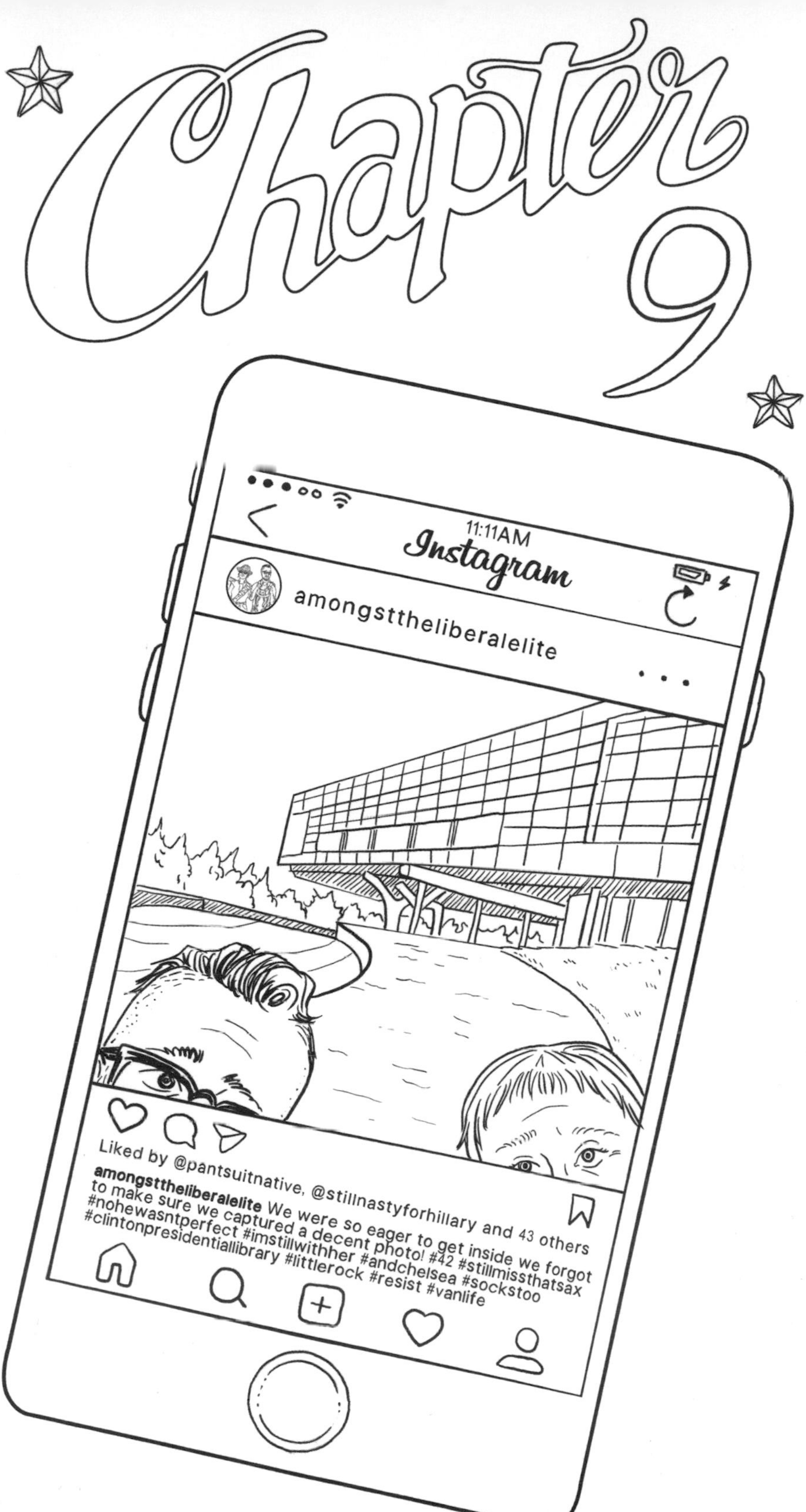
11:11AM
Instagram
amongsttheliberalelite
Liked by @pantsuitnative, @stillnastyforhillary and 43 others
amongsttheliberalelite We were so eager to get inside we forgot to make sure we captured a decent photo! #42 #stillmissthatsax #nohewasntperfect #imstillwithher #andchelsea #sockstoo #clintonpresidentiallibrary #littlerock #resist #vanlife

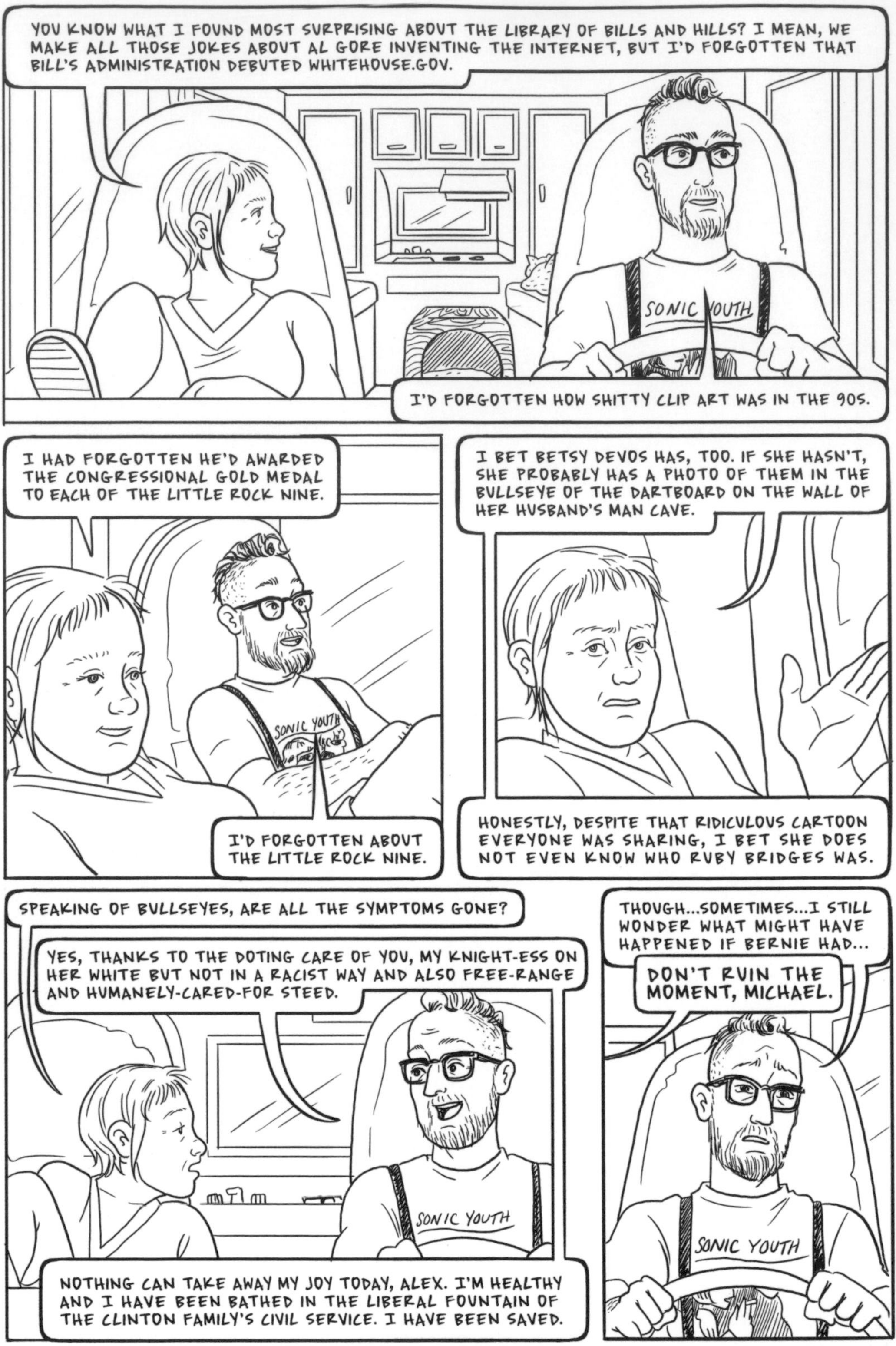

YOU KNOW WHAT I FOUND MOST SURPRISING ABOUT THE LIBRARY OF BILLS AND HILLS? I MEAN, WE MAKE ALL THOSE JOKES ABOUT AL GORE INVENTING THE INTERNET, BUT I'D FORGOTTEN THAT BILL'S ADMINISTRATION DEBUTED WHITEHOUSE.GOV.
SONIC YOUTH
I'D FORGOTTEN HOW SHITTY CLIP ART WAS IN THE 90S.
I HAD FORGOTTEN HE'D AWARDED THE CONGRESSIONAL GOLD MEDAL TO EACH OF THE LITTLE ROCK NINE.
SONIC YOUTH
I'D FORGOTTEN ABOUT THE LITTLE ROCK NINE.
I BET BETSY DEVOS HAS, TOO. IF SHE HASN'T, SHE PROBABLY HAS A PHOTO OF THEM IN THE BULLSEYE OF THE DARTBOARD ON THE WALL OF HER HUSBAND'S MAN CAVE.
HONESTLY, DESPITE THAT RIDICULOUS CARTOON EVERYONE WAS SHARING, I BET SHE DOES NOT EVEN KNOW WHO RUBY BRIDGES WAS.
SPEAKING OF BULLSEYES, ARE ALL THE SYMPTOMS GONE?
YES, THANKS TO THE DOTING CARE OF YOU, MY KNIGHT-ESS ON HER WHITE BUT NOT IN A RACIST WAY AND ALSO FREE-RANGE AND HUMANELY-CARED-FOR STEED.
SONIC YOUTH
NOTHING CAN TAKE AWAY MY JOY TODAY, ALEX. I'M HEALTHY AND I HAVE BEEN BATHED IN THE LIBERAL FOUNTAIN OF THE CLINTON FAMILY'S CIVIL SERVICE. I HAVE BEEN SAVED.
THOUGH...SOMETIMES...I STILL WONDER WHAT MIGHT HAVE HAPPENED IF BERNIE HAD...
DON'T RUIN THE MOMENT, MICHAEL.
SONIC YOUTH

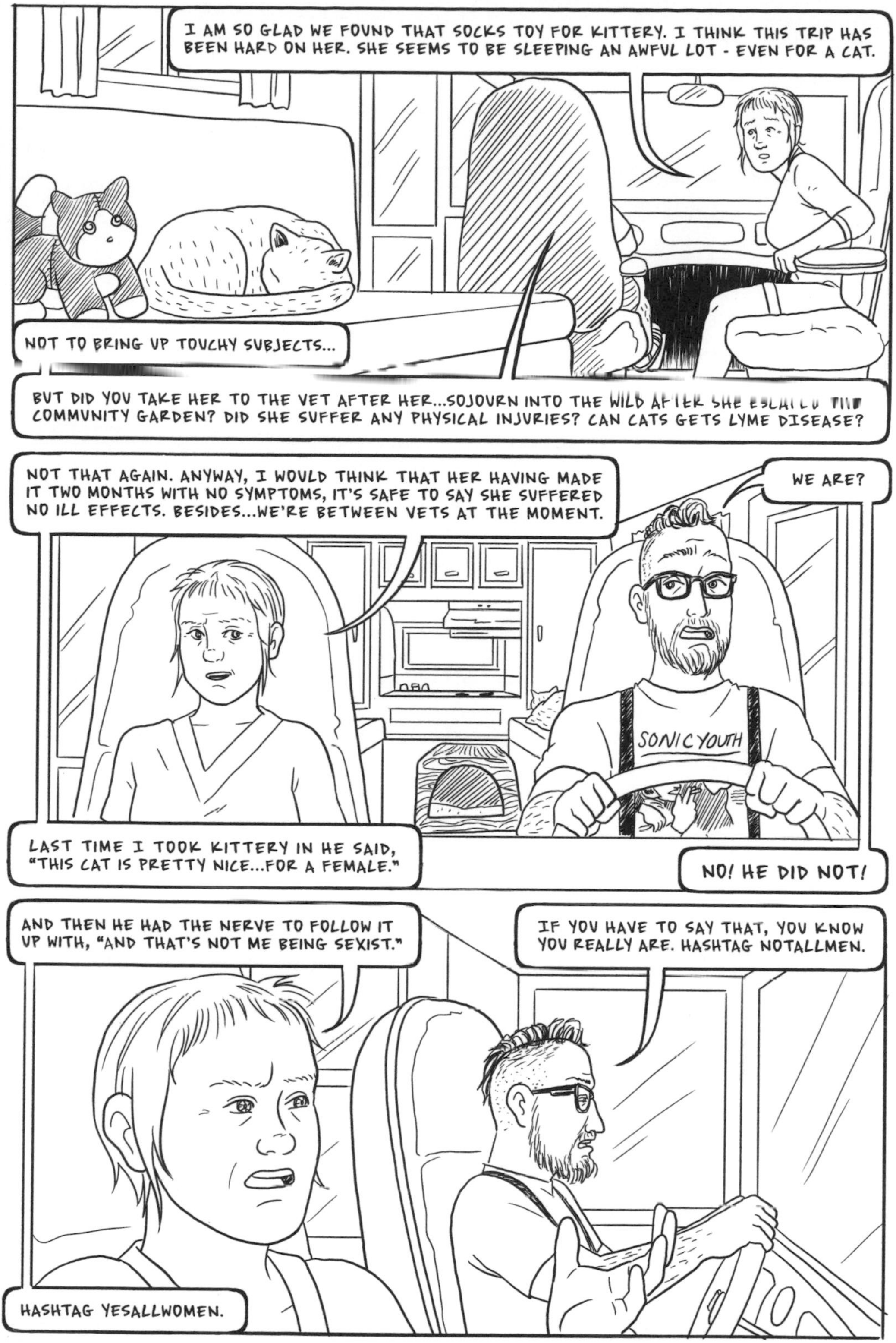
I AM SO GLAD WE FOUND THAT SOCKS TOY FOR KITTERY. I THINK THIS TRIP HAS BEEN HARD ON HER. SHE SEEMS TO BE SLEEPING AN AWFUL LOT - EVEN FOR A CAT.
NOT TO BRING UP TOUCHY SUBJECTS...
BUT DID YOU TAKE HER TO THE VET AFTER HER...SOJOURN INTO THE WILD AFTER SHE ESCAPED THE COMMUNITY GARDEN? DID SHE SUFFER ANY PHYSICAL INJURIES? CAN CATS GETS LYME DISEASE?
NOT THAT AGAIN. ANYWAY, I WOULD THINK THAT HER HAVING MADE IT TWO MONTHS WITH NO SYMPTOMS, IT'S SAFE TO SAY SHE SUFFERED NO ILL EFFECTS. BESIDES...WE'RE BETWEEN VETS AT THE MOMENT.
WE ARE?
SONIC YOUTH
LAST TIME I TOOK KITTERY IN HE SAID, "THIS CAT IS PRETTY NICE...FOR A FEMALE."
NO! HE DID NOT!
AND THEN HE HAD THE NERVE TO FOLLOW IT UP WITH, "AND THAT'S NOT ME BEING SEXIST."
IF YOU HAVE TO SAY THAT, YOU KNOW YOU REALLY ARE. HASHTAG NOTALLMEN.
HASHTAG YESALLWOMEN.

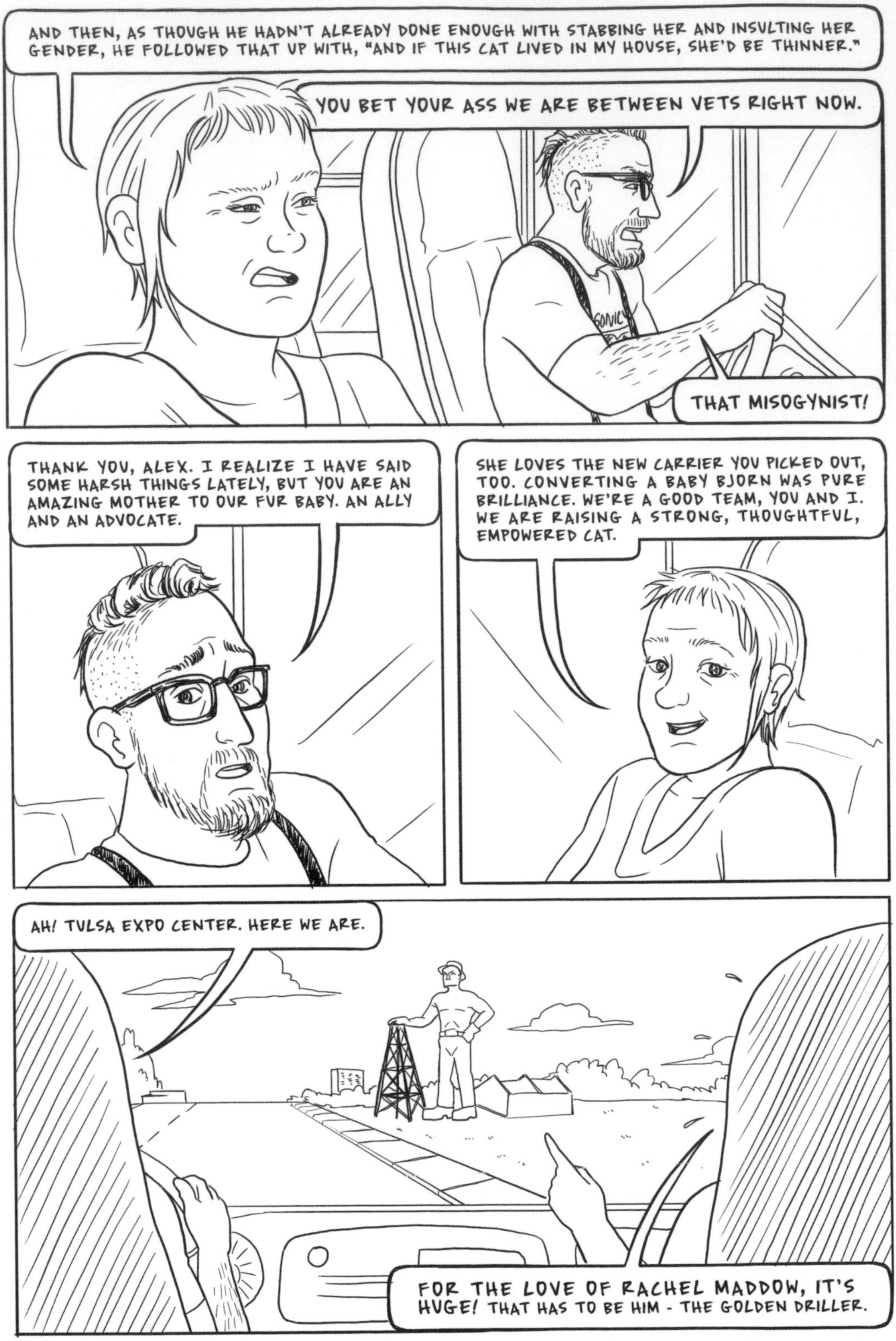
AND THEN, AS THOUGH HE HADN'T ALREADY DONE ENOUGH WITH STABBING HER AND INSULTING HER GENDER, HE FOLLOWED THAT UP WITH, "AND IF THIS CAT LIVED IN MY HOUSE, SHE'D BE THINNER."
YOU BET YOUR ASS WE ARE BETWEEN VETS RIGHT NOW.
THAT MISOGYNIST!
THANK YOU, ALEX. I REALIZE I HAVE SAID SOME HARSH THINGS LATELY, BUT YOU ARE AN AMAZING MOTHER TO OUR FUR BABY. AN ALLY AND AN ADVOCATE.
SHE LOVES THE NEW CARRIER YOU PICKED OUT, TOO. CONVERTING A BABY BJORN WAS PURE BRILLIANCE. WE'RE A GOOD TEAM, YOU AND I. WE ARE RAISING A STRONG, THOUGHTFUL, EMPOWERED CAT.
AH! TULSA EXPO CENTER. HERE WE ARE.
FOR THE LOVE OF RACHEL MADDOW, IT'S HUGE! THAT HAS TO BE HIM - THE GOLDEN DRILLER.

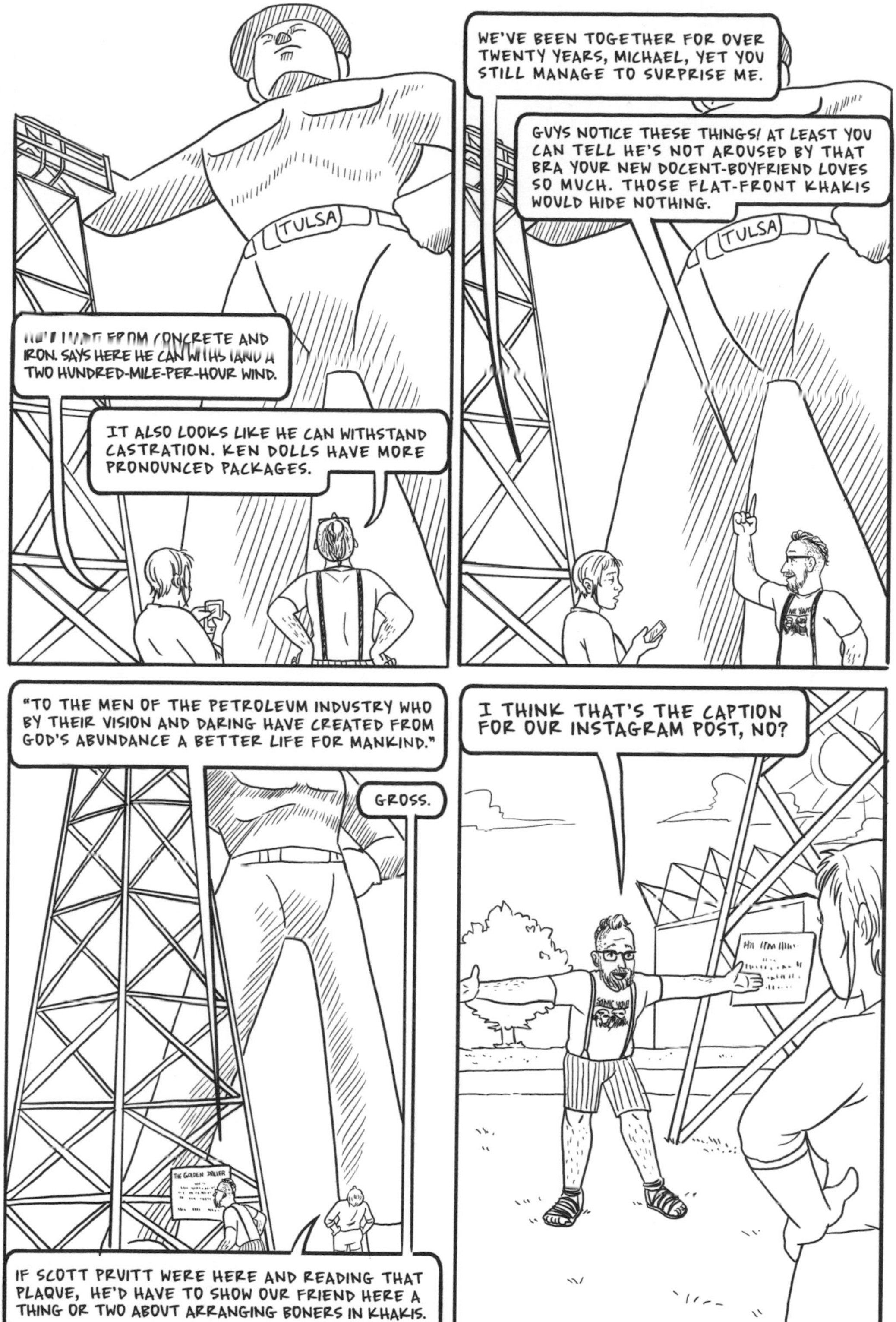
HE'S MADE FROM CONCRETE AND IRON. SAYS HERE HE CAN WITHSTAND A TWO HUNDRED-MILE-PER-HOUR WIND.
IT ALSO LOOKS LIKE HE CAN WITHSTAND CASTRATION. KEN DOLLS HAVE MORE PRONOUNCED PACKAGES.
TULSA
WE'VE BEEN TOGETHER FOR OVER TWENTY YEARS, MICHAEL, YET YOU STILL MANAGE TO SURPRISE ME.
GUYS NOTICE THESE THINGS! AT LEAST YOU CAN TELL HE'S NOT AROUSED BY THAT BRA YOUR NEW DOCENT-BOYFRIEND LOVES SO MUCH. THOSE FLAT-FRONT KHAKIS WOULD HIDE NOTHING.
"TO THE MEN OF THE PETROLEUM INDUSTRY WHO BY THEIR VISION AND DARING HAVE CREATED FROM GOD'S ABUNDANCE A BETTER LIFE FOR MANKIND."
GROSS.
THE GOLDEN DRILLER
IF SCOTT PRUITT WERE HERE AND READING THAT PLAQUE, HE'D HAVE TO SHOW OUR FRIEND HERE A THING OR TWO ABOUT ARRANGING BONERS IN KHAKIS.
I THINK THAT'S THE CAPTION FOR OUR INSTAGRAM POST, NO?

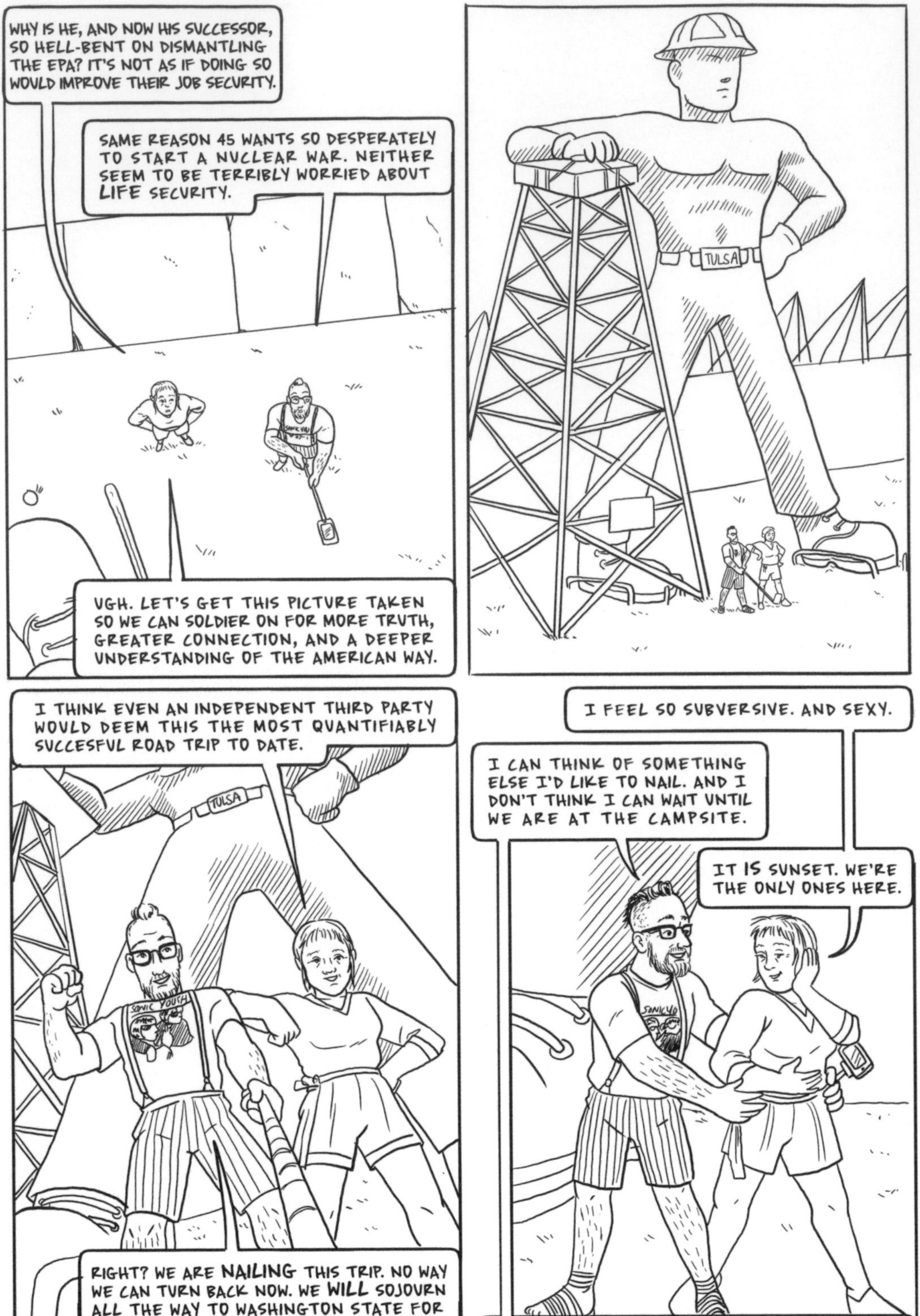
WHY IS HE, AND NOW HIS SUCCESSOR, SO HELL-BENT ON DISMANTLING THE EPA? IT'S NOT AS IF DOING SO WOULD IMPROVE THEIR JOB SECURITY.
SAME REASON 45 WANTS SO DESPERATELY TO START A NUCLEAR WAR. NEITHER SEEM TO BE TERRIBLY WORRIED ABOUT LIFE SECURITY.
SONIC YOUTH
UGH. LET'S GET THIS PICTURE TAKEN SO WE CAN SOLDIER ON FOR MORE TRUTH, GREATER CONNECTION, AND A DEEPER UNDERSTANDING OF THE AMERICAN WAY.
TULSA
I THINK EVEN AN INDEPENDENT THIRD PARTY WOULD DEEM THIS THE MOST QUANTIFIABLY SUCCESFUL ROAD TRIP TO DATE.
TULSA
SONIC YOUTH
RIGHT? WE ARE NAILING THIS TRIP. NO WAY WE CAN TURN BACK NOW. WE WILL SOJOURN ALL THE WAY TO WASHINGTON STATE FOR THE SAKE OF THE AMERICAN PEOPLE. NEVERTHELESS, WE PERSISTED!
I FEEL SO SUBVERSIVE. AND SEXY.
I CAN THINK OF SOMETHING ELSE I'D LIKE TO NAIL. AND I DON'T THINK I CAN WAIT UNTIL WE ARE AT THE CAMPSITE.
IT IS SUNSET. WE'RE THE ONLY ONES HERE.
LET'S DO SOME GOLDEN DRILLING OF OUR OWN.

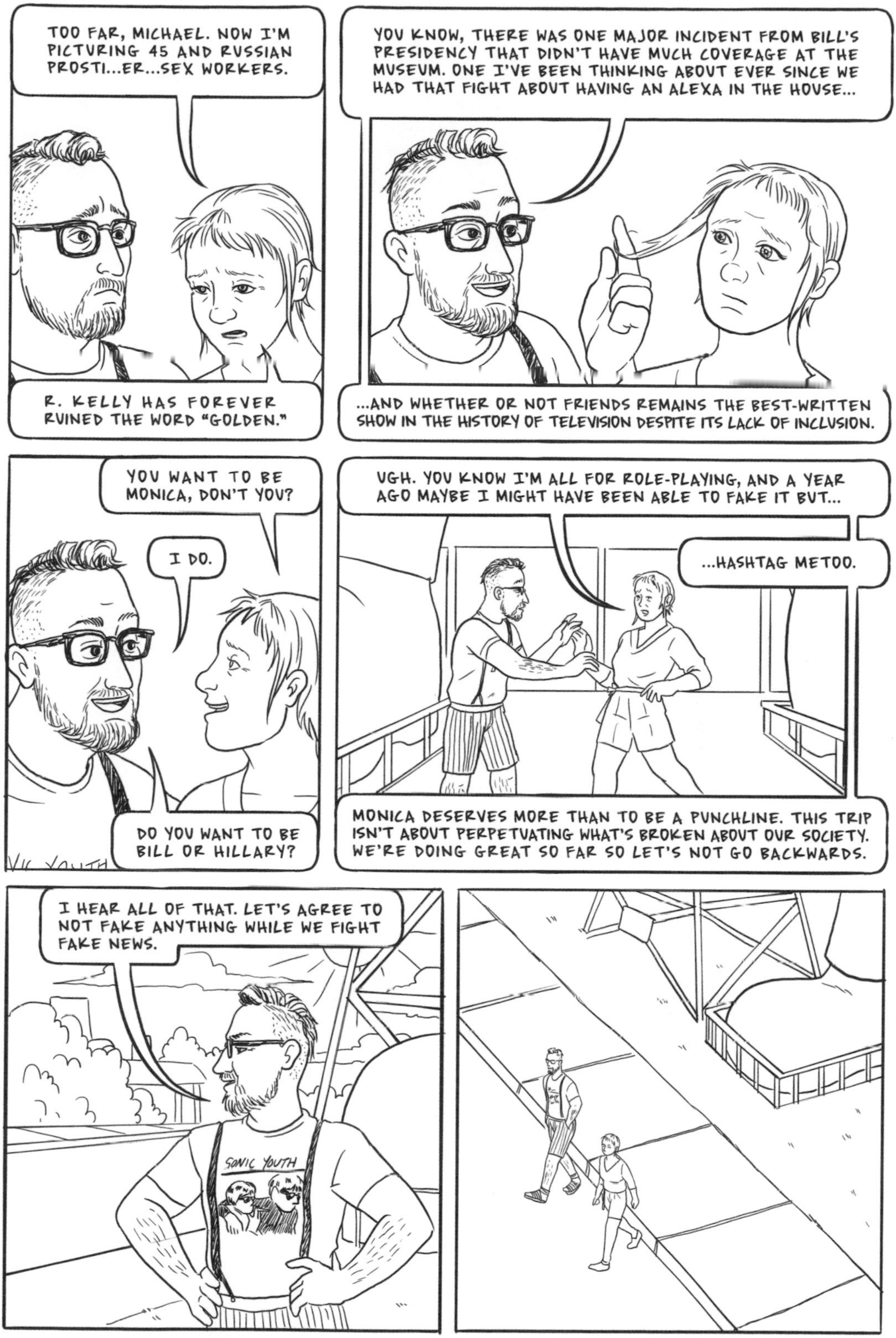
TOO FAR, MICHAEL. NOW I'M PICTURING 45 AND RUSSIAN PROSTI...ER...SEX WORKERS.
R. KELLY HAS FOREVER RUINED THE WORD "GOLDEN."
YOU KNOW, THERE WAS ONE MAJOR INCIDENT FROM BILL'S PRESIDENCY THAT DIDN'T HAVE MUCH COVERAGE AT THE MUSEUM. ONE I'VE BEEN THINKING ABOUT EVER SINCE WE HAD THAT FIGHT ABOUT HAVING AN ALEXA IN THE HOUSE...
...AND WHETHER OR NOT FRIENDS REMAINS THE BEST-WRITTEN SHOW IN THE HISTORY OF TELEVISION DESPITE ITS LACK OF INCLUSION.
YOU WANT TO BE MONICA, DON'T YOU?
I DO.
DO YOU WANT TO BE BILL OR HILLARY?
UGH. YOU KNOW I'M ALL FOR ROLE-PLAYING, AND A YEAR AGO MAYBE I MIGHT HAVE BEEN ABLE TO FAKE IT BUT...
...HASHTAG METOO.
MONICA DESERVES MORE THAN TO BE A PUNCHLINE. THIS TRIP ISN'T ABOUT PERPETUATING WHAT'S BROKEN ABOUT OUR SOCIETY. WE'RE DOING GREAT SO FAR SO LET'S NOT GO BACKWARDS.
I HEAR ALL OF THAT. LET'S AGREE TO NOT FAKE ANYTHING WHILE WE FIGHT FAKE NEWS.
SONIC YOUTH

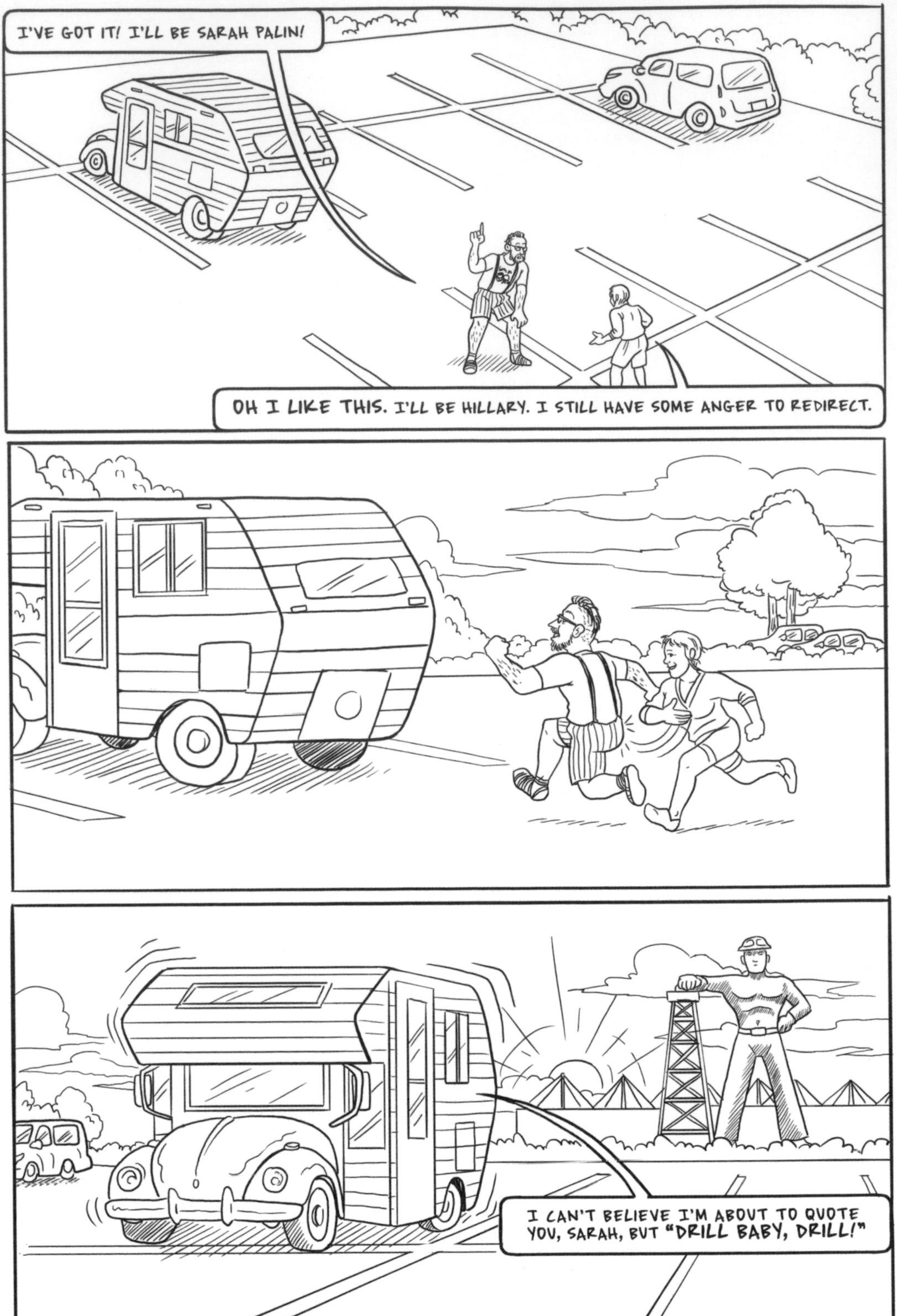
I'VE GOT IT! I'LL BE SARAH PALIN!
OH I LIKE THIS. I'LL BE HILLARY. I STILL HAVE SOME ANGER TO REDIRECT.
I CAN'T BELIEVE I'M ABOUT TO QUOTE YOU, SARAH, BUT "DRILL BABY, DRILL!"

Chapter 10

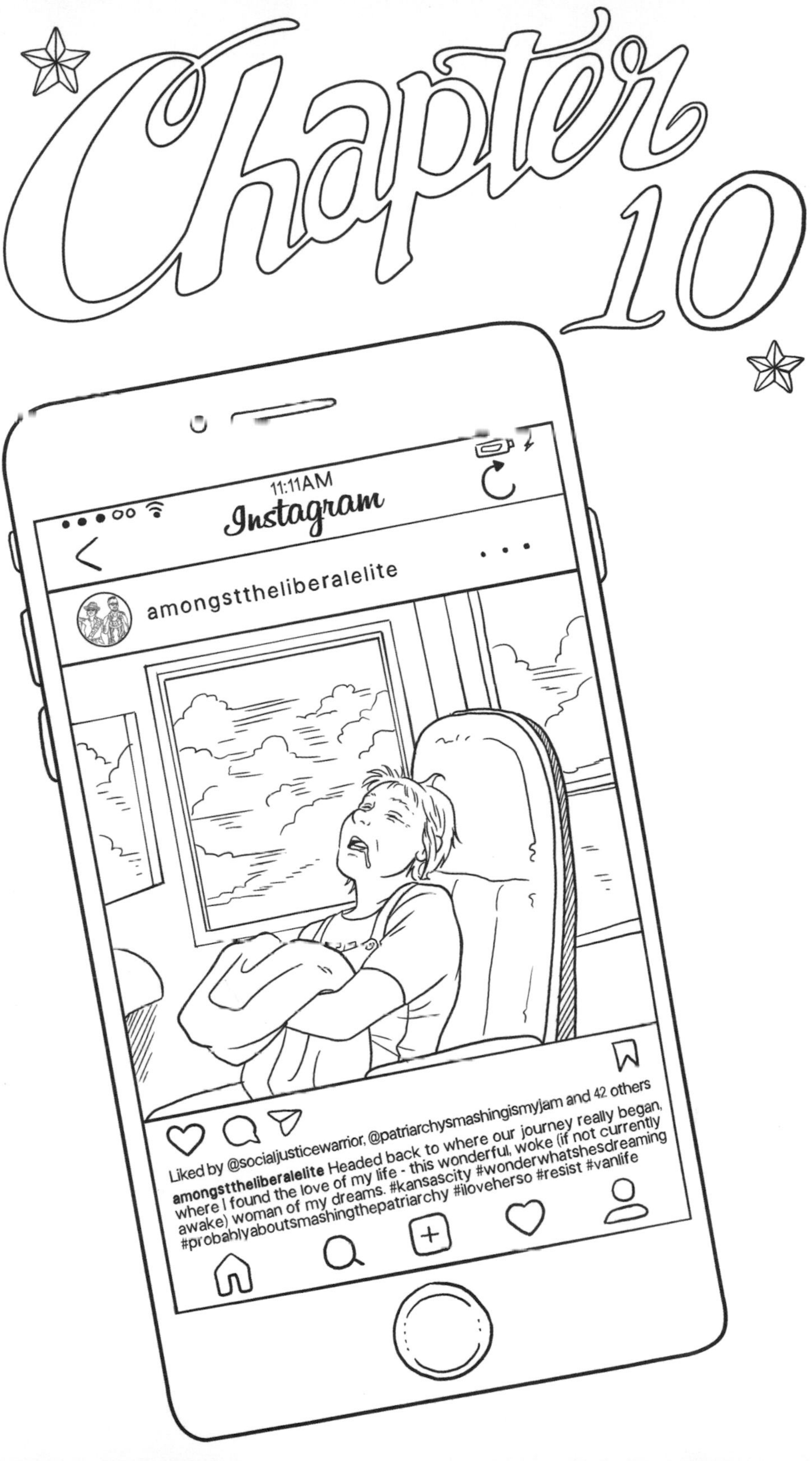
11:11AM
Instagram
amongsttheliberalelite
Liked by @socialjusticewarrior, @patriarchysmashingismyjam and 42 others
amongsttheliberalelite Headed back to where our journey really began, where I found the love of my life - this wonderful, woke (if not currently awake) woman of my dreams. #kansascity #wonderwhatshesdreaming #probablyaboutsmashingthepatriarchy #iloveherso #resist #vanlife

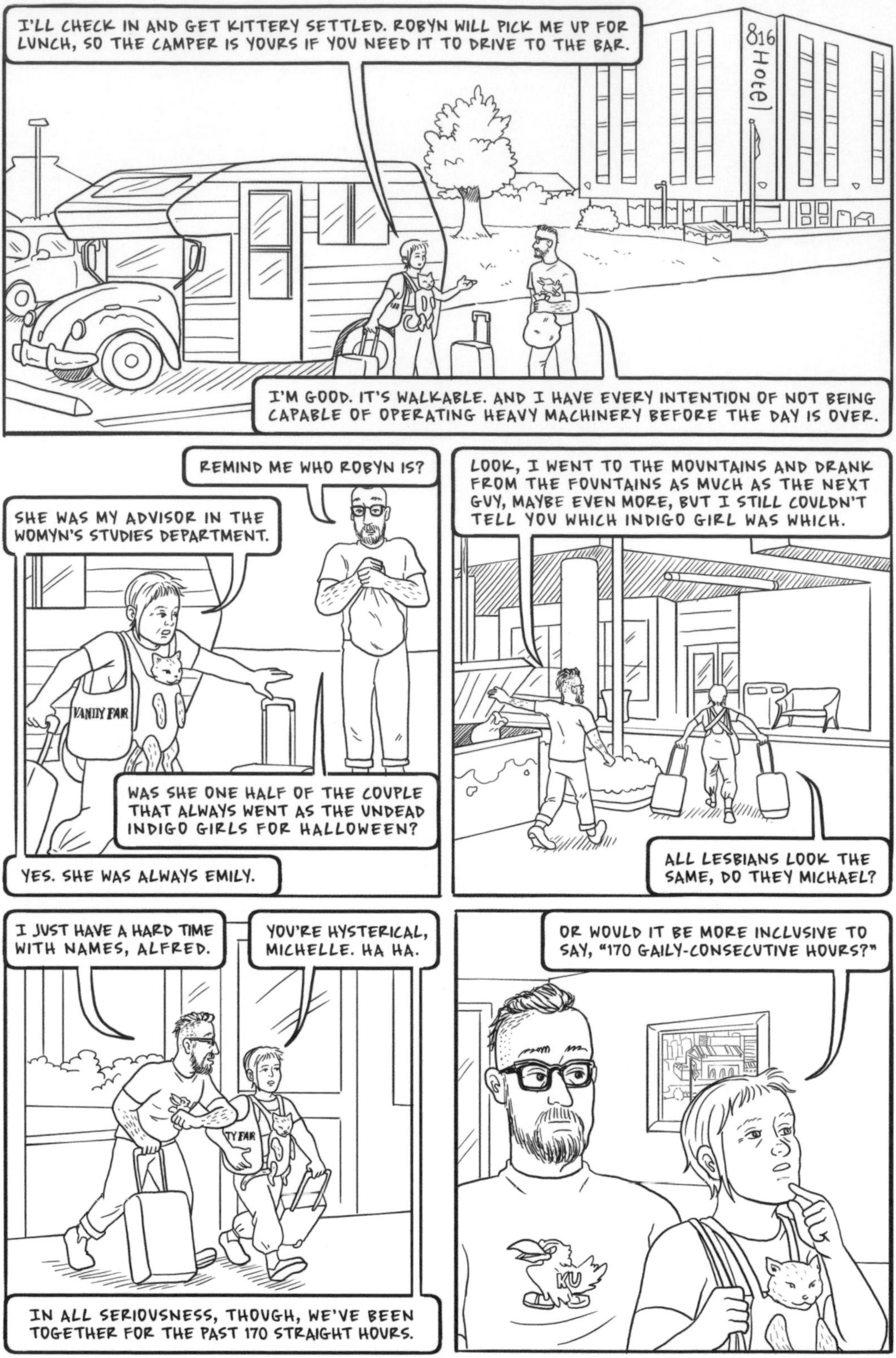
I'LL CHECK IN AND GET KITTERY SETTLED. ROBYN WILL PICK ME UP FOR LUNCH, SO THE CAMPER IS YOURS IF YOU NEED IT TO DRIVE TO THE BAR.
816 Hotel
I'M GOOD. IT'S WALKABLE. AND I HAVE EVERY INTENTION OF NOT BEING CAPABLE OF OPERATING HEAVY MACHINERY BEFORE THE DAY IS OVER.
REMIND ME WHO ROBYN IS?
SHE WAS MY ADVISOR IN THE WOMYN'S STUDIES DEPARTMENT.
VANITY FAIR
WAS SHE ONE HALF OF THE COUPLE THAT ALWAYS WENT AS THE UNDEAD INDIGO GIRLS FOR HALLOWEEN?
YES. SHE WAS ALWAYS EMILY.
LOOK, I WENT TO THE MOUNTAINS AND DRANK FROM THE FOUNTAINS AS MUCH AS THE NEXT GUY, MAYBE EVEN MORE, BUT I STILL COULDN'T TELL YOU WHICH INDIGO GIRL WAS WHICH.
ALL LESBIANS LOOK THE SAME, DO THEY MICHAEL?
I JUST HAVE A HARD TIME WITH NAMES, ALFRED.
YOU'RE HYSTERICAL, MICHELLE. HA HA.
TY FAIR
IN ALL SERIOUSNESS, THOUGH, WE'VE BEEN TOGETHER FOR THE PAST 170 STRAIGHT HOURS.
OR WOULD IT BE MORE INCLUSIVE TO SAY, "170 GAILY-CONSECUTIVE HOURS?"
KU

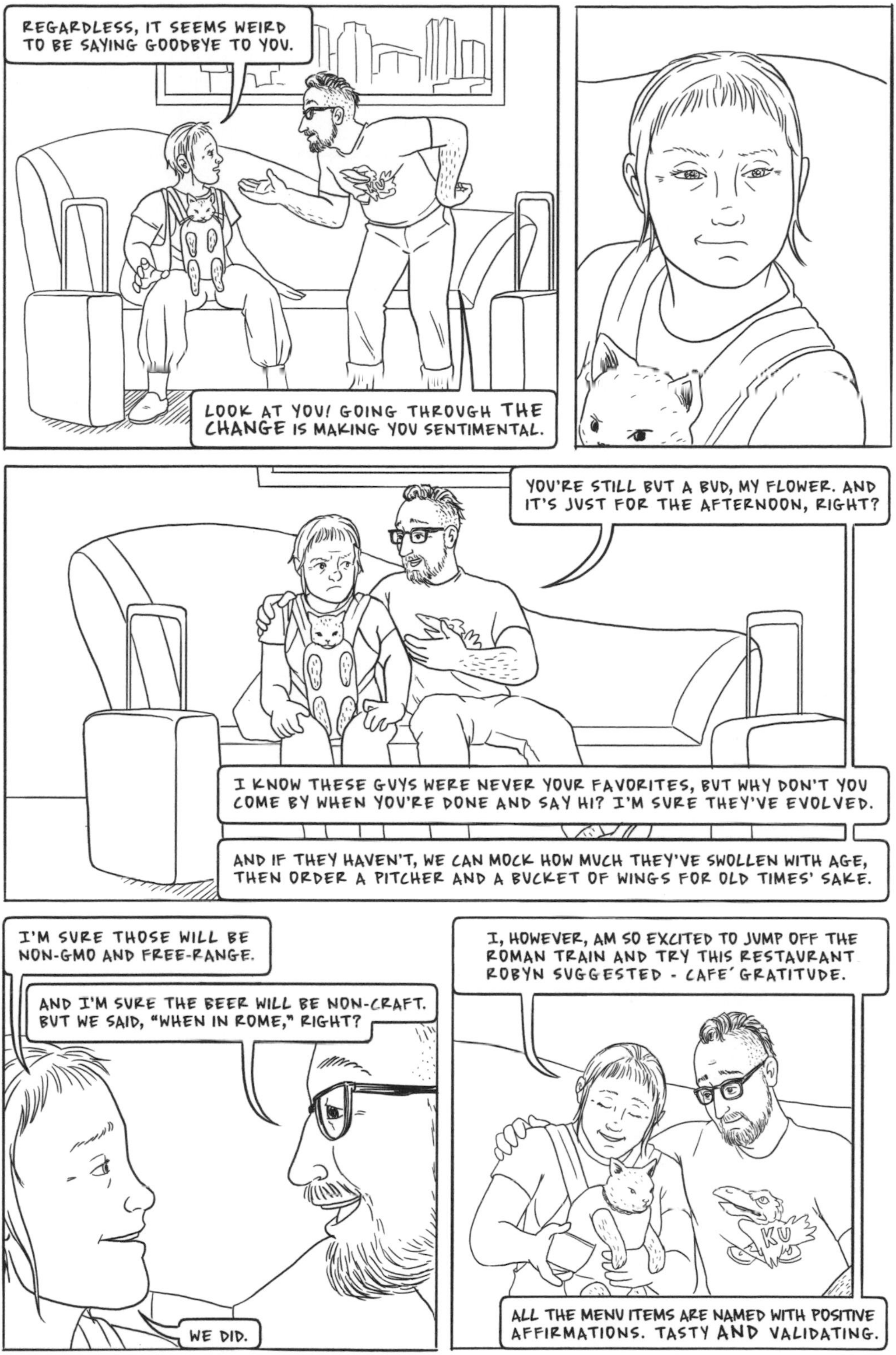
REGARDLESS, IT SEEMS WEIRD TO BE SAYING GOODBYE TO YOU.
LOOK AT YOU! GOING THROUGH THE CHANGE IS MAKING YOU SENTIMENTAL.
YOU'RE STILL BUT A BUD, MY FLOWER. AND IT'S JUST FOR THE AFTERNOON, RIGHT?
I KNOW THESE GUYS WERE NEVER YOUR FAVORITES, BUT WHY DON'T YOU COME BY WHEN YOU'RE DONE AND SAY HI? I'M SURE THEY'VE EVOLVED.
AND IF THEY HAVEN'T, WE CAN MOCK HOW MUCH THEY'VE SWOLLEN WITH AGE, THEN ORDER A PITCHER AND A BUCKET OF WINGS FOR OLD TIMES' SAKE.
I'M SURE THOSE WILL BE NON-GMO AND FREE-RANGE.
AND I'M SURE THE BEER WILL BE NON-CRAFT. BUT WE SAID, "WHEN IN ROME," RIGHT?
WE DID.
I, HOWEVER, AM SO EXCITED TO JUMP OFF THE ROMAN TRAIN AND TRY THIS RESTAURANT ROBYN SUGGESTED - CAFE´ GRATITUDE.
KU
ALL THE MENU ITEMS ARE NAMED WITH POSITIVE AFFIRMATIONS. TASTY AND VALIDATING.

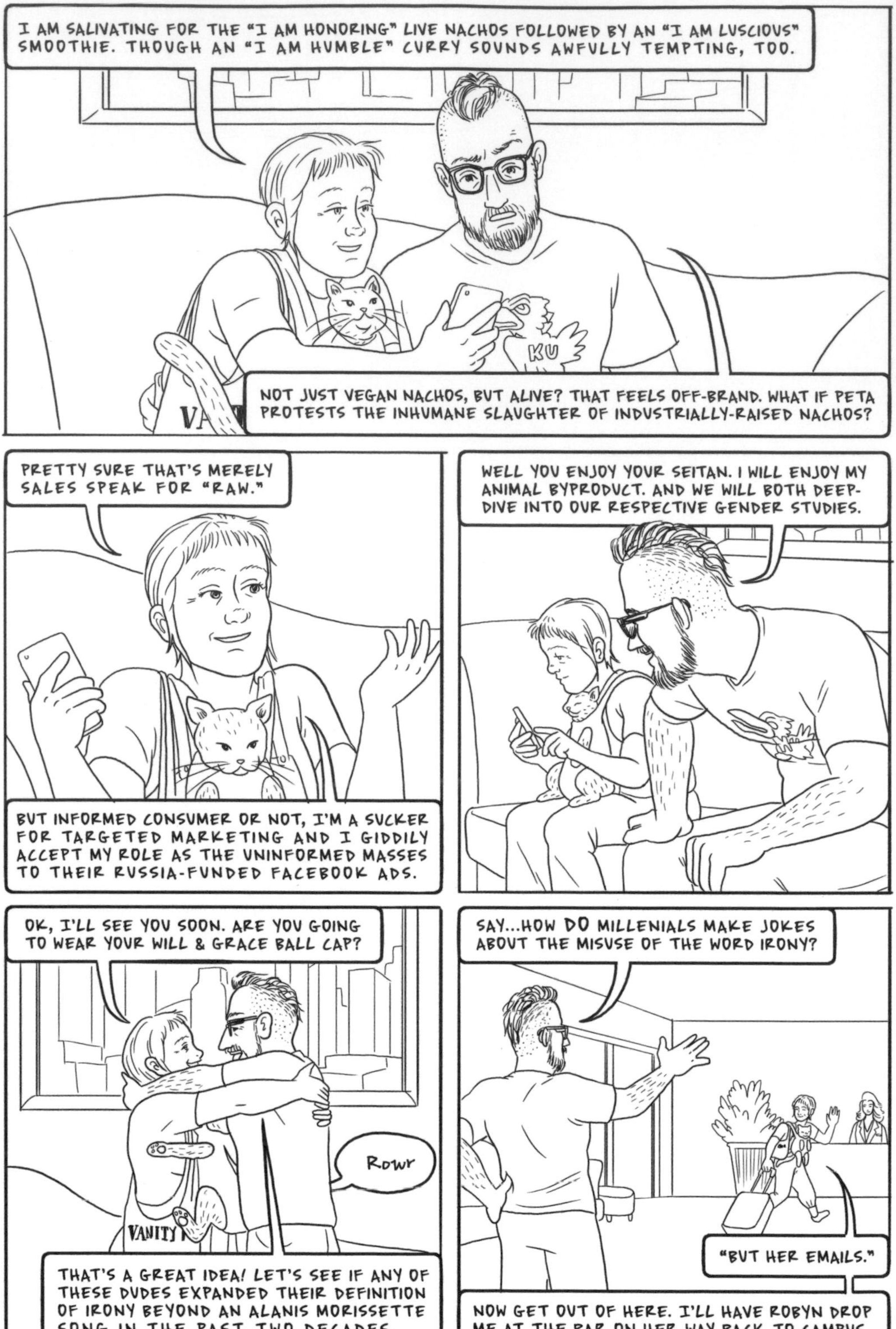
I AM SALIVATING FOR THE "I AM HONORING" LIVE NACHOS FOLLOWED BY AN "I AM LUSCIOUS" SMOOTHIE. THOUGH AN "I AM HUMBLE" CURRY SOUNDS AWFULLY TEMPTING, TOO.
KU
NOT JUST VEGAN NACHOS, BUT ALIVE? THAT FEELS OFF-BRAND. WHAT IF PETA PROTESTS THE INHUMANE SLAUGHTER OF INDUSTRIALLY-RAISED NACHOS?
PRETTY SURE THAT'S MERELY SALES SPEAK FOR "RAW."
BUT INFORMED CONSUMER OR NOT, I'M A SUCKER FOR TARGETED MARKETING AND I GIDDILY ACCEPT MY ROLE AS THE UNINFORMED MASSES TO THEIR RUSSIA-FUNDED FACEBOOK ADS.
WELL YOU ENJOY YOUR SEITAN. I WILL ENJOY MY ANIMAL BYPRODUCT. AND WE WILL BOTH DEEP-DIVE INTO OUR RESPECTIVE GENDER STUDIES.
OK, I'LL SEE YOU SOON. ARE YOU GOING TO WEAR YOUR WILL & GRACE BALL CAP?
Rowr
VANITY
THAT'S A GREAT IDEA! LET'S SEE IF ANY OF THESE DUDES EXPANDED THEIR DEFINITION OF IRONY BEYOND AN ALANIS MORISSETTE SONG IN THE PAST TWO DECADES.
SAY...HOW DO MILLENIALS MAKE JOKES ABOUT THE MISUSE OF THE WORD IRONY?
"BUT HER EMAILS."
NOW GET OUT OF HERE. I'LL HAVE ROBYN DROP ME AT THE BAR ON HER WAY BACK TO CAMPUS.

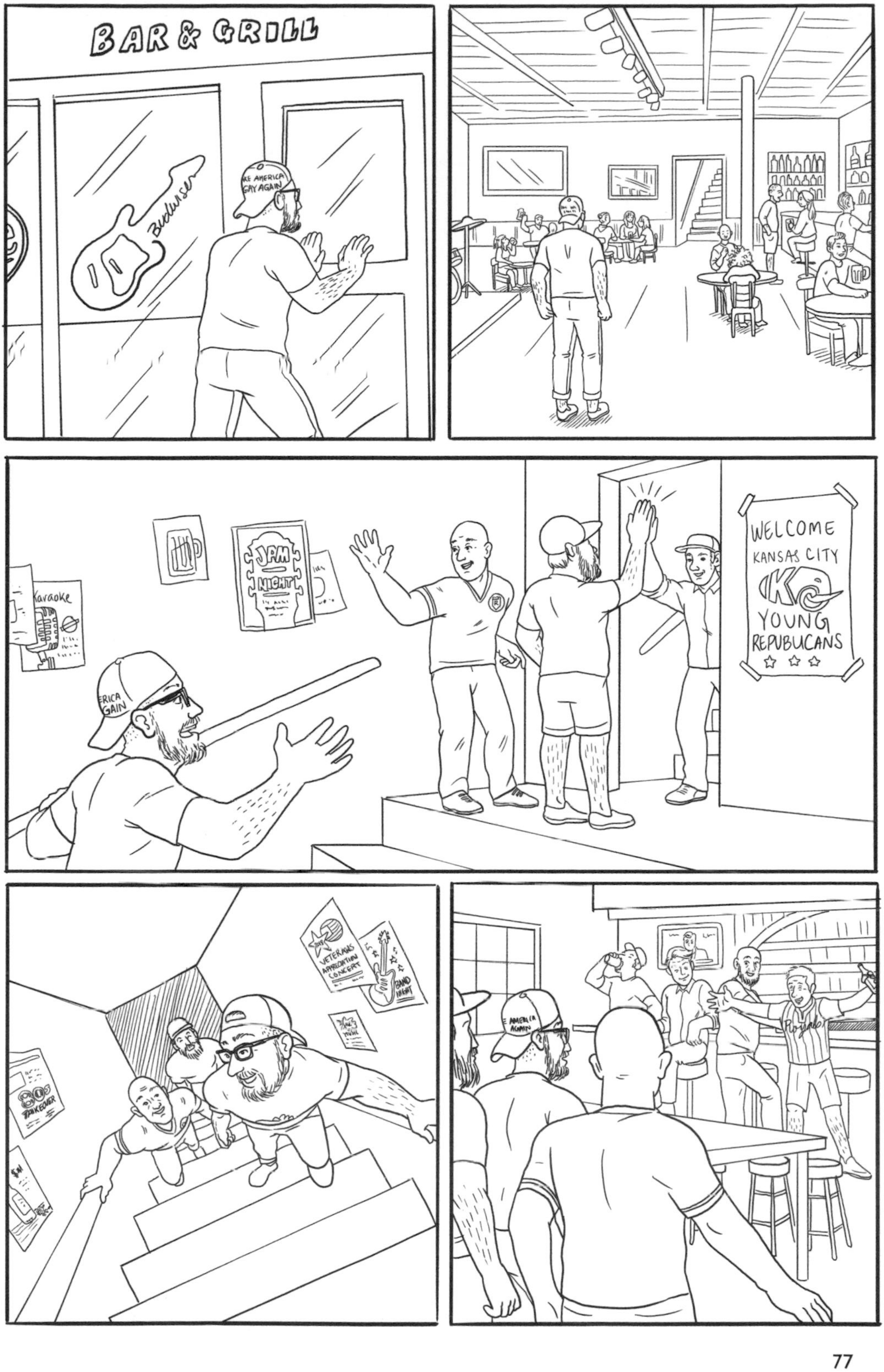
BAR & GRILL
Budweiser
JAM NIGHT
Karaoke
WELCOME
KANSAS CITY
YOUNG
REPUBUCANS
VETERANS APPRECIATION CONCERT
BAND NIGHT
80s TAKEOVER

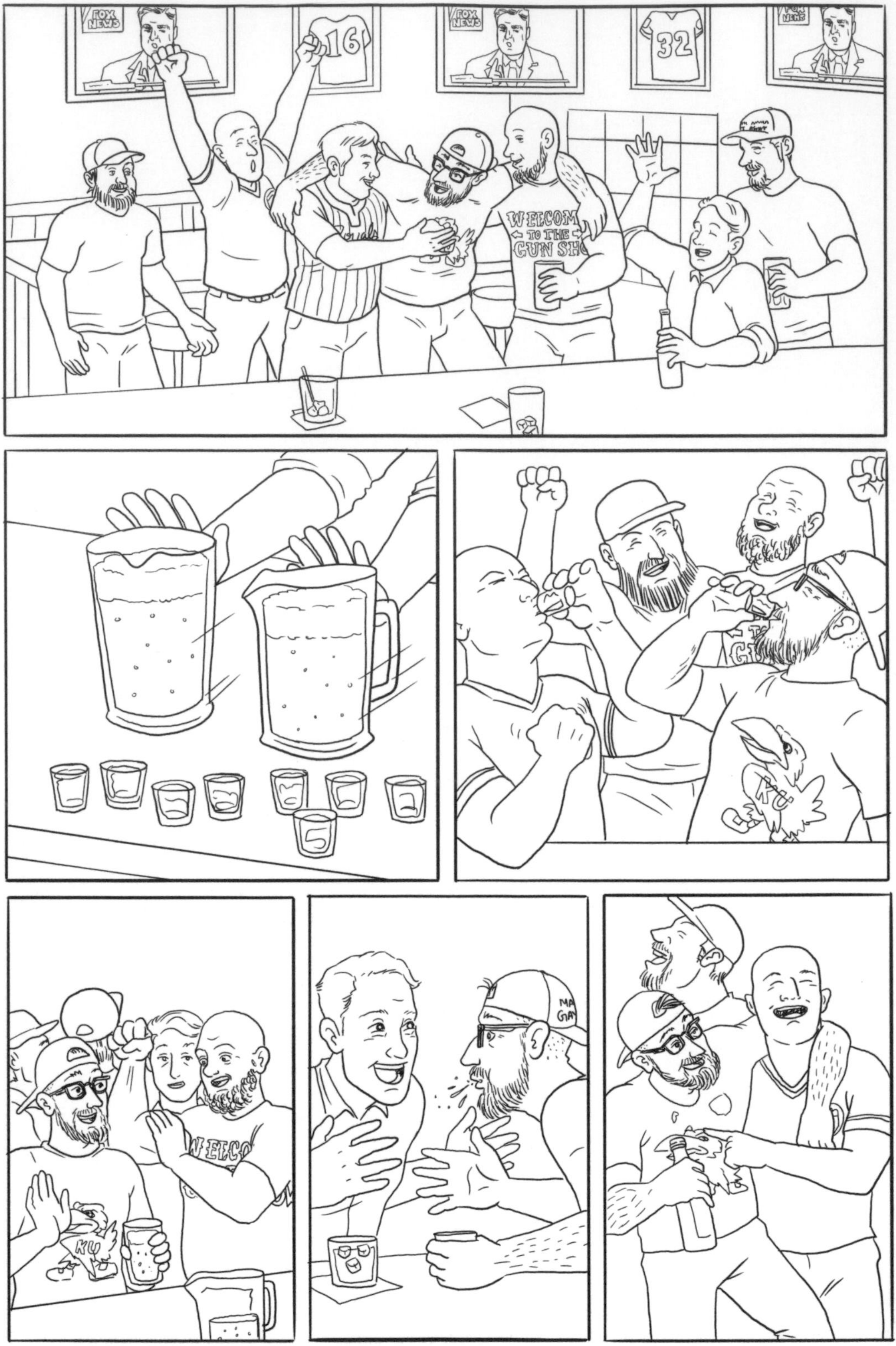
FOX NEWS
16
FOX NEWS
32
FOX NEWS
WELCOM
TO THE
GUN SHO
KU
WELCO
KU
MA
GAY

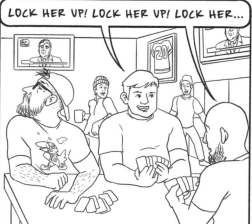

LOCK HER UP! LOCK HER UP! LOCK HER...

AMERICA FIRST! AMERICA FIRST! AMERICA...

LOCK HER UP! LOCK HER UP! LOCK HER UP!

AMER...

BAR & GRILL

Chapter 11

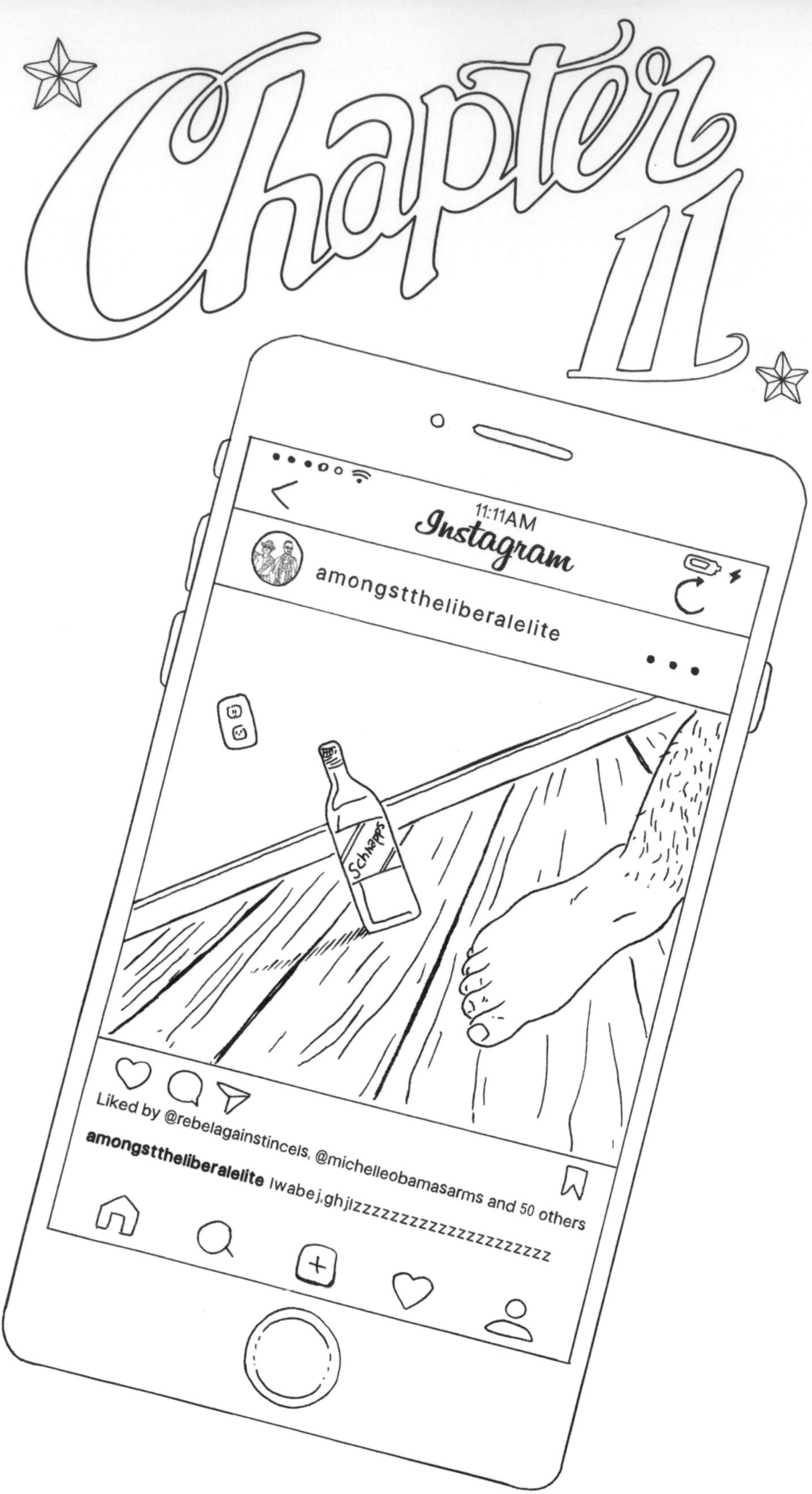
11:11AM
Instagram
amongsttheliberalelite
Schnapps
Liked by @rebelagainstincels, @michelleobamasarms and 50 others
amongsttheliberalelite Iwabej,ghjlzzzzzzzzzzzzzzzzzzzzz

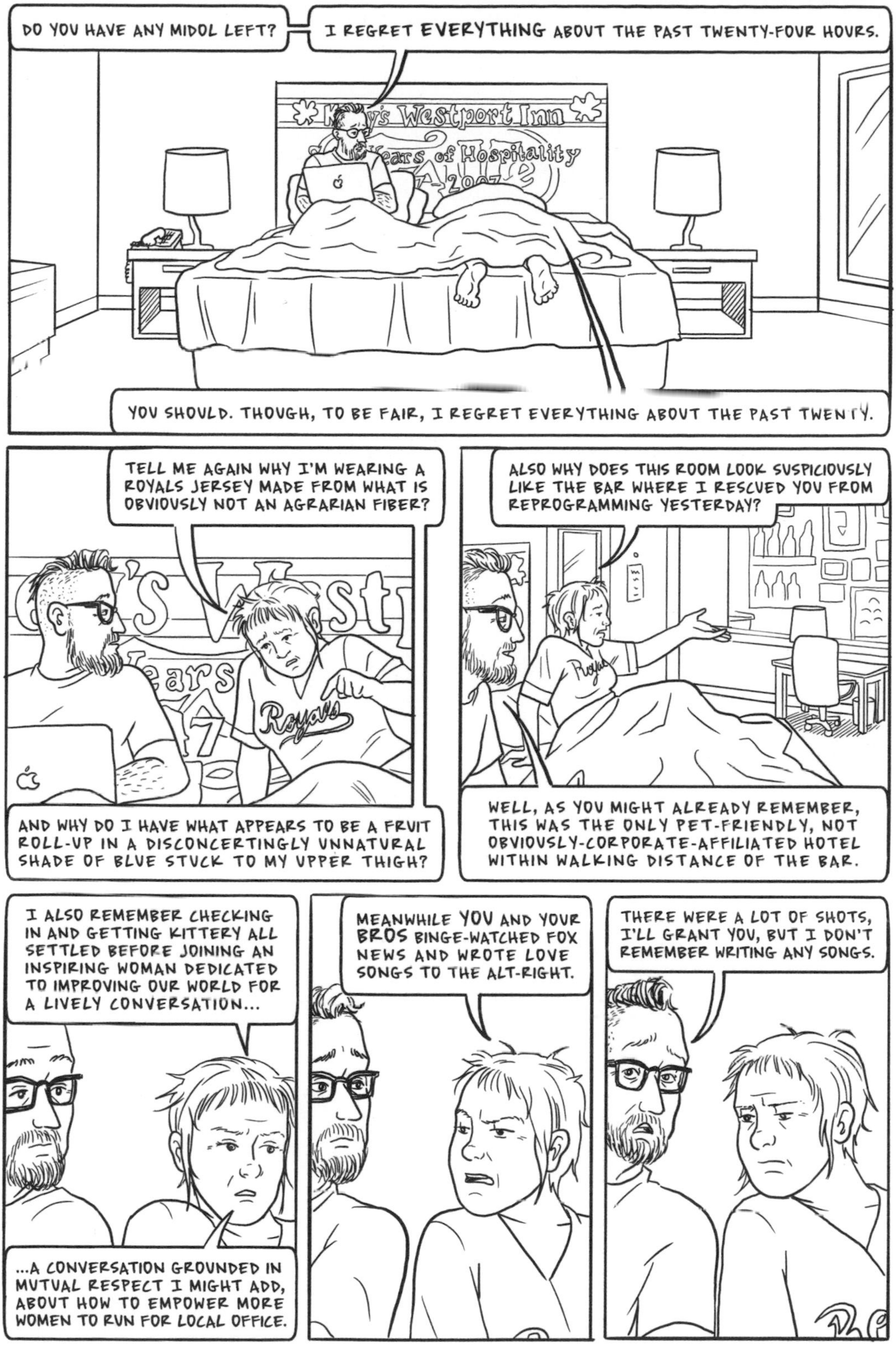
DO YOU HAVE ANY MIDOL LEFT?
I REGRET EVERYTHING ABOUT THE PAST TWENTY-FOUR HOURS.
YOU SHOULD. THOUGH, TO BE FAIR, I REGRET EVERYTHING ABOUT THE PAST TWENTY.
TELL ME AGAIN WHY I'M WEARING A ROYALS JERSEY MADE FROM WHAT IS OBVIOUSLY NOT AN AGRARIAN FIBER?
AND WHY DO I HAVE WHAT APPEARS TO BE A FRUIT ROLL-UP IN A DISCONCERTINGLY UNNATURAL SHADE OF BLUE STUCK TO MY UPPER THIGH?
ALSO WHY DOES THIS ROOM LOOK SUSPICIOUSLY LIKE THE BAR WHERE I RESCUED YOU FROM REPROGRAMMING YESTERDAY?
WELL, AS YOU MIGHT ALREADY REMEMBER, THIS WAS THE ONLY PET-FRIENDLY, NOT OBVIOUSLY-CORPORATE-AFFILIATED HOTEL WITHIN WALKING DISTANCE OF THE BAR.
I ALSO REMEMBER CHECKING IN AND GETTING KITTERY ALL SETTLED BEFORE JOINING AN INSPIRING WOMAN DEDICATED TO IMPROVING OUR WORLD FOR A LIVELY CONVERSATION...
...A CONVERSATION GROUNDED IN MUTUAL RESPECT I MIGHT ADD, ABOUT HOW TO EMPOWER MORE WOMEN TO RUN FOR LOCAL OFFICE.
MEANWHILE YOU AND YOUR BROS BINGE-WATCHED FOX NEWS AND WROTE LOVE SONGS TO THE ALT-RIGHT.
THERE WERE A LOT OF SHOTS, I'LL GRANT YOU, BUT I DON'T REMEMBER WRITING ANY SONGS.

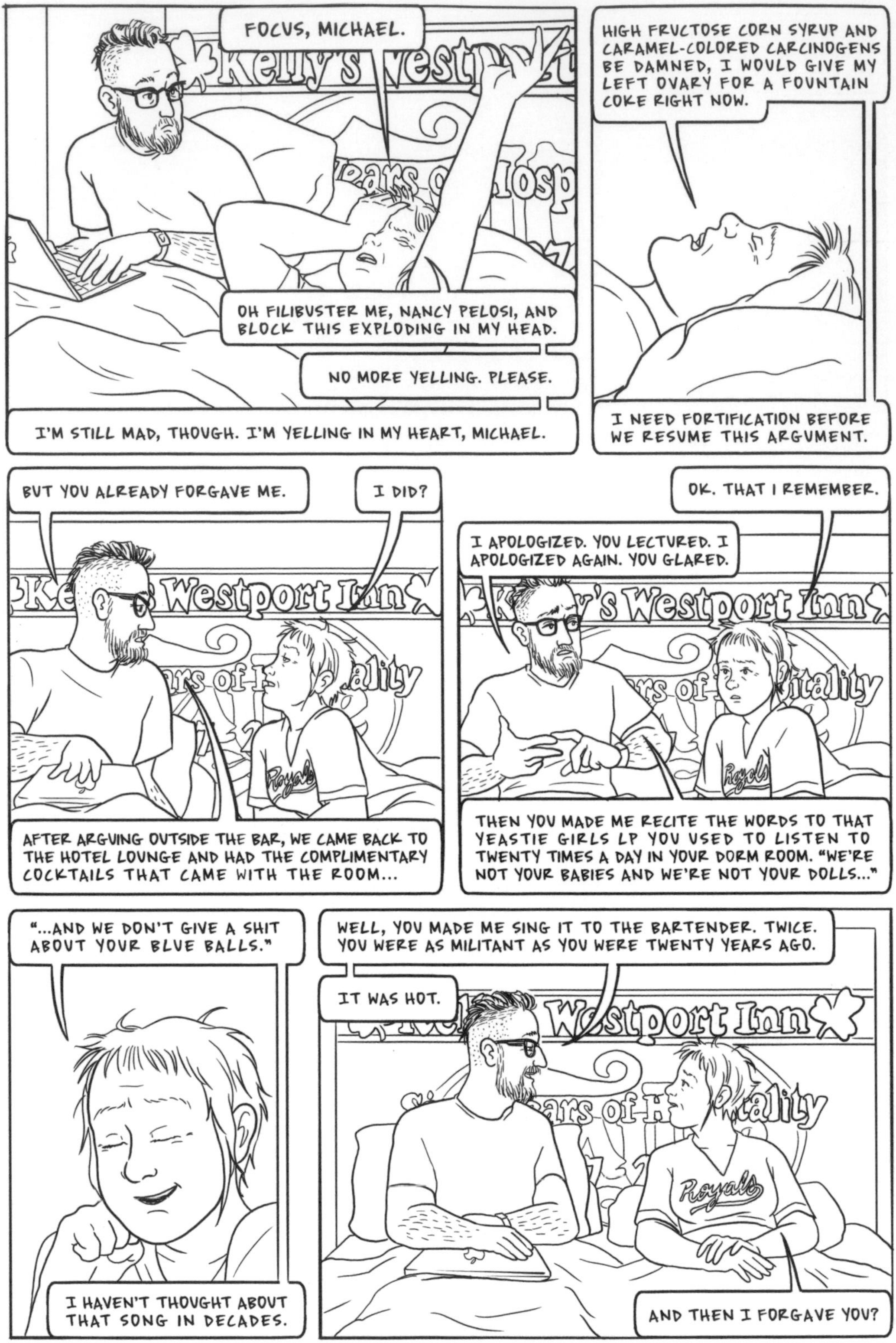
FOCUS, MICHAEL.
OH FILIBUSTER ME, NANCY PELOSI, AND BLOCK THIS EXPLODING IN MY HEAD.
NO MORE YELLING. PLEASE.
I'M STILL MAD, THOUGH. I'M YELLING IN MY HEART, MICHAEL.
HIGH FRUCTOSE CORN SYRUP AND CARAMEL-COLORED CARCINOGENS BE DAMNED, I WOULD GIVE MY LEFT OVARY FOR A FOUNTAIN COKE RIGHT NOW.
I NEED FORTIFICATION BEFORE WE RESUME THIS ARGUMENT.
BUT YOU ALREADY FORGAVE ME.
I DID?
AFTER ARGUING OUTSIDE THE BAR, WE CAME BACK TO THE HOTEL LOUNGE AND HAD THE COMPLIMENTARY COCKTAILS THAT CAME WITH THE ROOM...
OK. THAT I REMEMBER.
I APOLOGIZED. YOU LECTURED. I APOLOGIZED AGAIN. YOU GLARED.
THEN YOU MADE ME RECITE THE WORDS TO THAT YEASTIE GIRLS LP YOU USED TO LISTEN TO TWENTY TIMES A DAY IN YOUR DORM ROOM. "WE'RE NOT YOUR BABIES AND WE'RE NOT YOUR DOLLS..."
"...AND WE DON'T GIVE A SHIT ABOUT YOUR BLUE BALLS."
I HAVEN'T THOUGHT ABOUT THAT SONG IN DECADES.
WELL, YOU MADE ME SING IT TO THE BARTENDER. TWICE. YOU WERE AS MILITANT AS YOU WERE TWENTY YEARS AGO.
IT WAS HOT.
AND THEN I FORGAVE YOU?

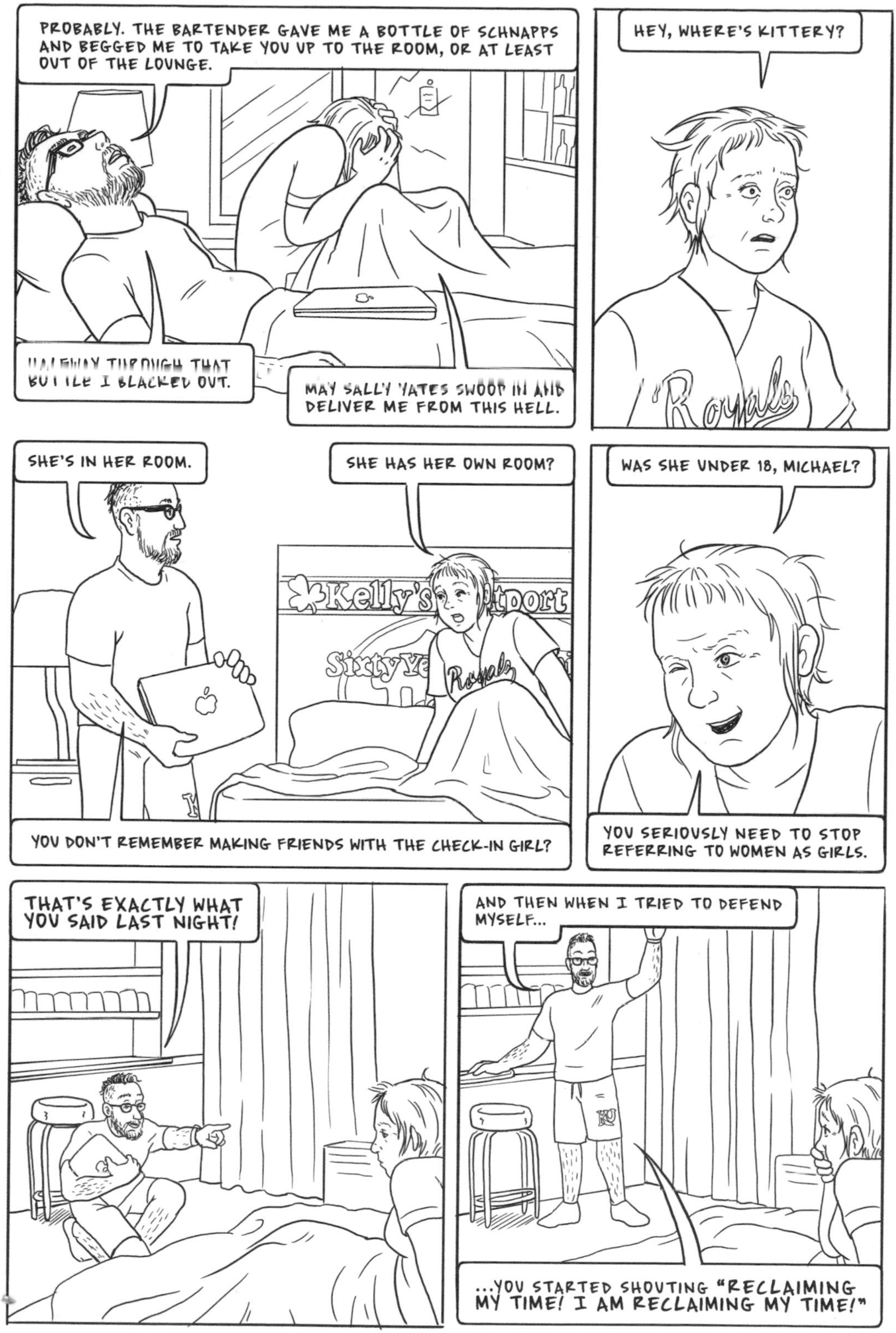
PROBABLY. THE BARTENDER GAVE ME A BOTTLE OF SCHNAPPS AND BEGGED ME TO TAKE YOU UP TO THE ROOM, OR AT LEAST OUT OF THE LOUNGE.
HALFWAY THROUGH THAT BOTTLE I BLACKED OUT.
MAY SALLY YATES SWOOP IN AND DELIVER ME FROM THIS HELL.
HEY, WHERE'S KITTERY?
SHE'S IN HER ROOM.
SHE HAS HER OWN ROOM?
YOU DON'T REMEMBER MAKING FRIENDS WITH THE CHECK-IN GIRL?
WAS SHE UNDER 18, MICHAEL?
YOU SERIOUSLY NEED TO STOP REFERRING TO WOMEN AS GIRLS.
THAT'S EXACTLY WHAT YOU SAID LAST NIGHT!
AND THEN WHEN I TRIED TO DEFEND MYSELF...
...YOU STARTED SHOUTING "RECLAIMING MY TIME! I AM RECLAIMING MY TIME!"

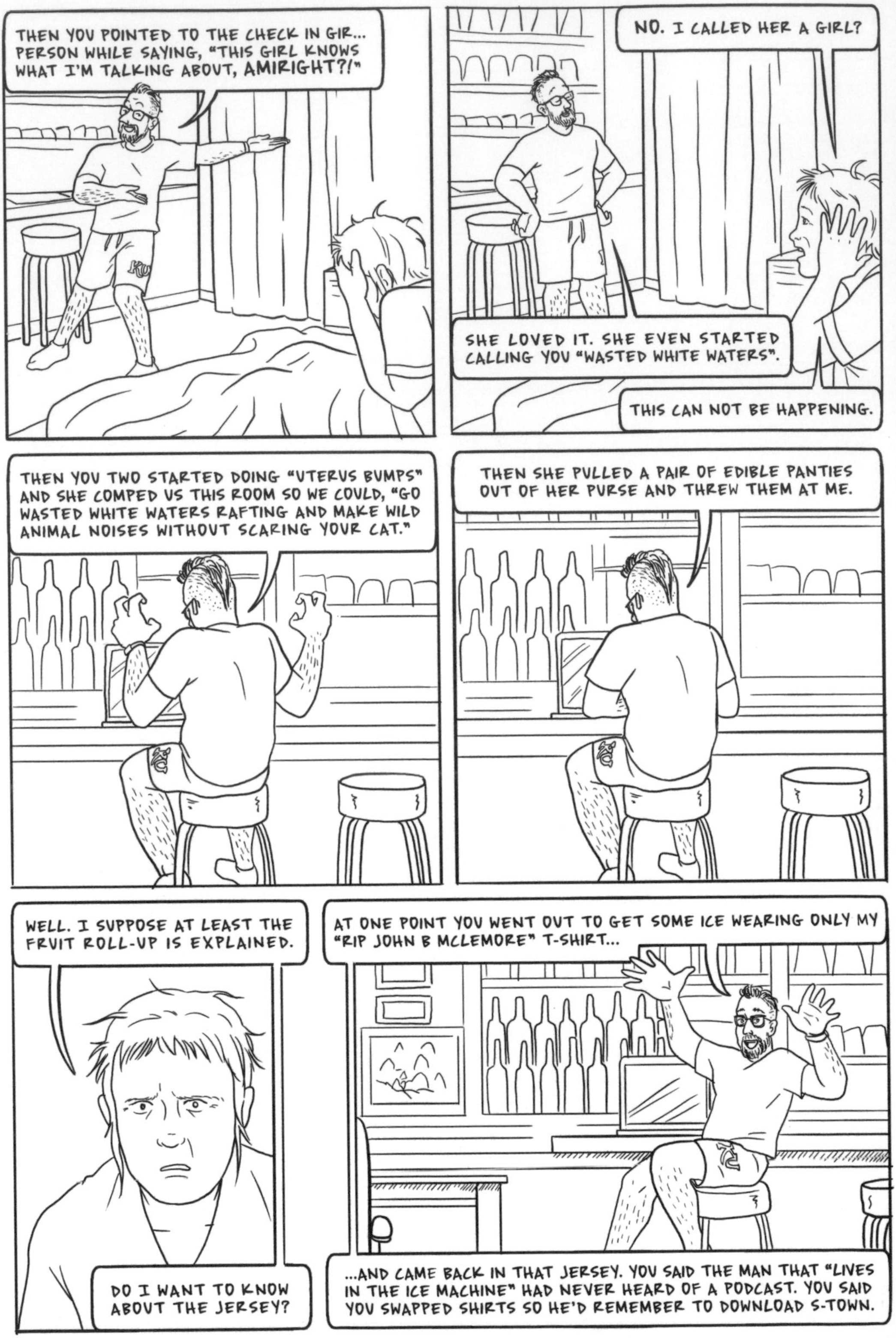
THEN YOU POINTED TO THE CHECK IN GIR... PERSON WHILE SAYING, "THIS GIRL KNOWS WHAT I'M TALKING ABOUT, AMIRIGHT?!"
NO. I CALLED HER A GIRL?
SHE LOVED IT. SHE EVEN STARTED CALLING YOU "WASTED WHITE WATERS".
THIS CAN NOT BE HAPPENING.
THEN YOU TWO STARTED DOING "UTERUS BUMPS" AND SHE COMPED US THIS ROOM SO WE COULD, "GO WASTED WHITE WATERS RAFTING AND MAKE WILD ANIMAL NOISES WITHOUT SCARING YOUR CAT."
THEN SHE PULLED A PAIR OF EDIBLE PANTIES OUT OF HER PURSE AND THREW THEM AT ME.
WELL. I SUPPOSE AT LEAST THE FRUIT ROLL-UP IS EXPLAINED.
DO I WANT TO KNOW ABOUT THE JERSEY?
AT ONE POINT YOU WENT OUT TO GET SOME ICE WEARING ONLY MY "RIP JOHN B MCLEMORE" T-SHIRT...
...AND CAME BACK IN THAT JERSEY. YOU SAID THE MAN THAT "LIVES IN THE ICE MACHINE" HAD NEVER HEARD OF A PODCAST. YOU SAID YOU SWAPPED SHIRTS SO HE'D REMEMBER TO DOWNLOAD S-TOWN.

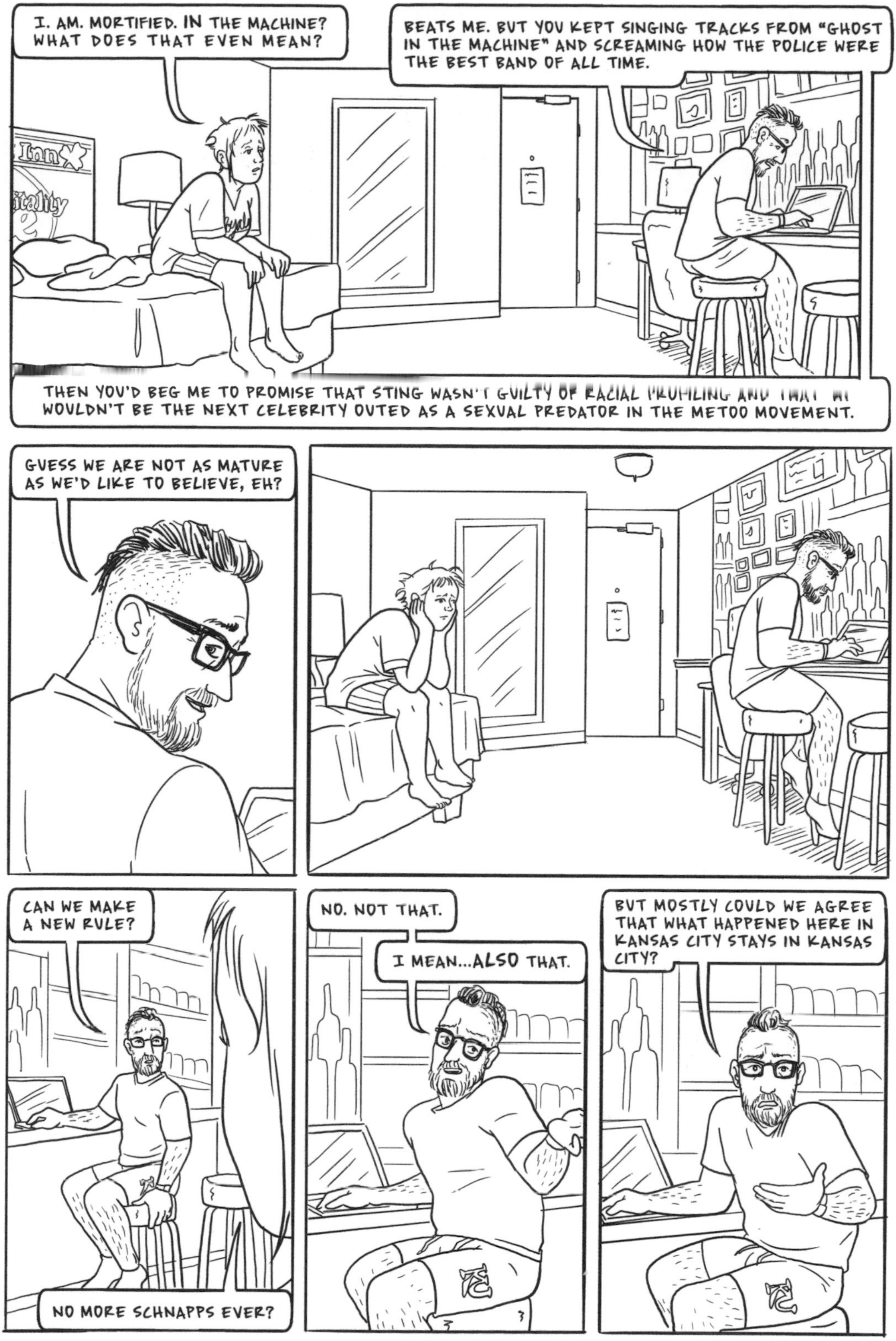
I. AM. MORTIFIED. IN THE MACHINE? WHAT DOES THAT EVEN MEAN?
BEATS ME. BUT YOU KEPT SINGING TRACKS FROM "GHOST IN THE MACHINE" AND SCREAMING HOW THE POLICE WERE THE BEST BAND OF ALL TIME.
THEN YOU'D BEG ME TO PROMISE THAT STING WASN'T GUILTY OF RACIAL PROFILING AND THAT HE WOULDN'T BE THE NEXT CELEBRITY OUTED AS A SEXUAL PREDATOR IN THE METOO MOVEMENT.
GUESS WE ARE NOT AS MATURE AS WE'D LIKE TO BELIEVE, EH?
CAN WE MAKE A NEW RULE?
NO MORE SCHNAPPS EVER?
NO. NOT THAT.
I MEAN...ALSO THAT.
BUT MOSTLY COULD WE AGREE THAT WHAT HAPPENED HERE IN KANSAS CITY STAYS IN KANSAS CITY?

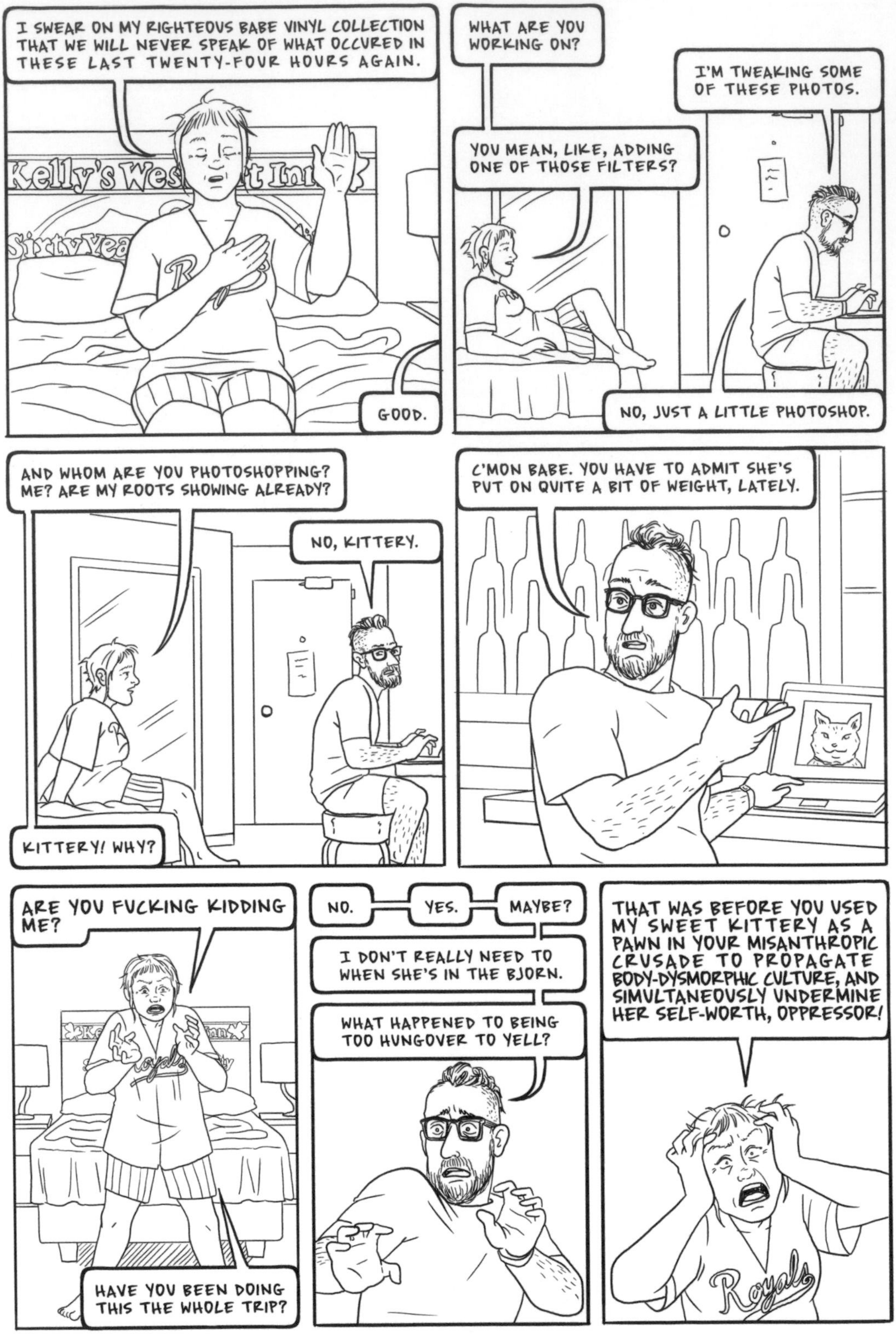
I SWEAR ON MY RIGHTEOUS BABE VINYL COLLECTION THAT WE WILL NEVER SPEAK OF WHAT OCCURED IN THESE LAST TWENTY-FOUR HOURS AGAIN.
Kelly's West... Inn
GOOD.
WHAT ARE YOU WORKING ON?
I'M TWEAKING SOME OF THESE PHOTOS.
YOU MEAN, LIKE, ADDING ONE OF THOSE FILTERS?
NO, JUST A LITTLE PHOTOSHOP.
AND WHOM ARE YOU PHOTOSHOPPING? ME? ARE MY ROOTS SHOWING ALREADY?
NO, KITTERY.
KITTERY! WHY?
C'MON BABE. YOU HAVE TO ADMIT SHE'S PUT ON QUITE A BIT OF WEIGHT, LATELY.
ARE YOU FUCKING KIDDING ME?
HAVE YOU BEEN DOING THIS THE WHOLE TRIP?
NO.
YES.
MAYBE?
I DON'T REALLY NEED TO WHEN SHE'S IN THE BJORN.
WHAT HAPPENED TO BEING TOO HUNGOVER TO YELL?
THAT WAS BEFORE YOU USED MY SWEET KITTERY AS A PAWN IN YOUR MISANTHROPIC CRUSADE TO PROPAGATE BODY-DYSMORPHIC CULTURE, AND SIMULTANEOUSLY UNDERMINE HER SELF-WORTH, OPPRESSOR!
Royals

I'M JUST SHOWING HER HOW GOOD SHE COULD LOOK IF SHE TRIED.

GASLIGHTING!

NO! I DON'T BLAME HER! OF COURSE SHE CAN'T HELP IT. HASHTAG VANLIFE IS SO VERY SEDENTARY.

SHE'S EITHER NAPPING IN THE CAMPER OR STRAPPED TO MY CHEST AT ALL TIMES.

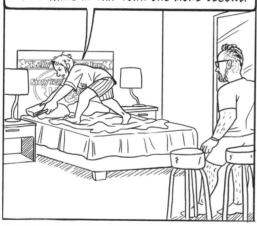

PACK UP. PACK UP EVERYTHING RIGHT NOW. WE ARE NOT STAYING IN THIS TOWN ONE MORE SECOND.

APPARENTLY THE REASON YOU CAN NEVER GO HOME AGAIN IS BECAUSE ONE REGRESSES TO A BORN-AGAIN, RACIST, BIGOTED, ETHNOCENTRIC, GOOD OLD BOY.

THERE MUST BE MISOGYNY IN THE WATER SUPPLY HERE.

PERSONALLY, I BLAME IT ON THE GLUTEN.

FROM HERE ON OUT, YOU ARE ON A COMPLICITY AND CARBOHYDRATE CLEANSE, MISTER.

ALSO, AS PENANCE FOR CRIMES AGAINST HITTERY CLINTON, WE WILL BE VISITING BOTH OF THE WORLD'S LARGEST BALLS OF TWINE.

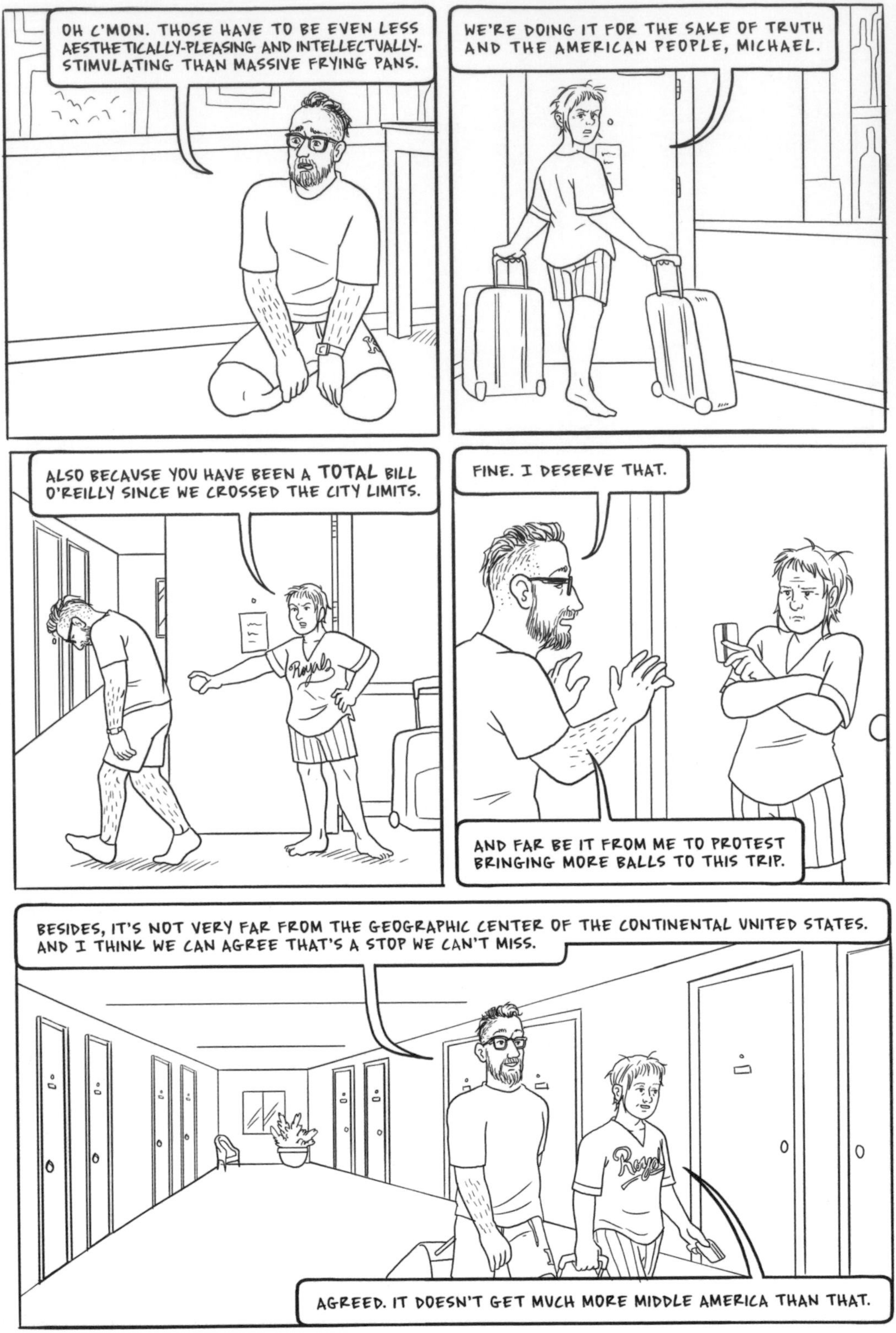

OH C'MON. THOSE HAVE TO BE EVEN LESS AESTHETICALLY-PLEASING AND INTELLECTUALLY-STIMULATING THAN MASSIVE FRYING PANS.
WE'RE DOING IT FOR THE SAKE OF TRUTH AND THE AMERICAN PEOPLE, MICHAEL.
ALSO BECAUSE YOU HAVE BEEN A TOTAL BILL O'REILLY SINCE WE CROSSED THE CITY LIMITS.
FINE. I DESERVE THAT.
AND FAR BE IT FROM ME TO PROTEST BRINGING MORE BALLS TO THIS TRIP.
BESIDES, IT'S NOT VERY FAR FROM THE GEOGRAPHIC CENTER OF THE CONTINENTAL UNITED STATES. AND I THINK WE CAN AGREE THAT'S A STOP WE CAN'T MISS.
AGREED. IT DOESN'T GET MUCH MORE MIDDLE AMERICA THAN THAT.

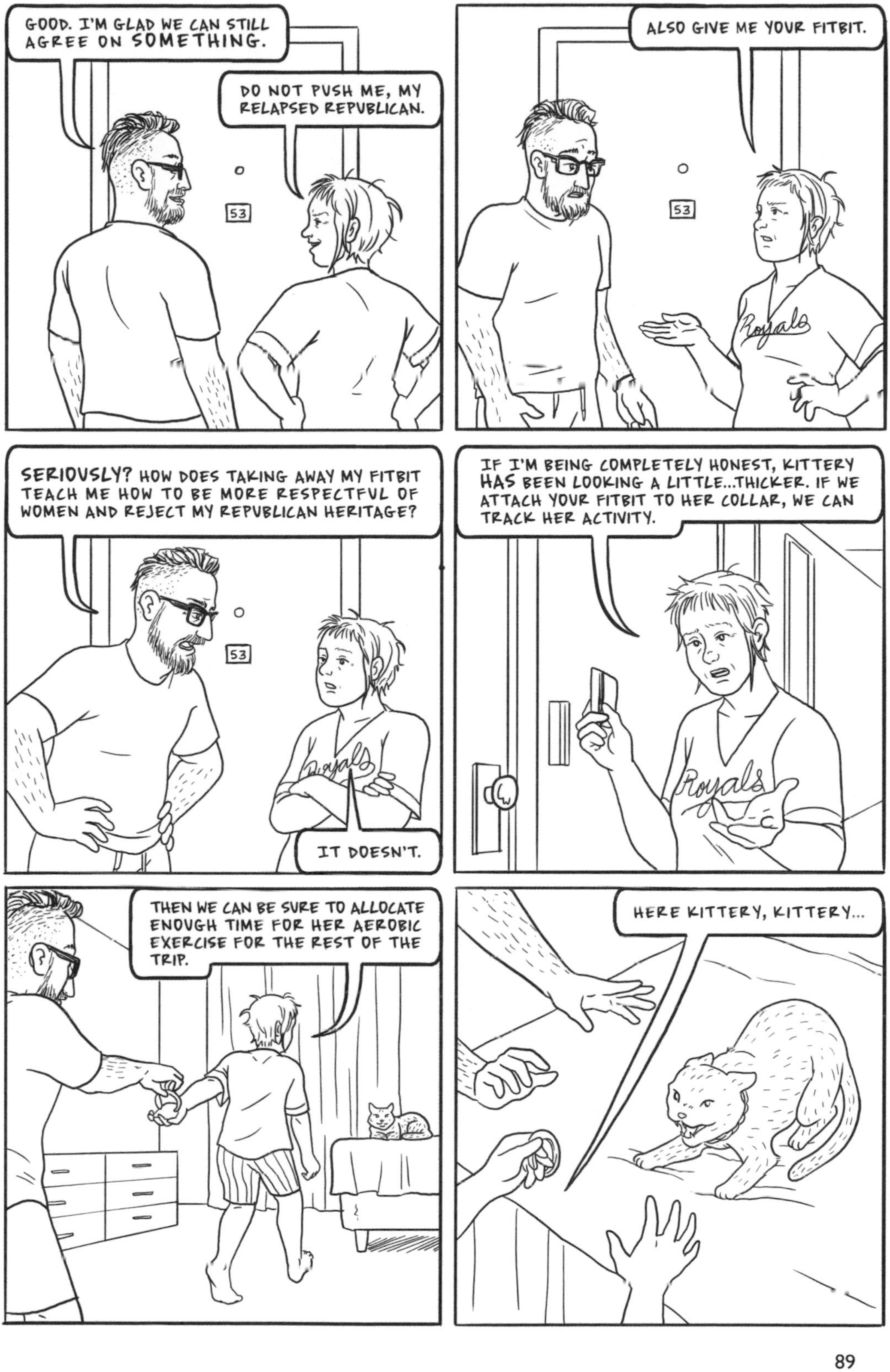
GOOD. I'M GLAD WE CAN STILL AGREE ON SOMETHING.
DO NOT PUSH ME, MY RELAPSED REPUBLICAN.
53
ALSO GIVE ME YOUR FITBIT.
53
Royals
SERIOUSLY? HOW DOES TAKING AWAY MY FITBIT TEACH ME HOW TO BE MORE RESPECTFUL OF WOMEN AND REJECT MY REPUBLICAN HERITAGE?
53
IT DOESN'T.
IF I'M BEING COMPLETELY HONEST, KITTERY HAS BEEN LOOKING A LITTLE...THICKER. IF WE ATTACH YOUR FITBIT TO HER COLLAR, WE CAN TRACK HER ACTIVITY.
Royals
THEN WE CAN BE SURE TO ALLOCATE ENOUGH TIME FOR HER AEROBIC EXERCISE FOR THE REST OF THE TRIP.
HERE KITTERY, KITTERY...

Chapter 12

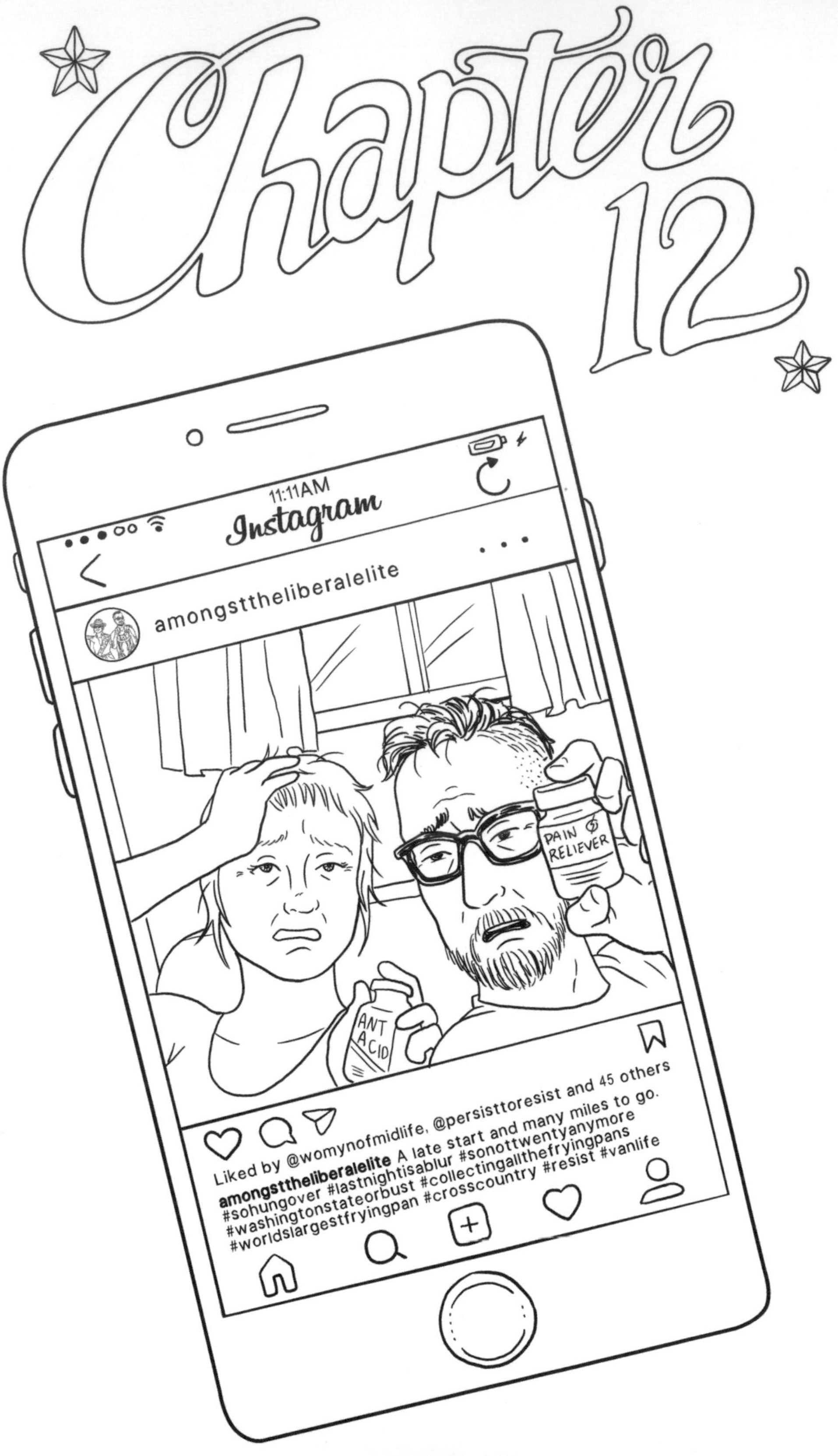
11:11AM
Instagram
amongstheliberalelite
amongsttheliberalelite
PAIN RELIEVER
ANT ACID
Liked by @womynofmidlife, @persisttoresist and 45 others
amongsttheliberalelite A late start and many miles to go. #sohungover #lastnightisablur #sonottwentyanymore #washingtonstateorbust #collectingallthefryingpans #worldslargestfryingpan #crosscountry #resist #vanlife

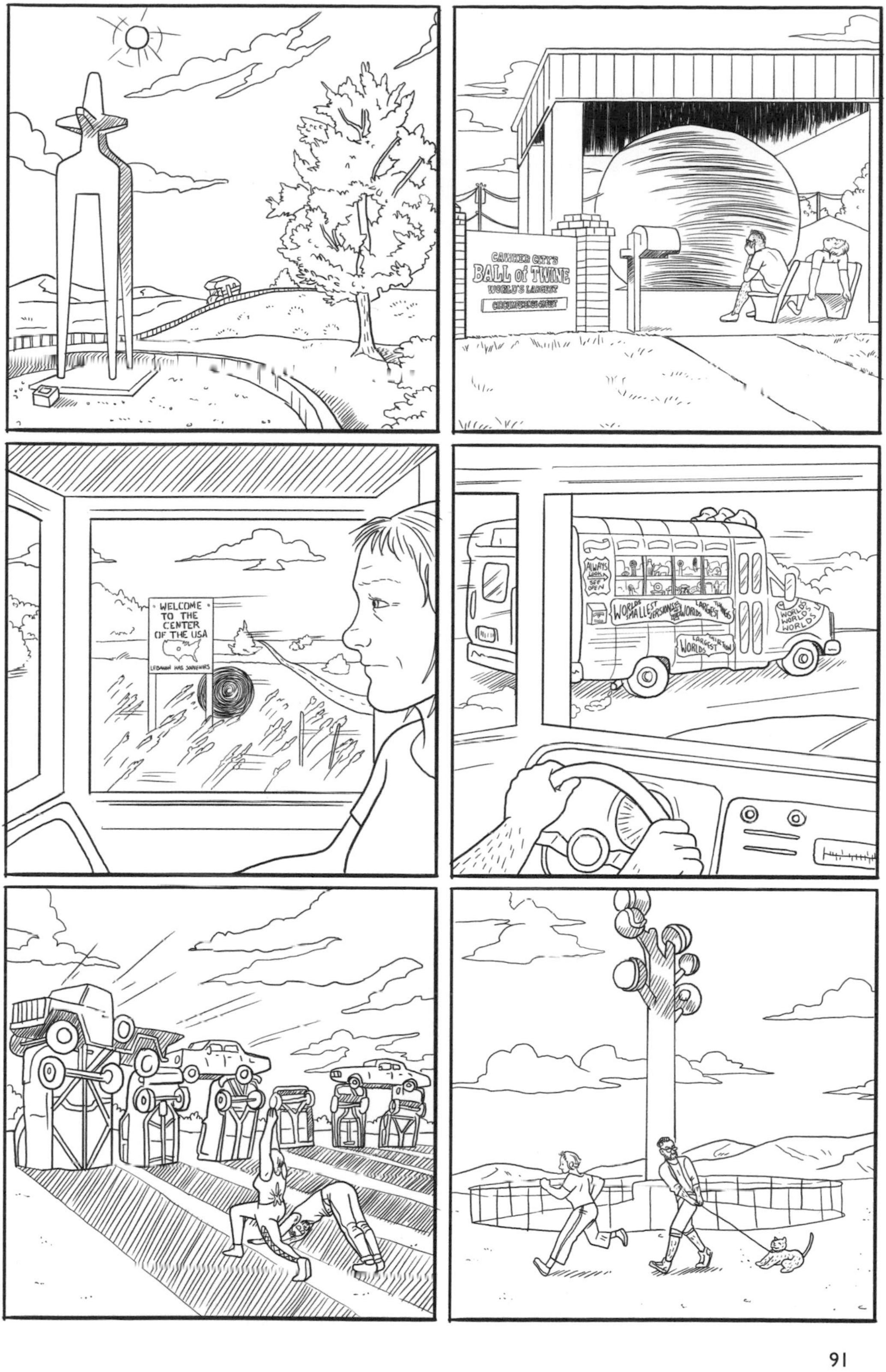
CAWKER CITY'S
BALL of TWINE
WORLD'S LARGEST
WELCOME TO THE CENTER OF THE USA
LEBANON HAS SOUVENIRS
ALWAYS LOOK SEE OPEN
WORLDS SMALLEST VERSIONS
WORLDS LARGEST THINGS
WORLDS WORLDS WORLDS

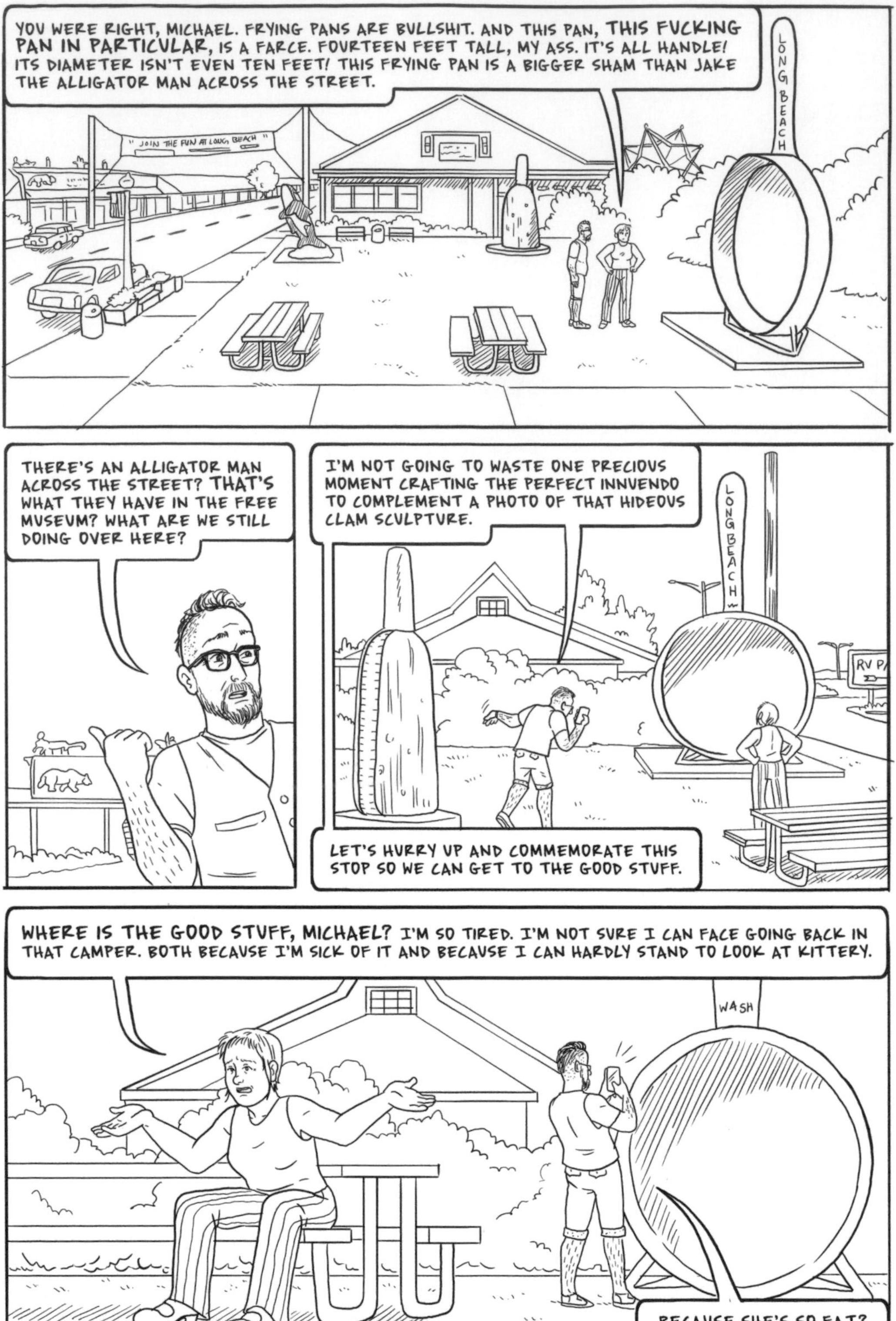

YOU WERE RIGHT, MICHAEL. FRYING PANS ARE BULLSHIT. AND THIS PAN, THIS FUCKING PAN IN PARTICULAR, IS A FARCE. FOURTEEN FEET TALL, MY ASS. IT'S ALL HANDLE! ITS DIAMETER ISN'T EVEN TEN FEET! THIS FRYING PAN IS A BIGGER SHAM THAN JAKE THE ALLIGATOR MAN ACROSS THE STREET.
LONG BEACH
" JOIN THE FUN AT LONG BEACH "
THERE'S AN ALLIGATOR MAN ACROSS THE STREET? THAT'S WHAT THEY HAVE IN THE FREE MUSEUM? WHAT ARE WE STILL DOING OVER HERE?
I'M NOT GOING TO WASTE ONE PRECIOUS MOMENT CRAFTING THE PERFECT INNVENDO TO COMPLEMENT A PHOTO OF THAT HIDEOUS CLAM SCULPTURE.
LONG BEACH
RV PA
LET'S HURRY UP AND COMMEMORATE THIS STOP SO WE CAN GET TO THE GOOD STUFF.
WHERE IS THE GOOD STUFF, MICHAEL? I'M SO TIRED. I'M NOT SURE I CAN FACE GOING BACK IN THAT CAMPER. BOTH BECAUSE I'M SICK OF IT AND BECAUSE I CAN HARDLY STAND TO LOOK AT KITTERY.
WASH
BECAUSE SHE'S SO FAT?

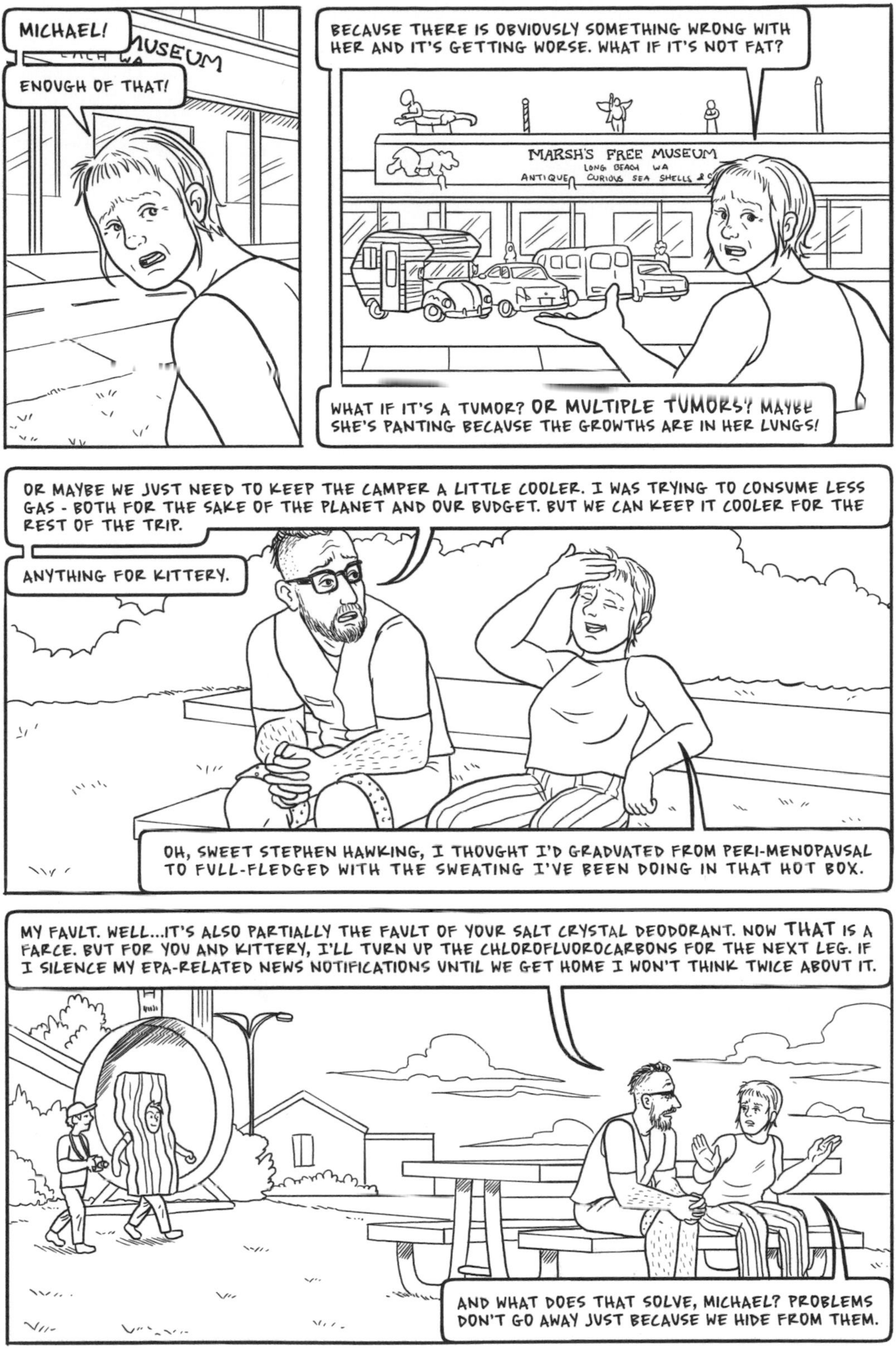
MICHAEL!
ENOUGH OF THAT!
MUSEUM
BECAUSE THERE IS OBVIOUSLY SOMETHING WRONG WITH HER AND IT'S GETTING WORSE. WHAT IF IT'S NOT FAT?
MARSH'S FREE MUSEUM
LONG BEACH WA
ANTIQUE CURIOUS SEA SHELLS
WHAT IF IT'S A TUMOR? OR MULTIPLE TUMORS? MAYBE SHE'S PANTING BECAUSE THE GROWTHS ARE IN HER LUNGS!
OR MAYBE WE JUST NEED TO KEEP THE CAMPER A LITTLE COOLER. I WAS TRYING TO CONSUME LESS GAS - BOTH FOR THE SAKE OF THE PLANET AND OUR BUDGET. BUT WE CAN KEEP IT COOLER FOR THE REST OF THE TRIP.
ANYTHING FOR KITTERY.
OH, SWEET STEPHEN HAWKING, I THOUGHT I'D GRADUATED FROM PERI-MENOPAUSAL TO FULL-FLEDGED WITH THE SWEATING I'VE BEEN DOING IN THAT HOT BOX.
MY FAULT. WELL...IT'S ALSO PARTIALLY THE FAULT OF YOUR SALT CRYSTAL DEODORANT. NOW THAT IS A FARCE. BUT FOR YOU AND KITTERY, I'LL TURN UP THE CHLOROFLUOROCARBONS FOR THE NEXT LEG. IF I SILENCE MY EPA-RELATED NEWS NOTIFICATIONS UNTIL WE GET HOME I WON'T THINK TWICE ABOUT IT.
AND WHAT DOES THAT SOLVE, MICHAEL? PROBLEMS DON'T GO AWAY JUST BECAUSE WE HIDE FROM THEM.

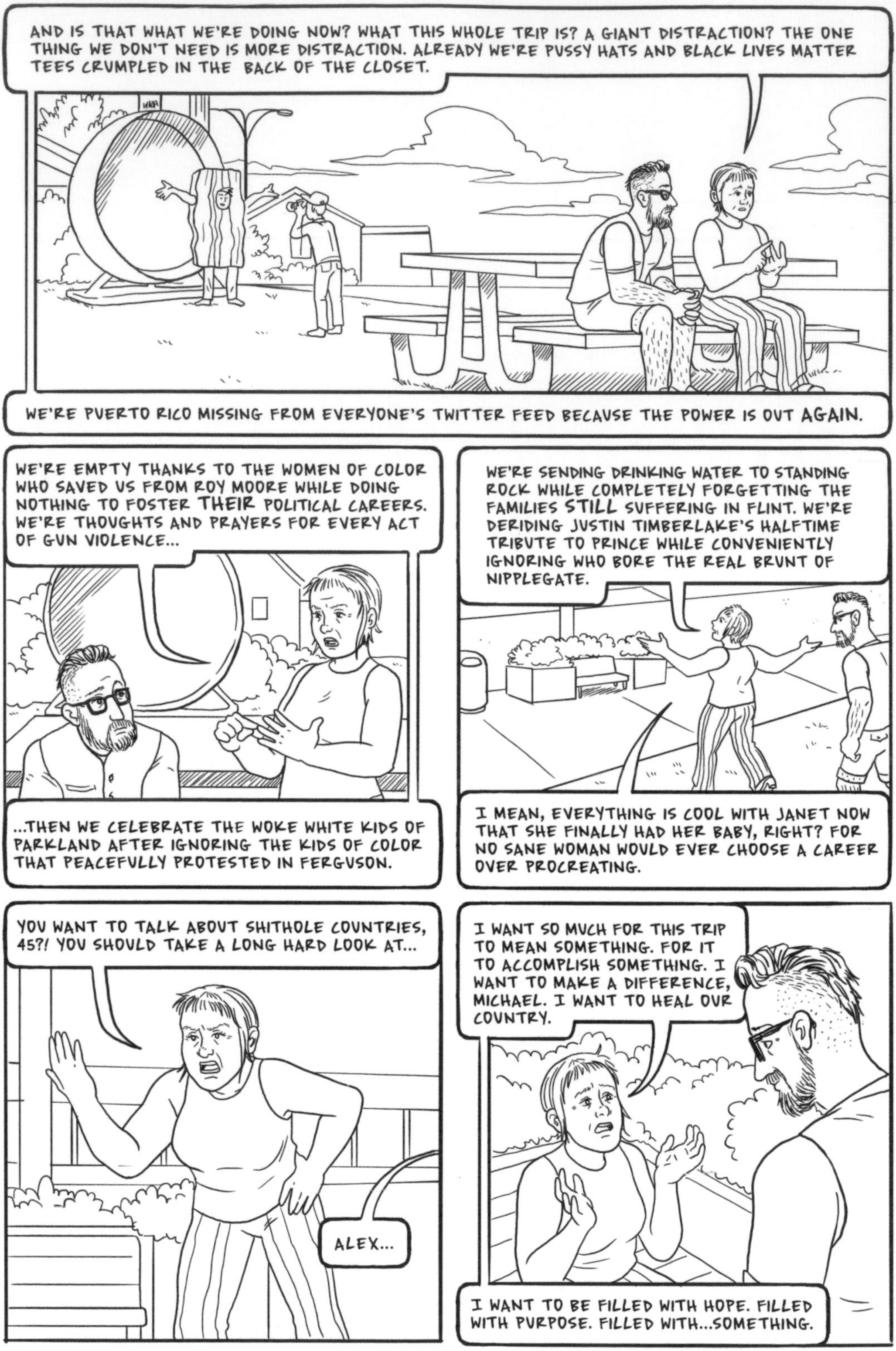
AND IS THAT WHAT WE'RE DOING NOW? WHAT THIS WHOLE TRIP IS? A GIANT DISTRACTION? THE ONE THING WE DON'T NEED IS MORE DISTRACTION. ALREADY WE'RE PUSSY HATS AND BLACK LIVES MATTER TEES CRUMPLED IN THE BACK OF THE CLOSET.
WE'RE PUERTO RICO MISSING FROM EVERYONE'S TWITTER FEED BECAUSE THE POWER IS OUT AGAIN.
WE'RE EMPTY THANKS TO THE WOMEN OF COLOR WHO SAVED US FROM ROY MOORE WHILE DOING NOTHING TO FOSTER THEIR POLITICAL CAREERS. WE'RE THOUGHTS AND PRAYERS FOR EVERY ACT OF GUN VIOLENCE...
...THEN WE CELEBRATE THE WOKE WHITE KIDS OF PARKLAND AFTER IGNORING THE KIDS OF COLOR THAT PEACEFULLY PROTESTED IN FERGUSON.
WE'RE SENDING DRINKING WATER TO STANDING ROCK WHILE COMPLETELY FORGETTING THE FAMILIES STILL SUFFERING IN FLINT. WE'RE DERIDING JUSTIN TIMBERLAKE'S HALFTIME TRIBUTE TO PRINCE WHILE CONVENIENTLY IGNORING WHO BORE THE REAL BRUNT OF NIPPLEGATE.
I MEAN, EVERYTHING IS COOL WITH JANET NOW THAT SHE FINALLY HAD HER BABY, RIGHT? FOR NO SANE WOMAN WOULD EVER CHOOSE A CAREER OVER PROCREATING.
YOU WANT TO TALK ABOUT SHITHOLE COUNTRIES, 45?! YOU SHOULD TAKE A LONG HARD LOOK AT...
ALEX...
I WANT SO MUCH FOR THIS TRIP TO MEAN SOMETHING. FOR IT TO ACCOMPLISH SOMETHING. I WANT TO MAKE A DIFFERENCE, MICHAEL. I WANT TO HEAL OUR COUNTRY.
I WANT TO BE FILLED WITH HOPE. FILLED WITH PURPOSE. FILLED WITH...SOMETHING.

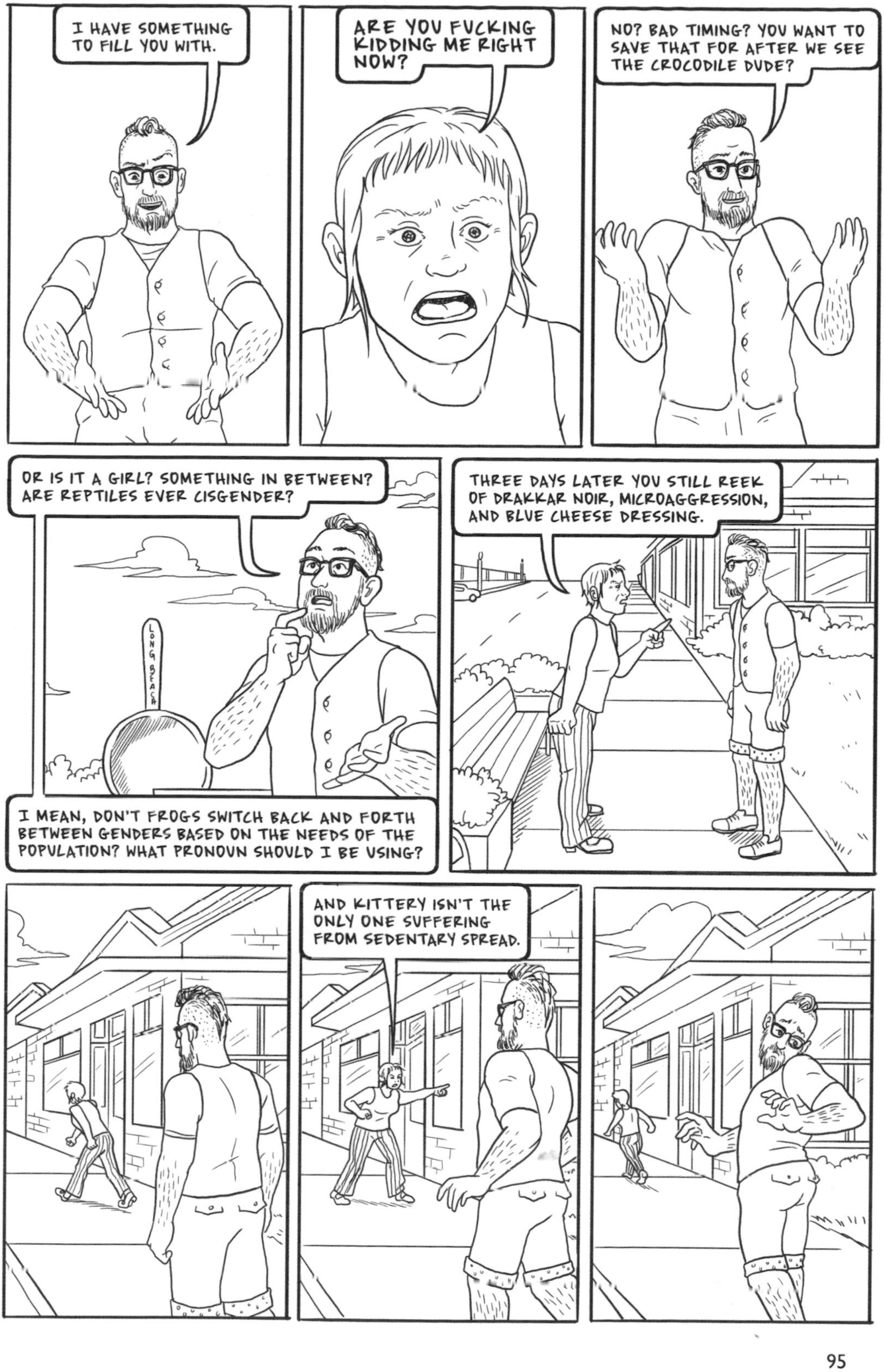
I HAVE SOMETHING TO FILL YOU WITH.
ARE YOU FUCKING KIDDING ME RIGHT NOW?
NO? BAD TIMING? YOU WANT TO SAVE THAT FOR AFTER WE SEE THE CROCODILE DUDE?
OR IS IT A GIRL? SOMETHING IN BETWEEN? ARE REPTILES EVER CISGENDER?
LONG BEACH
I MEAN, DON'T FROGS SWITCH BACK AND FORTH BETWEEN GENDERS BASED ON THE NEEDS OF THE POPULATION? WHAT PRONOUN SHOULD I BE USING?
THREE DAYS LATER YOU STILL REEK OF DRAKKAR NOIR, MICROAGGRESSION, AND BLUE CHEESE DRESSING.
AND KITTERY ISN'T THE ONLY ONE SUFFERING FROM SEDENTARY SPREAD.

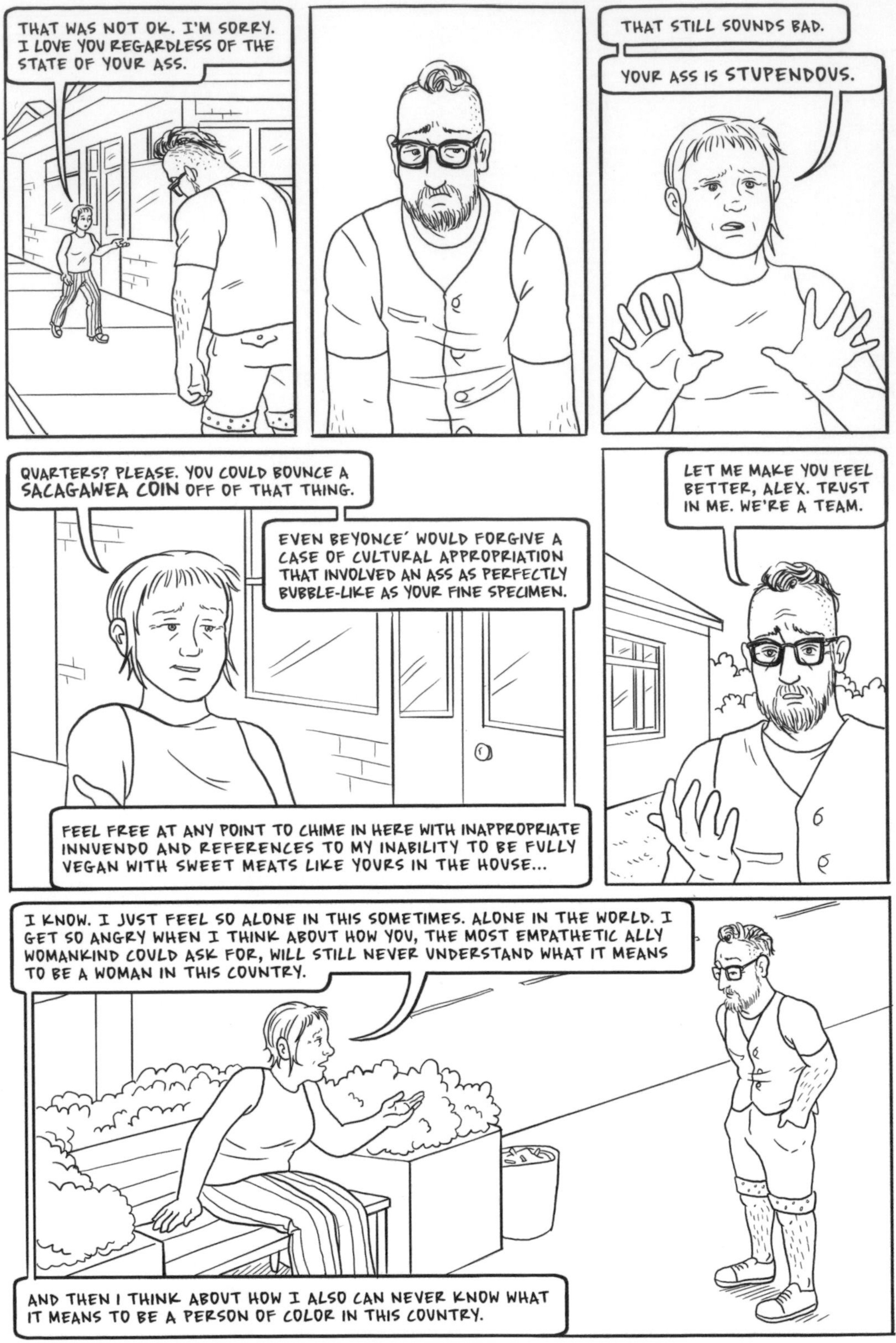
THAT WAS NOT OK. I'M SORRY. I LOVE YOU REGARDLESS OF THE STATE OF YOUR ASS.
THAT STILL SOUNDS BAD.
YOUR ASS IS STUPENDOUS.
QUARTERS? PLEASE. YOU COULD BOUNCE A SACAGAWEA COIN OFF OF THAT THING.
EVEN BEYONCE´ WOULD FORGIVE A CASE OF CULTURAL APPROPRIATION THAT INVOLVED AN ASS AS PERFECTLY BUBBLE-LIKE AS YOUR FINE SPECIMEN.
FEEL FREE AT ANY POINT TO CHIME IN HERE WITH INAPPROPRIATE INNVENDO AND REFERENCES TO MY INABILITY TO BE FULLY VEGAN WITH SWEET MEATS LIKE YOURS IN THE HOUSE...
LET ME MAKE YOU FEEL BETTER, ALEX. TRUST IN ME. WE'RE A TEAM.
I KNOW. I JUST FEEL SO ALONE IN THIS SOMETIMES. ALONE IN THE WORLD. I GET SO ANGRY WHEN I THINK ABOUT HOW YOU, THE MOST EMPATHETIC ALLY WOMANKIND COULD ASK FOR, WILL STILL NEVER UNDERSTAND WHAT IT MEANS TO BE A WOMAN IN THIS COUNTRY.
AND THEN I THINK ABOUT HOW I ALSO CAN NEVER KNOW WHAT IT MEANS TO BE A PERSON OF COLOR IN THIS COUNTRY.

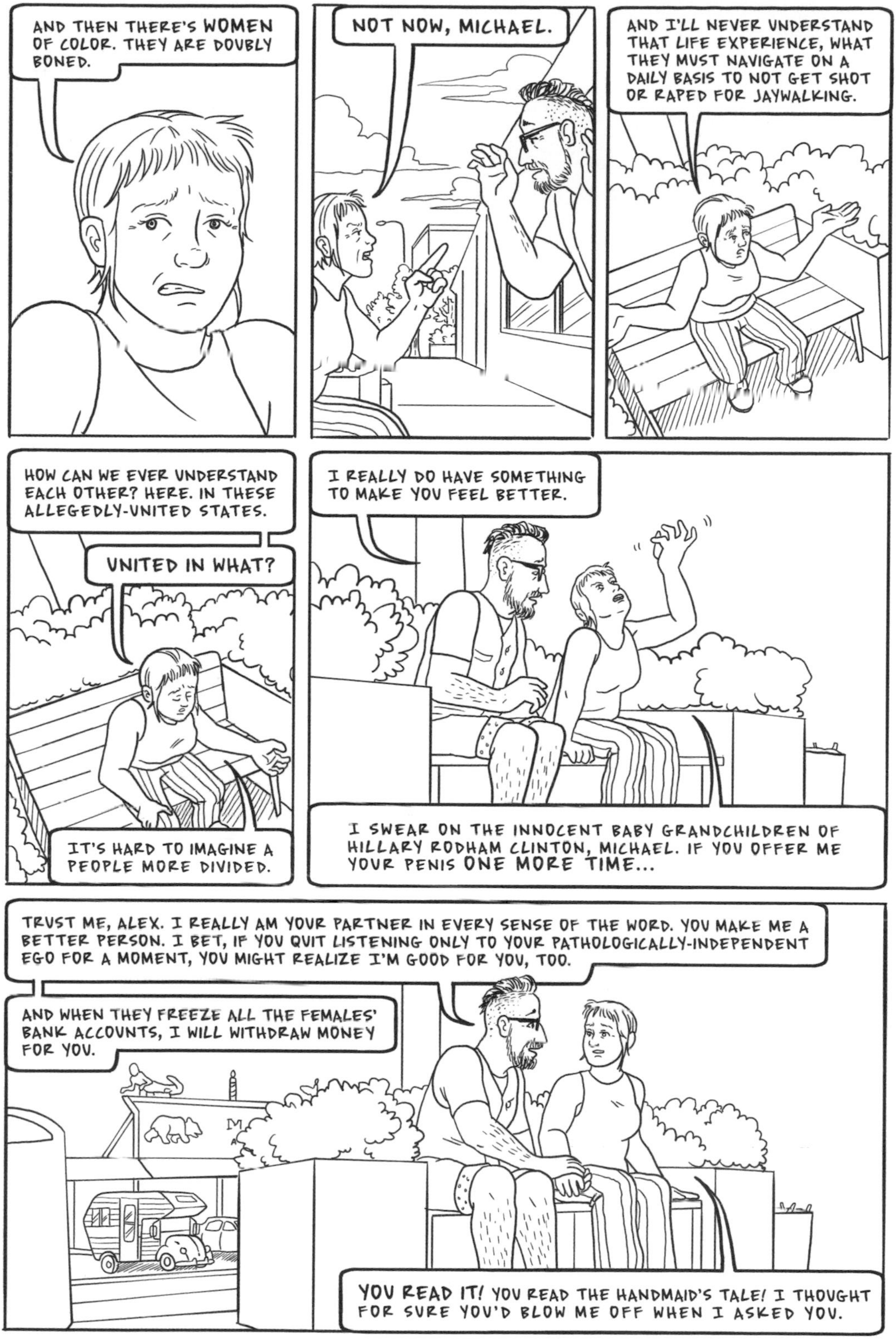

AND THEN THERE'S WOMEN OF COLOR. THEY ARE DOUBLY BONED.
NOT NOW, MICHAEL.
AND I'LL NEVER UNDERSTAND THAT LIFE EXPERIENCE, WHAT THEY MUST NAVIGATE ON A DAILY BASIS TO NOT GET SHOT OR RAPED FOR JAYWALKING.
HOW CAN WE EVER UNDERSTAND EACH OTHER? HERE. IN THESE ALLEGEDLY-UNITED STATES.
UNITED IN WHAT?
IT'S HARD TO IMAGINE A PEOPLE MORE DIVIDED.
I REALLY DO HAVE SOMETHING TO MAKE YOU FEEL BETTER.
I SWEAR ON THE INNOCENT BABY GRANDCHILDREN OF HILLARY RODHAM CLINTON, MICHAEL. IF YOU OFFER ME YOUR PENIS ONE MORE TIME...
TRUST ME, ALEX. I REALLY AM YOUR PARTNER IN EVERY SENSE OF THE WORD. YOU MAKE ME A BETTER PERSON. I BET, IF YOU QUIT LISTENING ONLY TO YOUR PATHOLOGICALLY-INDEPENDENT EGO FOR A MOMENT, YOU MIGHT REALIZE I'M GOOD FOR YOU, TOO.
AND WHEN THEY FREEZE ALL THE FEMALES' BANK ACCOUNTS, I WILL WITHDRAW MONEY FOR YOU.
YOU READ IT! YOU READ THE HANDMAID'S TALE! I THOUGHT FOR SURE YOU'D BLOW ME OFF WHEN I ASKED YOU.

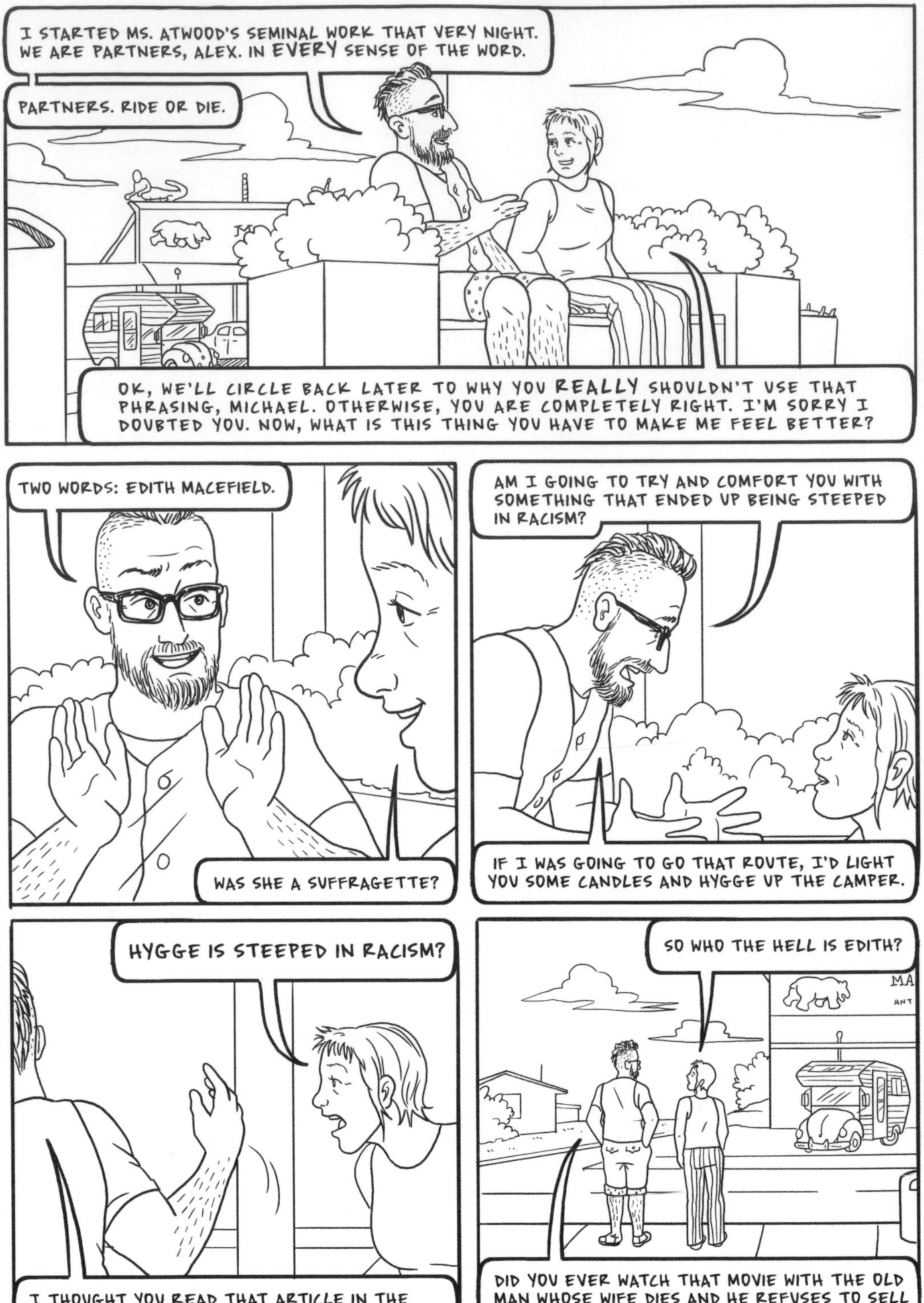
I STARTED MS. ATWOOD'S SEMINAL WORK THAT VERY NIGHT. WE ARE PARTNERS, ALEX. IN EVERY SENSE OF THE WORD.
PARTNERS. RIDE OR DIE.
OK, WE'LL CIRCLE BACK LATER TO WHY YOU REALLY SHOULDN'T USE THAT PHRASING, MICHAEL. OTHERWISE, YOU ARE COMPLETELY RIGHT. I'M SORRY I DOUBTED YOU. NOW, WHAT IS THIS THING YOU HAVE TO MAKE ME FEEL BETTER?
TWO WORDS: EDITH MACEFIELD.
WAS SHE A SUFFRAGETTE?
AM I GOING TO TRY AND COMFORT YOU WITH SOMETHING THAT ENDED UP BEING STEEPED IN RACISM?
IF I WAS GOING TO GO THAT ROUTE, I'D LIGHT YOU SOME CANDLES AND HYGGE UP THE CAMPER.
HYGGE IS STEEPED IN RACISM?
I THOUGHT YOU READ THAT ARTICLE IN THE GAURDIAN LAST YEAR, TOO. HYGGE IS AS RACIST AS JEFF SESSIONS. BUT AT LEAST SESSIONS ALLOWS SOME POLITICAL CONVERSATIONS TO TAKE PLACE.
SO WHO THE HELL IS EDITH?
DID YOU EVER WATCH THAT MOVIE WITH THE OLD MAN WHOSE WIFE DIES AND HE REFUSES TO SELL HIS HOUSE THEN TIES A BUNCH OF BALLOONS TO IT...AND I SEEM TO RECALL SOMETHING ABOUT TALKING DOGS?

THE ONE WHERE THE ONLY FEMALE CHARACTER DIES IN THE OPENING MONTAGE? GOOD LUCK PASSING THE BECHDEL TEST ON **THAT** ONE, PIXAR.

YES. BUT I WANT YOU TO FOCUS ON THE HOUSE. THERE WAS SOME KOCH BROTHER-ESQUE EVIL REAL ESTATE DEVELOPER AFTER IT. ALL HIS NEIGHBORS SOLD AND THEIR PLACES WERE TORN DOWN AND REPLACED WITH SKYSCRAPERS. BUT THERE WAS THIS ONE SWEET LITTLE HOUSE IN THE MIDDLE OF ALL THAT GLASS AND STEEL SCREAMING, "RESIST!" WITH ITS ADORABLE GINGERBREAD DETAILS. DO YOU REMEMBER IT?

I DO. I'VE ALWAYS WANTED A FRONT PORCH.

WELL, ALLEGEDLY THEY BASED THAT HOUSE ON EDITH'S. SOME BIG DEVELOPMENT COMPANY WANTED TO BUY HER OUT BUT SHE NEVER SOLD AND THEY HAD TO BUILD A MALL AROUND HER.

SO THEY TOOK THE STORY OF A DEFIANT, COURAGEOUS WOMAN AND RECAST HER AS AN OLD WHITE MAN?

STILL, THOUGH... I'D LOVE TO MEET HER.

OH SHE HAS LESS OF A PULSE THAN HARVEY WEINSTEIN'S PROFILE ON J-DATE.

BUT THE HOUSE IS STILL THERE. CAN YOU PICTURE IT, ALEX?

MARSH'S FREE M
LONG BEACH, WA
ANTIQUES CURIOUS SEAS

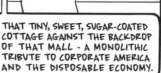

THAT TINY, SWEET, SUGAR-COATED COTTAGE AGAINST THE BACKDROP OF THAT MALL - A MONOLITHIC TRIBUTE TO CORPORATE AMERICA AND THE DISPOSABLE ECONOMY.

BUT ALSO THERE'S A TRADER JOE'S AROUND THE CORNER AND WE CAN STOCK UP ON FLAXSEED OIL.

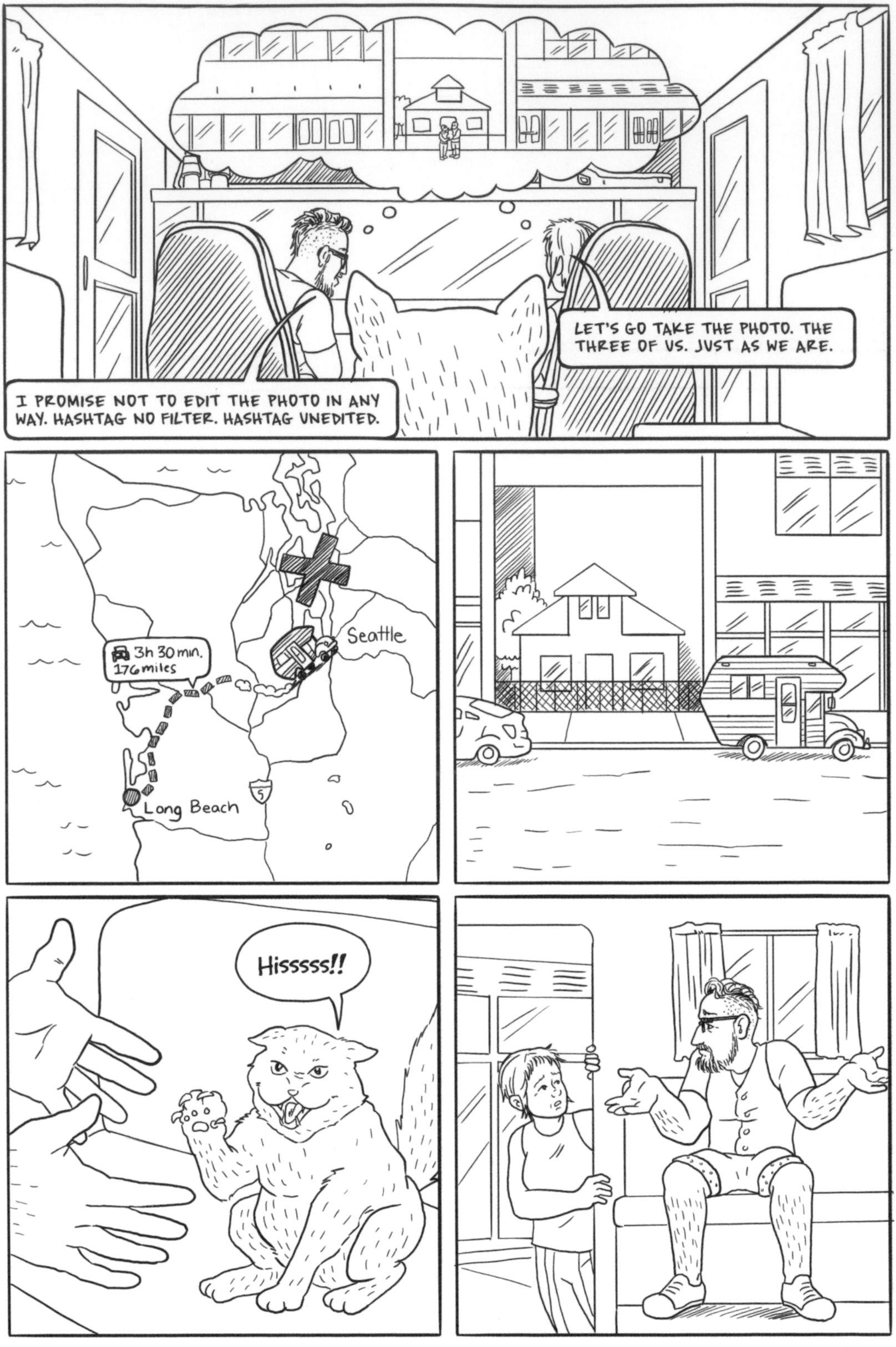
LET'S GO TAKE THE PHOTO. THE THREE OF US. JUST AS WE ARE.
I PROMISE NOT TO EDIT THE PHOTO IN ANY WAY. HASHTAG NO FILTER. HASHTAG UNEDITED.
3h 30 min.
176 miles
Seattle
Long Beach
5
Hisssss!!

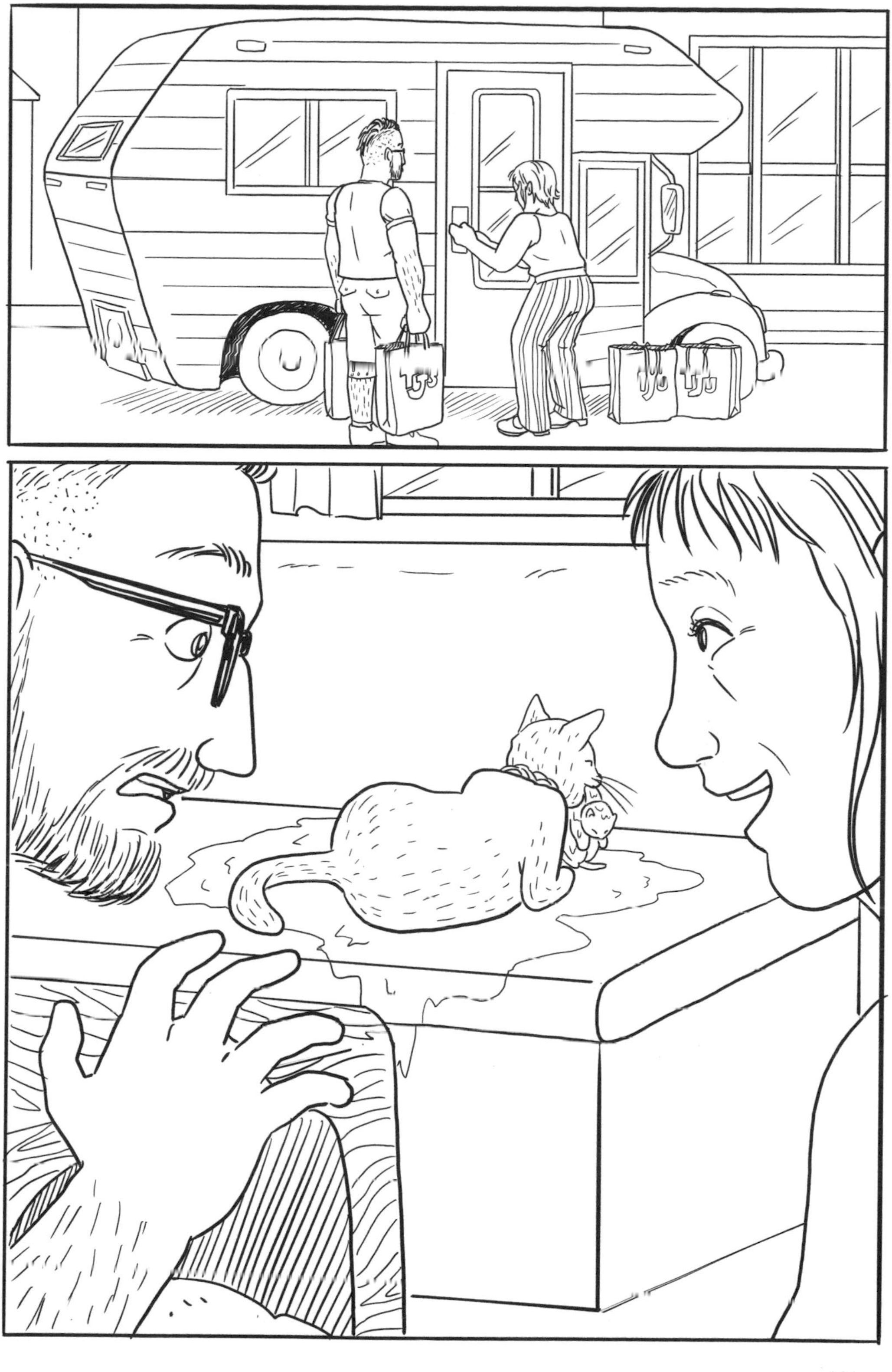

Chapter 13

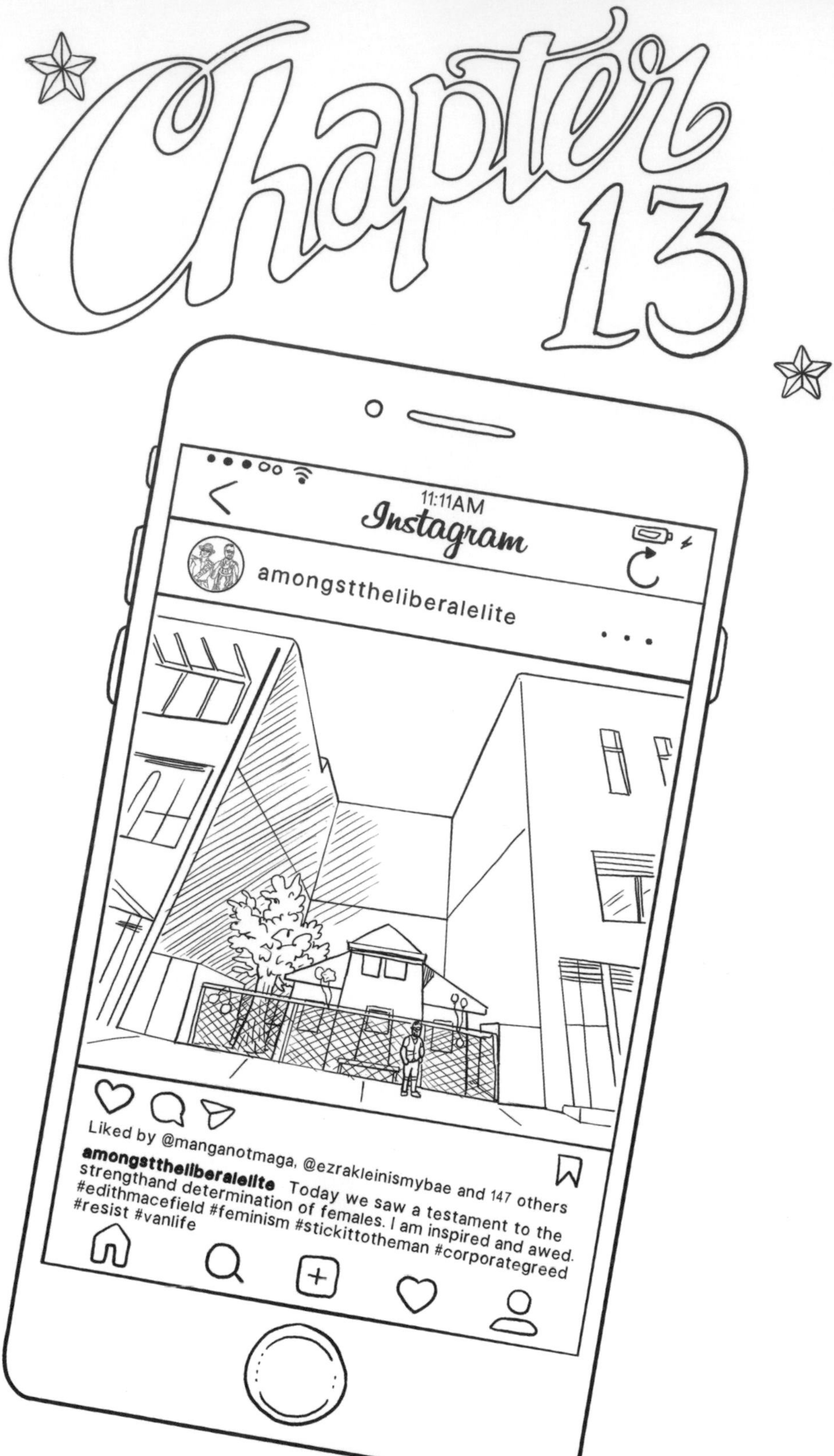

11:11AM
Instagram
amongsttheliberalelite
Liked by @manganotmaga, @ezrakleinismybae and 147 others
amongsttheliberalelite Today we saw a testament to the strengthand determination of females. I am inspired and awed.
#edithmacefield #feminism #stickittotheman #corporategreed
#resist #vanlife

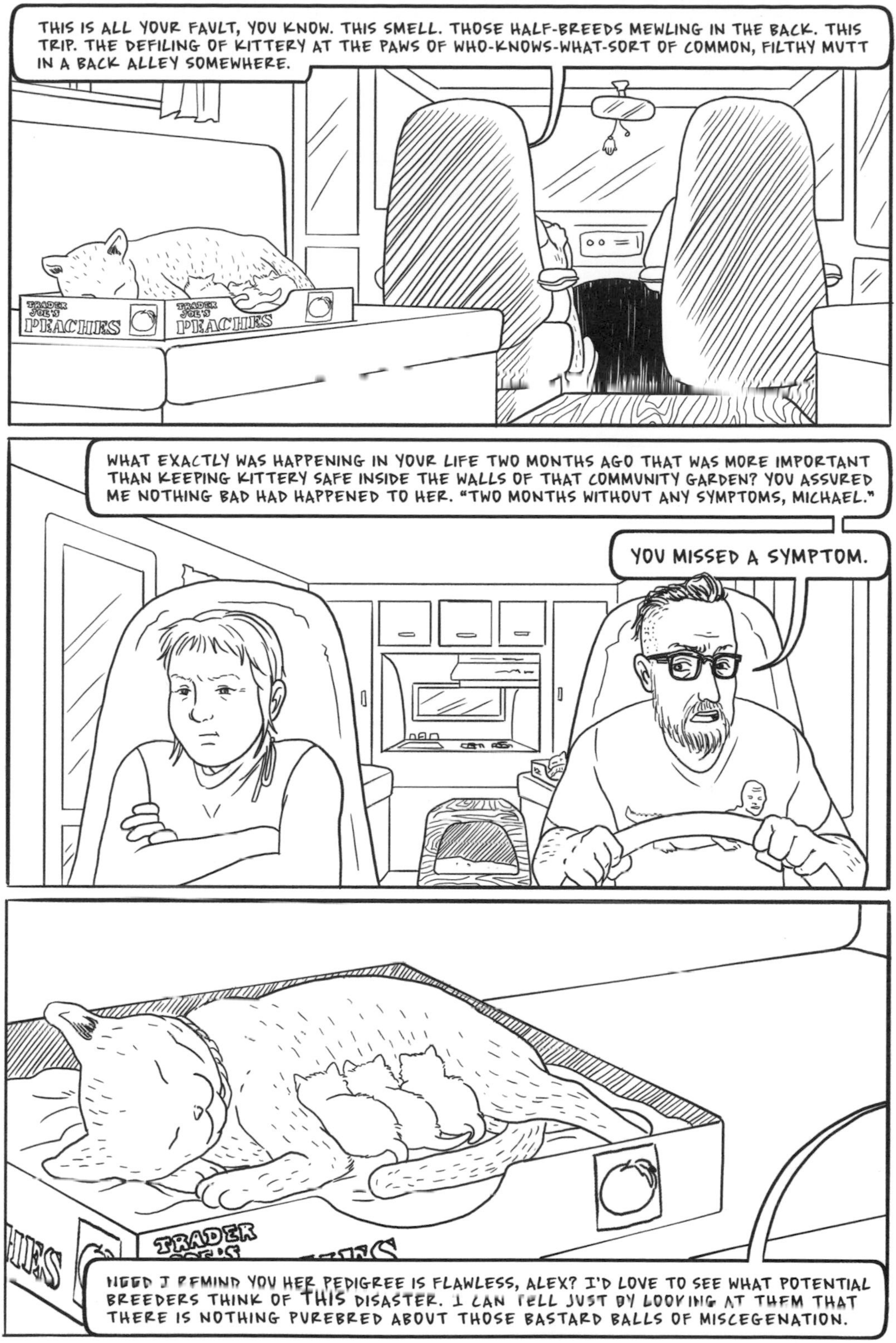
THIS IS ALL YOUR FAULT, YOU KNOW. THIS SMELL. THOSE HALF-BREEDS MEWLING IN THE BACK. THIS TRIP. THE DEFILING OF KITTERY AT THE PAWS OF WHO-KNOWS-WHAT-SORT OF COMMON, FILTHY MUTT IN A BACK ALLEY SOMEWHERE.
TRADER JOE'S PEACHES
TRADER JOE'S PEACHES
WHAT EXACTLY WAS HAPPENING IN YOUR LIFE TWO MONTHS AGO THAT WAS MORE IMPORTANT THAN KEEPING KITTERY SAFE INSIDE THE WALLS OF THAT COMMUNITY GARDEN? YOU ASSURED ME NOTHING BAD HAD HAPPENED TO HER. "TWO MONTHS WITHOUT ANY SYMPTOMS, MICHAEL."
YOU MISSED A SYMPTOM.
TRADER
NEED I REMIND YOU HER PEDIGREE IS FLAWLESS, ALEX? I'D LOVE TO SEE WHAT POTENTIAL BREEDERS THINK OF THIS DISASTER. I CAN TELL JUST BY LOOKING AT THEM THAT THERE IS NOTHING PUREBRED ABOUT THOSE BASTARD BALLS OF MISCEGENATION.

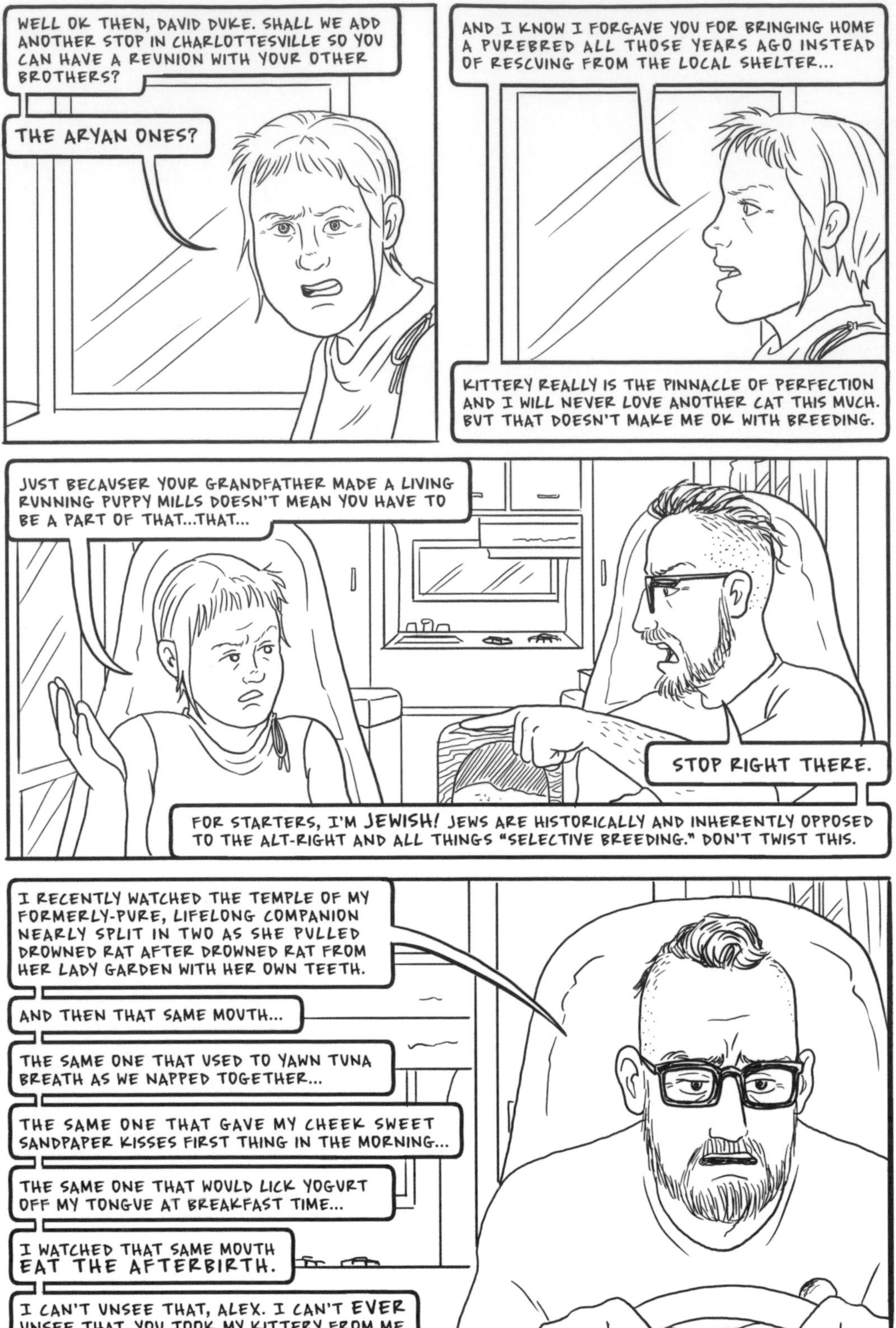
WELL OK THEN, DAVID DUKE. SHALL WE ADD ANOTHER STOP IN CHARLOTTESVILLE SO YOU CAN HAVE A REUNION WITH YOUR OTHER BROTHERS?
THE ARYAN ONES?
AND I KNOW I FORGAVE YOU FOR BRINGING HOME A PUREBRED ALL THOSE YEARS AGO INSTEAD OF RESCUING FROM THE LOCAL SHELTER...
KITTERY REALLY IS THE PINNACLE OF PERFECTION AND I WILL NEVER LOVE ANOTHER CAT THIS MUCH. BUT THAT DOESN'T MAKE ME OK WITH BREEDING.
JUST BECAUSER YOUR GRANDFATHER MADE A LIVING RUNNING PUPPY MILLS DOESN'T MEAN YOU HAVE TO BE A PART OF THAT...THAT...
STOP RIGHT THERE.
FOR STARTERS, I'M JEWISH! JEWS ARE HISTORICALLY AND INHERENTLY OPPOSED TO THE ALT-RIGHT AND ALL THINGS "SELECTIVE BREEDING." DON'T TWIST THIS.
I RECENTLY WATCHED THE TEMPLE OF MY FORMERLY-PURE, LIFELONG COMPANION NEARLY SPLIT IN TWO AS SHE PULLED DROWNED RAT AFTER DROWNED RAT FROM HER LADY GARDEN WITH HER OWN TEETH.
AND THEN THAT SAME MOUTH...
THE SAME ONE THAT USED TO YAWN TUNA BREATH AS WE NAPPED TOGETHER...
THE SAME ONE THAT GAVE MY CHEEK SWEET SANDPAPER KISSES FIRST THING IN THE MORNING...
THE SAME ONE THAT WOULD LICK YOGURT OFF MY TONGUE AT BREAKFAST TIME...
I WATCHED THAT SAME MOUTH EAT THE AFTERBIRTH.
I CAN'T UNSEE THAT, ALEX. I CAN'T EVER UNSEE THAT. YOU TOOK MY KITTERY FROM ME.

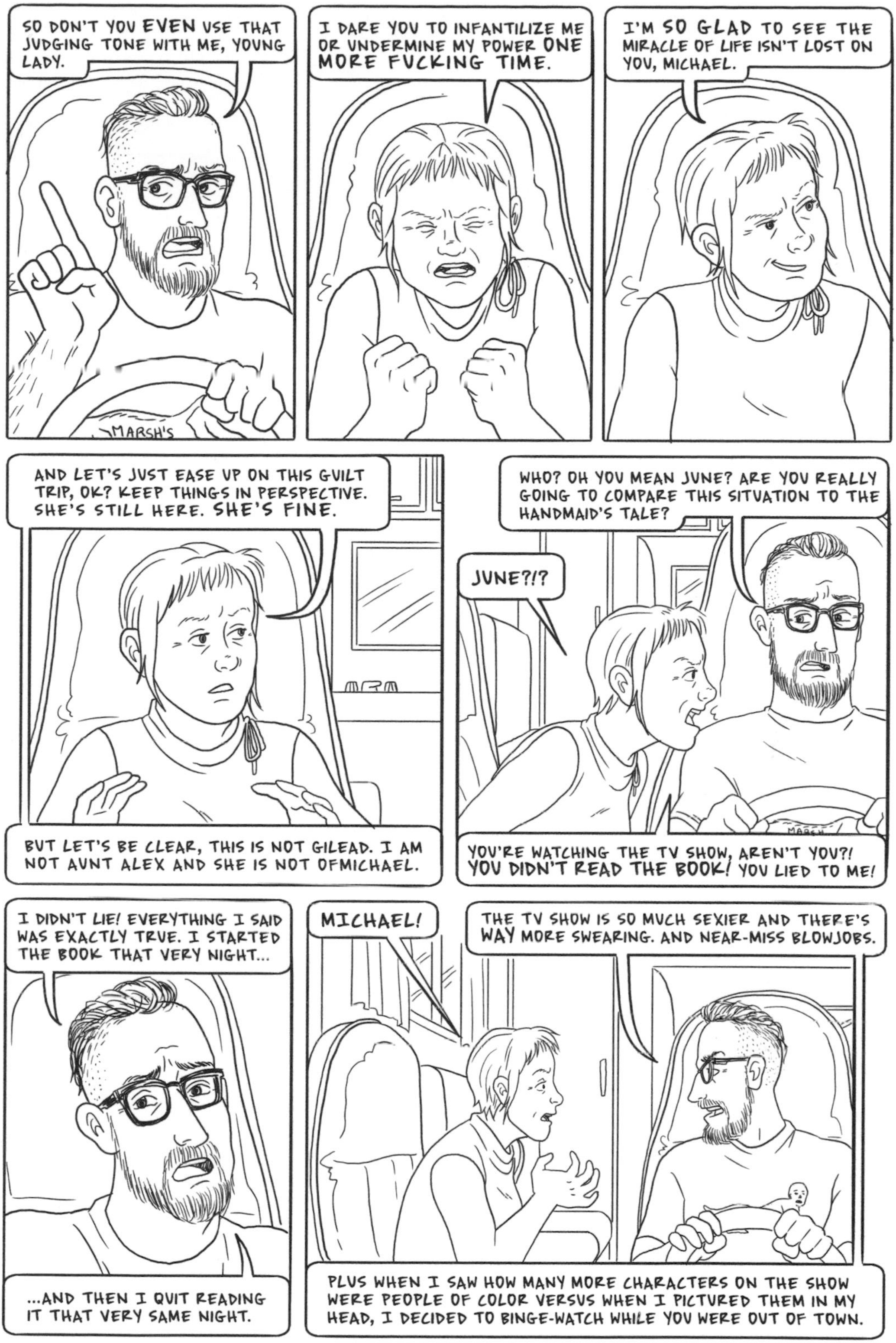
SO DON'T YOU EVEN USE THAT JUDGING TONE WITH ME, YOUNG LADY.
MARSH'S
I DARE YOU TO INFANTILIZE ME OR UNDERMINE MY POWER ONE MORE FUCKING TIME.
I'M SO GLAD TO SEE THE MIRACLE OF LIFE ISN'T LOST ON YOU, MICHAEL.
AND LET'S JUST EASE UP ON THIS GUILT TRIP, OK? KEEP THINGS IN PERSPECTIVE. SHE'S STILL HERE. SHE'S FINE.
BUT LET'S BE CLEAR, THIS IS NOT GILEAD. I AM NOT AUNT ALEX AND SHE IS NOT OFMICHAEL.
WHO? OH YOU MEAN JUNE? ARE YOU REALLY GOING TO COMPARE THIS SITUATION TO THE HANDMAID'S TALE?
JUNE?!?
YOU'RE WATCHING THE TV SHOW, AREN'T YOU?! YOU DIDN'T READ THE BOOK! YOU LIED TO ME!
I DIDN'T LIE! EVERYTHING I SAID WAS EXACTLY TRUE. I STARTED THE BOOK THAT VERY NIGHT...
...AND THEN I QUIT READING IT THAT VERY SAME NIGHT.
MICHAEL!
THE TV SHOW IS SO MUCH SEXIER AND THERE'S WAY MORE SWEARING. AND NEAR-MISS BLOWJOBS.
PLUS WHEN I SAW HOW MANY MORE CHARACTERS ON THE SHOW WERE PEOPLE OF COLOR VERSUS WHEN I PICTURED THEM IN MY HEAD, I DECIDED TO BINGE-WATCH WHILE YOU WERE OUT OF TOWN.

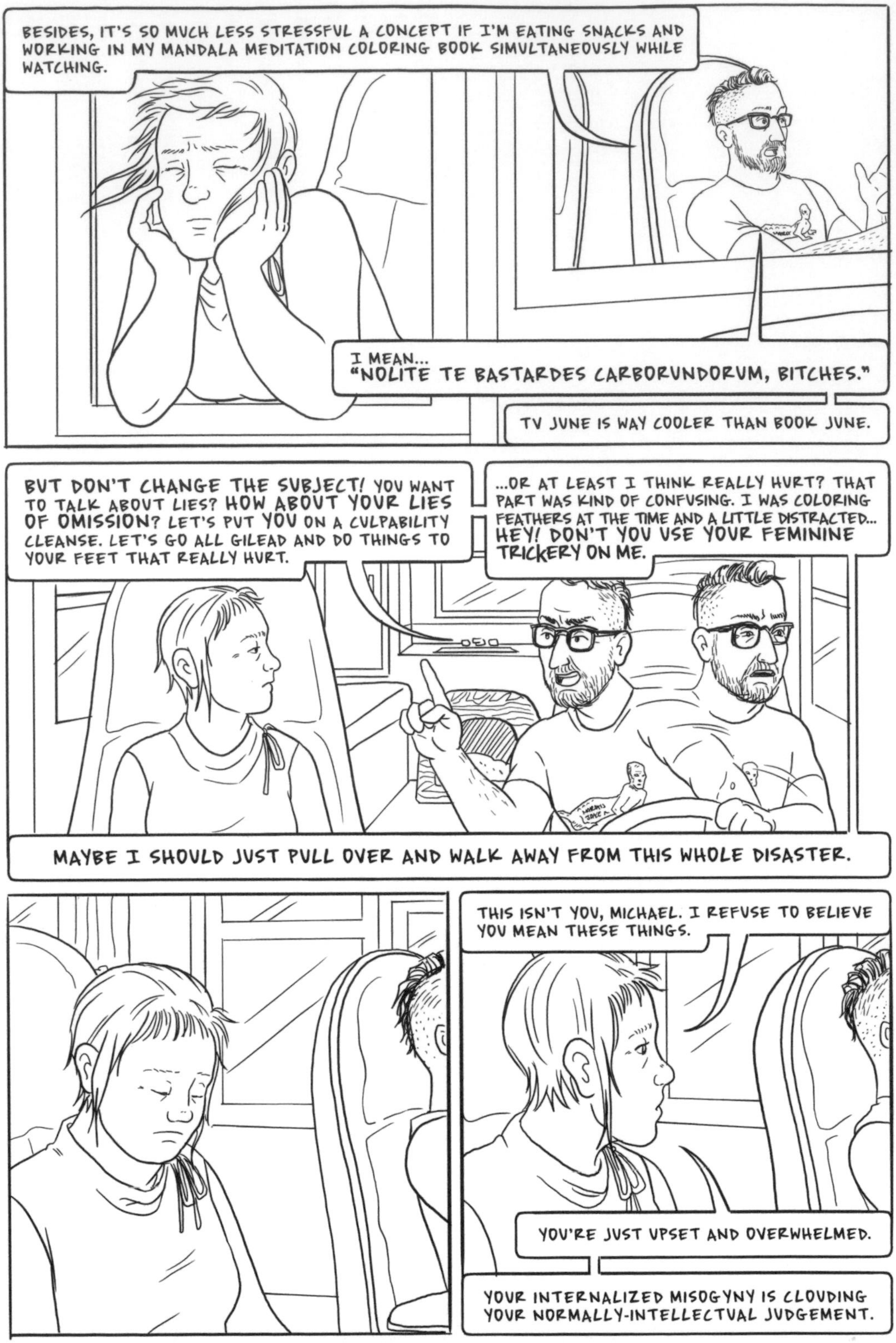

BESIDES, IT'S SO MUCH LESS STRESSFUL A CONCEPT IF I'M EATING SNACKS AND WORKING IN MY MANDALA MEDITATION COLORING BOOK SIMULTANEOUSLY WHILE WATCHING.
I MEAN... "NOLITE TE BASTARDES CARBORUNDORUM, BITCHES."
TV JUNE IS WAY COOLER THAN BOOK JUNE.
BUT DON'T CHANGE THE SUBJECT! YOU WANT TO TALK ABOUT LIES? HOW ABOUT YOUR LIES OF OMISSION? LET'S PUT YOU ON A CULPABILITY CLEANSE. LET'S GO ALL GILEAD AND DO THINGS TO YOUR FEET THAT REALLY HURT.
...OR AT LEAST I THINK REALLY HURT? THAT PART WAS KIND OF CONFUSING. I WAS COLORING FEATHERS AT THE TIME AND A LITTLE DISTRACTED... HEY! DON'T YOU USE YOUR FEMININE TRICKERY ON ME.
MAYBE I SHOULD JUST PULL OVER AND WALK AWAY FROM THIS WHOLE DISASTER.
THIS ISN'T YOU, MICHAEL. I REFUSE TO BELIEVE YOU MEAN THESE THINGS.
YOU'RE JUST UPSET AND OVERWHELMED.
YOUR INTERNALIZED MISOGYNY IS CLOUDING YOUR NORMALLY-INTELLECTUAL JUDGEMENT.

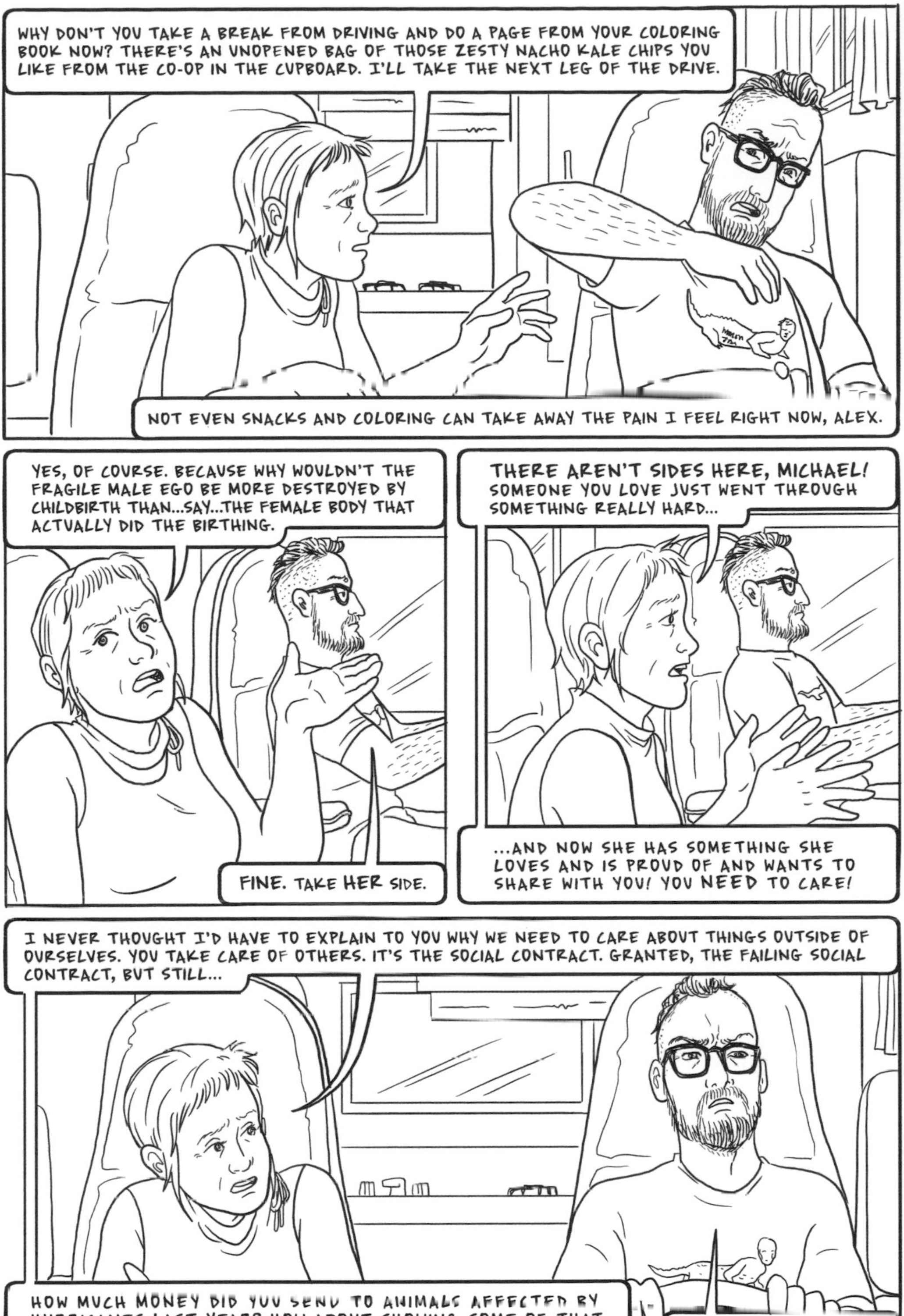
WHY DON'T YOU TAKE A BREAK FROM DRIVING AND DO A PAGE FROM YOUR COLORING BOOK NOW? THERE'S AN UNOPENED BAG OF THOSE ZESTY NACHO KALE CHIPS YOU LIKE FROM THE CO-OP IN THE CUPBOARD. I'LL TAKE THE NEXT LEG OF THE DRIVE.
NOT EVEN SNACKS AND COLORING CAN TAKE AWAY THE PAIN I FEEL RIGHT NOW, ALEX.
YES, OF COURSE. BECAUSE WHY WOULDN'T THE FRAGILE MALE EGO BE MORE DESTROYED BY CHILDBIRTH THAN...SAY...THE FEMALE BODY THAT ACTUALLY DID THE BIRTHING.
FINE. TAKE HER SIDE.
THERE AREN'T SIDES HERE, MICHAEL! SOMEONE YOU LOVE JUST WENT THROUGH SOMETHING REALLY HARD...
...AND NOW SHE HAS SOMETHING SHE LOVES AND IS PROUD OF AND WANTS TO SHARE WITH YOU! YOU NEED TO CARE!
I NEVER THOUGHT I'D HAVE TO EXPLAIN TO YOU WHY WE NEED TO CARE ABOUT THINGS OUTSIDE OF OURSELVES. YOU TAKE CARE OF OTHERS. IT'S THE SOCIAL CONTRACT. GRANTED, THE FAILING SOCIAL CONTRACT, BUT STILL...
HOW MUCH MONEY DID YOU SEND TO ANIMALS AFFECTED BY HURRICANES LAST YEAR? HOW ABOUT SHOWING SOME OF THAT SAME EMPATHY FOR THE CAT SHARING THE SAME AIR WITH YOU?
NO. CROOKED KITTERY.

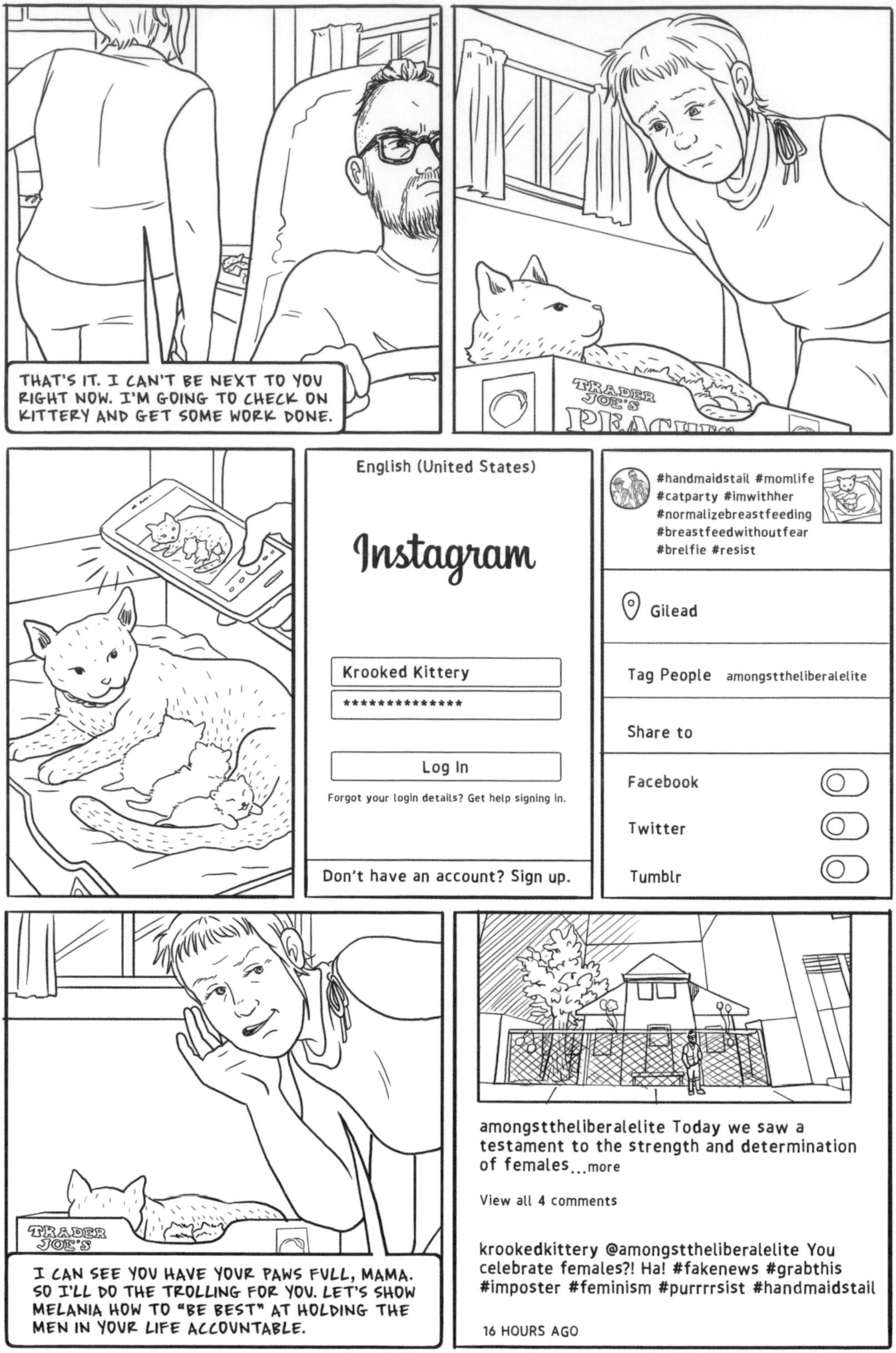
THAT'S IT. I CAN'T BE NEXT TO YOU RIGHT NOW. I'M GOING TO CHECK ON KITTERY AND GET SOME WORK DONE.
TRADER JOE'S
English (United States)
Instagram
Krooked Kittery
****
Log In
Forgot your login details? Get help signing in.
Don't have an account? Sign up.
#handmaidstail #momlife #catparty #imwithher #normalizebreastfeeding #breastfeedwithoutfear #brelfie #resist
Gilead
Tag People amongsttheliberalelite
Share to
Facebook
Twitter
Tumblr
TRADER JOE'S
I CAN SEE YOU HAVE YOUR PAWS FULL, MAMA. SO I'LL DO THE TROLLING FOR YOU. LET'S SHOW MELANIA HOW TO "BE BEST" AT HOLDING THE MEN IN YOUR LIFE ACCOUNTABLE.
amongsttheliberalelite Today we saw a testament to the strength and determination of females...more
View all 4 comments
krookedkittery @amongsttheliberalelite You celebrate females?! Ha! #fakenews #grabthis #imposter #feminism #purrrrsist #handmaidstail
16 HOURS AGO

Chapter 14

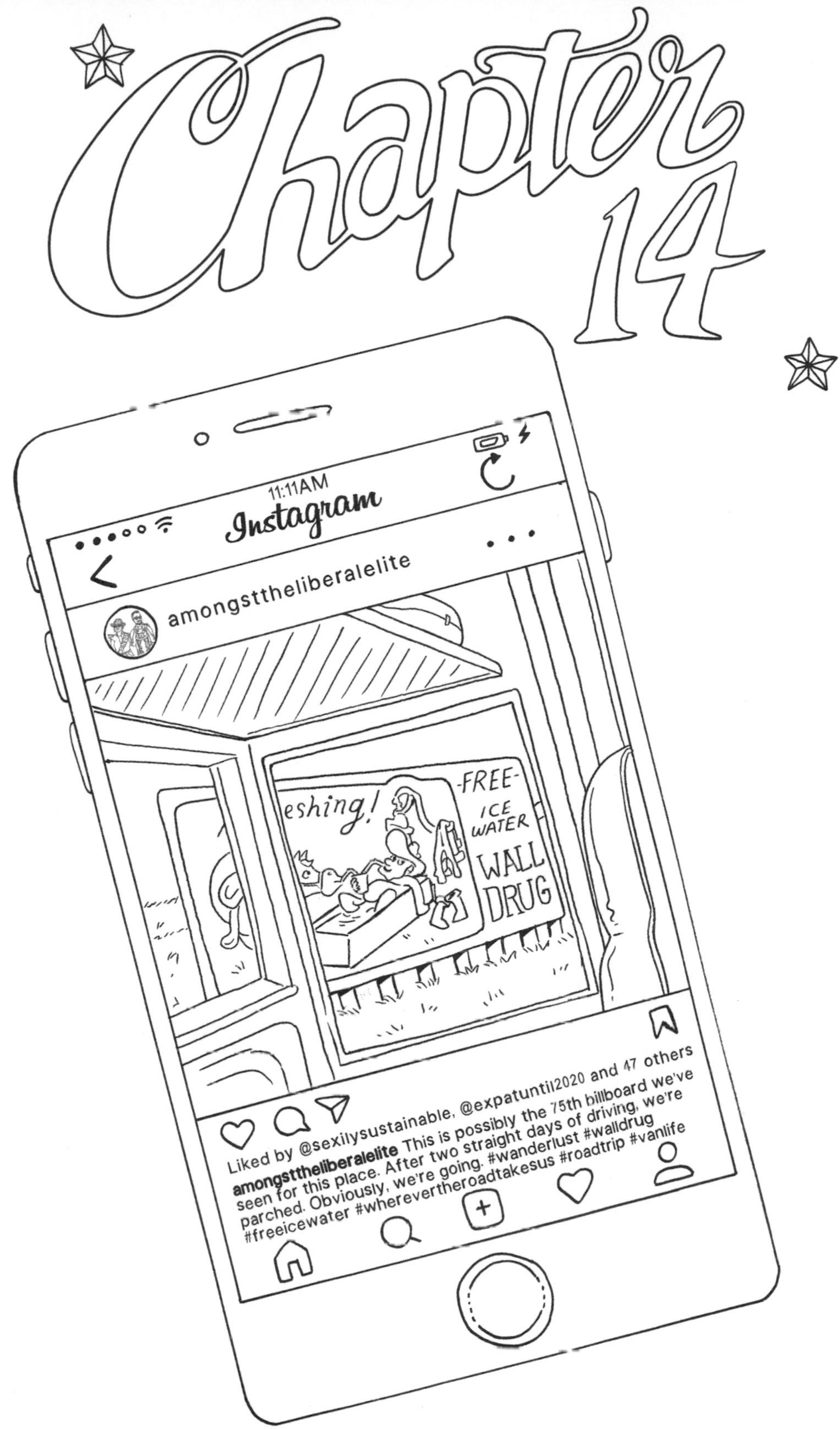
11:11AM
Instagram
amongsttheliberalelite
amongsttheliberalelite
eshing!
-FREE-
ICE WATER
WALL DRUG
Liked by @sexilysustainable, @expatuntil2020 and 47 others
amongsttheliberalelite This is possibly the 75th billboard we've seen for this place. After two straight days of driving, we're parched. Obviously, we're going. #wanderlust #walldrug #freeicewater #wherevertheroadtakesus #roadtrip #vanlife

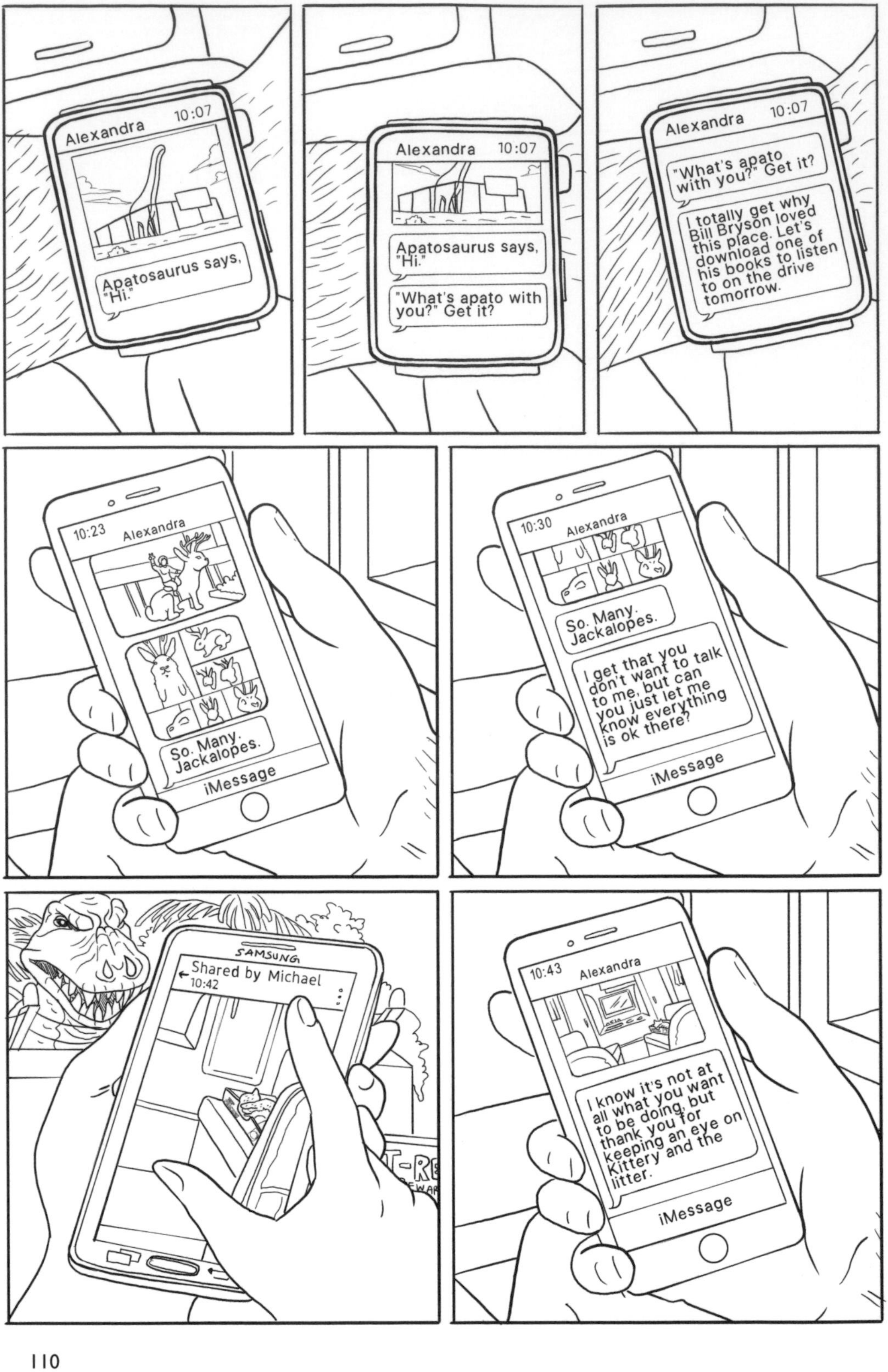
Alexandra
10:07
Apatosaurus says, "Hi."
Alexandra
10:07
Apatosaurus says, "Hi."
"What's apato with you?" Get it?
Alexandra
10:07
"What's apato with you?" Get it?
I totally get why Bill Bryson loved this place. Let's download one of his books to listen to on the drive tomorrow.
10:23
Alexandra
So. Many. Jackalopes.
iMessage
10:30
Alexandra
So. Many. Jackalopes.
I get that you don't want to talk to me, but can you just let me know everything is ok there?
iMessage
SAMSUNG
Shared by Michael
10:42
10:43
Alexandra
I know it's not at all what you want to be doing, but thank you for keeping an eye on Kittery and the litter.
iMessage

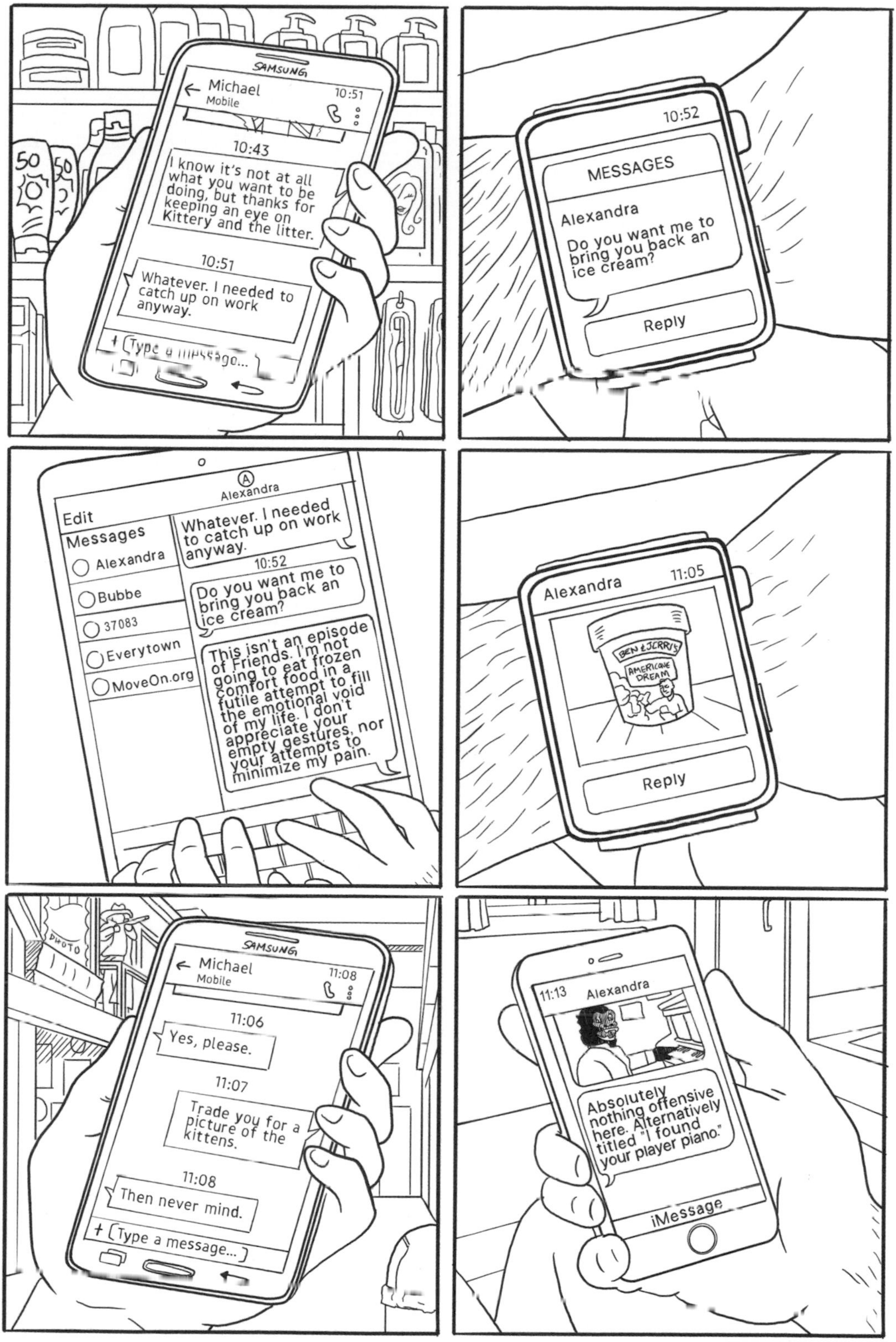
SAMSUNG
Michael
Mobile
10:51
10:43
I know it's not at all what you want to be doing, but thanks for keeping an eye on Kittery and the litter.
10:51
Whatever. I needed to catch up on work anyway.
Type a message...
10:52
MESSAGES
Alexandra
Do you want me to bring you back an ice cream?
Reply
Alexandra
Edit
Messages
Alexandra
Bubbe
37083
Everytown
MoveOn.org
Whatever. I needed to catch up on work anyway.
10:52
Do you want me to bring you back an ice cream?
This isn't an episode of Friends. I'm not going to eat frozen comfort food in a futile attempt to fill the emotional void of my life. I don't appreciate your empty gestures, nor your attempts to minimize my pain.
Alexandra
11:05
BEN & JERRY'S
AMERICONE DREAM
Reply
PHOTO
SAMSUNG
Michael
Mobile
11:08
11:06
Yes, please.
11:07
Trade you for a picture of the kittens.
11:08
Then never mind.
Type a message...
11:13
Alexandra
Absolutely nothing offensive here. Alternatively titled "I found your player piano."
iMessage

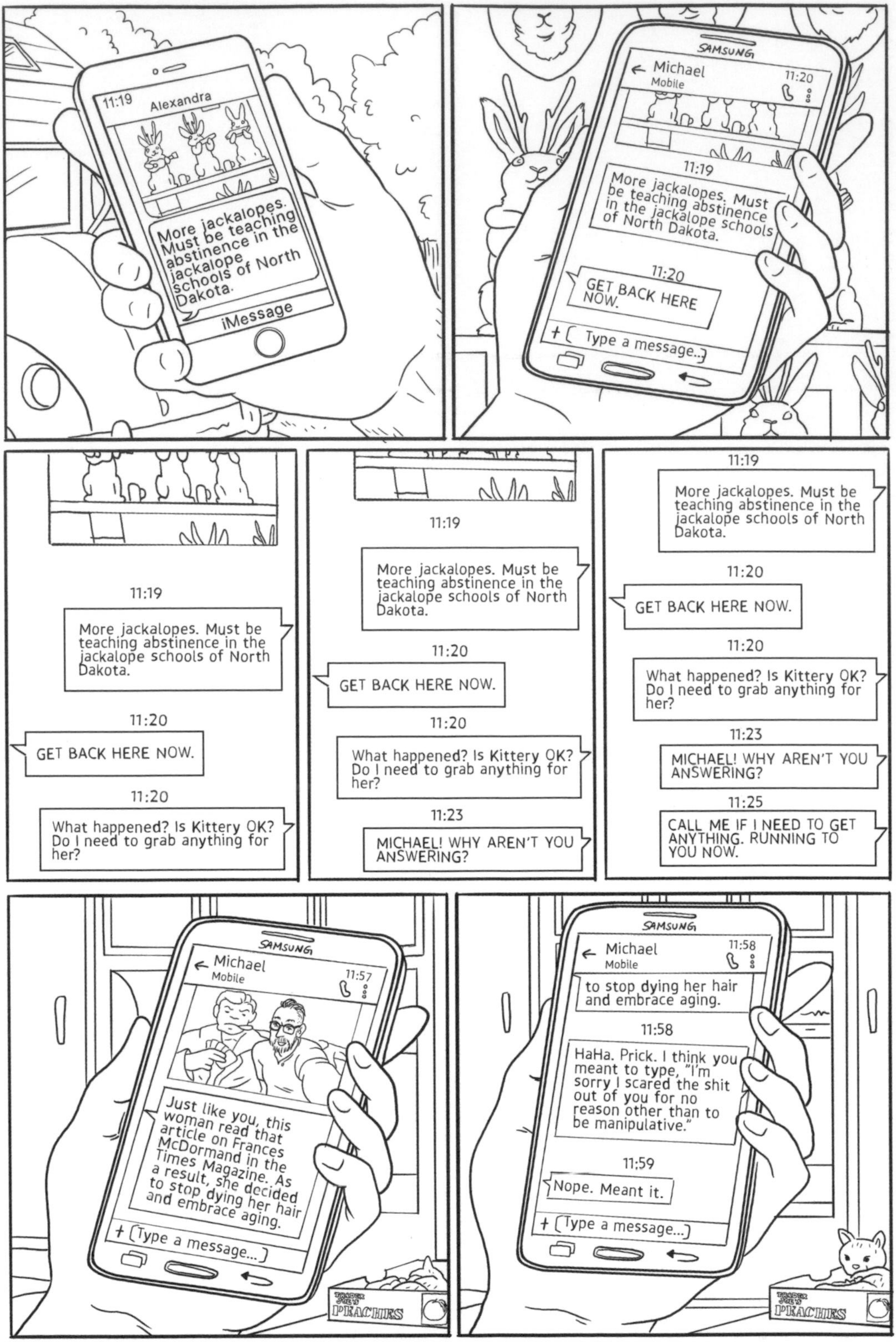

11:19
Alexandra
More jackalopes. Must be teaching abstinence in the jackalope schools of North Dakota.
iMessage
SAMSUNG
Michael
Mobile
11:20
11:19
More jackalopes. Must be teaching abstinence in the jackalope schools of North Dakota.
11:20
GET BACK HERE NOW.
Type a message...
11:19
More jackalopes. Must be teaching abstinence in the jackalope schools of North Dakota.
11:20
GET BACK HERE NOW.
11:20
What happened? Is Kittery OK? Do I need to grab anything for her?
11:19
More jackalopes. Must be teaching abstinence in the jackalope schools of North Dakota.
11:20
GET BACK HERE NOW.
11:20
What happened? Is Kittery OK? Do I need to grab anything for her?
11:23
MICHAEL! WHY AREN'T YOU ANSWERING?
11:19
More jackalopes. Must be teaching abstinence in the jackalope schools of North Dakota.
11:20
GET BACK HERE NOW.
11:20
What happened? Is Kittery OK? Do I need to grab anything for her?
11:23
MICHAEL! WHY AREN'T YOU ANSWERING?
11:25
CALL ME IF I NEED TO GET ANYTHING. RUNNING TO YOU NOW.
SAMSUNG
Michael
Mobile
11:57
Just like you, this woman read that article on Frances McDormand in the Times Magazine. As a result, she decided to stop dying her hair and embrace aging.
Type a message...
TRADER JOE'S
PEACHES
SAMSUNG
Michael
Mobile
11:58
to stop dying her hair and embrace aging.
11:58
HaHa. Prick. I think you meant to type, "I'm sorry I scared the shit out of you for no reason other than to be manipulative."
11:59
Nope. Meant it.
Type a message...
TRADER JOE'S
PEACHES

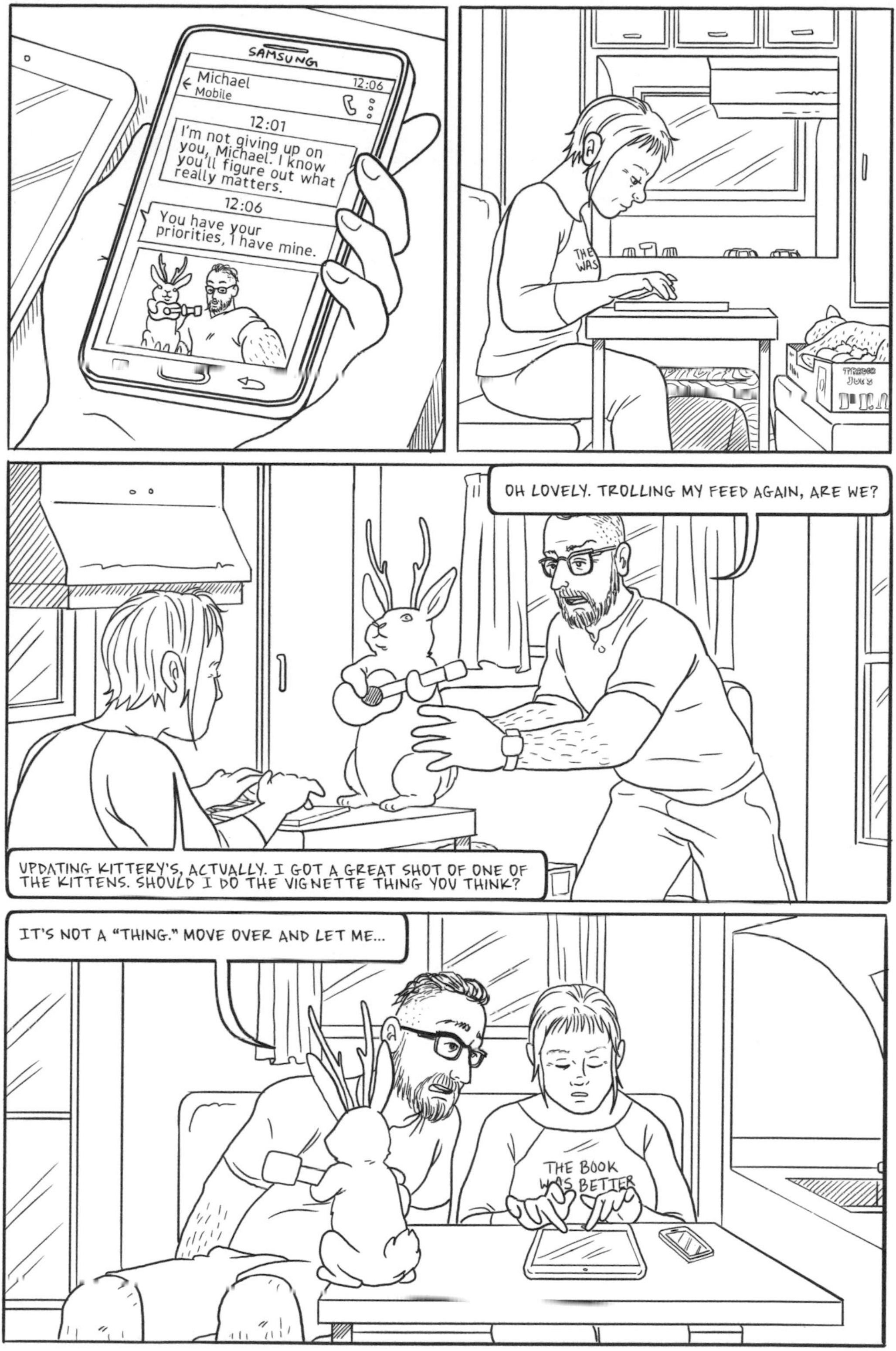
SAMSUNG
Michael
Mobile
12:06
12:01
I'm not giving up on you, Michael. I know you'll figure out what really matters.
12:06
You have your priorities, I have mine.
OH LOVELY. TROLLING MY FEED AGAIN, ARE WE?
UPDATING KITTERY'S, ACTUALLY. I GOT A GREAT SHOT OF ONE OF THE KITTENS. SHOULD I DO THE VIGNETTE THING YOU THINK?
IT'S NOT A "THING." MOVE OVER AND LET ME...
THE BOOK WAS BETTER

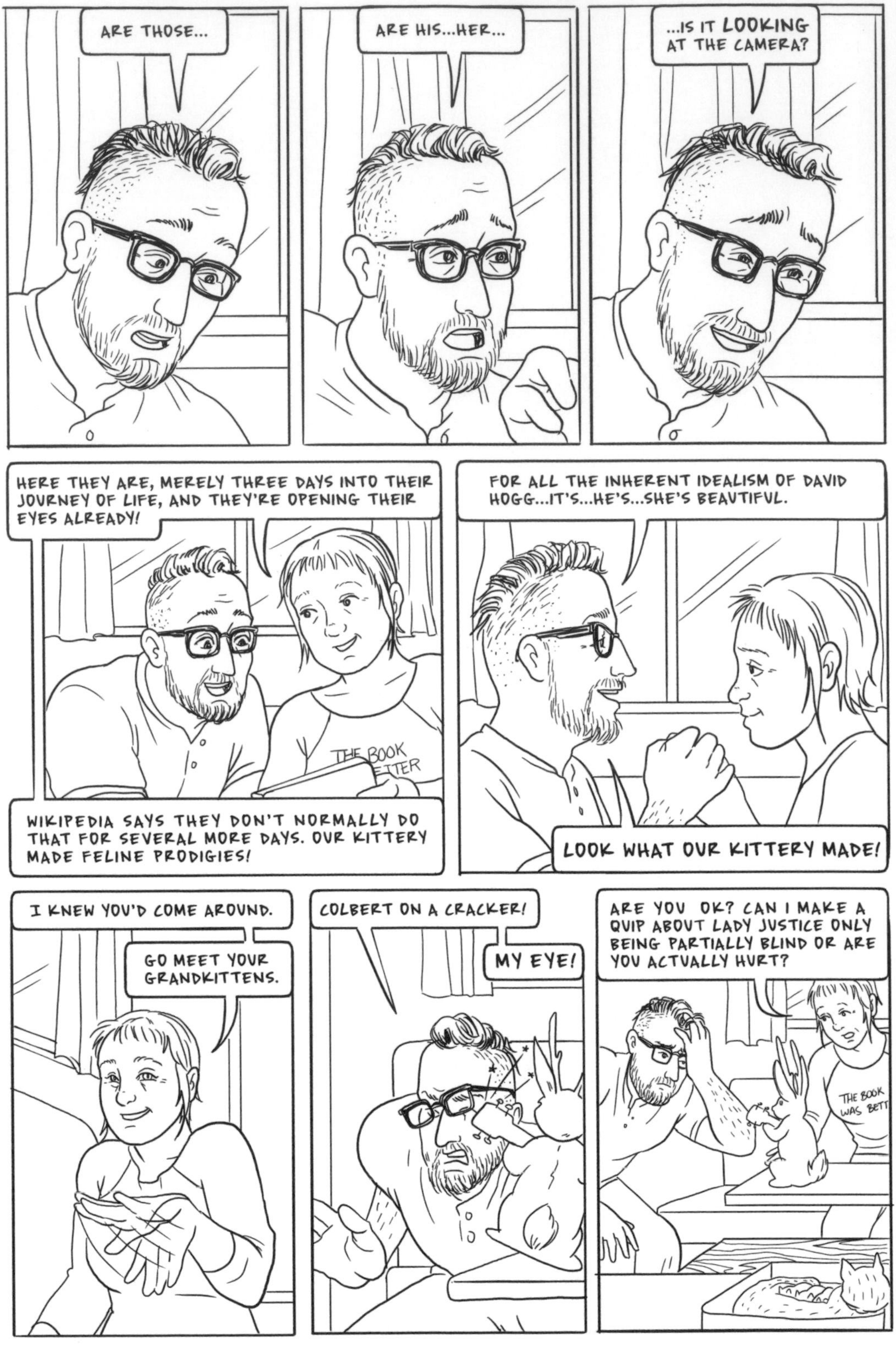
ARE THOSE...
ARE HIS...HER...
...IS IT LOOKING AT THE CAMERA?
HERE THEY ARE, MERELY THREE DAYS INTO THEIR JOURNEY OF LIFE, AND THEY'RE OPENING THEIR EYES ALREADY!
WIKIPEDIA SAYS THEY DON'T NORMALLY DO THAT FOR SEVERAL MORE DAYS. OUR KITTERY MADE FELINE PRODIGIES!
FOR ALL THE INHERENT IDEALISM OF DAVID HOGG...IT'S...HE'S...SHE'S BEAUTIFUL.
LOOK WHAT OUR KITTERY MADE!
I KNEW YOU'D COME AROUND.
GO MEET YOUR GRANDKITTENS.
COLBERT ON A CRACKER!
MY EYE!
ARE YOU OK? CAN I MAKE A QUIP ABOUT LADY JUSTICE ONLY BEING PARTIALLY BLIND OR ARE YOU ACTUALLY HURT?
THE BOOK WAS BETT

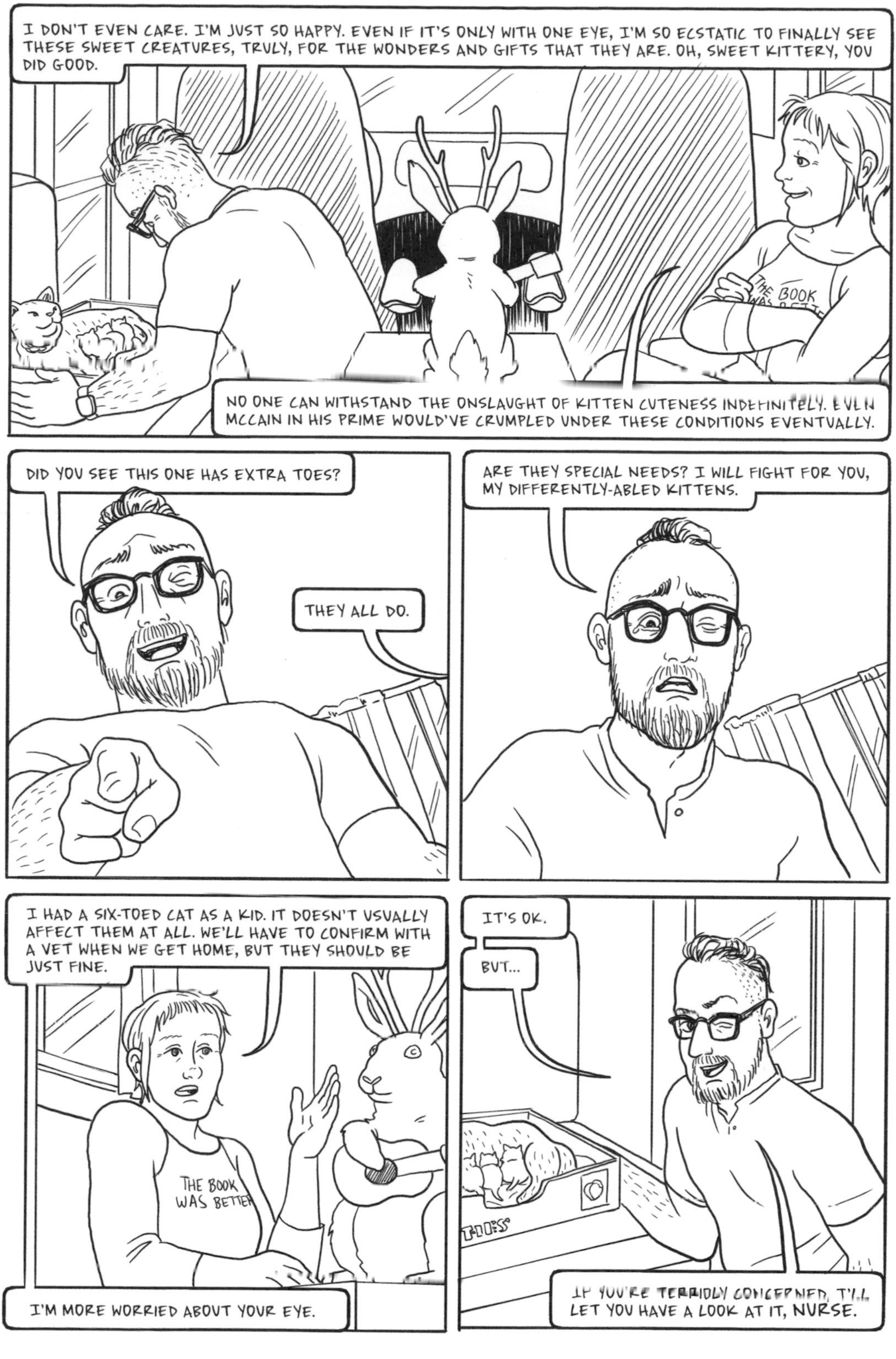
I DON'T EVEN CARE. I'M JUST SO HAPPY. EVEN IF IT'S ONLY WITH ONE EYE, I'M SO ECSTATIC TO FINALLY SEE THESE SWEET CREATURES, TRULY, FOR THE WONDERS AND GIFTS THAT THEY ARE. OH, SWEET KITTERY, YOU DID GOOD.
THE BOOK WAS BETTER
NO ONE CAN WITHSTAND THE ONSLAUGHT OF KITTEN CUTENESS INDEFINITELY. EVEN MCCAIN IN HIS PRIME WOULD'VE CRUMPLED UNDER THESE CONDITIONS EVENTUALLY.
DID YOU SEE THIS ONE HAS EXTRA TOES?
THEY ALL DO.
ARE THEY SPECIAL NEEDS? I WILL FIGHT FOR YOU, MY DIFFERENTLY-ABLED KITTENS.
I HAD A SIX-TOED CAT AS A KID. IT DOESN'T USUALLY AFFECT THEM AT ALL. WE'LL HAVE TO CONFIRM WITH A VET WHEN WE GET HOME, BUT THEY SHOULD BE JUST FINE.
THE BOOK WAS BETTER
I'M MORE WORRIED ABOUT YOUR EYE.
IT'S OK.
BUT...
IF YOU'RE TERRIBLY CONCERNED, I'LL LET YOU HAVE A LOOK AT IT, NURSE.

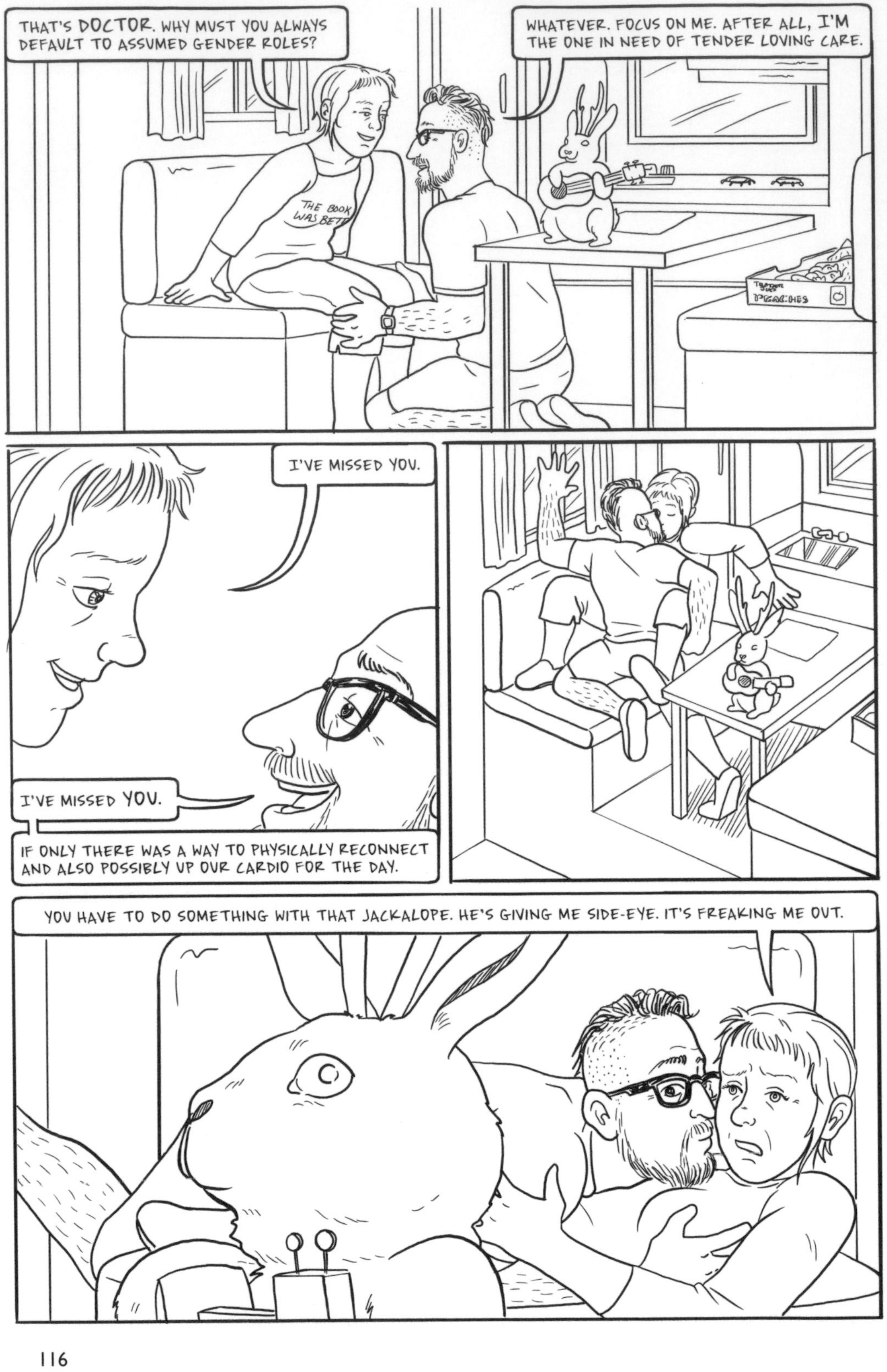
THAT'S DOCTOR. WHY MUST YOU ALWAYS DEFAULT TO ASSUMED GENDER ROLES?
WHATEVER. FOCUS ON ME. AFTER ALL, I'M THE ONE IN NEED OF TENDER LOVING CARE.
THE BOOK WAS BETT
PEACHES
I'VE MISSED YOU.
I'VE MISSED YOU.
IF ONLY THERE WAS A WAY TO PHYSICALLY RECONNECT AND ALSO POSSIBLY UP OUR CARDIO FOR THE DAY.
YOU HAVE TO DO SOMETHING WITH THAT JACKALOPE. HE'S GIVING ME SIDE-EYE. IT'S FREAKING ME OUT.

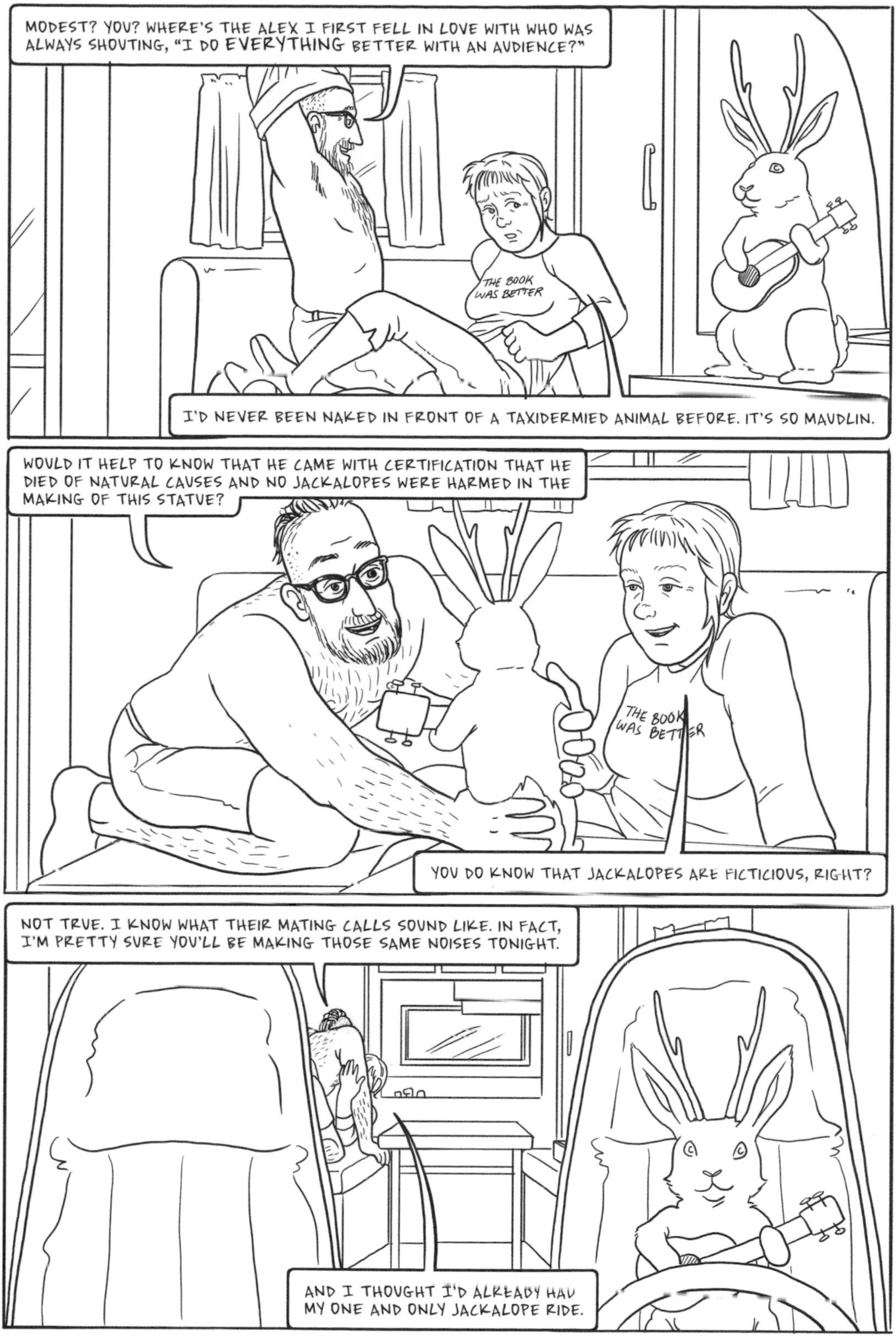

MODEST? YOU? WHERE'S THE ALEX I FIRST FELL IN LOVE WITH WHO WAS ALWAYS SHOUTING, "I DO EVERYTHING BETTER WITH AN AUDIENCE?"
THE BOOK WAS BETTER
I'D NEVER BEEN NAKED IN FRONT OF A TAXIDERMIED ANIMAL BEFORE. IT'S SO MAUDLIN.
WOULD IT HELP TO KNOW THAT HE CAME WITH CERTIFICATION THAT HE DIED OF NATURAL CAUSES AND NO JACKALOPES WERE HARMED IN THE MAKING OF THIS STATUE?
THE BOOK WAS BETTER
YOU DO KNOW THAT JACKALOPES ARE FICTICIOUS, RIGHT?
NOT TRUE. I KNOW WHAT THEIR MATING CALLS SOUND LIKE. IN FACT, I'M PRETTY SURE YOU'LL BE MAKING THOSE SAME NOISES TONIGHT.
AND I THOUGHT I'D ALREADY HAD MY ONE AND ONLY JACKALOPE RIDE.

Chapter 15

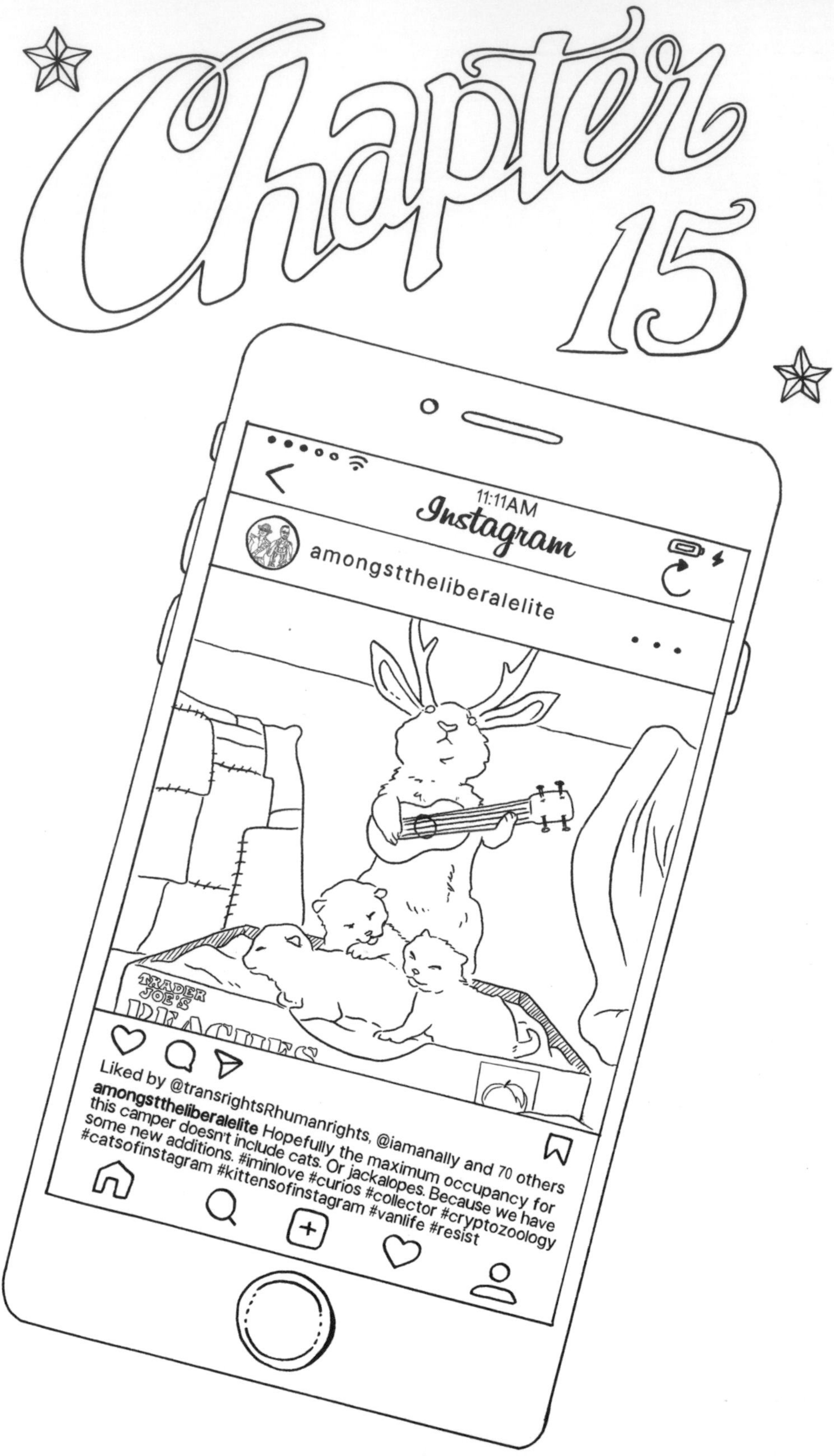
11:11AM
Instagram
amongsttheliberalelite
TRADER JOE'S
PEACHES
Liked by @transrightsRhumanrights, @iamanally and 70 others
amongsttheliberalelite Hopefully the maximum occupancy for this camper doesn't include cats. Or jackalopes. Because we have some new additions. #iminlove #curios #collector #cryptozoology #catsofinstagram #kittensofinstagram #vanlife #resist

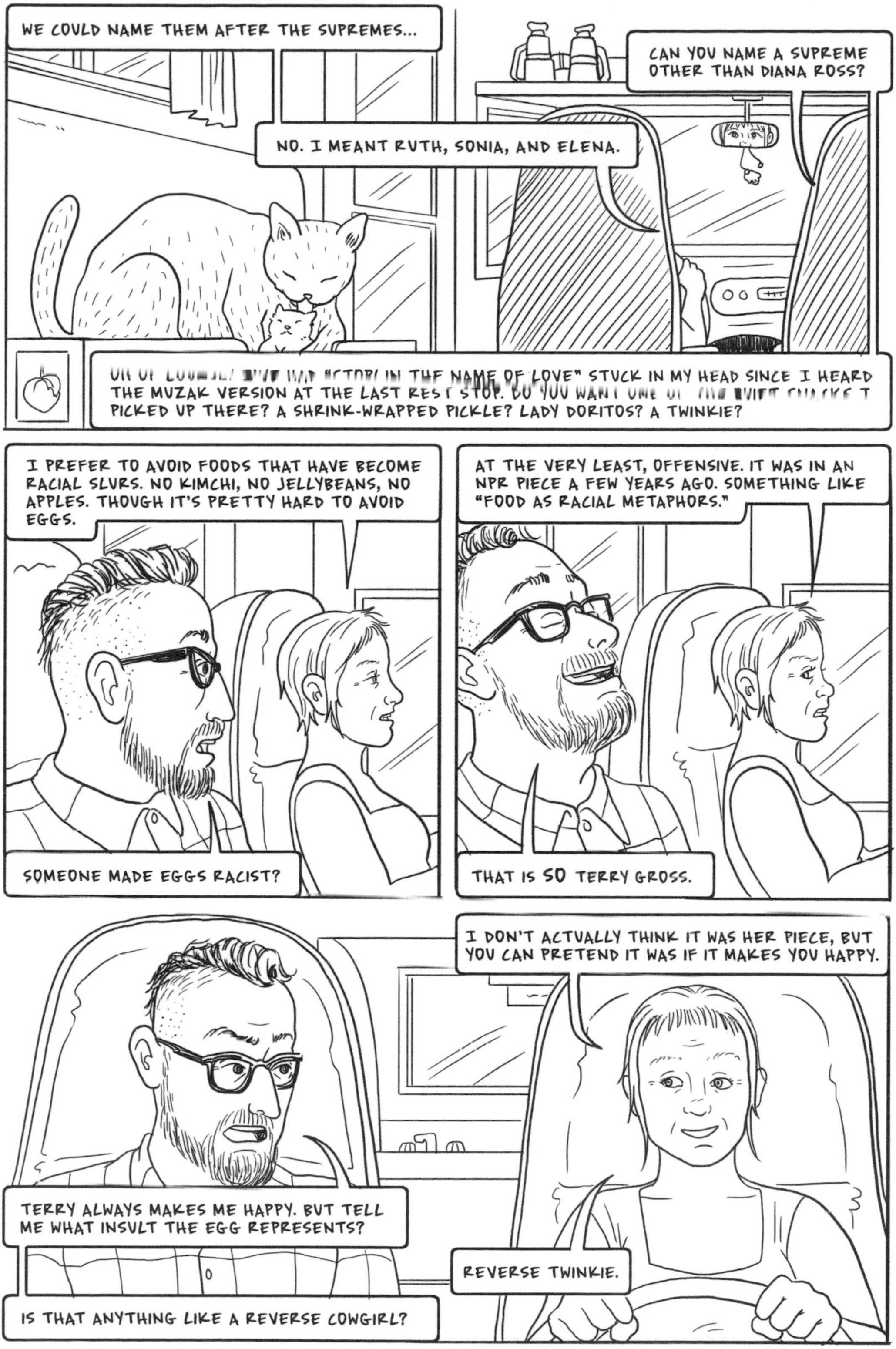

WE COULD NAME THEM AFTER THE SUPREMES...
CAN YOU NAME A SUPREME OTHER THAN DIANA ROSS?
NO. I MEANT RUTH, SONIA, AND ELENA.
IN THE NAME OF LOVE” STUCK IN MY HEAD SINCE I HEARD THE MUZAK VERSION AT THE LAST REST STOP. PICKED UP THERE? A SHRINK-WRAPPED PICKLE? LADY DORITOS? A TWINKIE?
I PREFER TO AVOID FOODS THAT HAVE BECOME RACIAL SLURS. NO KIMCHI, NO JELLYBEANS, NO APPLES. THOUGH IT'S PRETTY HARD TO AVOID EGGS.
SOMEONE MADE EGGS RACIST?
AT THE VERY LEAST, OFFENSIVE. IT WAS IN AN NPR PIECE A FEW YEARS AGO. SOMETHING LIKE “FOOD AS RACIAL METAPHORS.”
THAT IS SO TERRY GROSS.
I DON'T ACTUALLY THINK IT WAS HER PIECE, BUT YOU CAN PRETEND IT WAS IF IT MAKES YOU HAPPY.
TERRY ALWAYS MAKES ME HAPPY. BUT TELL ME WHAT INSULT THE EGG REPRESENTS?
REVERSE TWINKIE.
IS THAT ANYTHING LIKE A REVERSE COWGIRL?

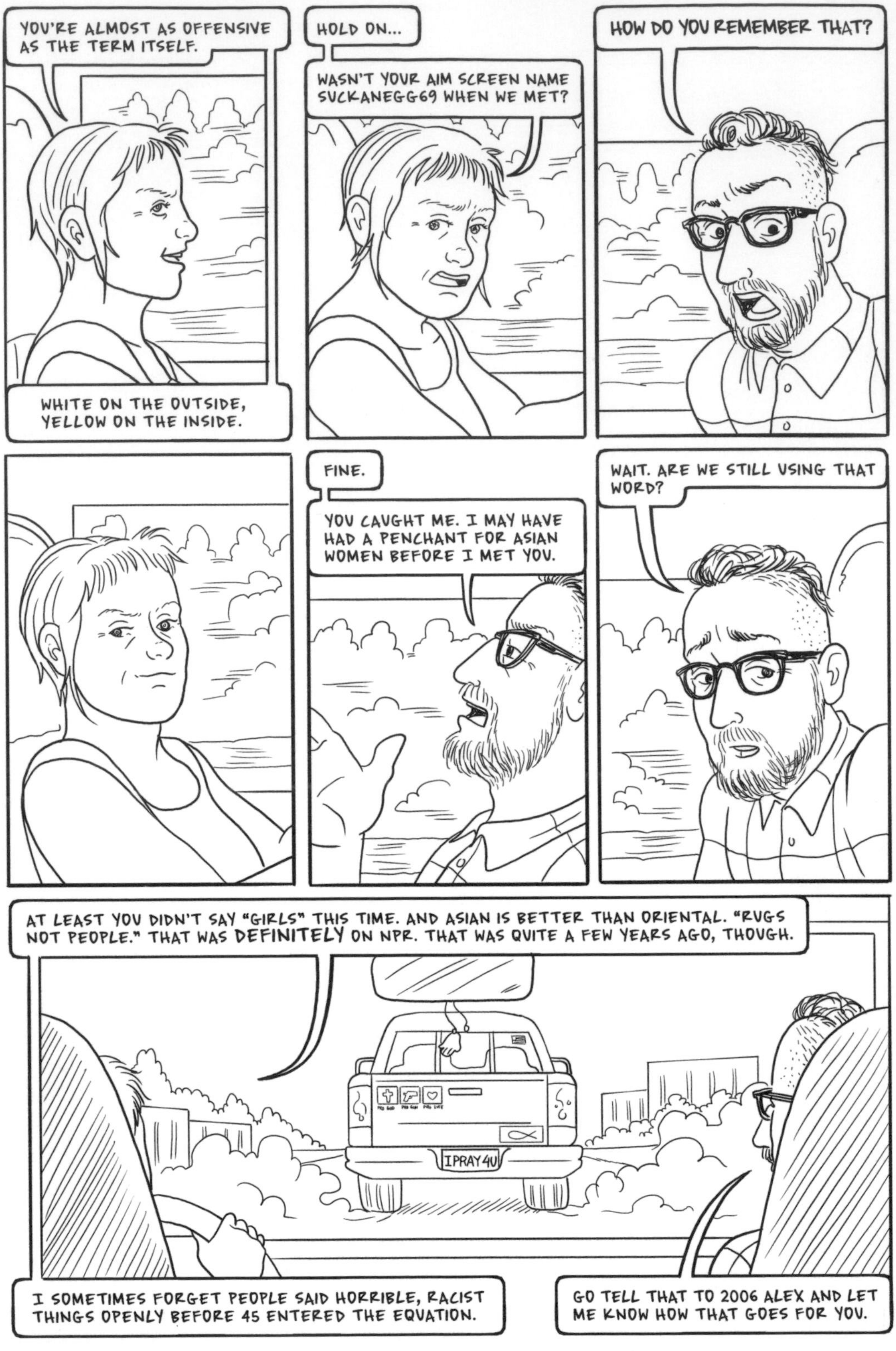
YOU'RE ALMOST AS OFFENSIVE AS THE TERM ITSELF.
WHITE ON THE OUTSIDE, YELLOW ON THE INSIDE.
HOLD ON...
WASN'T YOUR AIM SCREEN NAME SUCKANEGG69 WHEN WE MET?
HOW DO YOU REMEMBER THAT?
FINE.
YOU CAUGHT ME. I MAY HAVE HAD A PENCHANT FOR ASIAN WOMEN BEFORE I MET YOU.
WAIT. ARE WE STILL USING THAT WORD?
AT LEAST YOU DIDN'T SAY "GIRLS" THIS TIME. AND ASIAN IS BETTER THAN ORIENTAL. "RUGS NOT PEOPLE." THAT WAS DEFINITELY ON NPR. THAT WAS QUITE A FEW YEARS AGO, THOUGH.
IPRAY4U
I SOMETIMES FORGET PEOPLE SAID HORRIBLE, RACIST THINGS OPENLY BEFORE 45 ENTERED THE EQUATION.
GO TELL THAT TO 2006 ALEX AND LET ME KNOW HOW THAT GOES FOR YOU.

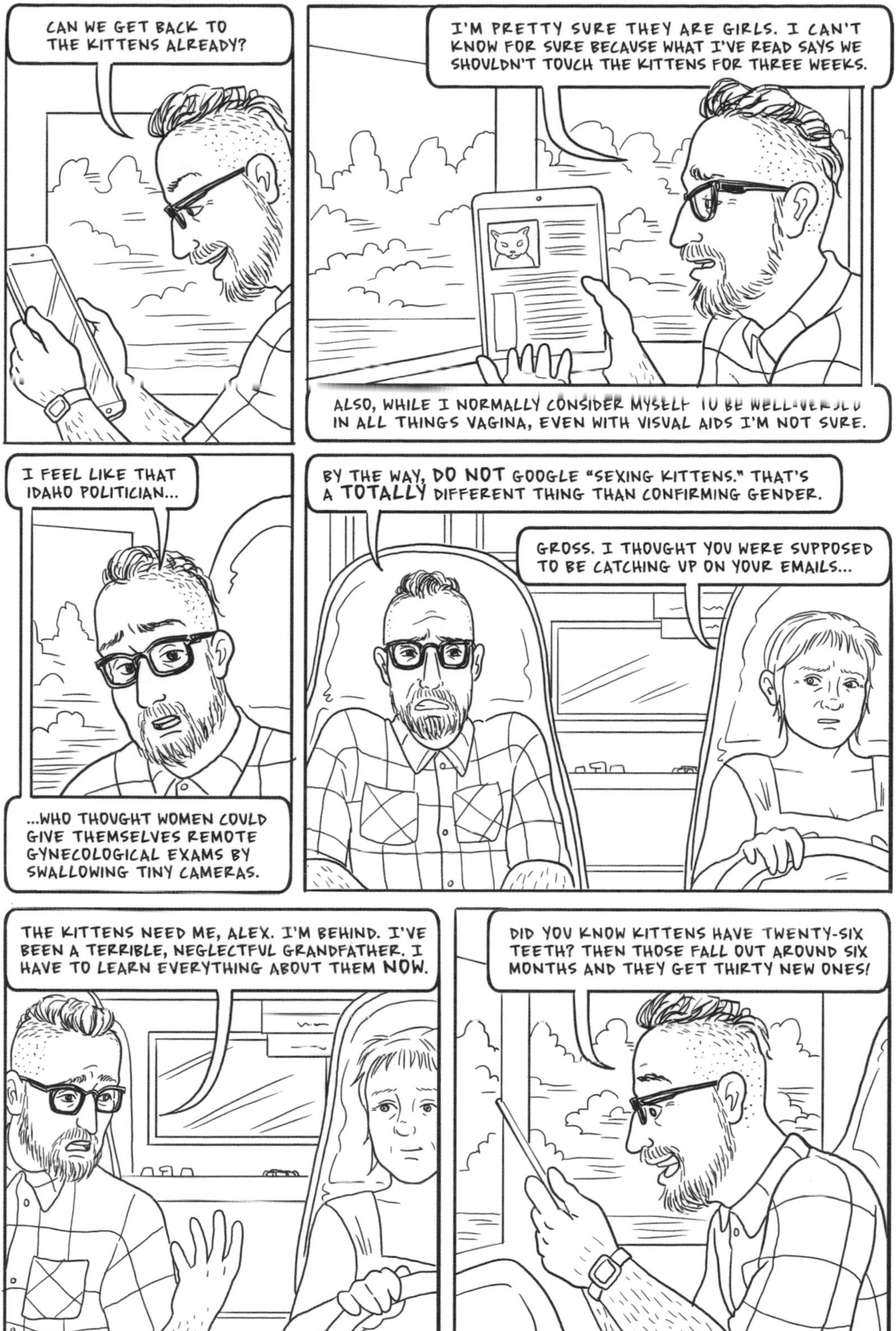

CAN WE GET BACK TO THE KITTENS ALREADY?
I'M PRETTY SURE THEY ARE GIRLS. I CAN'T KNOW FOR SURE BECAUSE WHAT I'VE READ SAYS WE SHOULDN'T TOUCH THE KITTENS FOR THREE WEEKS.
ALSO, WHILE I NORMALLY CONSIDER MYSELF TO BE WELL-VERSED IN ALL THINGS VAGINA, EVEN WITH VISUAL AIDS I'M NOT SURE.
I FEEL LIKE THAT IDAHO POLITICIAN...
...WHO THOUGHT WOMEN COULD GIVE THEMSELVES REMOTE GYNECOLOGICAL EXAMS BY SWALLOWING TINY CAMERAS.
BY THE WAY, DO NOT GOOGLE "SEXING KITTENS." THAT'S A TOTALLY DIFFERENT THING THAN CONFIRMING GENDER.
GROSS. I THOUGHT YOU WERE SUPPOSED TO BE CATCHING UP ON YOUR EMAILS...
THE KITTENS NEED ME, ALEX. I'M BEHIND. I'VE BEEN A TERRIBLE, NEGLECTFUL GRANDFATHER. I HAVE TO LEARN EVERYTHING ABOUT THEM NOW.
DID YOU KNOW KITTENS HAVE TWENTY-SIX TEETH? THEN THOSE FALL OUT AROUND SIX MONTHS AND THEY GET THIRTY NEW ONES!

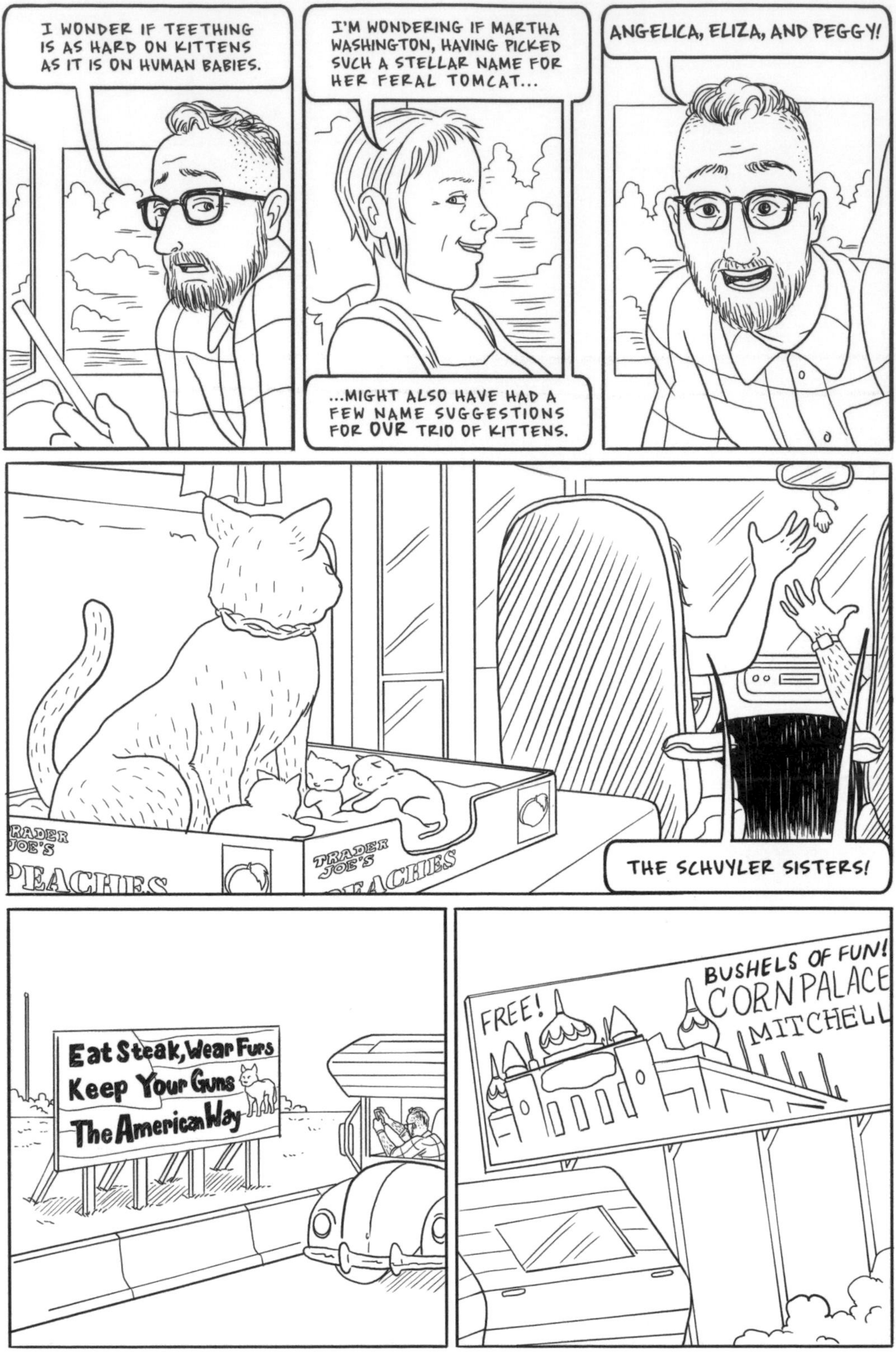
I WONDER IF TEETHING IS AS HARD ON KITTENS AS IT IS ON HUMAN BABIES.
I'M WONDERING IF MARTHA WASHINGTON, HAVING PICKED SUCH A STELLAR NAME FOR HER FERAL TOMCAT...
...MIGHT ALSO HAVE HAD A FEW NAME SUGGESTIONS FOR OUR TRIO OF KITTENS.
ANGELICA, ELIZA, AND PEGGY!
TRADER JOE'S
PEACHES
TRADER JOE'S
PEACHES
THE SCHUYLER SISTERS!
Eat Steak, Wear Furs
Keep Your Guns
The American Way
BUSHELS OF FUN!
FREE!
CORN PALACE
MITCHELL

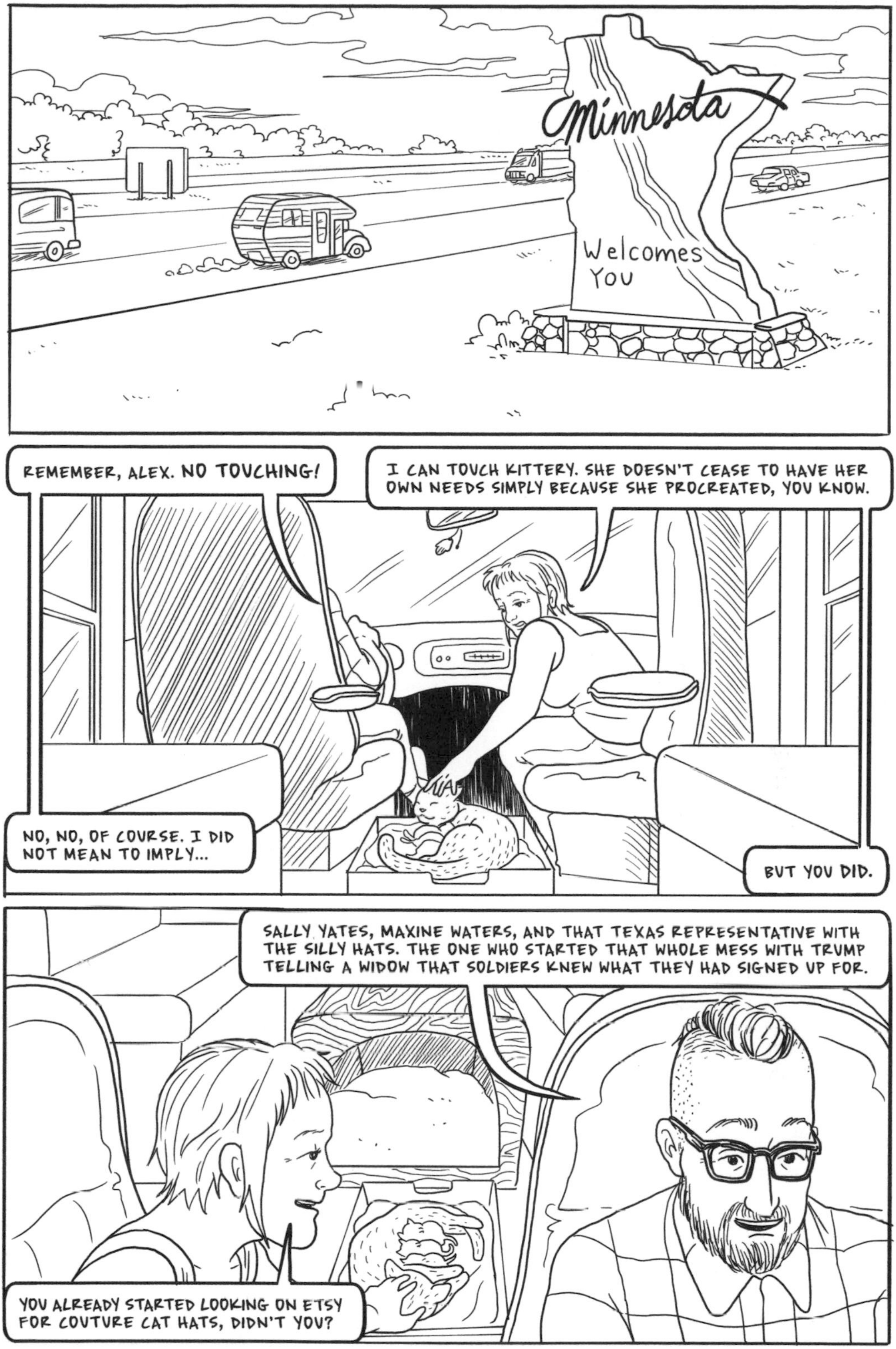
Minnesota
Welcomes You
REMEMBER, ALEX. NO TOUCHING!
I CAN TOUCH KITTERY. SHE DOESN'T CEASE TO HAVE HER OWN NEEDS SIMPLY BECAUSE SHE PROCREATED, YOU KNOW.
NO, NO, OF COURSE. I DID NOT MEAN TO IMPLY...
BUT YOU DID.
SALLY YATES, MAXINE WATERS, AND THAT TEXAS REPRESENTATIVE WITH THE SILLY HATS. THE ONE WHO STARTED THAT WHOLE MESS WITH TRUMP TELLING A WIDOW THAT SOLDIERS KNEW WHAT THEY HAD SIGNED UP FOR.
YOU ALREADY STARTED LOOKING ON ETSY FOR COUTURE CAT HATS, DIDN'T YOU?

I PLEAD THE FIFTH.

KATE MCKINNON, MELISSA MCCARTHY, AND LESLIE JONES?

MY FEELINGS FOR LESLIE ARE FAR TOO LUSTFUL FOR ME TO BE COMFORTABLE USING HER NAME TO BECKON TO OUR LITTLES.

YOU'RE STILL HAUNTED BY THAT "SEXING KITTENS" INTERNET SEARCH, AREN'T YOU?

TORMENTED.

I FEEL LIKE THE NAMES SHOULD SOMEHOW BE REPRESENTATIVE OF THIS TRIP. MAYBE DAKOTA, CAROLINA, AND...

IDAHO.

THEN EVERY TIME YOU CALL FOR IDAHO, I CAN SCREAM, "YEAH YOU DA HO!"

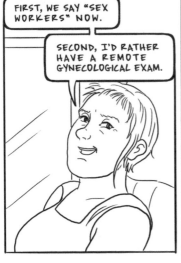

FIRST, WE SAY "SEX WORKERS" NOW.

SECOND, I'D RATHER HAVE A REMOTE GYNECOLOGICAL EXAM.

MICHAEL!

THAT WAS HYPERBOLE, NOT AN INVITATION FOR CUNNILINGUS.

YOU'RE JOSTLING THE KITTENS ON THE RUMBLE STRIPS.

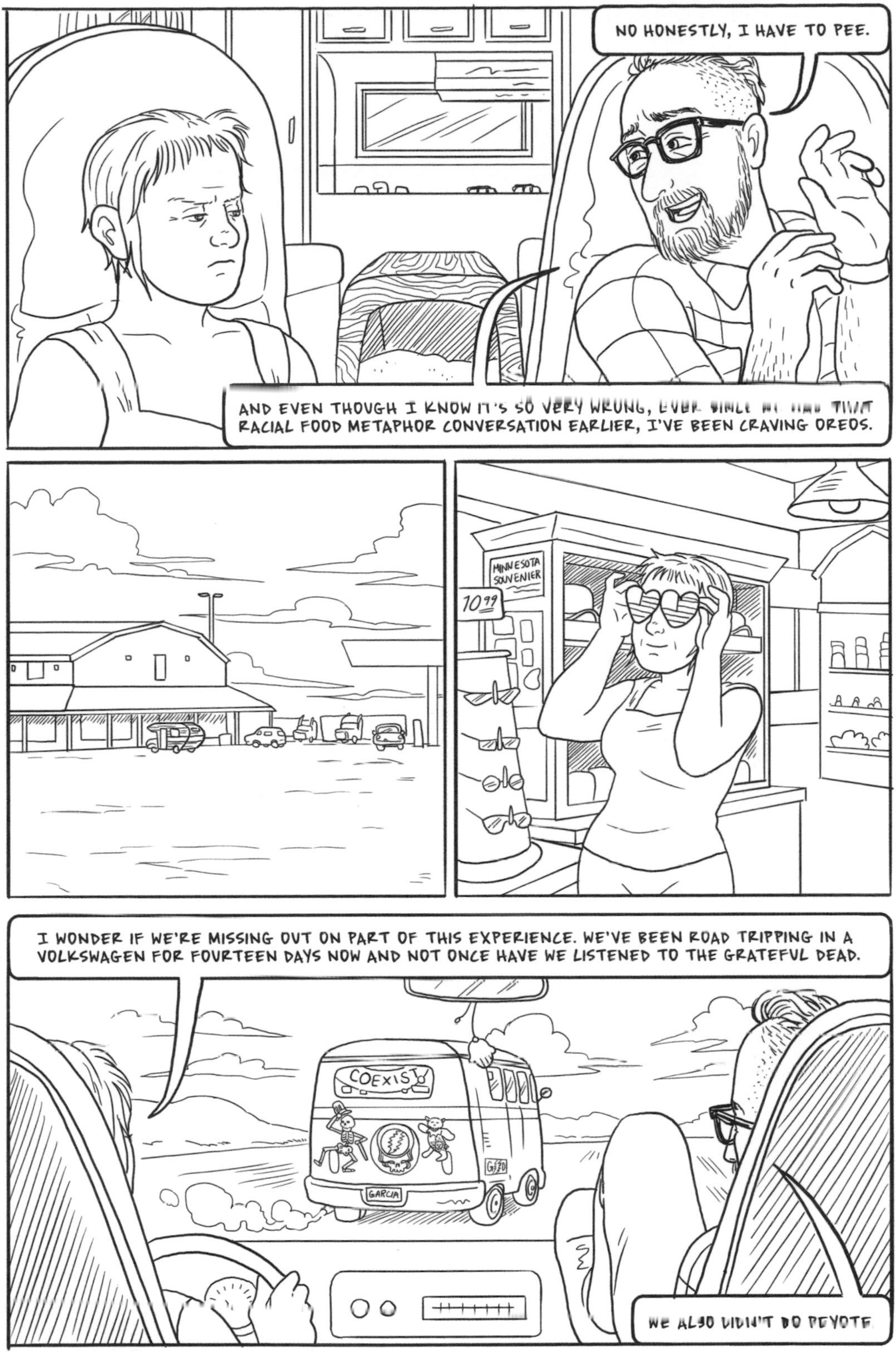

NO HONESTLY, I HAVE TO PEE.
AND EVEN THOUGH I KNOW IT'S SO VERY WRONG, EVER SINCE WE HAD THAT RACIAL FOOD METAPHOR CONVERSATION EARLIER, I'VE BEEN CRAVING OREOS.
MINNESOTA SOUVENIER
10.99
I WONDER IF WE'RE MISSING OUT ON PART OF THIS EXPERIENCE. WE'VE BEEN ROAD TRIPPING IN A VOLKSWAGEN FOR FOURTEEN DAYS NOW AND NOT ONCE HAVE WE LISTENED TO THE GRATEFUL DEAD.
COEXIST
GARCIA
WE ALSO DIDN'T DO PEYOTE.

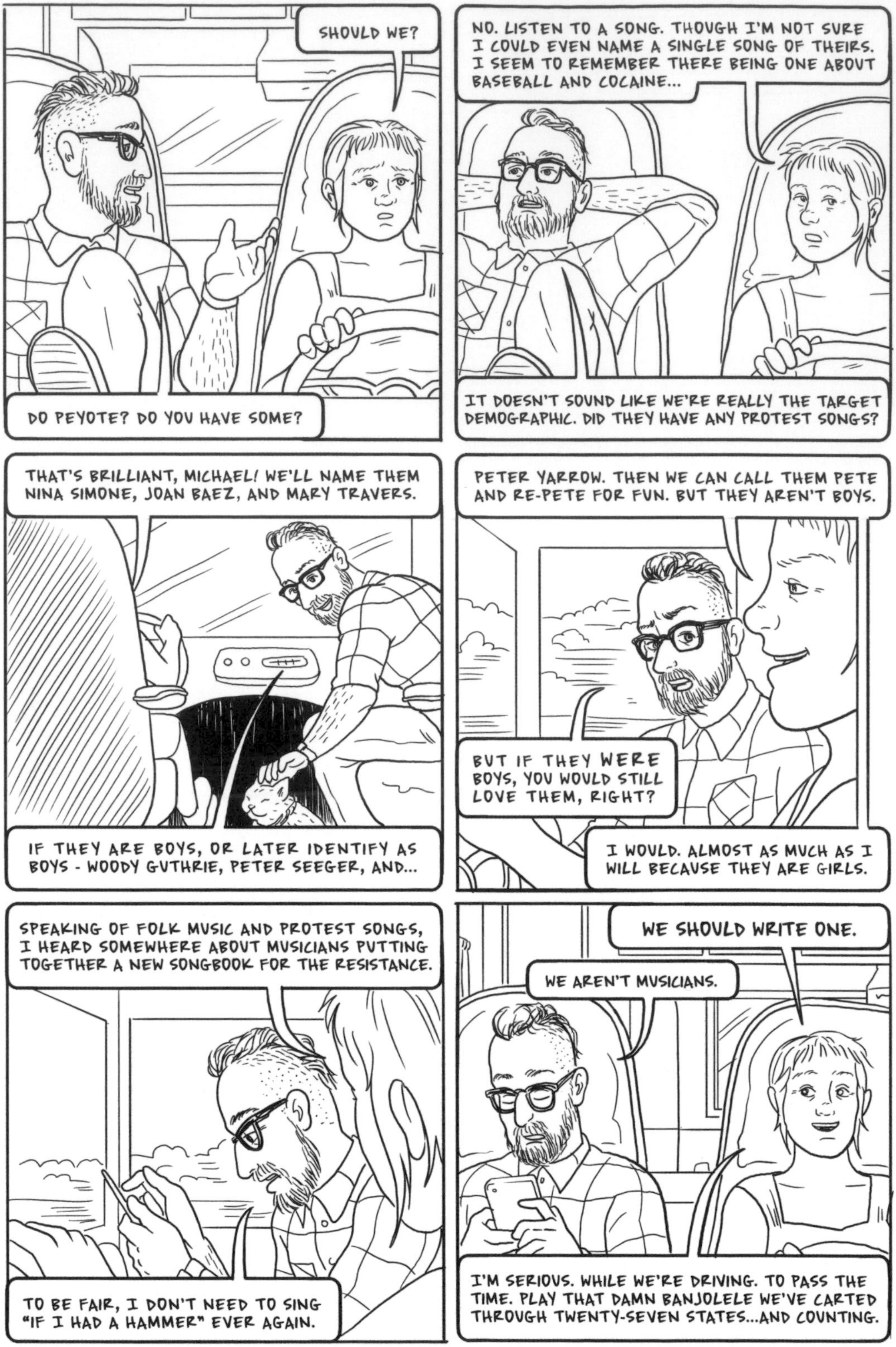
SHOULD WE?
DO PEYOTE? DO YOU HAVE SOME?
NO. LISTEN TO A SONG. THOUGH I'M NOT SURE I COULD EVEN NAME A SINGLE SONG OF THEIRS. I SEEM TO REMEMBER THERE BEING ONE ABOUT BASEBALL AND COCAINE...
IT DOESN'T SOUND LIKE WE'RE REALLY THE TARGET DEMOGRAPHIC. DID THEY HAVE ANY PROTEST SONGS?
THAT'S BRILLIANT, MICHAEL! WE'LL NAME THEM NINA SIMONE, JOAN BAEZ, AND MARY TRAVERS.
IF THEY ARE BOYS, OR LATER IDENTIFY AS BOYS - WOODY GUTHRIE, PETER SEEGER, AND...
PETER YARROW. THEN WE CAN CALL THEM PETE AND RE-PETE FOR FUN. BUT THEY AREN'T BOYS.
BUT IF THEY WERE BOYS, YOU WOULD STILL LOVE THEM, RIGHT?
I WOULD. ALMOST AS MUCH AS I WILL BECAUSE THEY ARE GIRLS.
SPEAKING OF FOLK MUSIC AND PROTEST SONGS, I HEARD SOMEWHERE ABOUT MUSICIANS PUTTING TOGETHER A NEW SONGBOOK FOR THE RESISTANCE.
TO BE FAIR, I DON'T NEED TO SING "IF I HAD A HAMMER" EVER AGAIN.
WE SHOULD WRITE ONE.
WE AREN'T MUSICIANS.
I'M SERIOUS. WHILE WE'RE DRIVING. TO PASS THE TIME. PLAY THAT DAMN BANJOLELE WE'VE CARTED THROUGH TWENTY-SEVEN STATES...AND COUNTING.

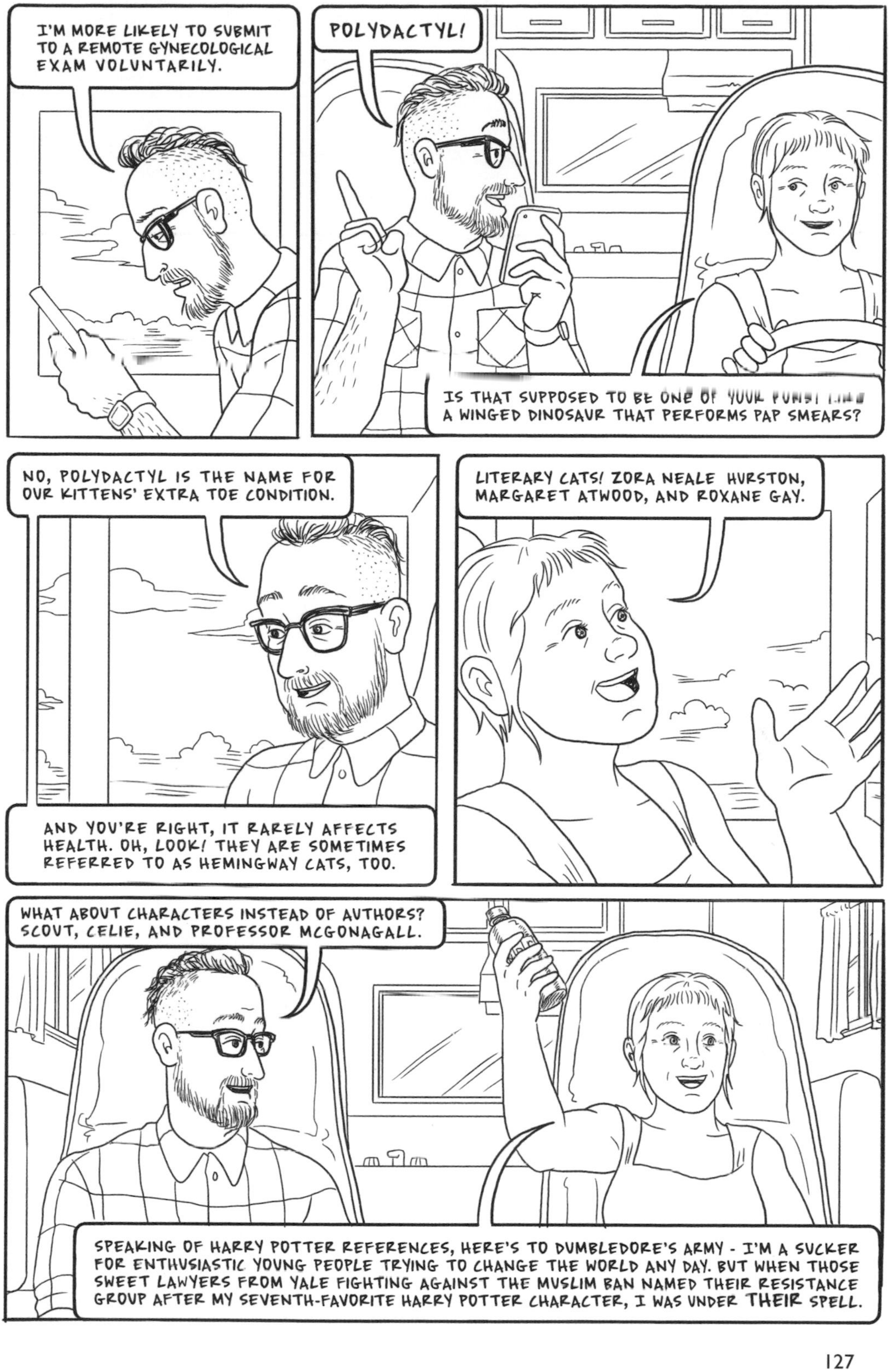
I'M MORE LIKELY TO SUBMIT TO A REMOTE GYNECOLOGICAL EXAM VOLUNTARILY.
POLYDACTYL!
IS THAT SUPPOSED TO BE ONE OF YOUR PUNS?
A WINGED DINOSAUR THAT PERFORMS PAP SMEARS?
NO, POLYDACTYL IS THE NAME FOR OUR KITTENS' EXTRA TOE CONDITION.
AND YOU'RE RIGHT, IT RARELY AFFECTS HEALTH. OH, LOOK! THEY ARE SOMETIMES REFERRED TO AS HEMINGWAY CATS, TOO.
LITERARY CATS! ZORA NEALE HURSTON, MARGARET ATWOOD, AND ROXANE GAY.
WHAT ABOUT CHARACTERS INSTEAD OF AUTHORS? SCOUT, CELIE, AND PROFESSOR MCGONAGALL.
SPEAKING OF HARRY POTTER REFERENCES, HERE'S TO DUMBLEDORE'S ARMY - I'M A SUCKER FOR ENTHUSIASTIC YOUNG PEOPLE TRYING TO CHANGE THE WORLD ANY DAY. BUT WHEN THOSE SWEET LAWYERS FROM YALE FIGHTING AGAINST THE MUSLIM BAN NAMED THEIR RESISTANCE GROUP AFTER MY SEVENTH-FAVORITE HARRY POTTER CHARACTER, I WAS UNDER THEIR SPELL.

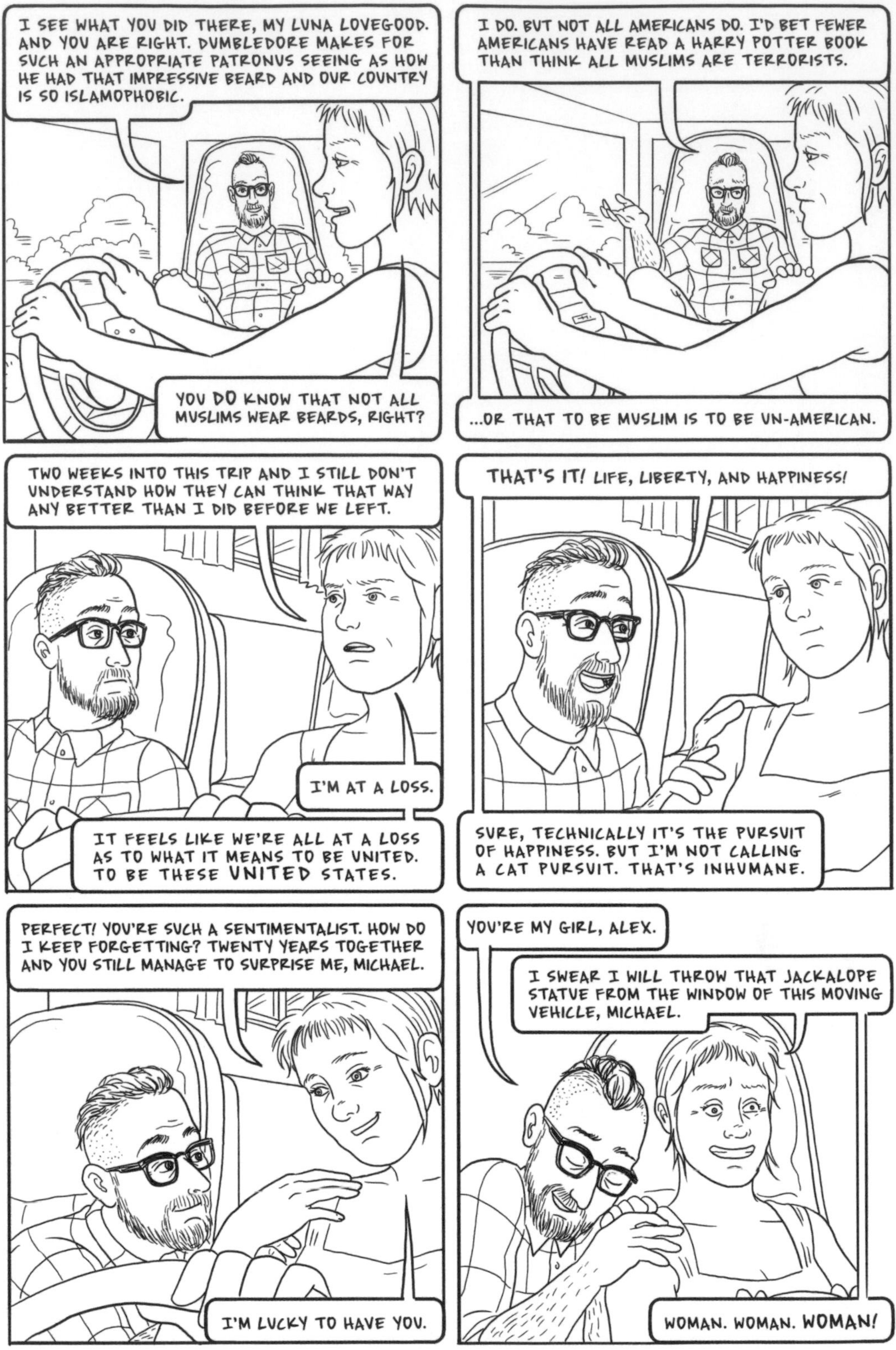
I SEE WHAT YOU DID THERE, MY LUNA LOVEGOOD. AND YOU ARE RIGHT. DUMBLEDORE MAKES FOR SUCH AN APPROPRIATE PATRONUS SEEING AS HOW HE HAD THAT IMPRESSIVE BEARD AND OUR COUNTRY IS SO ISLAMOPHOBIC.
YOU DO KNOW THAT NOT ALL MUSLIMS WEAR BEARDS, RIGHT?
I DO. BUT NOT ALL AMERICANS DO. I'D BET FEWER AMERICANS HAVE READ A HARRY POTTER BOOK THAN THINK ALL MUSLIMS ARE TERRORISTS.
...OR THAT TO BE MUSLIM IS TO BE UN-AMERICAN.
TWO WEEKS INTO THIS TRIP AND I STILL DON'T UNDERSTAND HOW THEY CAN THINK THAT WAY ANY BETTER THAN I DID BEFORE WE LEFT.
I'M AT A LOSS.
IT FEELS LIKE WE'RE ALL AT A LOSS AS TO WHAT IT MEANS TO BE UNITED. TO BE THESE UNITED STATES.
THAT'S IT! LIFE, LIBERTY, AND HAPPINESS!
SURE, TECHNICALLY IT'S THE PURSUIT OF HAPPINESS. BUT I'M NOT CALLING A CAT PURSUIT. THAT'S INHUMANE.
PERFECT! YOU'RE SUCH A SENTIMENTALIST. HOW DO I KEEP FORGETTING? TWENTY YEARS TOGETHER AND YOU STILL MANAGE TO SURPRISE ME, MICHAEL.
I'M LUCKY TO HAVE YOU.
YOU'RE MY GIRL, ALEX.
I SWEAR I WILL THROW THAT JACKALOPE STATUE FROM THE WINDOW OF THIS MOVING VEHICLE, MICHAEL.
WOMAN. WOMAN. WOMAN!

Chapter 16

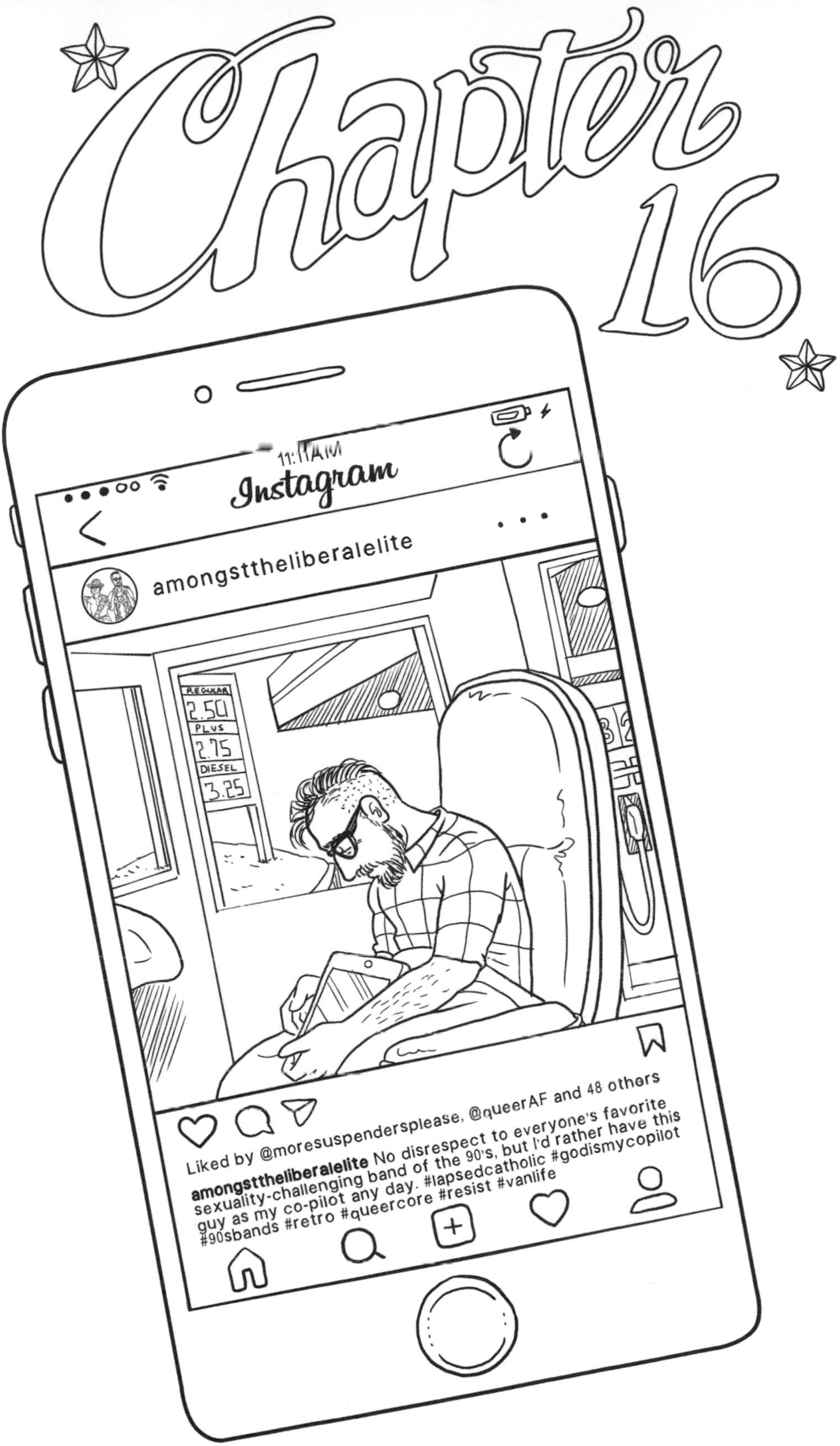
11:11AM
Instagram
amongsttheliberalelite
REGULAR
2.50
PLUS
2.75
DIESEL
3.25
Liked by @moresuspendersplease, @queerAF and 48 others
amongsttheliberalelite No disrespect to everyone's favorite sexuality-challenging band of the 90's, but I'd rather have this guy as my co-pilot any day. #lapsedcatholic #godismycopilot #90sbands #retro #queercore #resist #vanlife

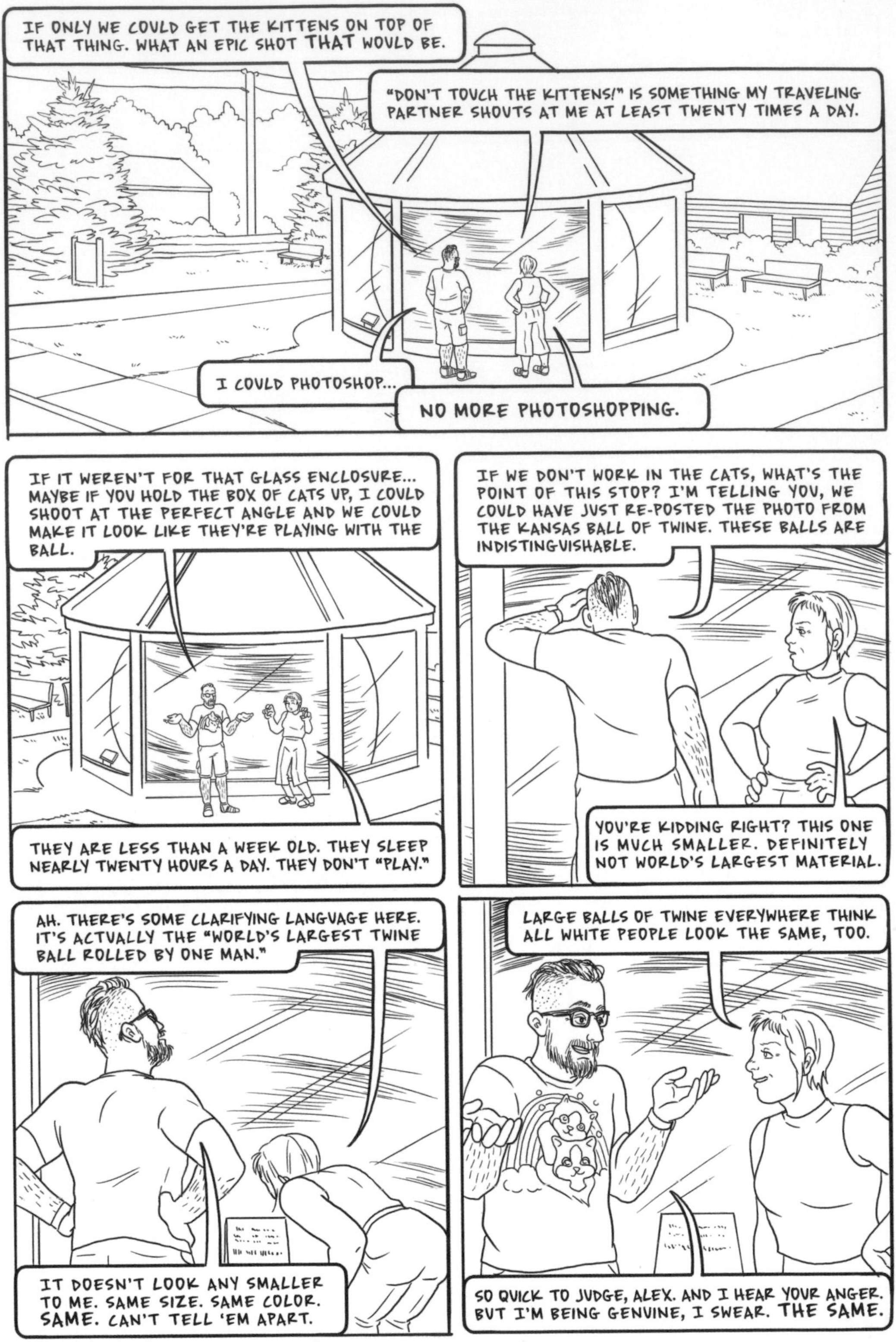
IF ONLY WE COULD GET THE KITTENS ON TOP OF THAT THING. WHAT AN EPIC SHOT THAT WOULD BE.
"DON'T TOUCH THE KITTENS!" IS SOMETHING MY TRAVELING PARTNER SHOUTS AT ME AT LEAST TWENTY TIMES A DAY.
I COULD PHOTOSHOP...
NO MORE PHOTOSHOPPING.
IF IT WEREN'T FOR THAT GLASS ENCLOSURE... MAYBE IF YOU HOLD THE BOX OF CATS UP, I COULD SHOOT AT THE PERFECT ANGLE AND WE COULD MAKE IT LOOK LIKE THEY'RE PLAYING WITH THE BALL.
THEY ARE LESS THAN A WEEK OLD. THEY SLEEP NEARLY TWENTY HOURS A DAY. THEY DON'T "PLAY."
IF WE DON'T WORK IN THE CATS, WHAT'S THE POINT OF THIS STOP? I'M TELLING YOU, WE COULD HAVE JUST RE-POSTED THE PHOTO FROM THE KANSAS BALL OF TWINE. THESE BALLS ARE INDISTINGUISHABLE.
YOU'RE KIDDING RIGHT? THIS ONE IS MUCH SMALLER. DEFINITELY NOT WORLD'S LARGEST MATERIAL.
AH. THERE'S SOME CLARIFYING LANGUAGE HERE. IT'S ACTUALLY THE "WORLD'S LARGEST TWINE BALL ROLLED BY ONE MAN."
IT DOESN'T LOOK ANY SMALLER TO ME. SAME SIZE. SAME COLOR. SAME. CAN'T TELL 'EM APART.
LARGE BALLS OF TWINE EVERYWHERE THINK ALL WHITE PEOPLE LOOK THE SAME, TOO.
SO QUICK TO JUDGE, ALEX. AND I HEAR YOUR ANGER. BUT I'M BEING GENUINE, I SWEAR. THE SAME.

MAYBE WE NEED TO LOOK AT YOUR EYE INJURY A BIT CLOSER. THIS IS A PLEXIGLASS DOME. KANSAS HAD AN OPEN-AIR GAZEBO.

I THOUGHT THAT WAS THE NORTH CAROLINA FRYING PAN.

NO, YOU'RE THINKING OF...WAIT...NO. DAMMIT. YOU ARE RIGHT. THERE WAS A GAZEBO AROUND THAT FRYING PAN.

DO YOU THINK IT'S POSSIBLE THAT OUR INABILITY TO KEEP ANY OF THESE STRAIGHT IS A SIGN WE SHOULD JUST GO HOME, FIND A NEW VET, AND GET THE CATS CHECKED OUT?

WHAT WOULD IT TAKE TO CONVINCE YOU THAT THIS BALL IS SMALLER THAN THE ONE IN KANSAS?

I KNOW BALLS.

ONE IS ALWAYS SMALLER.

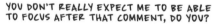

YOU DON'T REALLY EXPECT ME TO BE ABLE TO FOCUS AFTER THAT COMMENT, DO YOU?

UGH. YOU ARE WORSE THAN A PRINCIPAL WHO WON'T ALLOW FEMALE STUDENTS TO WEAR TANK TOPS FOR FEAR THE BOYS WILL SPONTANEOUSLY RAPE THEM.

NICE DEFLECTION. ANY CHANCE YOU'RE PANICKING ABOUT THE TRIP BEING ALMOST OVER? NOT READY TO RETURN TO CIVILIAN LIFE?

WE HAVEN'T EVEN TOUCHED ON THE PLIGHT OF OUR VETERANS.

I MISS OUR BED MORE THAN I MISS SEEING BO OBAMA RUMPING ACROSS THE SOUTH LAWN. I WANT TO GO HOME. BUT I DON'T FEEL LIKE I'VE EARNED IT YET.

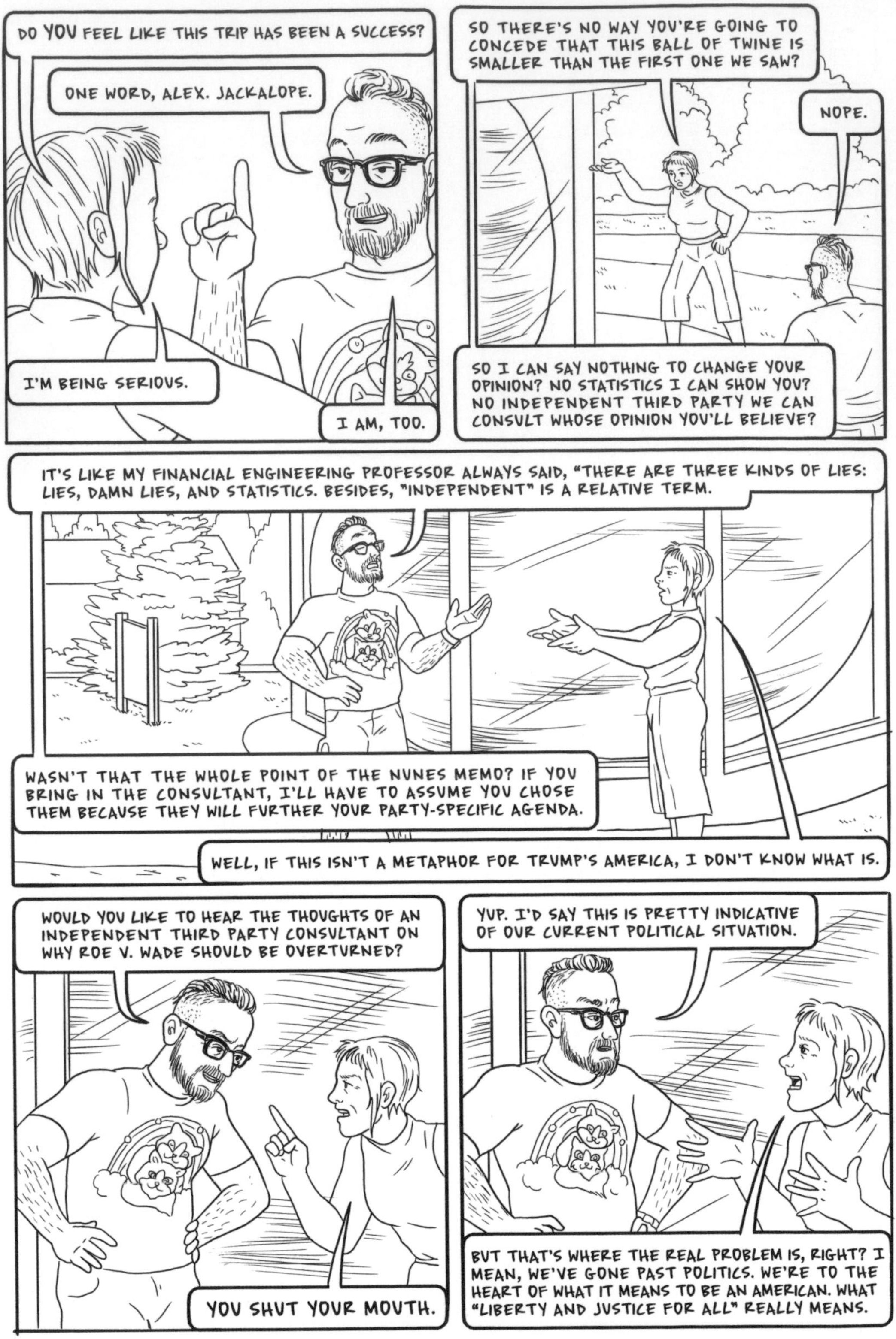
DO YOU FEEL LIKE THIS TRIP HAS BEEN A SUCCESS?
ONE WORD, ALEX. JACKALOPE.
I'M BEING SERIOUS.
I AM, TOO.
SO THERE'S NO WAY YOU'RE GOING TO CONCEDE THAT THIS BALL OF TWINE IS SMALLER THAN THE FIRST ONE WE SAW?
NOPE.
SO I CAN SAY NOTHING TO CHANGE YOUR OPINION? NO STATISTICS I CAN SHOW YOU? NO INDEPENDENT THIRD PARTY WE CAN CONSULT WHOSE OPINION YOU'LL BELIEVE?
IT'S LIKE MY FINANCIAL ENGINEERING PROFESSOR ALWAYS SAID, "THERE ARE THREE KINDS OF LIES: LIES, DAMN LIES, AND STATISTICS. BESIDES, "INDEPENDENT" IS A RELATIVE TERM.
WASN'T THAT THE WHOLE POINT OF THE NUNES MEMO? IF YOU BRING IN THE CONSULTANT, I'LL HAVE TO ASSUME YOU CHOSE THEM BECAUSE THEY WILL FURTHER YOUR PARTY-SPECIFIC AGENDA.
WELL, IF THIS ISN'T A METAPHOR FOR TRUMP'S AMERICA, I DON'T KNOW WHAT IS.
WOULD YOU LIKE TO HEAR THE THOUGHTS OF AN INDEPENDENT THIRD PARTY CONSULTANT ON WHY ROE V. WADE SHOULD BE OVERTURNED?
YOU SHUT YOUR MOUTH.
YUP. I'D SAY THIS IS PRETTY INDICATIVE OF OUR CURRENT POLITICAL SITUATION.
BUT THAT'S WHERE THE REAL PROBLEM IS, RIGHT? I MEAN, WE'VE GONE PAST POLITICS. WE'RE TO THE HEART OF WHAT IT MEANS TO BE AN AMERICAN. WHAT "LIBERTY AND JUSTICE FOR ALL" REALLY MEANS.

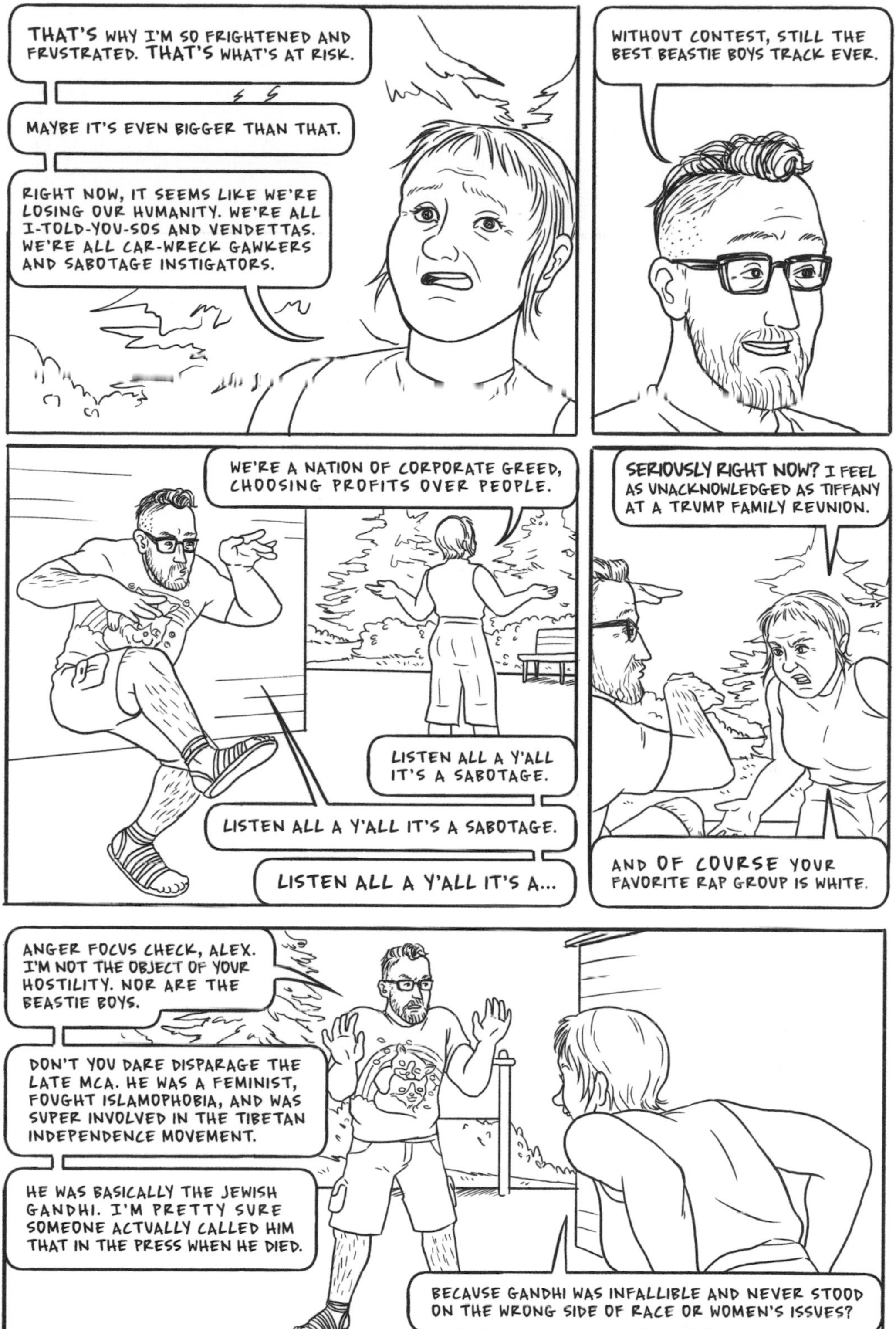
THAT'S WHY I'M SO FRIGHTENED AND FRUSTRATED. THAT'S WHAT'S AT RISK.
MAYBE IT'S EVEN BIGGER THAN THAT.
RIGHT NOW, IT SEEMS LIKE WE'RE LOSING OUR HUMANITY. WE'RE ALL I-TOLD-YOU-SOS AND VENDETTAS. WE'RE ALL CAR-WRECK GAWKERS AND SABOTAGE INSTIGATORS.
WITHOUT CONTEST, STILL THE BEST BEASTIE BOYS TRACK EVER.
WE'RE A NATION OF CORPORATE GREED, CHOOSING PROFITS OVER PEOPLE.
LISTEN ALL A Y'ALL IT'S A SABOTAGE.
LISTEN ALL A Y'ALL IT'S A SABOTAGE.
LISTEN ALL A Y'ALL IT'S A...
SERIOUSLY RIGHT NOW? I FEEL AS UNACKNOWLEDGED AS TIFFANY AT A TRUMP FAMILY REUNION.
AND OF COURSE YOUR FAVORITE RAP GROUP IS WHITE.
ANGER FOCUS CHECK, ALEX. I'M NOT THE OBJECT OF YOUR HOSTILITY. NOR ARE THE BEASTIE BOYS.
DON'T YOU DARE DISPARAGE THE LATE MCA. HE WAS A FEMINIST, FOUGHT ISLAMOPHOBIA, AND WAS SUPER INVOLVED IN THE TIBETAN INDEPENDENCE MOVEMENT.
HE WAS BASICALLY THE JEWISH GANDHI. I'M PRETTY SURE SOMEONE ACTUALLY CALLED HIM THAT IN THE PRESS WHEN HE DIED.
BECAUSE GANDHI WAS INFALLIBLE AND NEVER STOOD ON THE WRONG SIDE OF RACE OR WOMEN'S ISSUES?

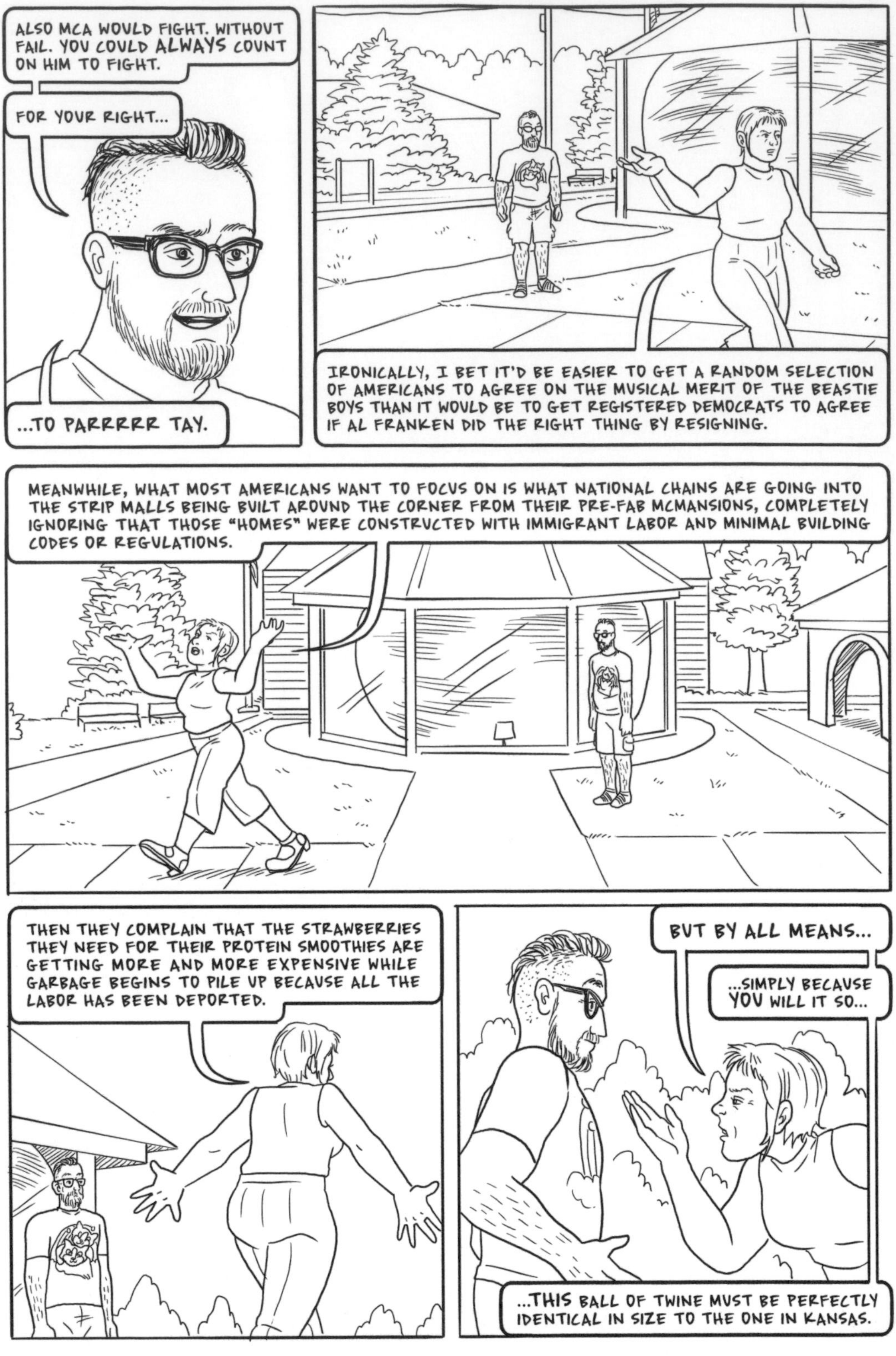
ALSO MCA WOULD FIGHT. WITHOUT FAIL. YOU COULD ALWAYS COUNT ON HIM TO FIGHT.
FOR YOUR RIGHT...
...TO PARRRRR TAY.
IRONICALLY, I BET IT'D BE EASIER TO GET A RANDOM SELECTION OF AMERICANS TO AGREE ON THE MUSICAL MERIT OF THE BEASTIE BOYS THAN IT WOULD BE TO GET REGISTERED DEMOCRATS TO AGREE IF AL FRANKEN DID THE RIGHT THING BY RESIGNING.
MEANWHILE, WHAT MOST AMERICANS WANT TO FOCUS ON IS WHAT NATIONAL CHAINS ARE GOING INTO THE STRIP MALLS BEING BUILT AROUND THE CORNER FROM THEIR PRE-FAB MCMANSIONS, COMPLETELY IGNORING THAT THOSE "HOMES" WERE CONSTRUCTED WITH IMMIGRANT LABOR AND MINIMAL BUILDING CODES OR REGULATIONS.
THEN THEY COMPLAIN THAT THE STRAWBERRIES THEY NEED FOR THEIR PROTEIN SMOOTHIES ARE GETTING MORE AND MORE EXPENSIVE WHILE GARBAGE BEGINS TO PILE UP BECAUSE ALL THE LABOR HAS BEEN DEPORTED.
BUT BY ALL MEANS...
...SIMPLY BECAUSE YOU WILL IT SO...
...THIS BALL OF TWINE MUST BE PERFECTLY IDENTICAL IN SIZE TO THE ONE IN KANSAS.

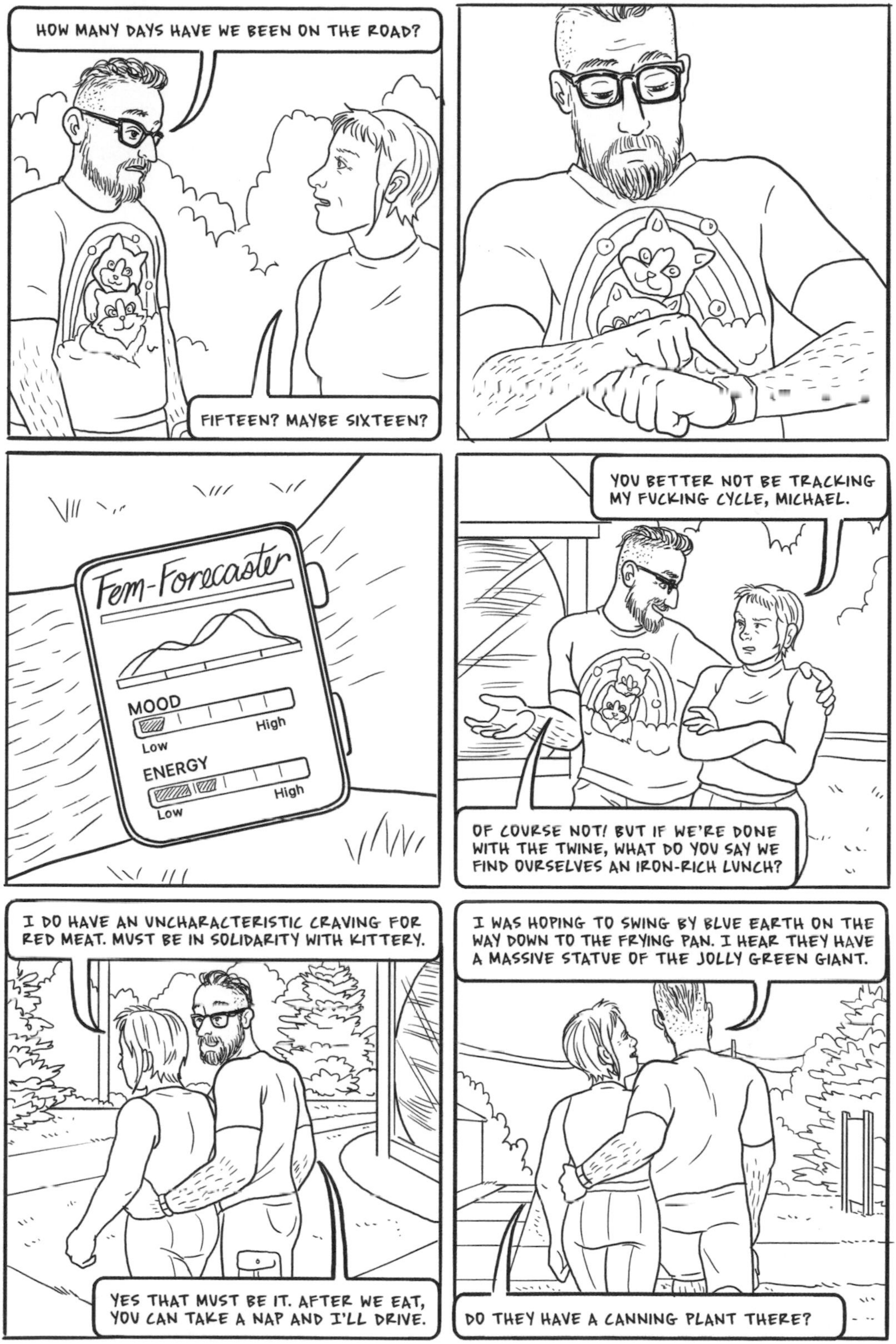
HOW MANY DAYS HAVE WE BEEN ON THE ROAD?
FIFTEEN? MAYBE SIXTEEN?
Fem-Forecaster
MOOD
Low
High
ENERGY
Low
High
YOU BETTER NOT BE TRACKING MY FUCKING CYCLE, MICHAEL.
OF COURSE NOT! BUT IF WE'RE DONE WITH THE TWINE, WHAT DO YOU SAY WE FIND OURSELVES AN IRON-RICH LUNCH?
I DO HAVE AN UNCHARACTERISTIC CRAVING FOR RED MEAT. MUST BE IN SOLIDARITY WITH KITTERY.
YES THAT MUST BE IT. AFTER WE EAT, YOU CAN TAKE A NAP AND I'LL DRIVE.
I WAS HOPING TO SWING BY BLUE EARTH ON THE WAY DOWN TO THE FRYING PAN. I HEAR THEY HAVE A MASSIVE STATUE OF THE JOLLY GREEN GIANT.
DO THEY HAVE A CANNING PLANT THERE?

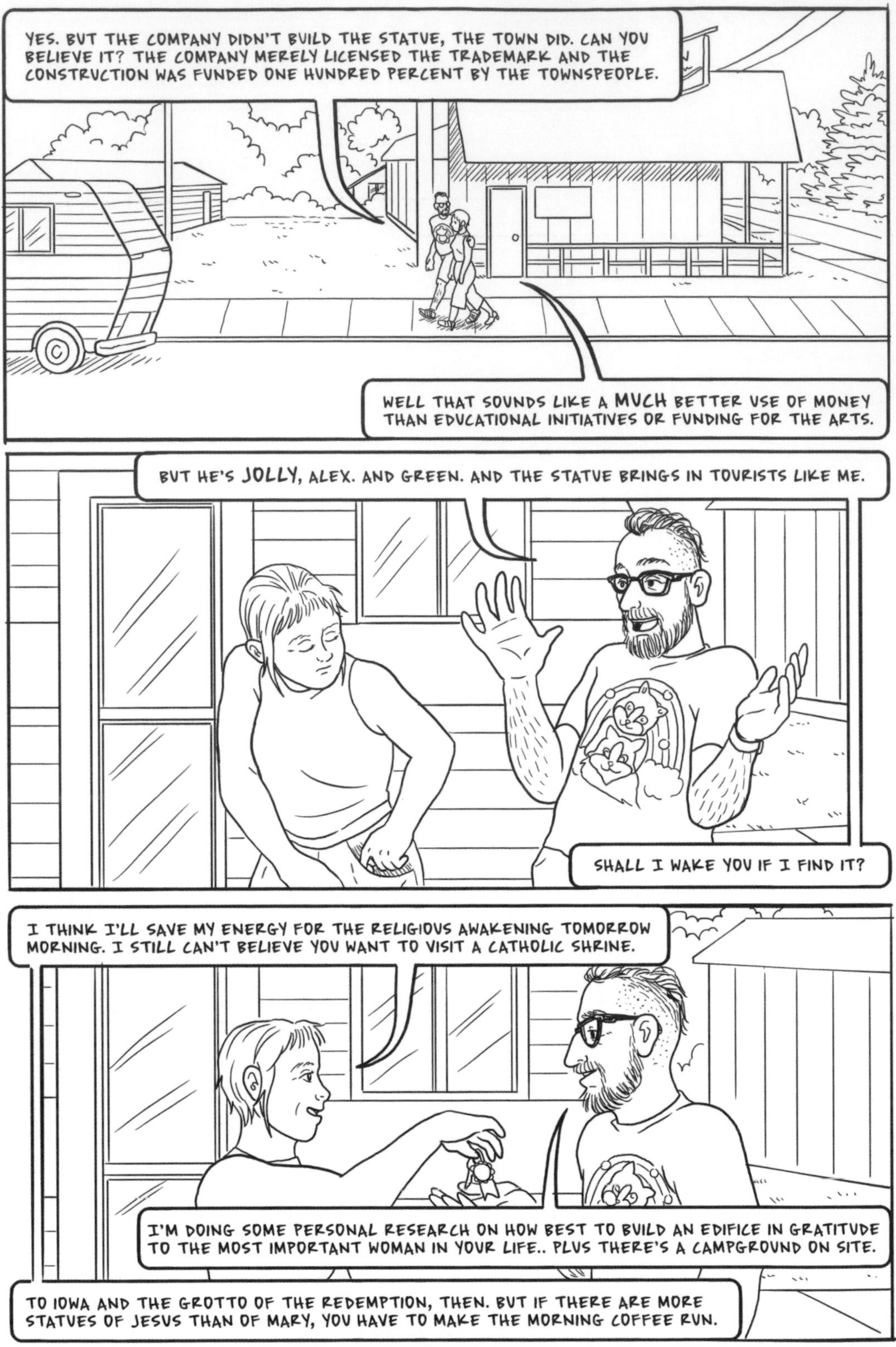
YES. BUT THE COMPANY DIDN'T BUILD THE STATUE, THE TOWN DID. CAN YOU BELIEVE IT? THE COMPANY MERELY LICENSED THE TRADEMARK AND THE CONSTRUCTION WAS FUNDED ONE HUNDRED PERCENT BY THE TOWNSPEOPLE.
WELL THAT SOUNDS LIKE A MUCH BETTER USE OF MONEY THAN EDUCATIONAL INITIATIVES OR FUNDING FOR THE ARTS.
BUT HE'S JOLLY, ALEX. AND GREEN. AND THE STATUE BRINGS IN TOURISTS LIKE ME.
SHALL I WAKE YOU IF I FIND IT?
I THINK I'LL SAVE MY ENERGY FOR THE RELIGIOUS AWAKENING TOMORROW MORNING. I STILL CAN'T BELIEVE YOU WANT TO VISIT A CATHOLIC SHRINE.
I'M DOING SOME PERSONAL RESEARCH ON HOW BEST TO BUILD AN EDIFICE IN GRATITUDE TO THE MOST IMPORTANT WOMAN IN YOUR LIFE.. PLUS THERE'S A CAMPGROUND ON SITE.
TO IOWA AND THE GROTTO OF THE REDEMPTION, THEN. BUT IF THERE ARE MORE STATUES OF JESUS THAN OF MARY, YOU HAVE TO MAKE THE MORNING COFFEE RUN.

Chapter 17

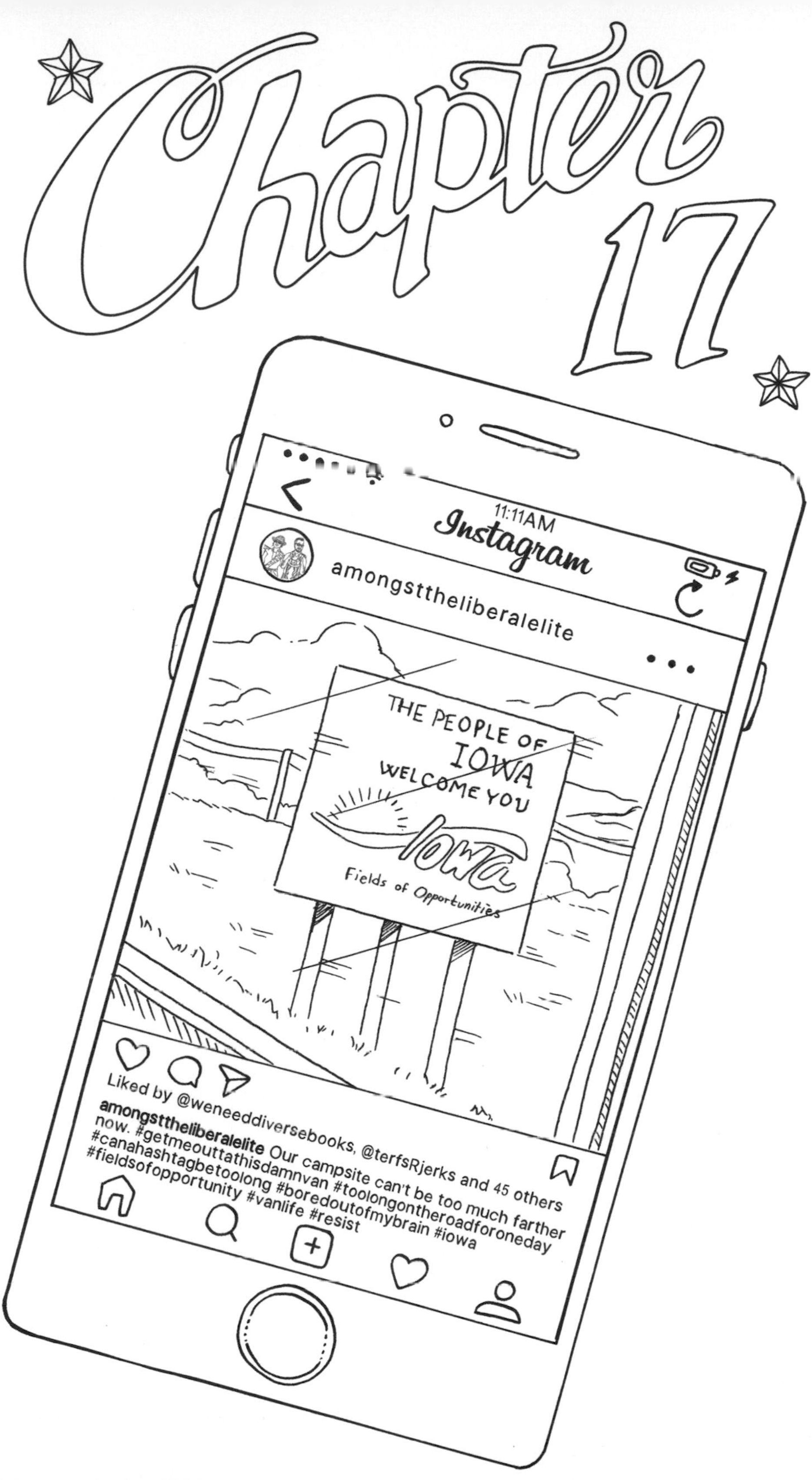

11:11AM
Instagram
amongsttheliberalelite
THE PEOPLE OF IOWA WELCOME YOU
Iowa
Fields of Opportunities
Liked by @weneeddiversebooks, @terfsRjerks and 45 others
amongsttheliberalelite Our campsite can't be too much farther now. #getmeouttathisdamnvan #toolongontheroadforoneday #canahashtagbetoolong #boredoutofmybrain #iowa #fieldsofopportunity #vanlife #resist

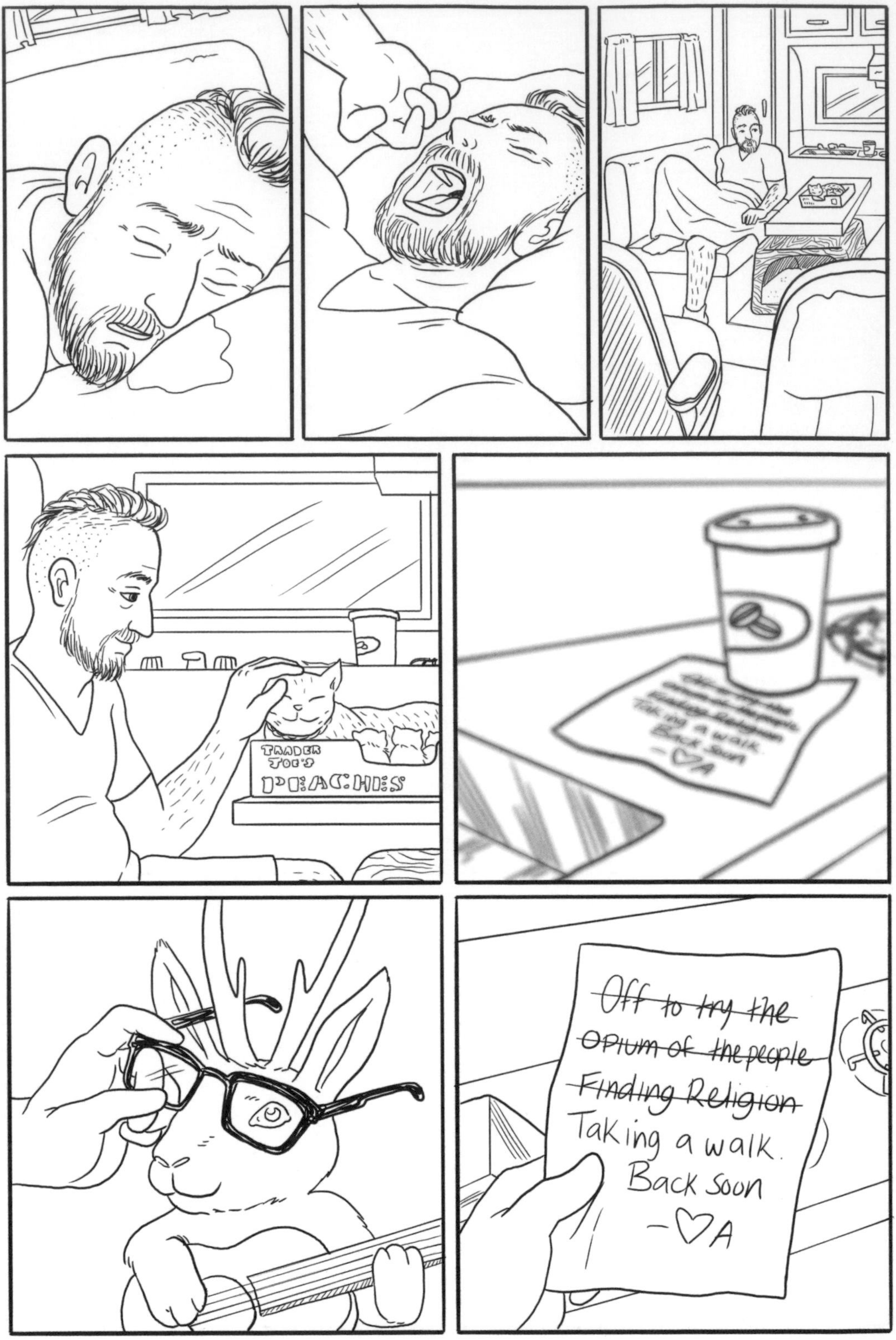
TRADER JOE'S
PEACHES
~~Off to try the~~
~~Opium of the people~~
~~Finding Religion~~
Taking a walk.
Back Soon
—♡A

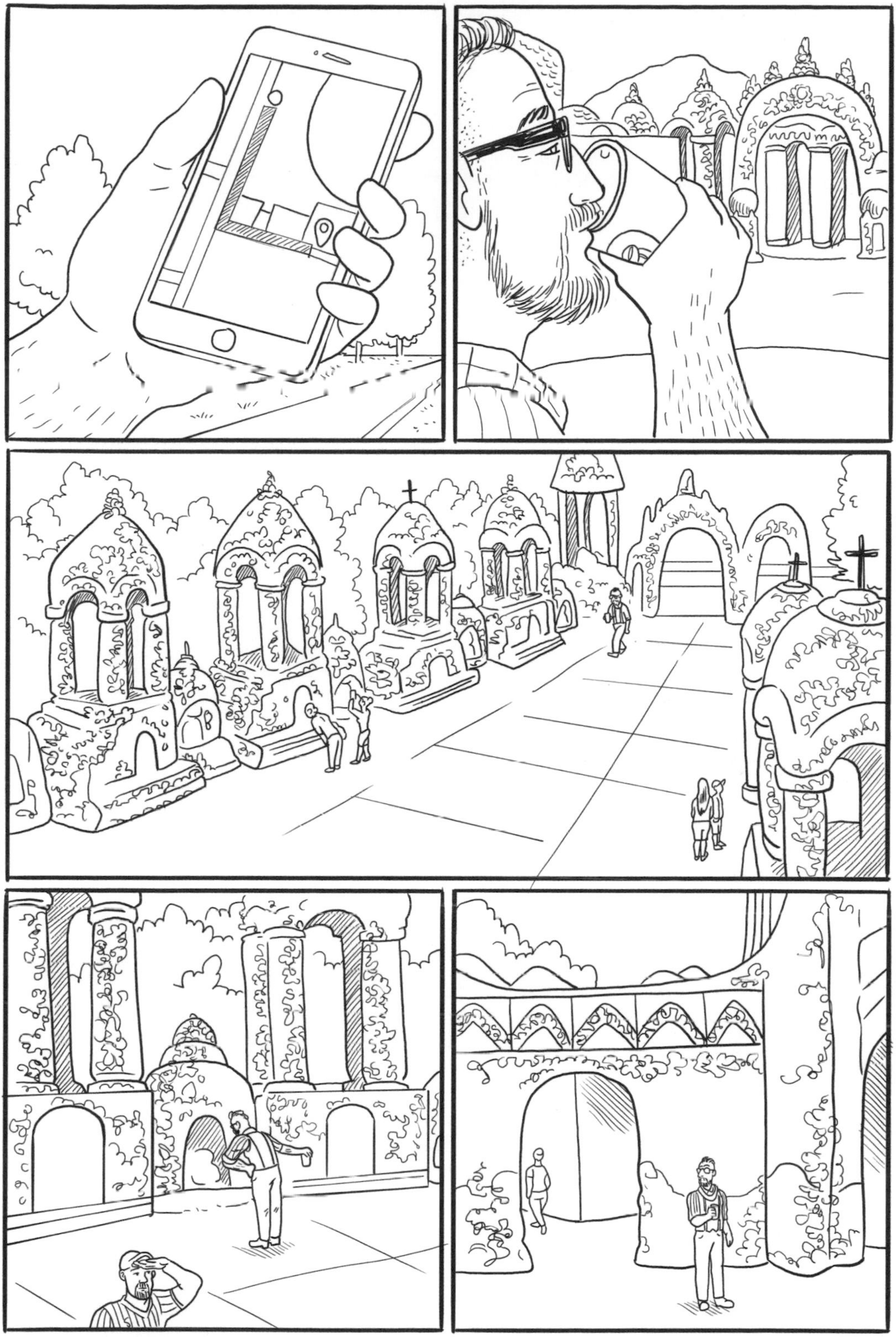

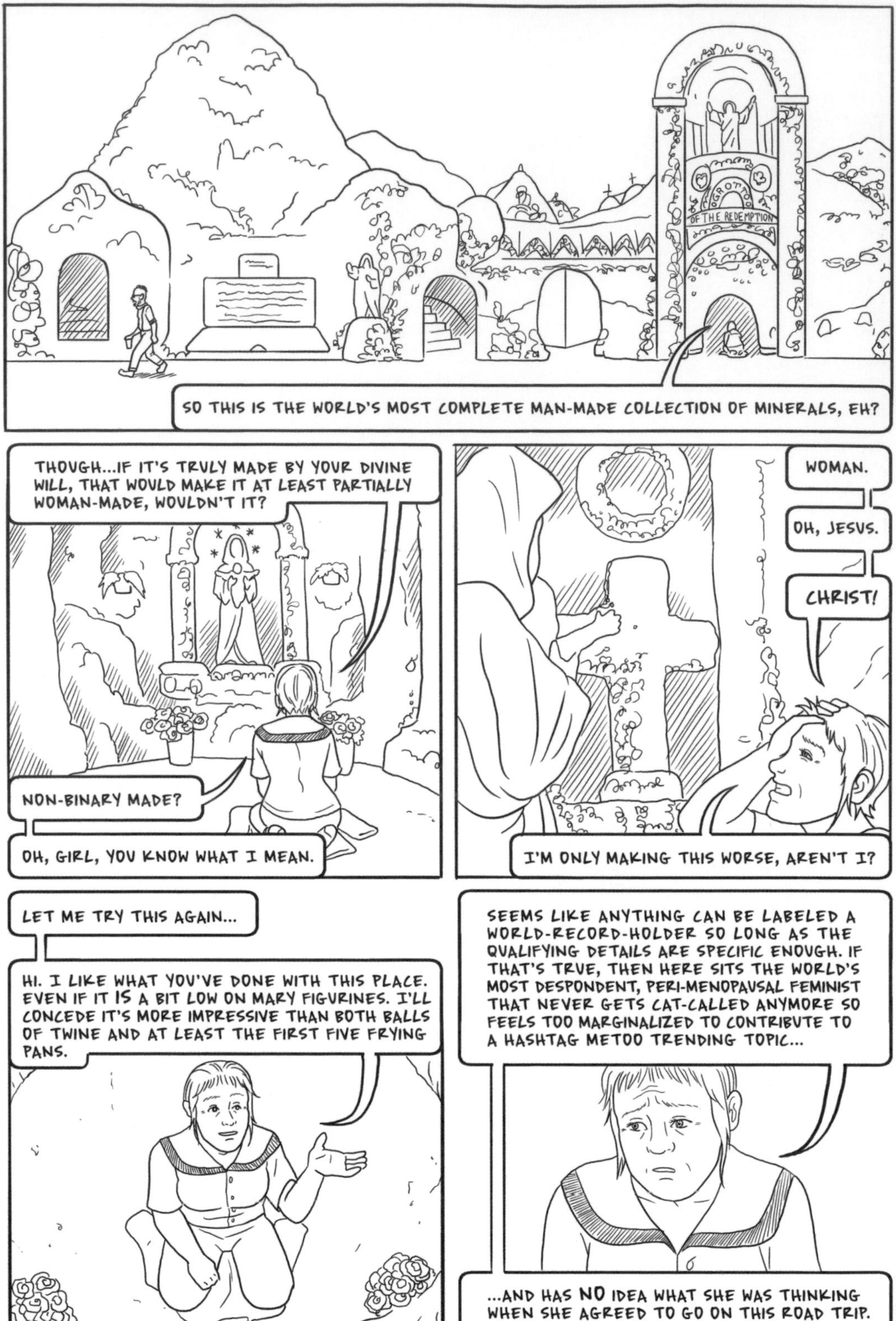

GROTTO OF THE REDEMPTION
SO THIS IS THE WORLD'S MOST COMPLETE MAN-MADE COLLECTION OF MINERALS, EH?
THOUGH...IF IT'S TRULY MADE BY YOUR DIVINE WILL, THAT WOULD MAKE IT AT LEAST PARTIALLY WOMAN-MADE, WOULDN'T IT?
NON-BINARY MADE?
OH, GIRL, YOU KNOW WHAT I MEAN.
WOMAN.
OH, JESUS.
CHRIST!
I'M ONLY MAKING THIS WORSE, AREN'T I?
LET ME TRY THIS AGAIN...
HI. I LIKE WHAT YOU'VE DONE WITH THIS PLACE. EVEN IF IT IS A BIT LOW ON MARY FIGURINES. I'LL CONCEDE IT'S MORE IMPRESSIVE THAN BOTH BALLS OF TWINE AND AT LEAST THE FIRST FIVE FRYING PANS.
SEEMS LIKE ANYTHING CAN BE LABELED A WORLD-RECORD-HOLDER SO LONG AS THE QUALIFYING DETAILS ARE SPECIFIC ENOUGH. IF THAT'S TRUE, THEN HERE SITS THE WORLD'S MOST DESPONDENT, PERI-MENOPAUSAL FEMINIST THAT NEVER GETS CAT-CALLED ANYMORE SO FEELS TOO MARGINALIZED TO CONTRIBUTE TO A HASHTAG METOO TRENDING TOPIC...
...AND HAS NO IDEA WHAT SHE WAS THINKING WHEN SHE AGREED TO GO ON THIS ROAD TRIP.

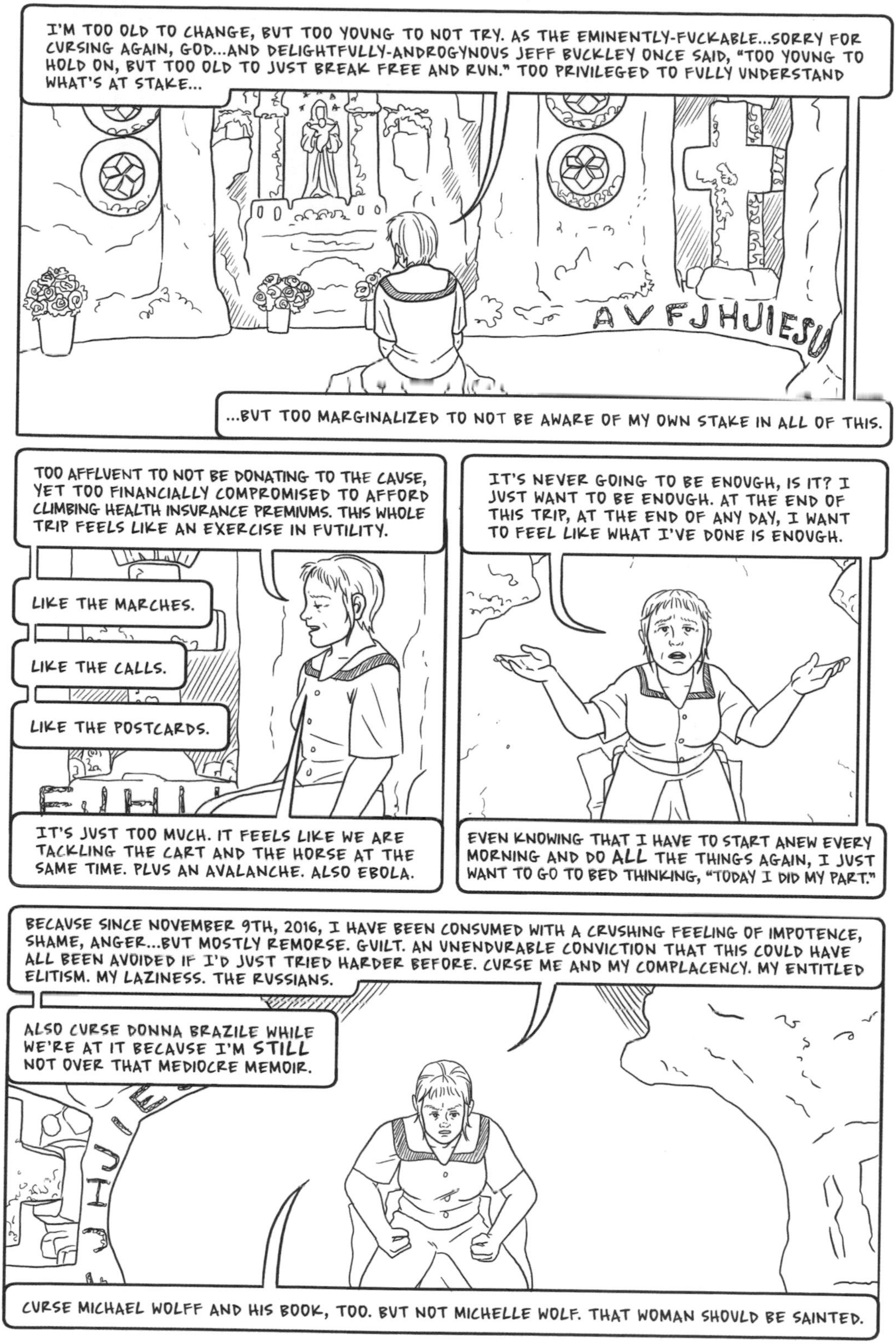
I'M TOO OLD TO CHANGE, BUT TOO YOUNG TO NOT TRY. AS THE EMINENTLY-FUCKABLE...SORRY FOR CURSING AGAIN, GOD...AND DELIGHTFULLY-ANDROGYNOUS JEFF BUCKLEY ONCE SAID, "TOO YOUNG TO HOLD ON, BUT TOO OLD TO JUST BREAK FREE AND RUN." TOO PRIVILEGED TO FULLY UNDERSTAND WHAT'S AT STAKE...
AVFJHUIESU
...BUT TOO MARGINALIZED TO NOT BE AWARE OF MY OWN STAKE IN ALL OF THIS.
TOO AFFLUENT TO NOT BE DONATING TO THE CAUSE, YET TOO FINANCIALLY COMPROMISED TO AFFORD CLIMBING HEALTH INSURANCE PREMIUMS. THIS WHOLE TRIP FEELS LIKE AN EXERCISE IN FUTILITY.
LIKE THE MARCHES.
LIKE THE CALLS.
LIKE THE POSTCARDS.
IT'S JUST TOO MUCH. IT FEELS LIKE WE ARE TACKLING THE CART AND THE HORSE AT THE SAME TIME. PLUS AN AVALANCHE. ALSO EBOLA.
IT'S NEVER GOING TO BE ENOUGH, IS IT? I JUST WANT TO BE ENOUGH. AT THE END OF THIS TRIP, AT THE END OF ANY DAY, I WANT TO FEEL LIKE WHAT I'VE DONE IS ENOUGH.
EVEN KNOWING THAT I HAVE TO START ANEW EVERY MORNING AND DO ALL THE THINGS AGAIN, I JUST WANT TO GO TO BED THINKING, "TODAY I DID MY PART."
BECAUSE SINCE NOVEMBER 9TH, 2016, I HAVE BEEN CONSUMED WITH A CRUSHING FEELING OF IMPOTENCE, SHAME, ANGER...BUT MOSTLY REMORSE. GUILT. AN UNENDURABLE CONVICTION THAT THIS COULD HAVE ALL BEEN AVOIDED IF I'D JUST TRIED HARDER BEFORE. CURSE ME AND MY COMPLACENCY. MY ENTITLED ELITISM. MY LAZINESS. THE RUSSIANS.
ALSO CURSE DONNA BRAZILE WHILE WE'RE AT IT BECAUSE I'M STILL NOT OVER THAT MEDIOCRE MEMOIR.
CURSE MICHAEL WOLFF AND HIS BOOK, TOO. BUT NOT MICHELLE WOLF. THAT WOMAN SHOULD BE SAINTED.

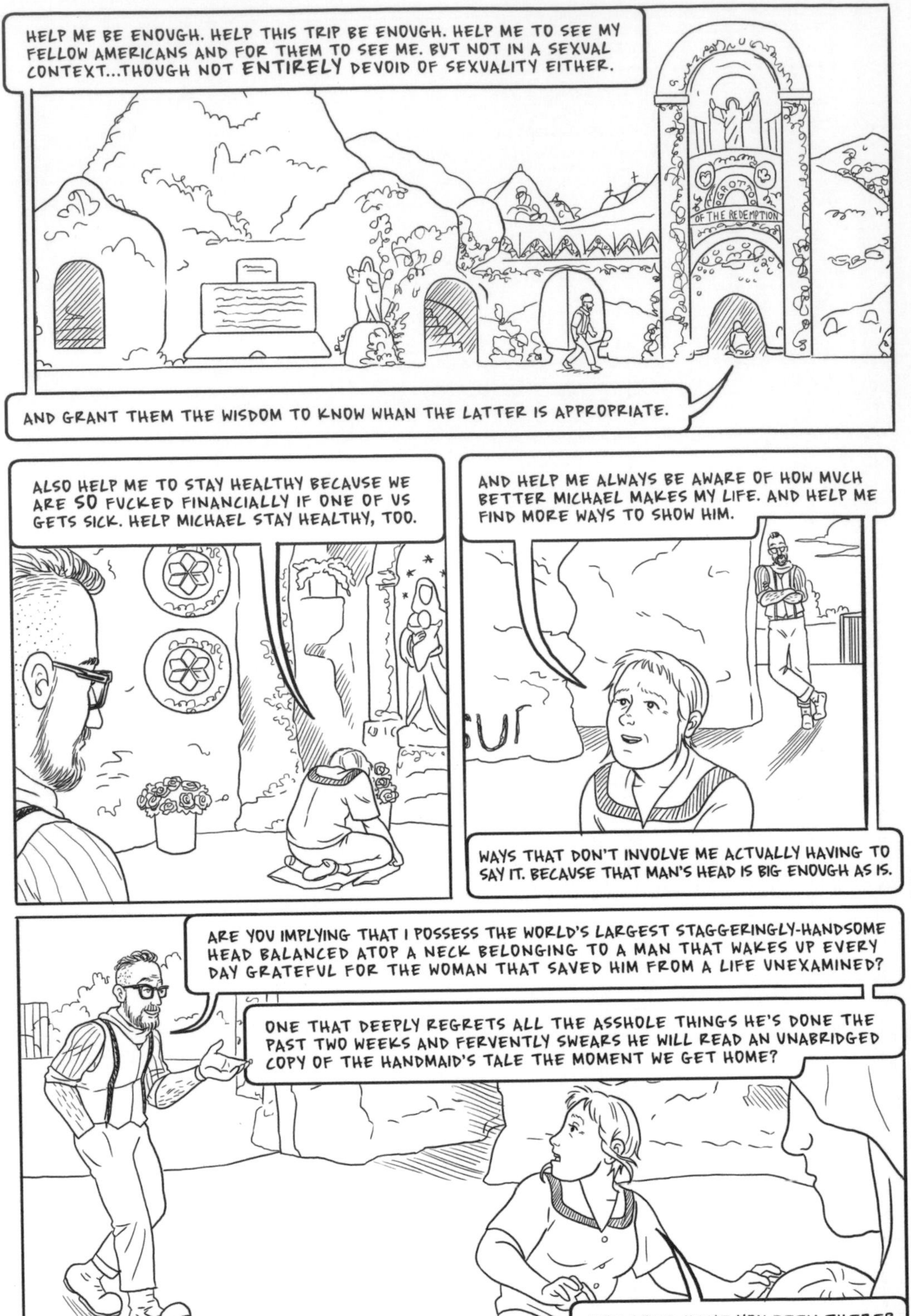
HELP ME BE ENOUGH. HELP THIS TRIP BE ENOUGH. HELP ME TO SEE MY FELLOW AMERICANS AND FOR THEM TO SEE ME. BUT NOT IN A SEXUAL CONTEXT...THOUGH NOT ENTIRELY DEVOID OF SEXUALITY EITHER.
GROTTO OF THE REDEMPTION
AND GRANT THEM THE WISDOM TO KNOW WHAN THE LATTER IS APPROPRIATE.
ALSO HELP ME TO STAY HEALTHY BECAUSE WE ARE SO FUCKED FINANCIALLY IF ONE OF US GETS SICK. HELP MICHAEL STAY HEALTHY, TOO.
AND HELP ME ALWAYS BE AWARE OF HOW MUCH BETTER MICHAEL MAKES MY LIFE. AND HELP ME FIND MORE WAYS TO SHOW HIM.
WAYS THAT DON'T INVOLVE ME ACTUALLY HAVING TO SAY IT. BECAUSE THAT MAN'S HEAD IS BIG ENOUGH AS IS.
ARE YOU IMPLYING THAT I POSSESS THE WORLD'S LARGEST STAGGERINGLY-HANDSOME HEAD BALANCED ATOP A NECK BELONGING TO A MAN THAT WAKES UP EVERY DAY GRATEFUL FOR THE WOMAN THAT SAVED HIM FROM A LIFE UNEXAMINED?
ONE THAT DEEPLY REGRETS ALL THE ASSHOLE THINGS HE'S DONE THE PAST TWO WEEKS AND FERVENTLY SWEARS HE WILL READ AN UNABRIDGED COPY OF THE HANDMAID'S TALE THE MOMENT WE GET HOME?
HOW LONG HAVE YOU BEEN THERE?

LONG ENOUGH. WERE YOU TALKING TO WHOM I THINK YOU WERE TALKING TO?

MAYBE? I'M NOT SURE IF SHE WAS LISTENING, OR IF SHE'S EVEN THERE. OR IF ANYTHING I COULD SAY WOULD MAKE A DIFFERENCE EITHER WAY.

HOW DO YOU FEEL?

CATHOLIC?

EMPTY. UNWORTHY. RESTLESS. TERRIFIED.

MAYBE A LITTLE.

AND THAT'S WHY YOU'RE KNEELING AMIDST FOUR MILLION DOLLARS OF JEWELS EMBEDDED IN GLOBS OF CONCRETE?

DO YOU WANT ME TO TRY MY GUY, TOO? JUST IN CASE?

WOULD YOU? IT COULDN'T POSSIBLY HURT, RIGHT?

LET'S SEE. I'M RUSTY...

HEAR, O ISRAEL:

THE LORD IS OUR GOD, THE LORD IS ONE.

BLESSED BE THE NAME OF HIS GLORIOUS KINGDOM FOR EVER AND EVER...

Chapter 18

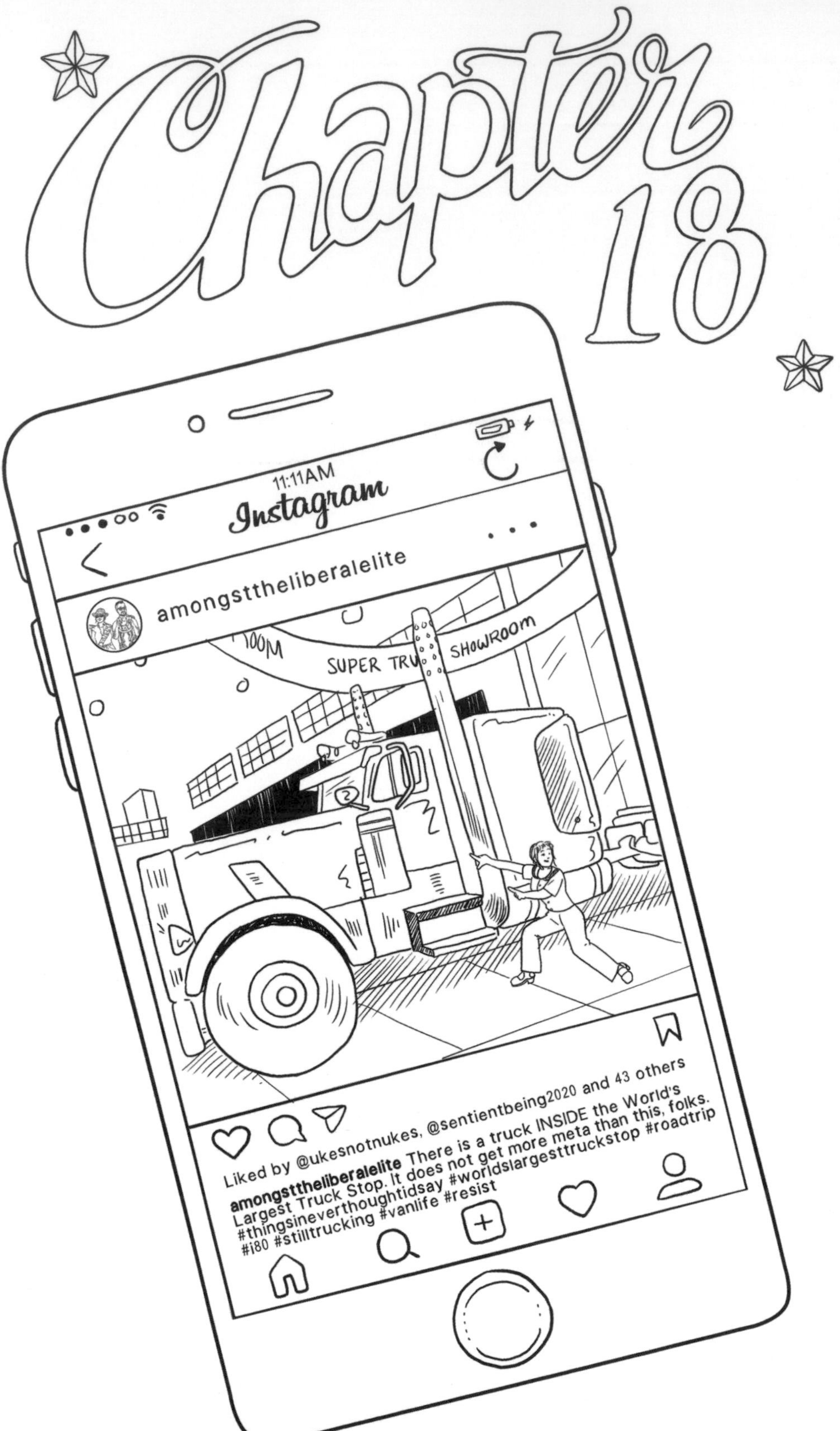

11:11AM
Instagram
amongsttheliberalelite
amongsttheliberalelite
OOM
SUPER TRU
SHOWROOM
Liked by @ukesnotnukes, @sentientbeing2020 and 43 others
amongsttheliberalelite There is a truck INSIDE the World's Largest Truck Stop. It does not get more meta than this, folks. #thingsineverthoughtidsay #worldslargesttruckstop #roadtrip #i80 #stilltrucking #vanlife #resist

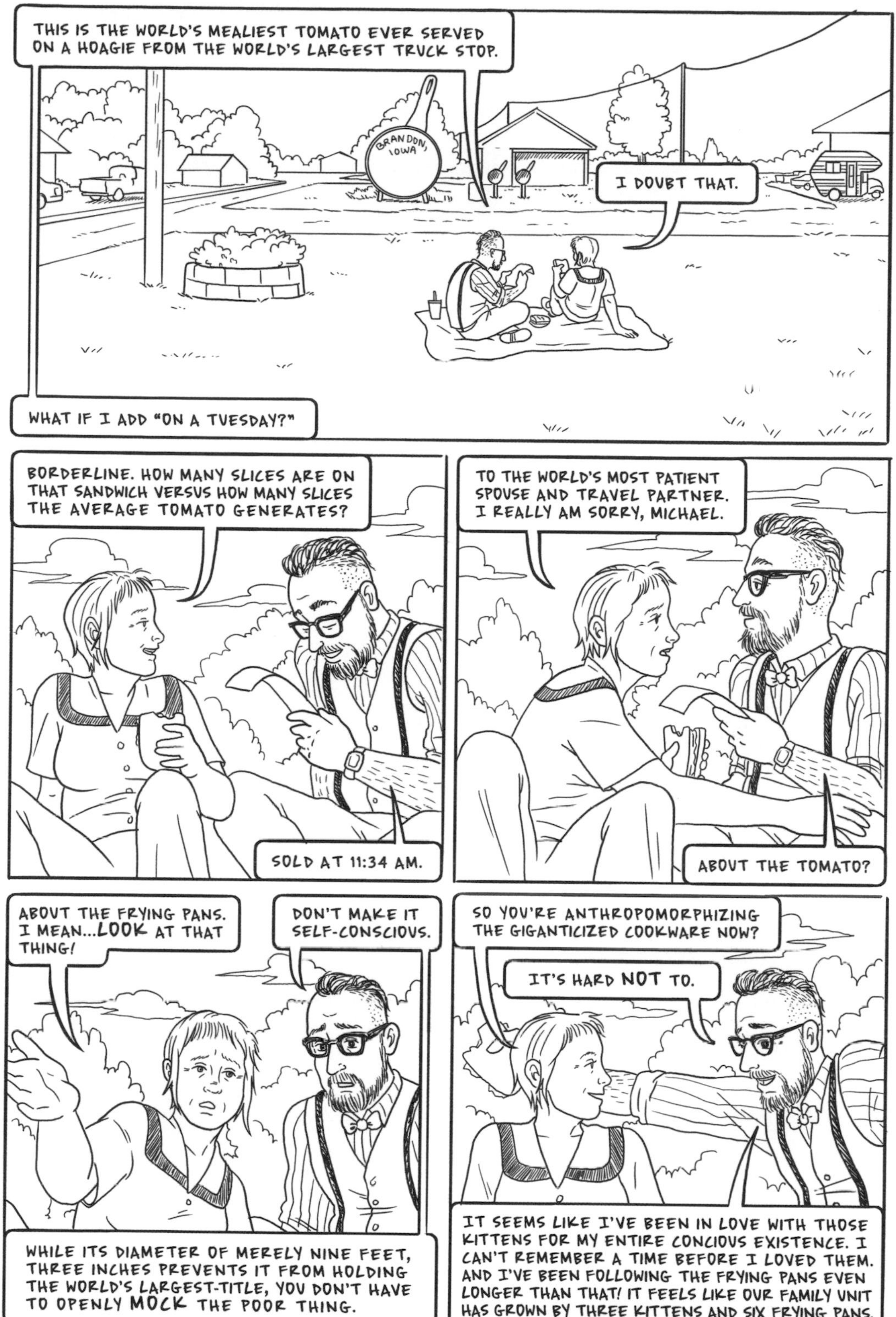

THIS IS THE WORLD'S MEALIEST TOMATO EVER SERVED ON A HOAGIE FROM THE WORLD'S LARGEST TRUCK STOP.
BRANDON, IOWA
I DOUBT THAT.
WHAT IF I ADD "ON A TUESDAY?"
BORDERLINE. HOW MANY SLICES ARE ON THAT SANDWICH VERSUS HOW MANY SLICES THE AVERAGE TOMATO GENERATES?
SOLD AT 11:34 AM.
TO THE WORLD'S MOST PATIENT SPOUSE AND TRAVEL PARTNER. I REALLY AM SORRY, MICHAEL.
ABOUT THE TOMATO?
ABOUT THE FRYING PANS. I MEAN...LOOK AT THAT THING!
DON'T MAKE IT SELF-CONSCIOUS.
WHILE ITS DIAMETER OF MERELY NINE FEET, THREE INCHES PREVENTS IT FROM HOLDING THE WORLD'S LARGEST-TITLE, YOU DON'T HAVE TO OPENLY MOCK THE POOR THING.
SO YOU'RE ANTHROPOMORPHIZING THE GIGANTICIZED COOKWARE NOW?
IT'S HARD NOT TO.
IT SEEMS LIKE I'VE BEEN IN LOVE WITH THOSE KITTENS FOR MY ENTIRE CONCIOUS EXISTENCE. I CAN'T REMEMBER A TIME BEFORE I LOVED THEM. AND I'VE BEEN FOLLOWING THE FRYING PANS EVEN LONGER THAN THAT! IT FEELS LIKE OUR FAMILY UNIT HAS GROWN BY THREE KITTENS AND SIX FRYING PANS.

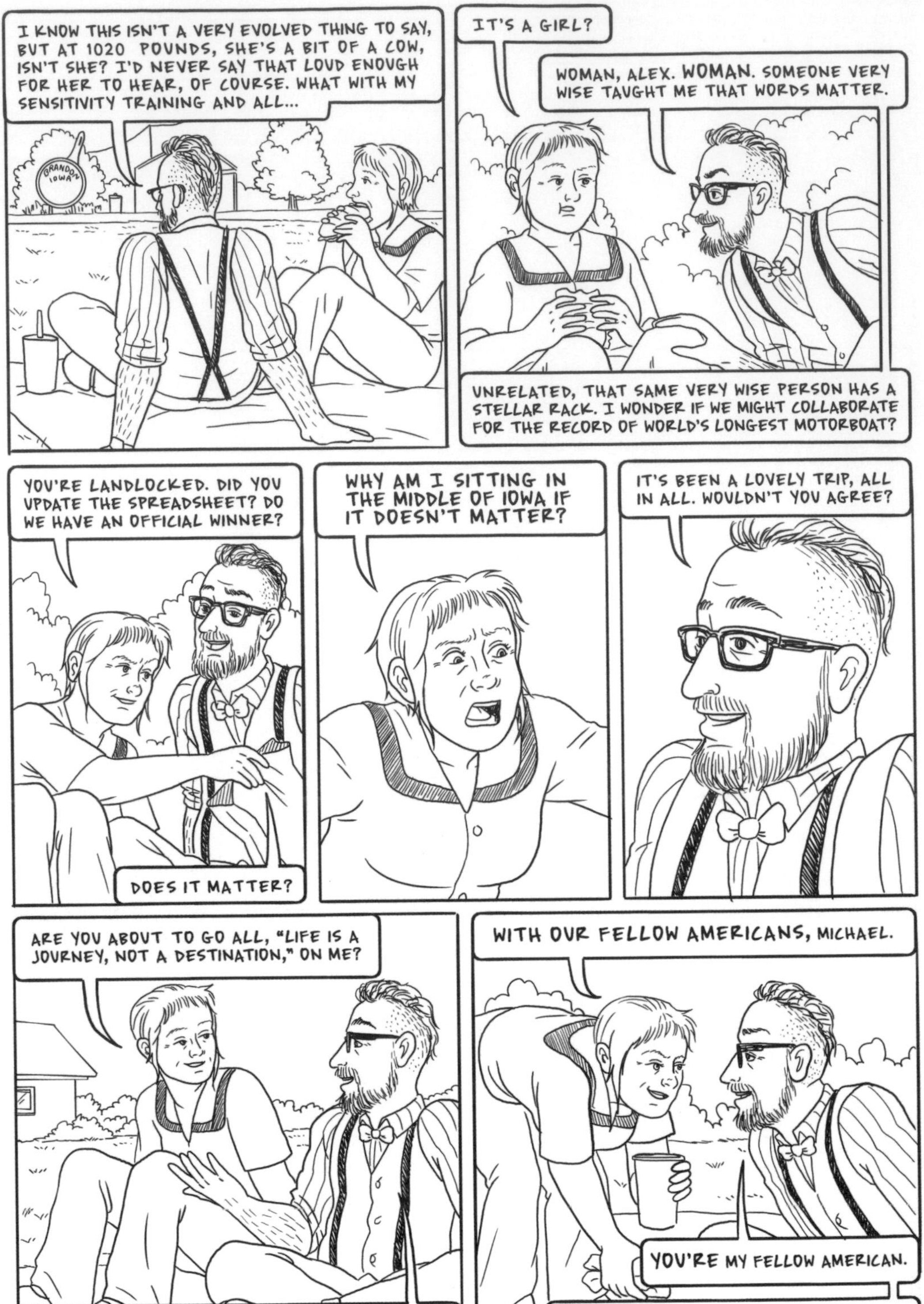

I KNOW THIS ISN'T A VERY EVOLVED THING TO SAY, BUT AT 1020 POUNDS, SHE'S A BIT OF A COW, ISN'T SHE? I'D NEVER SAY THAT LOUD ENOUGH FOR HER TO HEAR, OF COURSE. WHAT WITH MY SENSITIVITY TRAINING AND ALL...
GRANDON IOWA
IT'S A GIRL?
WOMAN, ALEX. WOMAN. SOMEONE VERY WISE TAUGHT ME THAT WORDS MATTER.
UNRELATED, THAT SAME VERY WISE PERSON HAS A STELLAR RACK. I WONDER IF WE MIGHT COLLABORATE FOR THE RECORD OF WORLD'S LONGEST MOTORBOAT?
YOU'RE LANDLOCKED. DID YOU UPDATE THE SPREADSHEET? DO WE HAVE AN OFFICIAL WINNER?
DOES IT MATTER?
WHY AM I SITTING IN THE MIDDLE OF IOWA IF IT DOESN'T MATTER?
IT'S BEEN A LOVELY TRIP, ALL IN ALL. WOULDN'T YOU AGREE?
ARE YOU ABOUT TO GO ALL, "LIFE IS A JOURNEY, NOT A DESTINATION," ON ME?
WELL ISN'T IT? WASN'T THAT OUR WHOLE GOAL? TO JOURNEY? TO UNDERSTAND? TO RECONNECT?
WITH OUR FELLOW AMERICANS, MICHAEL.
YOU'RE MY FELLOW AMERICAN.
I RECONNECTED WITH YOU IN AT LEAST EIGHT DIFFERENT STATES ON THIS TRIP.

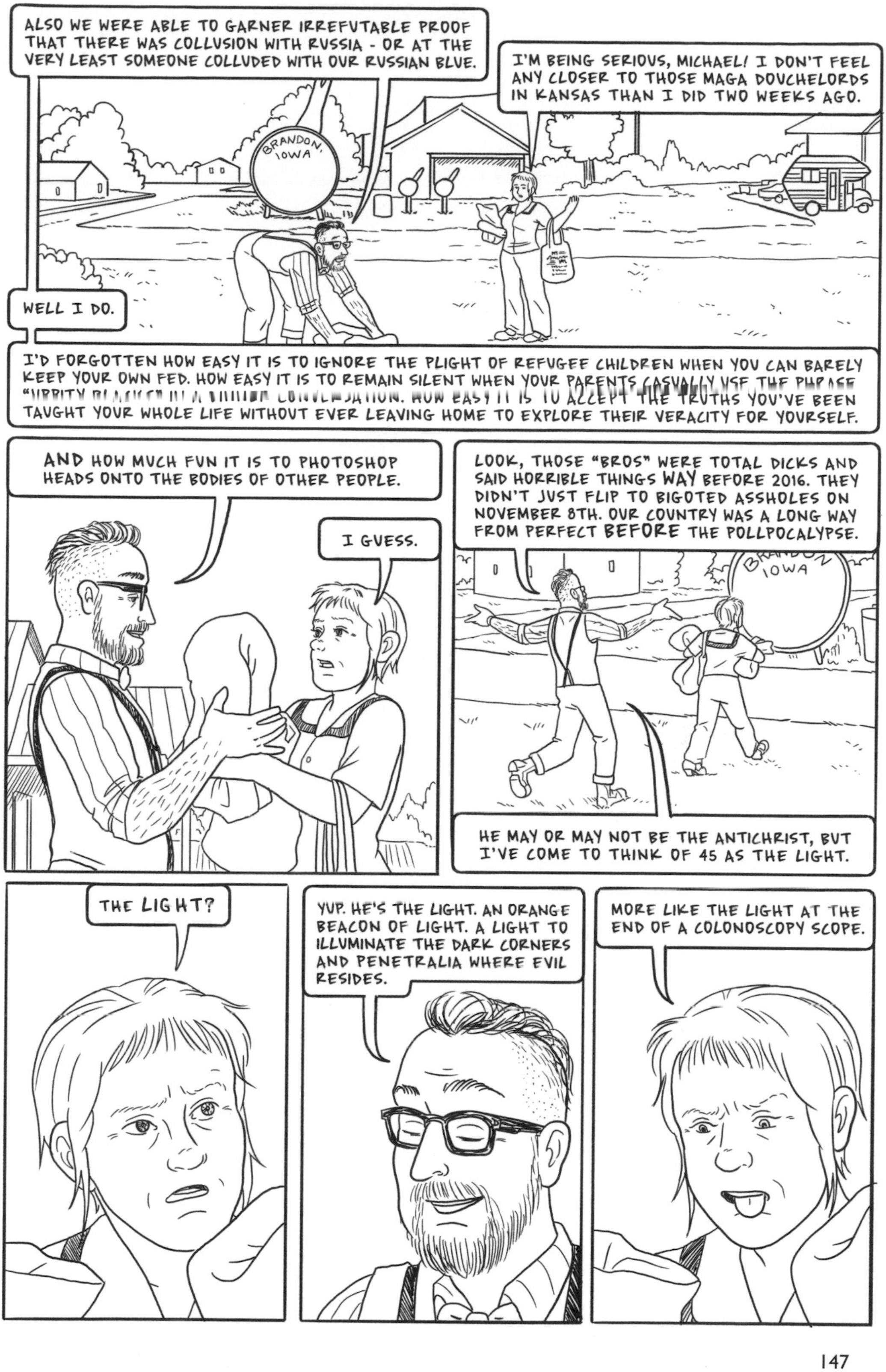
ALSO WE WERE ABLE TO GARNER IRREFUTABLE PROOF THAT THERE WAS COLLUSION WITH RUSSIA - OR AT THE VERY LEAST SOMEONE COLLUDED WITH OUR RUSSIAN BLUE.
I'M BEING SERIOUS, MICHAEL! I DON'T FEEL ANY CLOSER TO THOSE MAGA DOUCHELORDS IN KANSAS THAN I DID TWO WEEKS AGO.
BRANDON, IOWA
WELL I DO.
I'D FORGOTTEN HOW EASY IT IS TO IGNORE THE PLIGHT OF REFUGEE CHILDREN WHEN YOU CAN BARELY KEEP YOUR OWN FED. HOW EASY IT IS TO REMAIN SILENT WHEN YOUR PARENTS CASUALLY USE THE PHRASE “UPPITY BLACKS” IN A DINNER CONVERSATION. HOW EASY IT IS TO ACCEPT THE TRUTHS YOU'VE BEEN TAUGHT YOUR WHOLE LIFE WITHOUT EVER LEAVING HOME TO EXPLORE THEIR VERACITY FOR YOURSELF.
AND HOW MUCH FUN IT IS TO PHOTOSHOP HEADS ONTO THE BODIES OF OTHER PEOPLE.
I GUESS.
LOOK, THOSE “BROS” WERE TOTAL DICKS AND SAID HORRIBLE THINGS WAY BEFORE 2016. THEY DIDN'T JUST FLIP TO BIGOTED ASSHOLES ON NOVEMBER 8TH. OUR COUNTRY WAS A LONG WAY FROM PERFECT BEFORE THE POLLPOCALYPSE.
BRANDON IOWA
HE MAY OR MAY NOT BE THE ANTICHRIST, BUT I'VE COME TO THINK OF 45 AS THE LIGHT.
THE LIGHT?
YUP. HE'S THE LIGHT. AN ORANGE BEACON OF LIGHT. A LIGHT TO ILLUMINATE THE DARK CORNERS AND PENETRALIA WHERE EVIL RESIDES.
MORE LIKE THE LIGHT AT THE END OF A COLONOSCOPY SCOPE.

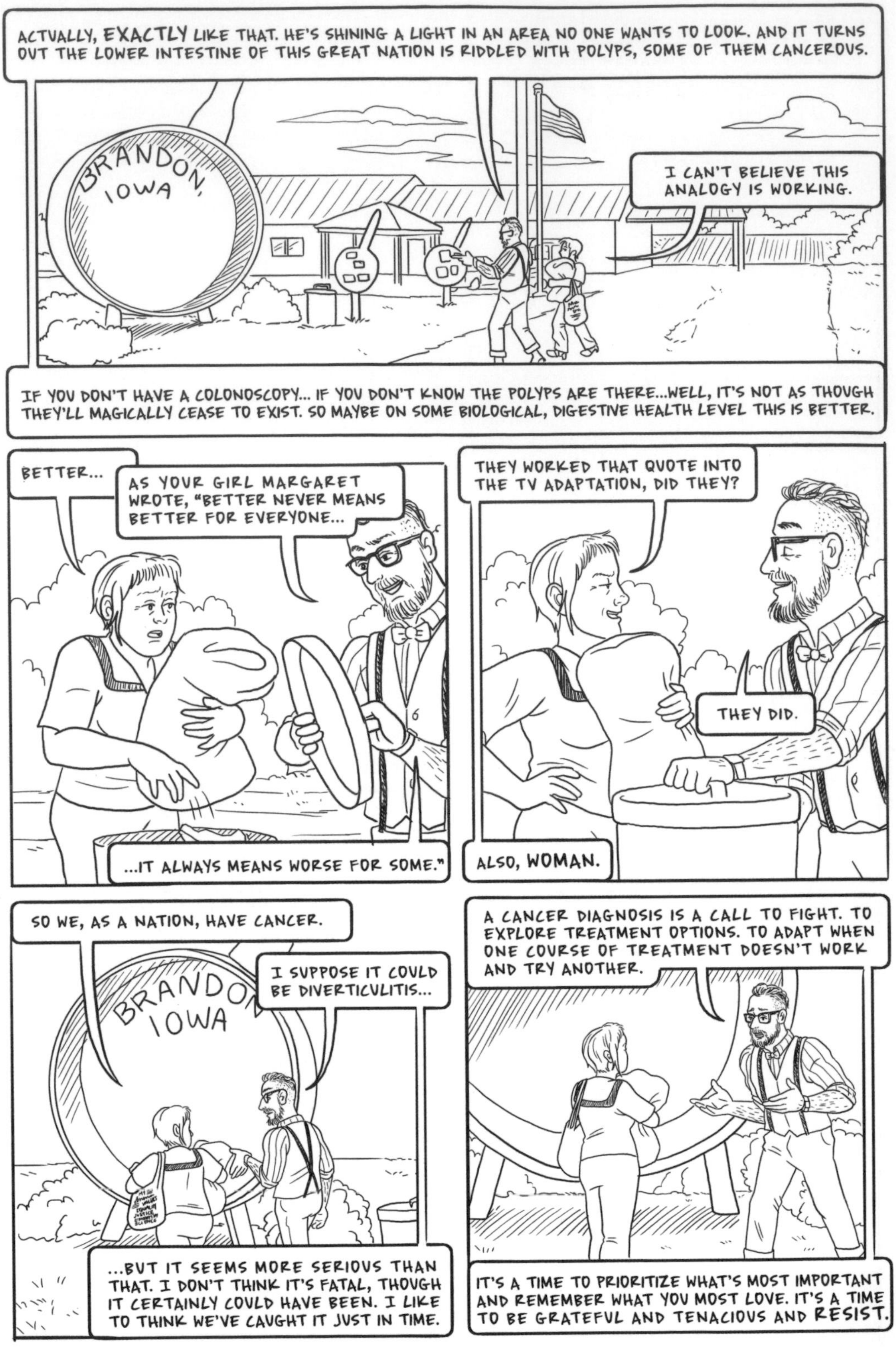
ACTUALLY, EXACTLY LIKE THAT. HE'S SHINING A LIGHT IN AN AREA NO ONE WANTS TO LOOK. AND IT TURNS OUT THE LOWER INTESTINE OF THIS GREAT NATION IS RIDDLED WITH POLYPS, SOME OF THEM CANCEROUS.
BRANDON, IOWA
I CAN'T BELIEVE THIS ANALOGY IS WORKING.
IF YOU DON'T HAVE A COLONOSCOPY... IF YOU DON'T KNOW THE POLYPS ARE THERE...WELL, IT'S NOT AS THOUGH THEY'LL MAGICALLY CEASE TO EXIST. SO MAYBE ON SOME BIOLOGICAL, DIGESTIVE HEALTH LEVEL THIS IS BETTER.
BETTER...
AS YOUR GIRL MARGARET WROTE, "BETTER NEVER MEANS BETTER FOR EVERYONE...
...IT ALWAYS MEANS WORSE FOR SOME."
THEY WORKED THAT QUOTE INTO THE TV ADAPTATION, DID THEY?
THEY DID.
ALSO, WOMAN.
SO WE, AS A NATION, HAVE CANCER.
I SUPPOSE IT COULD BE DIVERTICULITIS...
BRANDON IOWA
...BUT IT SEEMS MORE SERIOUS THAN THAT. I DON'T THINK IT'S FATAL, THOUGH IT CERTAINLY COULD HAVE BEEN. I LIKE TO THINK WE'VE CAUGHT IT JUST IN TIME.
A CANCER DIAGNOSIS IS A CALL TO FIGHT. TO EXPLORE TREATMENT OPTIONS. TO ADAPT WHEN ONE COURSE OF TREATMENT DOESN'T WORK AND TRY ANOTHER.
IT'S A TIME TO PRIORITIZE WHAT'S MOST IMPORTANT AND REMEMBER WHAT YOU MOST LOVE. IT'S A TIME TO BE GRATEFUL AND TENACIOUS AND RESIST.

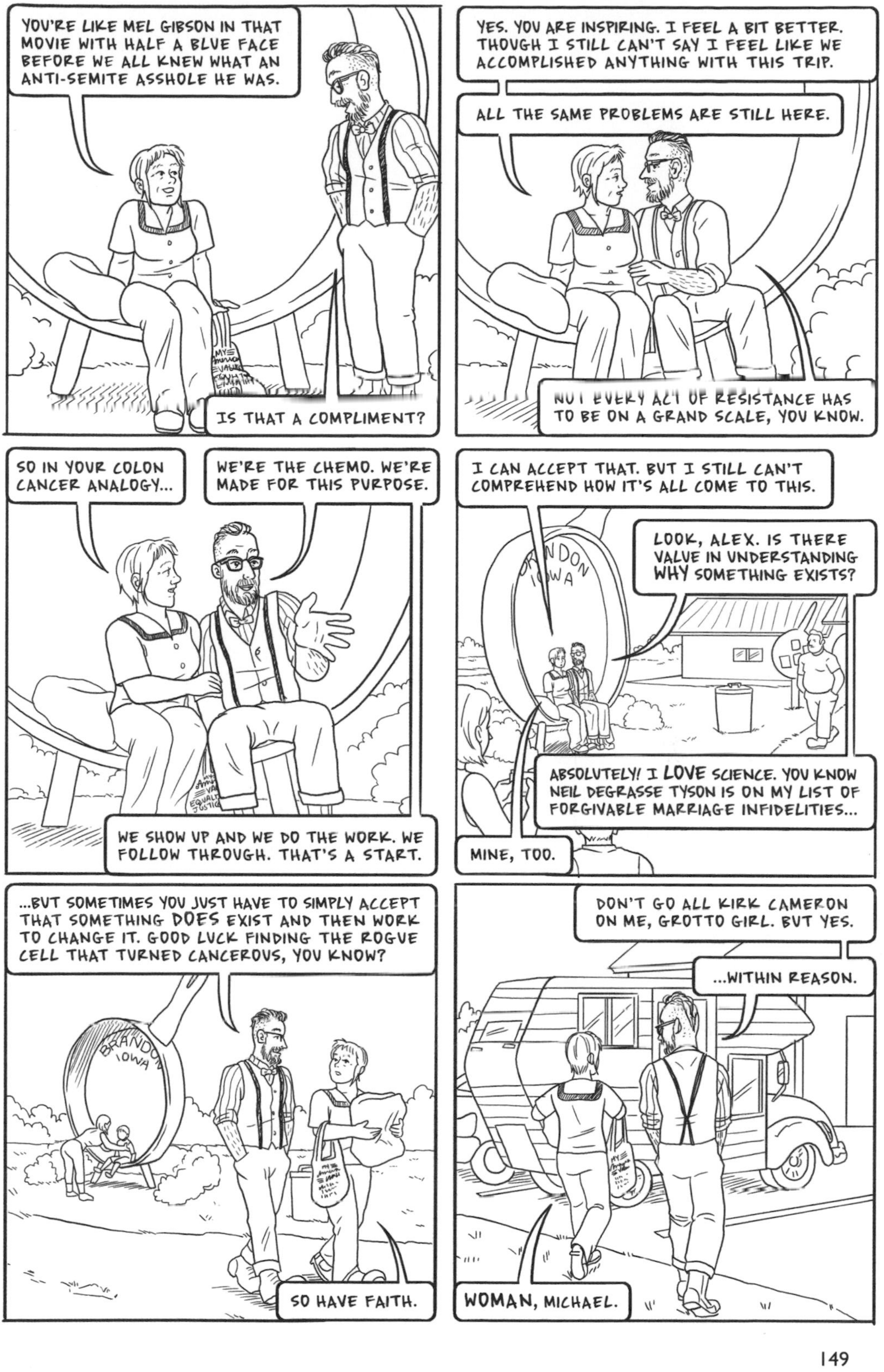
YOU'RE LIKE MEL GIBSON IN THAT MOVIE WITH HALF A BLUE FACE BEFORE WE ALL KNEW WHAT AN ANTI-SEMITE ASSHOLE HE WAS.
IS THAT A COMPLIMENT?
YES. YOU ARE INSPIRING. I FEEL A BIT BETTER. THOUGH I STILL CAN'T SAY I FEEL LIKE WE ACCOMPLISHED ANYTHING WITH THIS TRIP.
ALL THE SAME PROBLEMS ARE STILL HERE.
NOT EVERY ACT OF RESISTANCE HAS TO BE ON A GRAND SCALE, YOU KNOW.
SO IN YOUR COLON CANCER ANALOGY...
WE'RE THE CHEMO. WE'RE MADE FOR THIS PURPOSE.
WE SHOW UP AND WE DO THE WORK. WE FOLLOW THROUGH. THAT'S A START.
I CAN ACCEPT THAT. BUT I STILL CAN'T COMPREHEND HOW IT'S ALL COME TO THIS.
BRANDON IOWA
LOOK, ALEX. IS THERE VALUE IN UNDERSTANDING WHY SOMETHING EXISTS?
ABSOLUTELY! I LOVE SCIENCE. YOU KNOW NEIL DEGRASSE TYSON IS ON MY LIST OF FORGIVABLE MARRIAGE INFIDELITIES...
MINE, TOO.
...BUT SOMETIMES YOU JUST HAVE TO SIMPLY ACCEPT THAT SOMETHING DOES EXIST AND THEN WORK TO CHANGE IT. GOOD LUCK FINDING THE ROGUE CELL THAT TURNED CANCEROUS, YOU KNOW?
BRANDON IOWA
SO HAVE FAITH.
DON'T GO ALL KIRK CAMERON ON ME, GROTTO GIRL. BUT YES.
...WITHIN REASON.
WOMAN, MICHAEL.

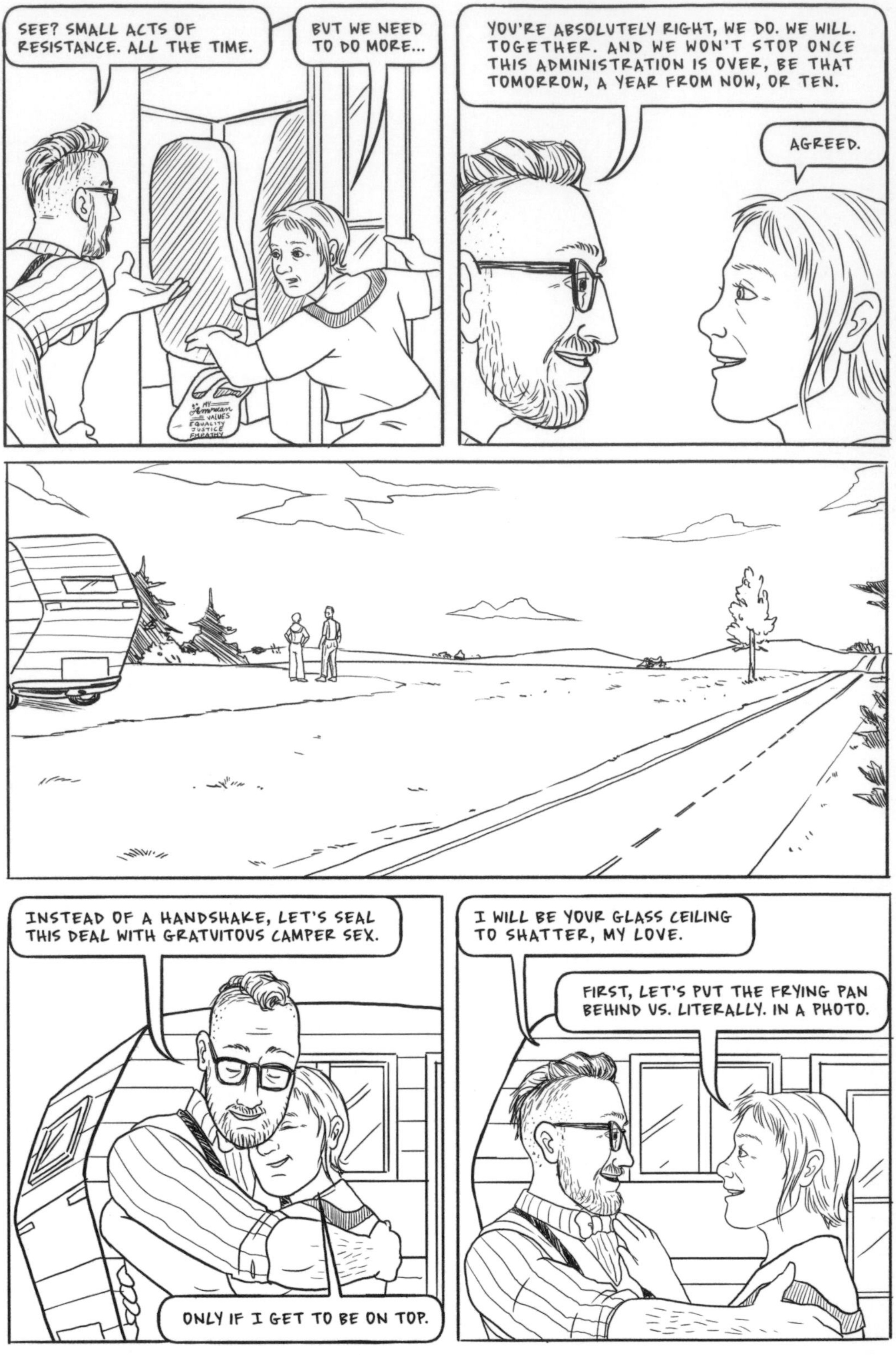
SEE? SMALL ACTS OF RESISTANCE. ALL THE TIME.
BUT WE NEED TO DO MORE...
YOU'RE ABSOLUTELY RIGHT, WE DO. WE WILL. TOGETHER. AND WE WON'T STOP ONCE THIS ADMINISTRATION IS OVER, BE THAT TOMORROW, A YEAR FROM NOW, OR TEN.
AGREED.
INSTEAD OF A HANDSHAKE, LET'S SEAL THIS DEAL WITH GRATUITOUS CAMPER SEX.
ONLY IF I GET TO BE ON TOP.
I WILL BE YOUR GLASS CEILING TO SHATTER, MY LOVE.
FIRST, LET'S PUT THE FRYING PAN BEHIND US. LITERALLY. IN A PHOTO.

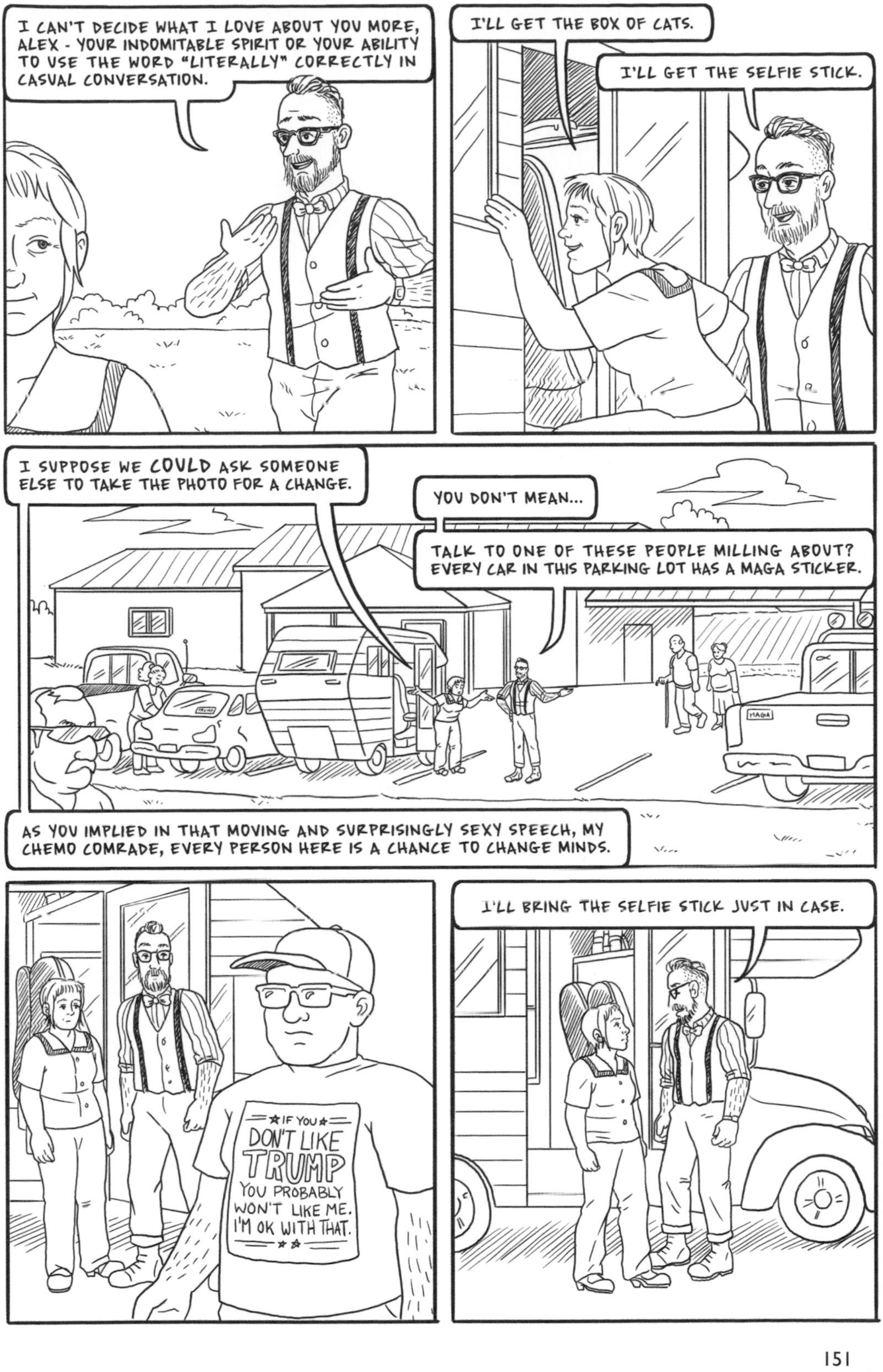

I CAN'T DECIDE WHAT I LOVE ABOUT YOU MORE, ALEX - YOUR INDOMITABLE SPIRIT OR YOUR ABILITY TO USE THE WORD "LITERALLY" CORRECTLY IN CASUAL CONVERSATION.
I'LL GET THE BOX OF CATS.
I'LL GET THE SELFIE STICK.
I SUPPOSE WE COULD ASK SOMEONE ELSE TO TAKE THE PHOTO FOR A CHANGE.
YOU DON'T MEAN...
TALK TO ONE OF THESE PEOPLE MILLING ABOUT? EVERY CAR IN THIS PARKING LOT HAS A MAGA STICKER.
TRUMP
MAGA
AS YOU IMPLIED IN THAT MOVING AND SURPRISINGLY SEXY SPEECH, MY CHEMO COMRADE, EVERY PERSON HERE IS A CHANCE TO CHANGE MINDS.
IF YOU DON'T LIKE TRUMP YOU PROBABLY WON'T LIKE ME. I'M OK WITH THAT.
I'LL BRING THE SELFIE STICK JUST IN CASE.

The End

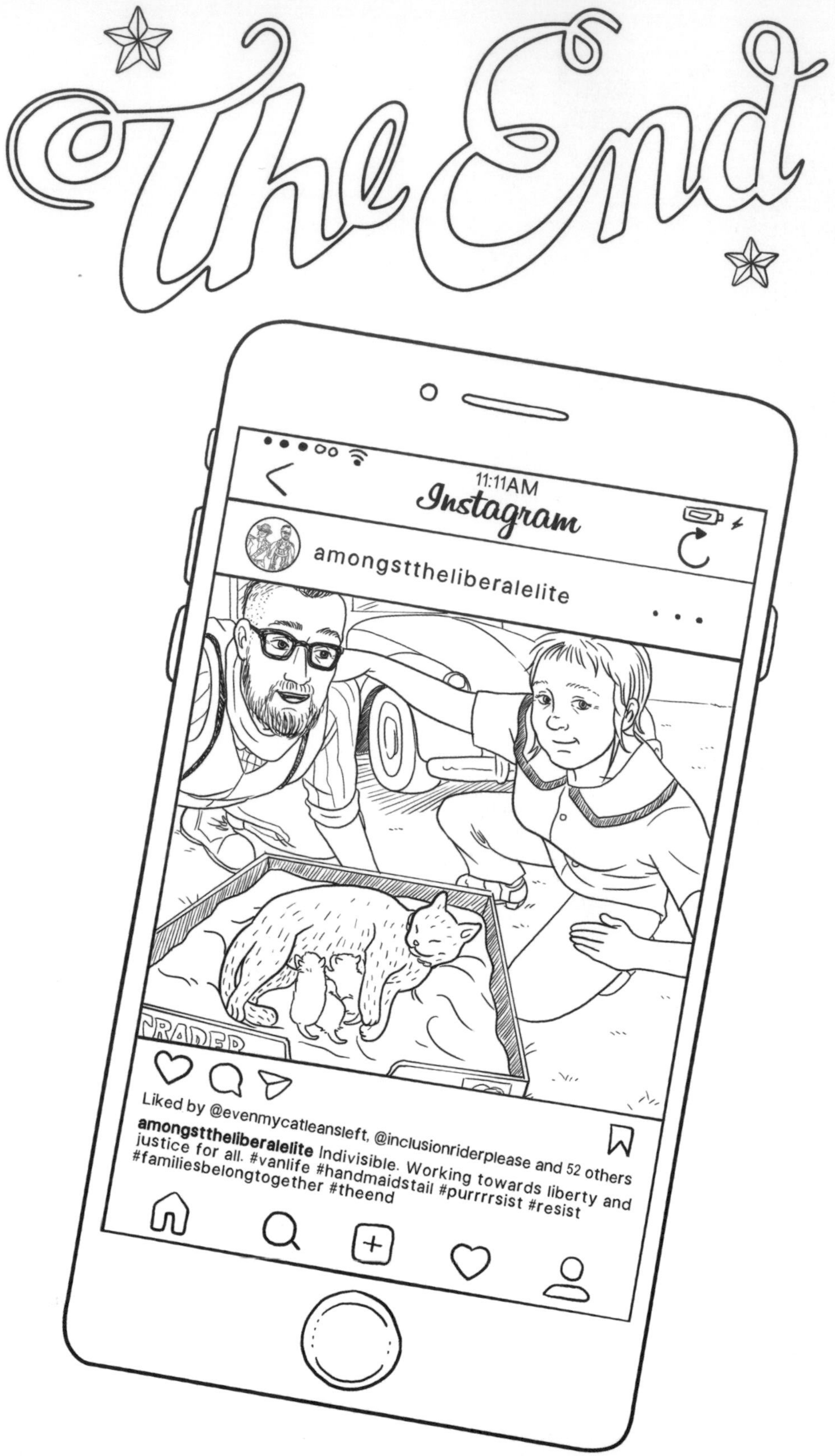

11:11AM
Instagram
amongsttheliberalelite
TRADER
Liked by @evenmycatleansleft, @inclusionriderplease and 52 others
amongsttheliberalelite Indivisible. Working towards liberty and justice for all. #vanlife #handmaidstail #purrrrsist #resist #familiesbelongtogether #theend

Elly Lonon:

A member of the Liberal Elite herself, Elly is still recovering from growing up in a red state. Born and raised in North Carolina, she moved to Manhattan for graduate school and to pursue a career in the music business. Weary from consistent marginalization by the patriarchy, she left both the industry and NYC, opting to work for a not-for-profit and moving to the suburbs of Jersey where living near a Superfund site promptly gave her cancer. Once in remission, she read far too many self-help books, learned to embrace life, and abandoned her previous career to write and procreate.

Joan Reilly:

Joan's work was featured most recently in *RESIST!*, a comics newspaper edited by Francoise Mouly and Nadja Spiegelman, and in *Draw the Line* (drawthelinecomics.com), an online anthology of comics promoting political action. Her comics and illustration have been published in many anthologies and literary magazines over the last two decades. She is a co-editor of *The Big Feminist BUT: Comics About the IFs, ANDs & BUTs of Feminism*, and created illustrations for the "Ask Marilyn" column in *Parade* magazine for over ten years. For more information, visit JoanReilly.com.

ACKNOWLEDGEMENTS

From Us Both:

Craig and Will and the powerHouse team — Thank you for embracing ukealope endpaper and shepherding this book onto shelves.

To our Elite Team:
• Miguel — no one has ever taken notes better. Thank you for loving this project and for your massive heart.
• Theresa — you landed in our laps at a full sprint and were a magical mind reader. Repeatedly. Even when we weren't sure what we were thinking ourselves!
• Sarah Oleksyk — for turning our script into joyful thumbnail sketches, imbued Kittery with wit, and answered late night logistical questions, endless thanks.
• Brooke Metzker — our skilled intern and intersectional feminist. Keep raising your voice.

To Tom Hart — thank you for your inspiration and beautiful work, but mostly thank you for Miguel. We say the same to Lauren Weinstein with deepest gratitude for sharing the magic of Theresa with us.

And to all the other artists who gave their time and thoughts on how to approach this project and its unique challenges (especially Kevin and Dan McCloskey), deepest thanks.

From Elly:

Meg and Cindy — it was always you. Thank you for the opportunity to choose Thompson Literary. To Arielle and David, The Book Doctors — Erma gave the world an awful lot, but her greatest gift to me was the two of you.

I know I already thanked my Village, but I also want to thank my Kilburn and every single person who offered to watch my kids. Also extra matrimonial points to Rocco for doubling down on all things domestic. Unless sex qualifies as domestic. Because there was definitely less of that as deadlines loomed.

To my fellow writers of HWP for enthusiastically brainstorming the literary collection of Alex and Michael. Thanks for encouraging my preparedness paranoia, Jen Mann and Gretchen Kelly. Melissa Romo, you showed me how it's done. To Liv, Lola, and Amanda — I don't know which of you I value more.

Emily McDowell - thank you for your kind words, your beautiful work, and the permission to feature your designs. Jen Pastiloff - thank you for your generous introduction.

To Jen Simon for reading every single McSweeney's column before it's published and for being my Jewru. And a HUGE thanks to Chris Monks and the entire McSweeney's team for not responding to my first pitch with your usual gentle, "I smiled several times but I'm afraid I'll have to pass."

To Vanessa Parvin — oh girl. WOMAN. There's not enough room here so I hope you just know what you've meant to this book and to me.

Most importantly, to Joan – thank you for loving Alex and Michael. Thank you for seeing even more within them than I could have ever fathomed. Thank you for laughing, crying, and laughing while crying with me. Never leave me, bish.

From Joan:

To Shannon O'Leary, my intrepid co-editor of The Big Feminist BUT, thank you for awakening the "SJW" in me, and for bravely volunteering to be my creative-collaboration guinea pig by re-cruiting me for that project. I know it was not always pleasant for you, and I am so glad that we are still friends anyway. That experience taught me so many ways to improve this one.

To Kevin McCloskey, thank you for welcoming me so warmly into the creative community of Kutztown.

To my dad, Bob Reilly, thank you for showing me the endless value and charm of being able to laugh at ourselves.

To Tracy Sane, thank you for giving me the freedom and encouragement to pursue my creative dreams, and for teasing me mercilessly as I do it.

To Elly, thank you for giving me the chance to concoct relatable earth-suits, outfits, expressions and gestures for these entities who seemingly sprang from your miraculous mind fully formed, and whom I now count among my chosen family, despite their fictional status. And thank you for holding everything so capably when I could not.

Amongst the Liberal Elite:
The Road Trip Exploring Societal Inequities Solidified by Trump (RESIST)

Published in the United States by powerHouse Books,
a division of powerHouse Cultural Entertainment, Inc.
32 Adams Street, Brooklyn, NY 11201-1021
e-mail: info@powerHouseBooks.com
website: www.powerHouseBooks.com

First edition, 2018

Library of Congress Control Number: 2018952334

ISBN 978-1-57687-905-4

Printed by Toppan Leefung

10 9 8 7 6 5 4 3 2 1

Printed and bound in China